THE JACOBITES AND RUSSIA

THE JACOBITES AND RUSSIA
1715–1750

REBECCA WILLS

TUCKWELL PRESS

First published in Great Britain in 2002 by
Tuckwell Press
The Mill House
Phantassie
East Linton
East Lothian EH40 3DG
Scotland

ISBN 1 86232 142 6

British Library Cataloguing in Publication Data

A catalogue record for this book is available
on request from the British Library

Typeset by Hewer Text Ltd, Edinburgh
Printed and bound by Cromwell Press, Trowbridge, Wiltshire

To my parents, Virginia and Peter,
for boundless love and patience

Contents

Illustrations   x
Acknowledgements   xi
Abbreviations   xii
Note on Transliteration   xiv
Note on Dates   xv
Map   xvi

Introduction   1
Preface: *Russia Through Foreign Eyes in the First Half
    of the Eighteenth Century*   6

PART ONE: THE REIGN OF PETER I, 1715–1725

1. *Jacobite Recruitment and Peter I, 1715–1725*   21
   Who were the Exiles?   21
   Russia's Reputation and Reality: 'Nothing at heart but
       the welfare of his subjects . . . ?'   25
   Career Opportunities for Naval Jacobites   27
   The Jacobites: A Select Elite   31
   Pay and Exploitation   33
2. *The Growth of the Jacobite Community in Russia and the
   Breakdown of Anglo-Russian Relations, 1715–1719*   38
   The Jacobite Tradition in Russia   38
   Jacobitism and Political Expediency   39
   Anglo-Russian Relations, 1715–1717   40
   Dr Robert Erskine and Russo-Jacobite Diplomacy, 1716–1717   41
   Dr Robert Erskine, Peter I and Jacobite Recruitment   49
   The Jacobites and the Anglo-Russian Diplomatic Rupture of 1719   56
3. *The Climax of Jacobite Diplomacy, 1720–1725*   68
   1720, A Year of Change   68
   The Tables Turn: Russia and the Atterbury Plot, 1721–1722   69
   Daniel O'Brien: The First Envoy Extraordinary and
   Minister Plenipotentiary from King James III to Emperor Peter I,
       1722–1724   77
   Daniel O'Brien's Mission, 1723–1724   82
   Aftermath: Kurakin and the Jacobites in France, 1724   89
   The Death of Peter I   90
   Conclusion   91

PART TWO: THE REIGN OF CATHERINE I, 1725–1727

4. *Agents and Intrigue*   97
   Threats from North and South   97
   The Return of William Hay   98
   Britain's Need for a Spy   99
   John Deane's Mission to St Petersburg   101
   The Aftermath of Deane's Mission: Spies and Jacobite Letters   106
   Ministerial Panic and Political Dissimulation   108
   'The Pretender and his Tools'   113
   British Confidence Undermined, 1726   114
   Quelling the Jacobite Threat?   119
   Jacobitism and International Hostility   121
   The Flame in the North   123
   The Flame Extinguished   124

PART THREE: THE REIGN OF PETER II, 1727–1730

5. *The Embassy of the Duke of Liria, 1727–1730*   129
   Bleak Prospects and Divided Loyalties   129
   Liria's Mission   130
   Jacobite Secrets   132
   Taking Risks   133
   The Treaty of Seville   135
   Liria and Britain   137
   Personal Loyalty: Conflict or Compromise?   138
   Liria's Recall and the Second Treaty of Vienna   139

PART FOUR: THE REIGN OF ANNA IVANOVNA, 1730–1740

6. *Jacobites and Politics, 1730–1740*   143
   The Collapse of the Anglo-French Alliance   143
   The War of the Polish Succession, 1733–1735   145
   Jacobite 'Ill Management'   149
   The War with Turkey, 1736–1739   152
   James Keith: Jacobite Exile or Russian General?   155
   James Keith's Visit to Britain   158
   Conclusion   162
7. *The Jacobite as Foreign Mercenary*   163
   The Myth of Foreign Favouritism   163
   A Haven for Foreign Mercenaries?   165
   The Russian Military in Crisis   166
   Foreigners and Military Legislation   167
   Legislation versus Practice   172
   Recruitment from the Royal Navy   174
   Jacobites and the Land Forces   181
   Selectivity and Success   186

8. *Jacobites in Battle, 1730–1740* 188
   Poland 189
   The Rhine Campaign 191
   The Crimea 192

PART FIVE: THE REGENCIES AND
THE REIGN OF ELISABETH, 1740–1750

9. *The End of An Era* 201
   Spark and Fire: Jacobite Attempts and the 1745 Rising 201
   Russian Domestic Turmoil, 1740–1741 204
   Jacobite Pawns and Politicians 207
   Elisabeth in Power 211
   Career Difficulties 212
   James Keith in Sweden 216
   Lord Hyndford's Offensive 221
   James Keith's Departure from Russia 226
   A Transfer of Allegiance 228
   Conclusion 231

   Bibliography 233
   Index 247

Illustrations

1. Peter the Great
2. Moscow, with the Kremlin
3. The German Quarter, Moscow
4. The old Tsar's Palace in the Kremlin
5. A Russian town
6. Plan of St Petersburg
7. View of St Petersburg
8. The Winter Palace in St Petersburg
9. The Empress Anna Ivanovna
10. The Empress Elizabeth Petrovna
11. James III, 'The Old Pretender'
12. Admiral Thomas Gordon
13. The Order of St Alexander Nevsky
14. Sir Henry Stirling of Ardoch
15. Miniatures of James III and his sons, Charles Edward and Henry Benedict
16. Field-Marshal Count Peter Lacy
17. James Keith, General-in-Chief of the Russian army
18. Kenneth Sutherland, 3rd Lord Duffus

Acknowledgements

In the course of my research I have been greatly helped by a number of people, particularly while working in the Russian archives in Moscow and St Petersburg. I would like to thank Dr Elena Belakon', Dr Boris Morozov, Dr Andrei Pavlov, Dr Sergei L'vov and the staff of the Russian Naval Archive, especially Dmitri Kopelev and Lyudmila Glazunova. Without their generosity and kindness my time in Russia would not have been nearly as enjoyable nor as productive. The staff of the National Archives of Scotland, the National Library of Scotland, Aberdeen University Library, the Bodleian Library, the Public Record Office, the British Library, the Scottish National Portrait Gallery, the National Museums of Scotland Library, the National Gallery in London, the National Galleries of Scotland and of Ireland, Marischal Museum and Blairs College, Aberdeen were also very helpful. I am grateful to Her Majesty the Queen for permission to use the collection of Stuart Papers at Windsor Castle. David Somervell, Professor Patrick O'Meara, Professor Lindsey Hughes, Ronald Baird, William Drummond-Moray of Abercairny, the Earl of Mar and Kellie, the Earl of Kintore and Neil Curtis kindly assisted in my search for illustrations and information. I would also like to thank Professor Paul Dukes of Aberdeen University, who first fired my enthusiasm for Jacobites in Russia, and Dr Paul Langford of Lincoln College, Oxford, who supervised the writing of the original thesis on which this book is based, Finally, my special thanks to Virginia, Peter and Mark Wills and Halcyon Martin for all their encouragement and help with proof-reading, printing and sourcing illustrations.

Abbreviations

AHR	American Historical Review
ALOII	Arkhiv Leningradskogo otdeleniya istoricheskogo instituta (Archive of the Leningrad Institute of History)
ASEER	American Slavonic and East European Review
AUR	Aberdeen University Review
AUL	Aberdeen University Library
AVPR	Arkhiv vneshnei politiki Rossii (Archive of Russian Foreign Affairs, Moscow).
BGO	Beiträge zur Geschichte Osteuropas
BL	British Library
CASS	Canadian and American Slavic Review
CH CUL	Cholomondeley (Houghton) Mss. Cambridge University Library
ChIOMU	Chtenie v Imperatorskom obshchestve pri Moskovskom universitete
CMRS	Cahiers du Monde Russe et Soviétique
DNB	Dictionary of National Biography
EHR	English Historical Review
ESR	European Studies Review
FOG	Forschungen zur Osteuropäischen Geschichte
GM	Gentleman's Magazine
Guildhall L.	Library of the Guildhall, London
HMC	Historical Manuscripts Commission
HJ	Historical Journal
HT	History Today
IAN	Izvestiya Akademiya Nauk
JGO	Jahrbücher für Geschichte Osteuropas
MM	Mariner's Mirror
NAS	National Archives of Scotland (formerly Scottish Record Office)
NBSS	Nationalnaya biblioteka Saltykova Shchedrina (St.Petersburg).
NLS	National Library of Scotland
NRS	Navy Records Society
OMS	Obshchi morskoi spisok
OSP	Oxford Slavonic Papers
PH	Parliamentary History
PRO	Public Record Office
RA	Russki Arkhiv
RA Stuart	Stuart Papers (Microform of Stuart Papers at Windsor Castle, Aberdeen University)

RBS	Russki biograficheski slovar'
RGADA	Rossiiski Gosudarstvenny arkhiv Drevnykh aktov (Russian State Archive of Ancient Acts, Moscow)
RGAVMF	Rossiiski Gosudarstvenny arkhiv Voenno-Morskogo flota (Russian State Naval Archive, St.Petersburg)
RGVIA	Rossiiski Gosudarstvenny Voenno-istoricheski arkhiv (Russian State Military Archive, Moscow)
RS	Russkaya starina
RSP	Calendar of the Royal Stuart Papers, 7 vols.
SEER	Slavonic and East European Review
SGER	Study Group for Eighteenth Century Russia
SHR	Scottish Historical Review
SHS	Scottish History Society
SIRIO	Sbornik Imperatorskogo Russkogo istoricheskogo obshchestva
SR	Slavic Review
VMU	Vestnik Moskovskogo Universiteta

When citing Russian archival sources I have used the Russian system of reference:

F = Fond (collection)
o = opis' (sub-collection)
d = delo (item)
ch. = chast' (part)
l = list (folio)

Note on Transliteration

In the transliteration of Russian I have followed a simple pattern in order to reduce technicalities to a minimum.

i = ий
ii = ии
y = ый or ий
ya = я
yu = ю
u = у
ts = ц
ch = ч
sh = ш
shch = щ
' = ь
The hard sign is omitted

Note on Dates

During the first half of the eighteenth century, until 31 December 1751[1], the Julian or Old Style calendar was used in Britain, while the Gregorian or New Style, which was eleven days ahead of the Julian, was in use everywhere in Europe but Sweden and Russia. In addition to this, the new year in Britain began on Lady Day, 25 March, rather than 1 January. In Russia the old Julian calendar continued to be used until the twentieth century. To avoid the confusion which the artificial adjustment of dates would inevitably cause, the letters of varied origins referred to in the text are dated as they were in the manuscript, according to the country in which they were written. Where diplomats have provided both Old and New Styles, these are given. However, the beginning of January is taken as the beginning of the year in every case. Unless otherwise stated, letters from Britain, Russia and Sweden are dated Old Style (o.s.), those from the rest of Europe in New Style (n.s.). Where ambiguity arises, this is clarified in the text.

---

1 Although the Julian calendar was corrected by omitting the eleven days between 2 and 14 September 1752, the 'Act for regulating the commencement of the year and for correcting the Calendar now in use' (24 George II, ch.23) took effect from 31 December 1751, commencing the year 1752 the following day.

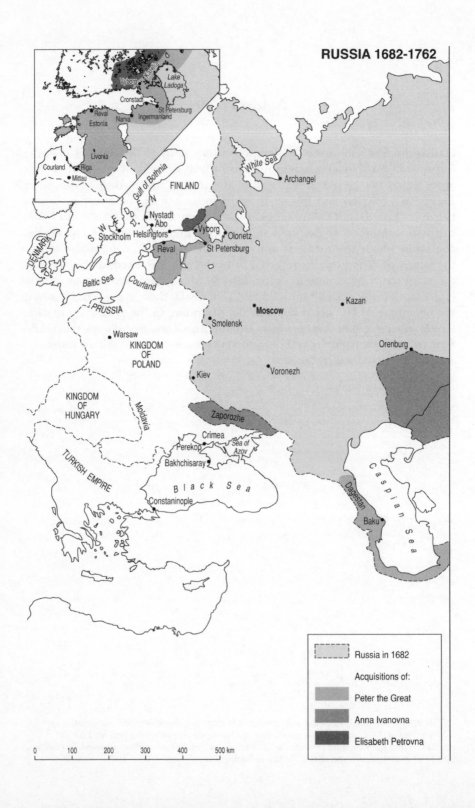

RUSSIA 1682-1762

Inset map labels:
Vyborg
Karelia
Lake Ladoga
Cronstadt
St Petersburg
Ingermanland
Reval
Estonia
Narva
Courland
Livonia
Riga
Mittau

Main map labels:
White Sea
Archangel
Gulf of Bothnia
FINLAND
Nystadt
Abo
Stockholm
Helsingfors
Vyborg
Olonetz
Reval
St Petersburg
S W E D E N
Baltic Sea
Courland
DENMARK
PRUSSIA
Warsaw
KINGDOM OF POLAND
Smolensk
Moscow
Kazan
Orenburg
KINGDOM OF HUNGARY
Moldavia
Kiev
Voronezh
TURKISH EMPIRE
Zaporozhe
Crimea
Perekop
Sea of Azov
Bakhchisaray
Black Sea
Constantinople
Dagestan
Caspian Sea
Baku

Legend:

Russia in 1682

Acquisitions of:

Peter the Great

Anna Ivanovna

Elisabeth Petrovna

0   100   200   300   400   500 km

Introduction

'Here's a health to the mysterious Czar
I hope he'll send us help from far
To end the work begun by Mar . . .'[1]

Between the Williamite Revolution of 1688–9 and the last Jacobite rising of 1745–6, each successive attempt to restore the House of Stuart to the British throne produced a crop of Jacobite refugees, forced to seek a safe haven and a secure livelihood wherever they could, in destinations as far apart as America, Spain and Russia. They numbered in thousands,[2] and the impact of their resettlement was considerable, particularly on the armies and navies of the countries in which they took refuge. So many of them carved out successful military careers on the Continent that one historian has observed that exiled Irish Jacobites alone, '. . . provided field marshals for all the major European powers in the first half of the eighteenth century'.[3] Scots and English Jacobites played an equally prominent role as mercenaries, particularly in France, Spain, Sweden, Italy, Austria and, of course, in Russia.

The importance of the diaspora, both in terms of its military and cultural influence abroad, and of its place in the saga of Jacobite intrigue and British foreign policy in the first half of the eighteenth century, has been frequently acknowledged. Eveline Cruickshanks, for example, has described the contribution of the diaspora abroad as, '. . . One of the most important aspects of Jacobitism in Europe and that perhaps most neglected by British historians', while Bruce Lenman has written that, '. . . the story of these forgotten and despised communities is as neglected as it is fascinating'.[4] Despite this recognition of the significance of the political and military role of Jacobite exiles in general, the subject is remarkably under-researched.

This book is an attempt to address this omission, at least with regard to Russia, arguably one of the most exciting of Jacobite destinations. The Russia to which the Jacobites came was a land emerging onto the eighteenth century

---

1 'Here's a Health to the Valiant Swede', J.Hogg, ed., *The Jacobite Relics of Scotland*, 2 vols., 2, pp.283–284.
2 Bruce Lenman estimated the number of Irish Jacobite émigrés after the surrender of Limerick to King William of Orange's troops in 1691 to be 12,000 soldiers and 4,000 dependants. B.Lenman, 'The Jacobite Diaspora', *History Today* 30 (1980), p.8; according to McLynn 5,000 Scots enlisted in the Royal Scots regiment in France which, it was hoped, would participate in the 1745 rising. F. McLynn, *The Jacobites*, p.136.
3 F.McLynn, *The Jacobites* (London, 1985), p.130. These included Maximilian Ulysses Browne and James Robert Nugent in the Imperial army, the Duke of Berwick and Charles O'Brien, Lord Clare in the French army.
4 E.Cruickshanks, *Ideology and Conspiracy: Aspects of Jacobitism 1689–1759* (Edinburgh, 1982), p.xi; B.Lenman, 'The Jacobite Diaspora', *History Today* 30 (1980), p.7.

European stage under the guidance and ambitions of Tsar Peter I, 'the Great', and his successors. Some of the peculiarities of the Russia these travellers must have experienced are described in a short historical sketch following this introduction. The principal objective of this study, however, is to investigate some of the fundamental questions to which even brief acquaintance with the military and political influence of the Jacobite diaspora would be expected to give rise. The answers, however, are relevant to the perception of Jacobitism as a phenomenon affecting European diplomacy on every level. For example, how was the 'Jacobite' identity, if there was one, preserved? To what extent, that is, did exiles select their destination on political, to what extent on professional or religious grounds? Was their loyalty to James III preserved in the host country, was it subsumed by a new allegiance to another monarch, or did it simply become irrelevant? Directly linked with the problem of changing identity is the extent to which the exiles remained actively involved in Jacobite politics, and thus the influence they were able to exert on the foreign policies both of their host country, and, in turn, of Britain. Conversely, did foreign powers merely feign support for the Jacobites as a symbol of their hostility against Britain, as a negotiating tool, or was military assistance a serious prospect? What did the Jacobites achieve in Russia and what influence did they have? This book considers these areas as they relate to Jacobites in Russia after the 1715 Jacobite rising, concentrating primarily on the military and political role which distinguished them from other foreign mercenaries.

In view of the revived attention which the Jacobite movement has received since the 1970's, the marked absence of scholarly work devoted to the diaspora, and thus of answers to these fundamental questions, is the more surprising. The debates which have divided recent historical opinion have been more concerned with defining the domestic parameters of Jacobitism. Eveline Cruickshanks, for example, has emphasised the key role of Jacobitism in Tory party politics as a reaction against proscription, while Linda Colley has tended to regard the link between Tories and Stuart supporters with more scepticism.[5] The political aspect of domestic Jacobitism has been examined by many others, including, for example, G.V Bennet, Daniel Szechi and Ian Christie, but the role of the diaspora in Jacobite diplomacy is largely neglected.[6]

The scant attention paid to the exiled communities by British historians may be due, in part, to the repeated failure of the Jacobites to elicit effective foreign support. Although A.F.Steuart, Frank McLynn, Paul Fritz and Jeremy Black have gone some way towards placing domestic Jacobitism in the context of European politics, examining both the relationship between Britain and

5 E.Cruickshanks, *Political Untouchables: The Tories and the '45* (London, 1979); L.Colley, *In Defiance of Oligarchy: The Tory Party, 1714–60* (Cambridge, 1982).

6 G.V.Bennet, *The Tory Crisis in Church and State, 1688–1730: The Career of Francis Atterbury, Bishop of Rochester* (Oxford, 1975); D.Szechi, *Jacobitism and Tory Politics 1710–14*, (Edinburgh, 1984), I. Christie, 'The Tory Party, Jacobitism and the 'Forty Five": A Note', *HJ* 30 (1987), pp.921–931.

Jacobites abroad, and the military achievements of exiles,[7] the subject has been more directly addressed outside Britain, for example by Claud Nordmann and Goran Behre.[8] A fascinating but as yet unpublished monograph of the life of Peter I of Russia's Jacobite General Patrick Gordon sheds some light on the early history of Jacobite links with Russia, and a short essay by Maurice Bruce considers a five-year period under Peter I.[9] Nevertheless, the role of the Jacobites in Russia in the first half of the eighteenth century remains virtually unknown, a reflection not only of the language barrier and of the inaccessibility of primary source material, but of a tendency to underestimate, and hence to neglect, Russia's significance in both Jacobite and British politics.

The year 1715, in which a Jacobite rising followed the succession of the first Hanoverian monarch, George I, to the British throne, and in which serious differences between the new King and Peter I of Russia dealt lasting damage to Anglo-Russian relations, forms the most suitable starting point for an investigation of the relationship between the Jacobites, Britain and Russia. Although the Jacobite movement began with the flight of James II to France in 1688, Russia's involvement as an enemy of Britain in European diplomacy, and hence its dominance in Jacobite conspiracy, became an issue only after 1715. Jacobite projects were hatched and communication with the exiled diaspora maintained through the exiled Jacobite Court, which, from 1689 until the treaty of Utrecht in 1713 necessitated the expulsion of Jacobites from France, was situated at St-Germain-en-Laye near Paris. James II was succeeded on his death in 1701 by his son James 'III', with whom the court moved in 1713 to Bar in Lorraine, in 1715 to Avignon, and finally in 1717 to Urbino in Italy. The birth of James III's sons, Charles Edward, the 'Young Pretender', and Henry Benedict, later Cardinal York, in 1720 and 1725 respectively, injected new hope into the Stuart cause, hope which approached fulfilment in the restoration attempts of the early 1740's.

The years between 1715 and 1750 marked the climax and decline of a Jacobite influence in Russia. The absence of a Jacobite insurrection in Britain for over twenty years after 1719 has led to a relative neglect of a large part of this interim period in terms of Jacobite activity on the Continent. This book relates the efforts of Jacobites in Russia to the wider projects of the Jacobite Court, and, in turn, to the changing state of European diplomatic alignments and to the likewise changeable interests of each Russian monarch.

7 A.F.Steuart, 'Sweden and the Jacobites, 1719–1720', *SHR* 23 (1927), pp.119–127; J.Black, *Jacobitism and British Foreign Policy under the First Two Georges*, Royal Stuart Papers 32 (Huntingdon, 1988); J.Black, 'Jacobitism and British Foreign Policy, 1731–5', in J.Black and E.Cruickshanks, eds., *The Jacobite Challenge*, (Edinburgh, 1988); F.McLynn, *The Jacobites* (London, 1985); P.Fritz, *The English Ministers and Jacobitism between the Rebellions of 1715 and 1745* (Toronto, 1975).

8 G.Behre, 'Gothenburg in Stuart War Strategy 1649–1760', in G.Simpson, ed., *Scotland and Scandinavia*, (Edinburgh, 1990), pp.107–118; C.Nordmann, 'Louis XIV and the Jacobites', in R.Hatton, *Louis XIV and Europe* (London, 1976).

9 Graeme P.Herd, 'General Patrick Gordon of Auchleuchries – a Scot in Seventeenth Century Russian Service', Unpubl. Ph.D.thesis (Aberdeen University, 1994); M.Bruce, 'Jacobite Relations with Peter the Great', *SEER* 14 (1936), pp.343–362.

During the most dynamic and encouraging period of Russo-Jacobite relations, which coincided roughly with the Anglo-Russian diplomatic rupture
from 1716 to 1730, Jacobite hope of Russian assistance lay, first, in the prospect
of a Russo-Swedish alliance against Britain, then in the support of France and
Russia within a Russo-French alliance, and, after Peter I's death in 1725, in an
anti-British Alliance of Vienna between Russia, Austria and Spain. The fact that
no military support was ultimately forthcoming is of only relative importance;
the damage dealt to British-Hanoverian interests by Jacobite diplomatic
activity, and the changes in British foreign policy prompted by a perceived
Russian-Jacobite threat, were evidence of the influence which a small number
of exiles was able to exert. Even after 1730, when the accession of Empress
Anna Ivanovna and the inception of better Anglo-Russian relations greatly
diminished the possibility of assistance from Russia, the Jacobites there could
not escape the repercussions of European politics.

Historians' lack of awareness of the relationship between Jacobitism and
Russia is the more remarkable, given the growing importance of Russia in
British foreign policy over the course of the century as a direct response to
Russia's rising military prominence in Europe. In 1718, Russia superseded
Sweden, which it was in the process of conquering, as the focus of Jacobite
attempts to obtain foreign support. As a power with a military capacity far
superior to that of Spain or Austria, Russia offered the dual prospect either of a
naval offensive on British coasts or of an invasion of George I's Hanoverian
possessions in northern Germany as part of a joint restoration attempt.
However, the physical distance of Russia from the centres of Jacobite authority
posed a unique problem in terms of communication, often forcing Jacobite
envoys to take the initiative without guidance. The demands of the Russian
monarchy for the unquestioned and absolute allegiance of its foreign subjects
greatly restricted the freedom of individuals to remain active Jacobites in the
face of Anglo-Russian amity after 1730.

The instability and sudden changes of power which characterised Russian
politics during the period posed an added threat to successful professionals in
Russia, acting as a disincentive to political involvement of any kind. Nevertheless, the great military achievements of individual Jacobites in Russian
service had inevitable political consequences, both for Jacobite hopes elsewhere in Europe, and for the military and political status of Russia. Although
an investigation of the role of the diaspora in, for example, France and Spain
would, by virtue of their greater accessibility to Jacobites and their proximity
both to Britain and to the exiled court, yield evidence of a greater number and
diversity of exiles, Russia remains a unique case. The exceptional career
opportunities offered in Russian military service, the talented individuals
who settled there, the changing, but always central, position of Russia in
British foreign policy, and, most importantly, a lack of published material
relating to Russia's role in European Jacobitism, make this study not only of
particular interest, but an important complement to existing work.

The geographical range of the subject necessitated the drawing together of diverse and hitherto unused or unconjoined source material from three principal areas, Russia, Britain, and the Jacobite Court in exile. This included diplomatic correspondence from archival sources in the British Library, the Bodleian Library, the Public Record Office, the Stuart Papers from the Royal Archive at Windsor, the National Archives of Scotland and the National Library of Scotland, as well as information on Russian military and political affairs from the Russian Archive of Ancient Acts (RGADA), the Russian Military Archive (RGVIA) and the Archive of Foreign Affairs (AVPR) in Moscow, and the Russian Naval Archive (RGAVMF) in St Petersburg. Secondary material, likewise, ranged in scope from British Jacobitism and British and Russian foreign policy to military, political and cultural affairs in Russia in the first half of the eighteenth century. The use of these sources for research uncovered a number of practical challenges, which, luckily, did not prove insurmountable. Perhaps most challenging was learning to decipher eighteenth-century cyrillic handwriting at the speed necessary to skim through quantities of archival material. Most satisfying was working out how to decode versions of Jacobite cipher to which there appears to be no extant key.

This book attempts first and foremost to extrapolate the international implications of Jacobite-Russian links by placing the political and military activities of individuals within the wider context of European diplomacy. This is, in part, because the attraction of Russia for the Jacobites lay largely in the opportunities it presented for a military career, and the principal impact of these military men was on the battlefield. There is no doubt, however, that Jacobites must also have experienced at first hand great changes in the social and cultural fabric of Russia during a period which brought momentous reforms fuelled by increasing contact with the West. Their personal impressions of daily life have not been recorded to the same extent and in such detail as have their military careers, and speculation as to how they might have lived is incidental to the main concern of the book. In order to redress the balance a little and provide a useful social background to the subject, the main body of the work is prefaced with a short historical sketch to provide a taste of what daily life might have been like for many of the Jacobites who made Russia their home.

PREFACE

Russia Through Foreign Eyes in the First Half of the Eighteenth Century

At the beginning of the eighteenth century Russia lagged behind many other European countries, including Britain, in terms of its industrial base, foreign trade, military framework and social and cultural development. Its sheer size, coupled with the remoteness of most of its rural population from the centres of power, posed an inevitable challenge to any attempt to instigate change. By 1722 Petrine Russia had 13 million inhabitants, of whom only 0.3% lived in urban areas. By 1742, territorial gains on the Baltic, Caspian and Black Seas had increased the population to 16 million,[1] and the Empire stretched from Karelia and the Polish border in the west to eastern Siberia. Power over this extensive territory was by necessity autocratic.[2] The Tsar (Emperor from 1721), conferred estates, together with the serfs tied to them, on loyal members of the nobility and eminent military men and up to 60% of the land area and its peasant population was owned by a small number of prominent families, whose status was entirely dependent on the will of the monarch.[3] Although successive rulers alternated in their choice of capital, the two centres of political, cultural and, later, of industrial power remained the land-locked city of Moscow, and St Petersburg, founded at the mouth of the Neva by Peter I in 1703 as his 'Window on the West'.

Despite these logistical and geographical impediments, the wide-ranging reforms instigated by Tsar Peter (1682–1725) brought Russia into the new century as a rising economic and military power, and one of increasing importance within European diplomacy. Peter's two unprecedented visits to western Europe in 1697–98 and 1716–17, which fuelled his desire to attract western technology and expertise, raised Russia's profile as an attractive destination for career-seeking, or simply curious, foreign visitors. This reputation was perpetuated by Peter's successors. Although there were no fewer than six changes of power in Russia during the first fifty years of the century, a political instability which inevitably varied the pace of progress, the internationalisation of cultural and intellectual life throughout Europe which characterised the Enlightenment period had a marked impact on Russian social and cultural development. Foreign visitors to

---

1 E.Donnert, *Russia in the Age of Enlightenment* (Leipzig, 1986), p.10.
2 James Keith, one of the Jacotibes who figures in this study and who was in Russia from 1728 to 1747, commented on this necessity that, '. . . Russia, where the genius of the nation, and the vast extent of the empire, demands a Souverain, and even an absolute one', J.Keith, *A Fragment of a memoir of Field-marshal James Keith, written by himself 1714–1734* (Edinburgh, 1843), p.84.
3 J.P. le Donne, 'Ruling Families in the Russian Political Order 1689–1725', *CMRS*, 28 (1987), pp.233–322.

Russia during the period were witness to and played a key role in this process of change.[4]

Major Cities

Jacobites were only some of the many foreigners to travel to Russia in the first half of the century. Most arrived in the port of Cronstadt by ship, travelled or sailed the short distance to St Petersburg and journeyed overland from there to Moscow and beyond. Many of them left detailed and colourful memoirs which convey an impression of the Russia they encountered.[5] Although military men, traders and adventurers reached far-flung destinations, the majority of foreigners remained close to the centres of power, Moscow, St Petersburg and neighbouring Cronstadt.

The city of St Petersburg and the port of Cronstadt were Petrine creations, constructed rapidly during the first years of the century at great human cost. Sir Francis Dashwood, who visited Russia in 1733 at the age of 25 recorded that he was, 'credibly, and by severall informed, that in building (or rather) laying the foundation of this town and Crownstad there were three hundred thousand men perished, by hunger and the air'.[6] Nevertheless, by the time of Peter's death in 1725 these astonishing feats of engineering and architecture were well-established and much admired by foreign visitors. Dashwood described the port of Cronstadt thus,

> I went over and viewed the Isle of Crownstad which is about five miles in length, the plan of the prodigious work is very regularly laid out . . . the Entrance into the Haven is excessive Strong . . . there are large Canals, well lined with stone, for to bring Ships or large Vessels, into the town . . . upon the South East, is a Haven, called the Merchants Haven, within the Outer Works, the fort stands distinct by itself, on the South, and all boats and Ships pass betwixt that and Crownstadt . . .[7]

By 1733 St Petersburg was a pleasant, well-appointed city, carrying on a bustling trade with the rest of Europe and with ready access to many western commodities. It certainly impressed Dashwood,

> At the entrance into the town is a long prospection of a Verst long, in which are two Triumphall Arches of Wood painted . . . the streets are

4 The contribution of foreigners to all aspects of Russian social, cultural and economic life has been extensively covered elsewhere. See, for example, E.Amburger, *Fremde und Einheimische in Wirtschafts und Kulturleben des Neuzeitlichen Russland* (Wiesbaden, 1982); A.G.Cross, *Russia under Western Eyes, 1553–1815* (London, 1971); A.G.Cross, *Anglo-Russica* (Oxford, 1993); E.Donnert, *Russia in the Age of Enlightenment* (Leipzig, 1986); J.G.Garrard, *The Eighteenth Century in Russia* (Oxford, 1973).

5 Among the most interesting British observations on the Russian scene from this period are memoirs by Peter Henry Bruce, Alexander Gordon, Francis Dashwood, John Cook, John Deane, John Bell, James Keith and James Spilman.

6 'Sir Francis Dashwood's Diary of his Visit to St Petersburg in 1733', *SEER*, 38 (1959–60), p.203.

7 'Sir Francis Dashwood's Diary', *SEER*, 38 (1959–60), p.200.

pretty well paved, streight, and of a good breadth in Severall there are canals, they say the Czar designed cutting canals through most of the streets, expecially opposite to the Palace which is now inhabited by her Majesty, called the Summer Palace, that being the reall town of St Petersburgh, where the exchange is, where the Merchants dayley resort, though not reside, as also the greatest part of the Shops, for retail commodities.[8]

John Cook, a Scots doctor who arrived three years later, commented favourably on the layout and sanitary arrangements of the city,

> . . . Where the streets (which are all broad, well paved, and formed in straight lines where possible) cut these canals there are built large draw-bridges, and that the common people may have no pretext for leaving nastiness in any part of the streets, convenient places are built upon the banks of the river and its canals; Besides, all houses which are built two stories high, and in straight lines, are well supplied with every conveniency to keep the city sweet and clean.[9]

Moscow, the ancient capital, steeped in Russia's history, was, by contrast, generally regarded as embodying more traditional values than its counterpart on the Baltic littoral. It was a city of contrasts, ancient military defences standing beside the eastern splendour of Russian Orthodoxy, the palaces of the aristocracy visible above the humble wooden huts of the ordinary people. One Scottish observer described his first impression of Moscow in 1713,

> Coming in view of it, in a clear sun-shine day, I never saw so glorious a sight as this city presented at a distance with the vast numbers of gilded domes and steeples; but my expectations were greatly disappointed when I entered it, finding only ill-built wooden houses and timber streets interspersed with churches and brick houses, with large courts and gardens, the habitations of the grandees and people of fortune.[10]

His description of the city is as the Jacobites would have seen it, and some of the buildings mentioned remain largely unaltered to this day,

> . . . it is divided into four parts; the first is called the Middle, or Red-Town, which is surrounded by a strong brick wall; part of it is taken up by the castle, called Kremelin, being two miles in circumference, and is inclosed [sic] by three strong walls, each higher than the other, with a deep ditch on the outside . . . The other part of this division, without the castle, is

---

8 'Sir Francis Dashwood's Diary', p.202.
9 J.Cook, *Voyages and Travels through the Russian Empire, Tartary and part of the Kingdom of Persia*, v.1, p.64.
10 P.H.Bruce, *Memoirs of Peter Henry Bruce Esq. A Military Officer in the services of Prussia, Russia and Great Britain*, (London, 1782), p.79; John Cook made an almost identical observation in 1737, J.Cook, *Voyages and Travels through the Russian Empire, Tartary and part of the Kingdom of Persia*, v.1, p.121.

mostly inhabited by the grandees; here also stands the grand market, which is a very large square, divided into streets, where the merchants have shops for the sale of goods . . . The second part . . . is called Zaargorod, and is surrounded by a strong wall with battlements . . . here are the czar's stables, a foundry for cannon and bells, the arsenal, prince Menshikov's palace, general Bruce's house and many other gentlemen's houses of rank . . . The third division is called Skorodom, or the House-Market . . . Here one may buy a wooden house of any dimensions, have it carried to the place where it is to stand, set up and ready to dwell in, the third day after the purchase . . . The fourth division is called Strelitza Slaboda, where the military are generally quartered . . .[11]

Moscow and St Petersburg alternated as the capital and imperial seat according to the whim of successive monarchs throughout the first half of the century, and members of the court moved between the two cities as the need arose.

The Russians

Foreigners' experiences of the Russian people themselves varied greatly, and there are accounts describing both extreme xenophobia and warm hospitality. One of the most entertaining examples of hostility towards foreigners relates to an incident which occurred in the late seventeenth century to Patrick Gordon, Peter I's Jacobite general[12] and was recounted by Alexander Gordon, a Jacobite in Petrine service in the eighteenth century,

Few nations are fond of foreigners; and the Russians in particular are too apt to despise them. When these gentlemen were warm with their liquor, some of them spoke very disrespectfully of foreigners in general, and of the Scots in particular; they even went to the length of personal abuse. Mr Gordon, who to his last hour had a strong passion for his country, could not hear it abused by any body, without resenting the insult. He modestly represented to them the injustice of such indiscriminate satire . . . acknowledged there were bad, but insisted there were also good men in all countries – begged they would not lay him under the disagreeable necessity of quarrelling with them, by enlarging further on such a grating subject . . . The mildness of his reproof, like oil poured upon the fire, only served to inflame these brave fellows, who exclaimed against foreigners and Scotland more than ever. When he could bear their insolence no longer, he gave the one who sat next to him a blow on the temple, which brought him on the floor; in an instant, he and the other five were upon Mr Gordon, and seemed to make him fall a victim to their national prejudice; but our Author not in the least intimidated by their number, in

11 P.H.Bruce, *Memoirs*, pp.79–81.
12 Patrick Gordon, who died in 1699, and whose fascinating life is outside the scope of this book, left extensive letters and diaries which have been thoroughly researched by G.Herd in 'General Patrick Gordon of Auchleuchries – A Scot in Seventeenth Century Russian Service', Unpubl. Ph.D. thesis (Aberdeen University, 1994).

a few minutes obliged them to retreat, and had the glory of the victory in this very unequal combat.[13]

Outbreaks of anti-foreign feeling did not, it would seem, subside with increased exposure to foreigners and western culture over the course of the century. Indeed, similar incidents were recorded during subsequent reigns, and are described later in this book. There were, however, contrasting perceptions of the natives. The Scots doctor John Cook, for example, was favourably impressed, and commented that, 'The Russians, formerly savage, but now civilised, are a brave, and virtuous people, their manners mild, and their judges just; nor are there in the world better officers and bolder men . . . In Russia nothing pleased me more than their easy and elegant civility and descretion to strangers'.[14] In general, antipathy towards foreigners appears to have been more the exception than the rule, at least on a personal level. Jacobite accounts would suggest that most Jacobites managed well in Russian society, not least, one might speculate, by virtue of the common cultural predilection for strong liquor as a prerequisite for successful social interaction.

The majority of foreigners, who were admitted for their technical skills or military expertise, enjoyed a lifestyle considerably better than that of the common Russian. The mass of the population lived in a greater or lesser degree of poverty, in marked contrast with those higher up the social hierarchy. John Deane, who served in the Russian Navy until 1722, commented that,

. . . the Russian population in general are incredibly dispirited, partly through the despotic power of their superiors; as also by their own mean, sordid way of living, being much addicted to salts and acids and extremely afflicted with the scurvy; and so accustomed to *bagnios* [banya or Russian steam bath] that unless they have recourse at least once a week to cleanse themselves, they are almost consumed with vermin.[15]

Nevertheless, it was from these people that the bulk of Russia's armies and navies were conscripted, and they formed the rank-and-file which foreign mercenaries led successfully in battle on so many occasions.

Crime and punishment

Perhaps not surprisingly given such widespread poverty, crime was rife throughout Russia. Peter Henry Bruce commented in 1713 that, 'Murders are so frequent in Moscow that few nights pass without some people being found dead in the streets in the morning'.[16] Similarly, in 1718 Moscow was described as 'a hotbed of brigandage, everything is devastated, the number of

---

13 A. Gordon, *The History of Peter the Great* (Aberdeen, 1755), pp.v,vi,vii.
14 J.Cook, *Voyages and Travels*, v.1, p.75.
15 J.Deane, *History of the Russian Fleet during the reign of Peter the Great by a Contemporary Englishman* (1724), ed. by Vice Admiral Cyprian A.G.Bridge, Navy Records Society 15 (London, 1899).
16 P.H.Bruce, *Memoirs*, p.94.

lawbreakers is multiplying, and executions never stop'.[17] It was also recorded that, 'The highways are also much infested by those Rasbonicks ['razboinik' or brigand], as they are called, which makes it very dangerous travelling in any part of Russia'.[18] Punishment for criminals was barbaric by British standards of the time. In 1733, for example, it was noted that, 'the punishment for Murderers &c is a Hook that is drove up betwixt their ribbs, bearded, and that manner they are hung up by a Gibbett till they dye . . .'[19] Clearly, although aspects of Russian life may have appeared superficially progressive, foreigners must constantly have been reminded of the barbaric past on which the new more western 'civilisation' was precariously perched.

Religion and foreign integration

Despite Russia's increased exposure to western technology and culture, the Russian Orthodox religion continued to pervade every aspect of Russian life and greatly affected the ability of foreigners to become integrated into Russian society. Religion largely determined where foreigners were permitted to live, particularly early in the century. Although most foreign mercenaries spent much of the fighting season travelling with the army or were based with one of the fleets on the Baltic, Black, Azov, Caspian or White Seas, the majority of foreigners were concentrated in Moscow and St Petersburg, where the distinction between Orthodox and non-Orthodox was subject to regulation.

As early as the reign of Ivan the Terrible, a colony of Western European immigrants settled on the River Yauza, near Moscow. As the influx of foreigners increased, however, and they began to build churches and purchase property within the walls of Moscow itself, the Orthodox community began to object to the proximity of foreign places of worship to Orthodox churches. In 1643 it was decreed that all foreign churches within the city be destroyed. From 1652, all non-Orthodox foreigners were obliged to transfer to a settlement known as the New German Quarter (Novaya Nemetskaya sloboda) on the bank of the Neglina. As foreign experts in all fields, from military men to doctors, translators, craftsmen, merchants, factory owners, teachers and ministers, were attracted to Russia and moved into the 'sloboda', so it became a cosmopolitan centre, with a standard of culture exceeding that beyond its walls, and with access to the imported comforts and amenities of Western Europe. Peter Henry Bruce described it in 1713,

> A great number of foreigners live in the city, as Greeks, Armenians, Persians, Turks and Tartars, and are allowed the public exercise of their religious worship. At a small distance from the city, stands a large suburb called Inoisemska Slaboda, or Foreign Town, where the English, Dutch and Germans live; there are four Protestant and one Roman Catholic

---

17 Field Marshal Sheremetev to Secretary of Peter I, 1718, in M.T.Florinsky, *Russia: A History and an Interpretation* (New York, 1955), v.1, pp.400–401.
18 P.H.Bruce, *Memoirs*, p.94.
19 'Sir Francis Dashwood's Diary', p.212.

church in it, but not [sic] of them are allowed to have steeples or use bells. It is pleasantly situated on the River Neglina, on the banks of which are a number of pleasure-houses with fine gardens; the famous general Le Fort, built a magnificent palace here; the people live very agreeably among themselves, without interfering with the natives except upon business . . . The czar, when in Moscow, used always to make one in their parties of pleasure and entertainments, and paid them frequent visits.[20]

One hundred foreign families have been identified by surname as inhabitants of the 'sloboda' during Peter I's reign.[21] The countries of origin best represented were Germany, Holland, Livonia and Scotland; as many as twenty-four families are believed to have been of Scottish descent although many of these first came to Russia earlier in the seventeenth century, well before the Jacobite period. St Petersburg also had a small German Quarter on Admiralty Island,

Above the admiralty stands the Inoisemska Slaboda, or Foreign Town, where all European foreigners live, and have several Protestant and one Roman Catholic meeting houses . . . This land was also low and marshy, but was drained and raised by digging several canals through it.[22]

Over the course of the century, however, in the wake of Petrine reform, the strict divide between Orthodox and foreign habitation was gradually eroded. During Peter I's reign Russians began to buy land and settle in the Moscow 'sloboda' and by 1745 383 of the 625 properties were owned by Russians.[23] The settlement survived extensive rebuilding after a terrible fire in May 1737 which severely damaged the German Quarter as well as much of Moscow.[24] Although no longer strictly confined to foreigners, the area continued to be known as the 'Nemetskaya sloboda' until the twentieth century.

Segregation did, however, pertain to other areas of landownership. According to a decree of the seventeenth century, which was renewed in 1714, non-Orthodox foreigners were not permitted to own land on which there were Orthodox serfs.[25] Although exceptions were made for certain prominent individuals, like General Patrick Gordon in the late seventeenth century, the majority of landowning foreigners in the eighteenth century were granted estates outwith Orthodox Russia.[26]

Apart from dictating, to some extent, where foreigners lived, Russian Orthodoxy exerted direct restrictions on opportunities for integration. The

---

20 P.H.Bruce, *Memoirs*, p.81.
21 E.Amburger, 'Die weiteren Schicksale der alten Einwohnerschaft der Moskauer Ausländer-Sloboda seit der Zeit Peters I', *JGO* NF 20 (1972), pp.279–281.
22 P.H.Bruce, *Memoirs*, p.118.
23 E.Amburger, 'Die weiteren Schicksale', p.285.
24 Rondeau to Harrington, 11/10/1737, *SIRIO* 80, pp.155–156.
25 H.H.Nolte, *Religiöse Toleranz in Russland 1600–1725* (1969), p.526.
26 The Jacobites James Keith and Peter Lacy were granted estates in Livonia.

Church was an inescapable element of life in Russia, and Peter Henry Bruce observed of Moscow that, 'It is generally computed there are in this city fifteen hundred churches, chapels and cloysters; this surprising number is accounted for by every grandee's having a chapel and priest of his own'.[27] Many foreign accounts comment with astonishment on the extent to which Russian Orthodox custom affected the population on a daily basis. In the words of one observer,

> there is no people of what sort, soever, that keep their fasts more vigorously than the Russians . . . there are, for the whole nation, four fasts in the year, of six weeks each fast, which is of great inconvenience, and kills great numbers in a year. One would think the Devill might have spared that invention in this Country, where the poor people are So very miserable in the best of times[28]

John Deane, who was with the fleet near St Petersburg at this time, was shocked by the effects of religious ritual on the Russian crews, which must have impacted adversely on their fighting ability.

> . . . their religion enjoins a strict observance of three annual fasts, amounting in the whole to fifteen weeks, besides every Wednesday and Friday throughout the year; and so tenacious is the ignorant superstitious multitude of this less essential part, that when great numbers of sick have been landed from aboard the Russian fleet, especially in these fasting seasons, and the Tsar has ordered a provision of fresh meat and set a guard to prevent the introducing all other support, many have actually perished rather than violate their ill-informed consciences in eating of prohibited viands.[29]

Other Russian Orthodox practices involved excesses of the opposite extreme, as Dashwood noted, 'perhaps there is no Country where the Papas (or Priests) not even in England, gett drunk so frequently as in this Country, and that mostly with Malt Brandy, though they have a liquor, made of Honey, that is very much used'.[30] Peter Henry Bruce observed of 'Butter Week' before Lent that the Russians, 'employ it with the most extravagant excess in drinking brandy and melted butter, which they pour down their throats in such amazing quantities, that one would imagine the least spark of fire would set their bodies in a flame.[31] The religious faith which dictated the life of the ordinary Russian to a deep level undoubtedly left a strong impression on all foreign visitors to Russia.

Attempts by Peter I and subsequent monarchs to contain the power of the Church notwithstanding, Church and State remained inextricably linked by

---

27 P.H.Bruce, *Memoirs*, p.116.
28 'Sir Francis Dashwood's Diary', p.211
29 J.Deane, *History of the Russian Fleet* , pp.104–105.
30 'Sir Francis Dashwood's Diary', p.211.
31 P.H.Bruce, *Memoirs*, p.106.

the sheer strength of religious faith throughout Orthodox Russia. Foreigners of all religions, with the exception of Jews, were permitted to reside in Russia, but the practice of non-Orthodox religion was more restricted, particularly during the early part of the century. The Orthodox Church did not officially sanction Catholic Mass, although it was occasionally tolerated in practice, and although Protestant churches had been permitted in Russia since the beginning of the seventeenth century, the first Catholic church did not appear until 1694. The erection of all non-Orthodox churches required the special permission of the Tsar.

Peter I recognised the importance of religious tolerance for the encouragement of foreign immigration and the development of Russia into a modern state. In 1689 he invited Huguenots to Russia on the promise of religious freedom, and his 1702 Tolerance Manifesto extended this promise to all creeds. He allowed his conquests in Livonia, Estonia and Finland to retain their Lutheran faith and sanctioned the building of stone churches by both Catholics and Protestants.[32] At his death in 1725 there were five Protestant parishes in St Petersburg, one at Kronstadt, two at Narva, three in Moscow, two at the iron works south of Moscow, two at Archangel and one in Astrakhan.[33] There were also several Catholic congregations, including one in St Petersburg. The number of foreign churches in St Petersburg was the same when Dashwood visited it in 1733,

> In St Petersburg there is sixteen Churches ten Russian and six foreign, for Strangers, in the Part, called Petersburgh there are three Russian, in the Admiralty Island there are four Russian and one Lutheran German Church, one reformed Dutch One French Catholick, and one reformed french, at Vasiliostoff [Vasilii Ostrov], one Russian and one German lutheran. In the Artillery quarters, two Russian and one German Lutheran.[34]

During the reigns of Anna Ivanovna and Elisabeth the freedom of western foreigners to practise their own religion was largely condoned, although proselityzing remained strictly illegal.

Despite this degree of latitude granted to western immigrants in the practice of religion, Russian Orthodoxy was directly equated with Russian nationality, and conversion to Orthodoxy was an essential precondition to any degree of integration. Indeed, to Russian eyes western religions ranked only marginally above the 'heathen' practices encountered in the south of the Empire. Recent or temporary incomers, labelled 'inozemcy' by Russians, were differentiated from 'nemtsy', (meaning 'Germans', lit. 'dumb', but applied to all western foreigners), who were the Non-Orthodox born in Russia. An increasing level of foreign integration was associated with a loss of individual freedoms. 'Nemtsy' and those who purchased Russian land were considered subjects of the Tsar and could only travel abroad for short periods with his permission, while

32 E.Amburger, *Geschichte des Protestantismus in Russland* (Stuttgart, 1961), p.38.
33 E.Amburger, *Geschichte des Protestantismus*, p.49.
34 'Sir Francis Dashwood's Diary', p.211.

Orthodox converts and those who entered Russian service on a permanent contract ceded completely the right to leave Russia.[35] These restrictions notwithstanding, a considerable number converted to Orthodoxy and eventually became completely russified.[36] Of these, the best known of British origin were James Daniel (Jakob Wilimovich) Bruce and his brother Robert, whose ancestor had left Scotland for Russia during the time of Cromwell. By Peter I's reign, both had converted to Orthodoxy and had integrated fully into Russian society. Most of the Jacobites with whom this book is concerned, however, did not convert, but either left Russia or died there in their original faith.

As might be expected, the marriage of Non-Orthodox foreigners to Russians was strictly prohibited under Church law until 1718, when the Orthodox Church recognised Protestant baptism.[37] In 1721, the Holy Synod permitted Non-Orthodox to take Orthodox spouses without converting, on the condition that the children be baptised in the Orthodox faith.[38] In view of the restrictions placed on integration, it is perhaps not surprising that many foreigners married their own kind. The 'Register of all the Christenings, Weddings and Burials in the English Congregation', a document begun in 1706 by Charles Thirlby, minister to the British Factory in Russia, and continued by his successors, recorded the births, marriages and deaths of a congregation which included many Germans and Scots. The British Factory was part of The Russia Company, a Chartered Company which was operating from London until as late as 1917.[39] The Factory and its congregation moved in 1723 from Moscow to St Petersburg with its minister Thomas Consett, and the Register provides a valuable record of the social fabric of a small foreign community. Between 1706 and 1750 39 marriages between foreigners are recorded, including that in 1726 between the Jacobite Sir Henry Stirling and Ann Gordon, daughter of the Jacobite Admiral Thomas Gordon.[40] There are several further instances of Jacobites in Russia choosing their spouses from other families sympathetic to the Jacobite cause. The Irish Jacobite Peter Lacy's two daughters married George Brown and Patrick Stuart, and Thomas Gordon's granddaughter Ann (daughter of Jean Young, née Gordon and John Young), married Lt.Thomas MacKenzie, who was a naval officer at Archangel in 1738, and it is recorded that she bore a son Thomas two years later.[41] The register is evidence of a close-knit

35 E.Amburger, 'Die weiteren Schicksale', p.275; H.H.Nolte, 'Religiöse Toleranz in Russland 1600–1725', in *JGO* (1969), 17, p.503; Platonov, *Moskva i Zapad* (Berlin, 1969), p.133.
36 E.Amburger, 'Die weiteren Schicksale', p.282.
37 H.H.Nolte, *Religiöse Toleranz in Russland 1600–1725*, Göttinger Bausteine zur Geschichtswissenschaft, 41 (Göttingen, 1969), p.188.
38 E.Amburger, *Geschichte des Protestantismus*, p.44.
39 For further details of the British Factory see, 'The Russia Company of London in the Eighteenth Century: the effective survival of a 'Regulated' Chartered Company, *The Guildhall Miscellany*, 4 (1973), pp.222–236.
40 'The Register of all the Christenings, Weddings and Burials in the English Congregation', Diocese of London, Register of the British Factory in Russia 1706–1815, Guildhall Library, MS.11192b.
41 T.Gordon to J.Young 24/4/1738, T.Gordon to J.Gordon 11/3/1740, GD24/1/855, ff.69,81.

ex-patriate community, frequently brought together by the occasion of a birth, marriage or death. Many children were born, but child mortality appears to have been high, as does the incidence of re-marriage following the death of a partner. Both Moscow and St Petersburg had their own cemeteries exclusively for non-Orthodox burials, which may still be visited today.

Education

Formal education in Russia was in its infancy in the early eighteenth century. John Milton, who had visited Russia towards the end of the seventeenth century, commented of the Russian people that, 'they have no learning, nor will suffer to be among them'.[42] By 1736 Admiral Thomas Gordon was less disparaging of the level of knowledge in Russia. John Cook recorded his conversation with Gordon at his home in Cronstadt,

> He said a knowledge of business was the best recommendation in that country, but at the same time an introduction to the principal overseers, made every thing more easy, and told me, that although Russia was but in its infancy in most branches of arts and learning, yet I would experience as smart an examination as in any country.[43]

During the first years of his reign Peter I had placed the existing Church schools at the service of the state and made them open to secular scholars. In 1698 he founded the school of navigation in Moscow, which was later moved to Azov. In 1701 a new artillery school and a school of mathematics and navigation were opened in Moscow. Among the foreign specialists appointed to teach at the school of mathematics and navigation were James Daniel Bruce and Henry Farquharson, both of Scots descent. A further school of military engineering was established in Moscow in 1713 and moved to St Petersburg in 1723, and a medical school was opened in Moscow in 1707 under the direction of the Scots Jacobite physician Robert Erskine.[44] Although Peter's attempts to educate the native population enjoyed mixed success, it is known that the children of foreigners were among the several thousand pupils who attended the new schools. Other foreigners either sent their sons to school in Britain or employed tutors for them in Russia, as the Russian gentry did.

Society and links with the West

It is probable, despite the frequent arrival of trading ships and the availability, albeit rather out-of-date, of western gazettes, that foreigners felt somewhat isolated from current affairs in western Europe. On one occasion Admiral Thomas Gordon asked his correspondent John Menzies in Paris,

---

42 John Milton, *A brief History of Muscovia: and of other less known Countries lying eastward of Russia as far as Cathay* (London, 1682), p.21.
43 J.Cook, *Voyages and Travels*, v.1, p.8.
44 For further details of educational institutions in Russia, see, for example, E.Donnert, *Russia in the Age of Enlightenment* (Leipzig, 1986), pp.53–94.

... now & then to refresh one with a line or two with what Passes in the world for we are heer[sic] at a Great Distance from those parts where matters of moment are transacted, and what we know is from second and third hands, which cannot be depended on.[45]

Many Western luxuries were certainly less available or more expensive in Russia than Britain, and had to be ordered periodically from abroad. In 1721, for example, Gordon asked William Cooper to bring over 'a chariot', as 'furniture is scarce to be had in this place and that very dear'.[46] Gordon's letters are filled with requests to friends in Scotland and abroad and Jacobite merchants at Rouen and Bordeaux for such items as 'wine and champagne', claret, prunes, vinegar, olives, anchovies, clothes, bedlinen, greyhounds, books, medicine and naval instruments.[47] James Keith, similarly, was sent Spanish sword blades, guns, Torrento wine, medicines, books, and even a Spanish servant by his brother, the Earl Marischal, in Spain.[48] If one had money and patience, however, most items could be acquired. An inventory of the furniture in Admiral Gordon's St Petersburg house, drawn up in preparation for use of the house by the French envoy Campredon, suggests that he lived in some comfort, and had many of the possessions one would expect of a man of his rank in the British navy.[49]

Foreigners in the main cities of Russia nevertheless enjoyed a lively social scene. Peter Henry Bruce observed that the residents of the German Quarter in Moscow had free access to entertainment,

As the country abounds with great plenty of every necessary of life, people live at a very cheap rate, and regale themselves with balls and entertainments, which they can furnish at a very small expence[sic]. In the summer time they carry tents and pitch them in the neighbouring woods, where they make merry with dancing on the green till night.[50]

These foreign cultural activities were, increasingly, shared by the highest ranks of Russian society,

The people of rank and fashion in Moscow having laid aside the old customs and manners of their fathers, now live very gay, dress in the French fashion, and converse with more freedom than formerly, and as the fair sex are allowed all manner of freedom in company, they live in a perpetual round of pleasure and diversion, spending most part of their time in balls and entertainments.[51]

By contrast, however, the lower classes were more traditional in their forms of entertainment,

45 T.Gordon to J.Menzies, n/d 1724, NAS GD24/1/859, f.287.
46 T.Gordon to W.Cooper, 5/1/1721, NAS GD24/1/859, f.272.
47 NAS GD24/1/855, f.80; GD24/1/859, ff.293, 298, 308, 335.
48 NAS GD156/62/2, ff.11,17,54,62.
49 'Inventory of furniture in T.Gordon's house', 22/4/1723, NAS GD24/1/854, f.42.
50 P.H.Bruce, *Memoirs*, p.81.
51 P.H.Bruce, *Memoirs*, p.84.

As for the second rank of the people, they still retain much of their old manner of living; at their entertainments none but the men appear; the master of the house waits on his guests till the dessert . . . when he takes his seat amongst them and does all he can to make them drunk, for it would be a great reflexion upon them if any of the company should get out of the house without being drunk.[52]

In addition to balls and private functions for their pleasure and entertainment, foreigners had, over the course of the century, increasing access to the fine arts. A generation of Russian painters, sculptors and engravers was gaining widespread recognition, and Russian literature was gaining ground, inspired by French and German writers and poets. Peter I encouraged the theatre as a medium for education and transformed the theatre in Red Square into a drama school. He employed musicians from Hamburg and Sweden, and established several orchestras. After his death theatrical and musical entertainment continued to enjoy popularity, and several operas were written and performed. In 1736, during the reign of Anna Ivanovna, Cook admired the theatre in St Petersburg and observed that, 'The Empress has a large playhouse in the city, with German and French actors; also a set of Italian singers'. Such cultural diversion was, however, strictly for the social elite, for, although it was commented that, 'No person pays for going to either plays or concerts', it was also the case that, 'none are allowed to enter, except such as have tickets by authority'.[53] When Elisabeth ascended the throne in 1741 cultural life flourished on a grander scale. French theatre and Italian opera began to be performed on a weekly basis in the grand court theatre built by Bartolomeo Carlo Rastrelli. By 1750 the cultural pursuits available to the foreigner in the major cities of Russia were beginning to approach those of cities elsewhere in Europe.

There is no doubt that eighteenth century Russia presented the foreigner with abundant opportunity for new experience and adventure, and it was in this spirit that many Jacobites travelled there. With its strong asiatic links and alien traditions it was a very different destination from that encountered by Jacobite exiles in, for example, Sweden, France and Spain. It is this world which forms the backdrop for the political and military activities of the Jacobites which follow.

52 P.H.Bruce, *Memoirs*, p.84.
53 J.Cook, *Voyages and Travels*, v.1, p.66.

PART ONE

The Reign of Peter I, 1715–1725

ONE

Jacobite Recruitment and Peter I, 1715–1725

The decade between the failed Jacobite Rising of 1715 and Peter I's death in 1725 saw the recruitment into Russian service of a wave of Jacobite exiles. There were a number of reasons why Russia was attractive to disaffected Britons during this period. Firstly, Peter I's reign was characterised by a high level of Russo-Jacobite political activity, the result of poor Anglo-Russian relations, which encouraged Jacobites to seek the Tsar's support for the restoration of James III to the British throne. Secondly, at this time Russia's growing armed forces offered great opportunities to men experienced in military affairs and in need of a career, from which the exiles were naturally in a position to benefit. Russia was, therefore, one of the most attractive of the destinations reached by the diaspora because its attraction for Jacobites combined the opportunity for the expression of Jacobite loyalty with the promise of good career prospects and material gain.

The extent to which allegiance to the Stuart cause provided Jacobites with an incentive to seek service in Russia, and whether they preserved this political identity while in exile, will be discussed at a later stage. Before examining the political motivations which brought some of these men to Russia, however, it is important to consider the quality and type of livelihood Russia offered in the context of their material and career requirements. The need to create a new livelihood in the host country was to most, after all, of immediate practical concern, and had direct bearing on the extent to which they could remain involved with the Stuart cause.

Who were the Exiles?

There is a generally-held view that the Jacobite diaspora resulting from the 1715 Rising was a largely aristocratic phenomenon. Bruce Lenman refers to the exiles as 'aristocratic Jacobite refugees'.[1] Frank McLynn describes 'the Jacobite diaspora' as '. . . aristocratic in character rather than bourgeois . . . It presented the peculiar spectacle of an entire section of a given aristocracy following its sovereign into exile'.[2] One Jacobite, Campbell of Glendarule, attempting in 1717 to categorise participants in the late Rising according to their financial needs, distinguished three main groups,

> . . . First, those attainted, as they are generally of the first rank and most useful to the King, will have difficulty to go home with any sort of security. Next, those having estates or any valuable conveniency in their own country, that have not rendered themselves exceeding obnoxious, will

---

1 Bruce Lenman, 'The Jacobite Diaspora', *History Today,* 30 (1980), p.8.
2 Frank McLynn, *The Jacobites* (London, 1985), p.136.

very readily take the hint and go home, in which they do well for many reasons . . . As to the third and last sort, and of the least import, an advice or hint will not so easily prevail with them. Their circumstances on this side render them easier than they have been at home or can be by returning now.[3]

Glendarule's letter indeed indicated that the exiles in most desperate straits were those '. . . of the first rank and most useful to the King', that is, the landed gentry rather than commoners. Among their number, of course, were the fifty-three Jacobites whose lands were to be forfeited to the Crown, forty-nine of these if they did not surrender themselves before June 1716.[4] The implication is that the aristocracy, to which many of the leaders of the Rising belonged, had most to lose as a result of the forfeiture of titles and estates, and once attainted became exiles in the true sense of the word.

A cursory glance at the diaspora in Russia would tend to confirm that titled and land-owning families were well represented. It included such as George Brown, a member of the Irish Jacobite family the Browns of Camus, Sir Henry Stirling of Ardoch and his uncle Dr Robert Erskine, who was a cousin of the Earl of Mar, James Fitzjames, Duke of Liria, son of the Duke of Berwick and grandson to James II himself, Duncan Robertson, younger brother of Alexander, 17th Laird of Struan and 13th Chief of the Clan Donnachaidh, Robert Fullarton, son of the Laird of Dudwick, Kenneth Sutherland, 3rd Lord Duffus, Alexander Gordon of Auchintoul, and James Keith, younger brother of the Earl Marischal of Scotland.

Of these men, however, only one, Lord Duffus, had actually been attainted and exiled for his participation in the 1715 Rising. The remainder were Jacobite exiles in a wider sense, some involved in the Rising, some opposed to the Hanoverian monarchy, who had left Britain to escape government reprisals on the disaffected.

If one is to use the term 'exile' in this looser sense, one must also reappraise the assumption that the diaspora was largely composed of gentry. Political disaffection as a motive for leaving Britain is at times difficult to distinguish from economic considerations. By 1715, many Roman Catholic landed families found themselves deeply in debt as a result of legal measures debarring Catholics from positions of responsibility in all areas of state employment, in both the military and civil services.[5] The accession of George I introduced similar penal laws designed to prevent Tories from holding office in the armed forces, the civil service, the judiciary and the Church.[6] Thus the only oppor-

---

3 Campbell of Glendarule to J.Paterson, Bordeaux, 19/11/1717, *Calendar of the Stuart Papers, Belonging to His Majesty the King*, Publications of the Historical Manuscripts Commission, 7 vols. (London, 1902–1923), 5, p.217.

4 Acts of Attainder were passed on a number of Jacobites in 1715 and subsequently. John, Earl of Mar, was attainted with the Marquis of Tullibardine, the Earl of Linlithgow and Lord Drummond on 17 February 1715, George, Earl Marischal together with the Earls of Seaforth, Southesk and Panmure on 17 May 1716. *Journals of the House of Lords*, 2 George I, pp. 294a, 350b.

5 B.Lenman, *The Jacobite Risings in Britain 1689–1746* (London, 1980), p.118.

6 E.Cruickshanks, *Political Untouchables: the Tories and the '45*, (London, 1979), p.4.

tunity for Jacobite Tories or Catholics to follow a career was '. . . in the service of foreign princes'.[7]

In Russia there was also a significant number of Jacobite exiles who had played no active part in the 1715 Rising, nor were of noble family. Many of these men had left or been expelled from the Royal Navy, some, like Thomas Gordon, had probably refused to take an oath of allegiance to George I.[8] Others, like Thomas Saunders had to leave, '. . . for having spoken ill of the Elector of Hanover and his government'.[9]

Another group of disaffected Britons of various social origins, including Jacobites, left British service for Russia as a result of a period of acute disillusionment in the British armed forces. Morale was at a particularly low ebb in 1717, and this was exacerbated in early 1718 when Tory and Whig opposition united and defeated the ministry to reduce the number of half-pay officers. The Jacobite George Home reported to the Earl of Mar that,

> . . . A great many of the sea half-pay officers are gone into the Muscovite and Swedish service and some of their land officers were beginning to take that course, which has startled the government not little.[10]

Although remaining in Britain posed no real risk to these men, they were forced abroad to seek employment, and became 'exiles' in this sense, their plight not directly related to their political beliefs.

By 1717, even Jacobites who had been exiled once for their involvement in the 1715 Rising and had settled as financial dependants of the exiled court were forced to seek a livelihood elsewhere. They were as much affected by material considerations as any driven abroad by lack of opportunity at home.[11] In May 1718, Thomas Bruce reported of Jacobites dependent on the exiled court that, '. . . All or most of them have run themselves into debt, having now

---

7 Lenman, *The Jacobite Risings in Britain*, p.118.

8 Thomas Gordon was so opposed to the Union and the amalgamation of the Scots with the English navy that it was said in 1707 that he 'would soon be obliged to quit the service because he refuses to take the oath of abjuration, which is going, in consequence of the union to be imposed on all officers' (Earl of Erroll to N.Hooke, in M. Bulloch, *The Gay Gordons* (London, 1908), p.63). Although he evaded this fate in 1707, he might well have refused to take an oath of loyalty to King George, and certainly left the British Navy illegally. Many years later, in 1740, when he was applying to Lord Golovin for permission to retire to Scotland, he referred to the fact that, 'When I left Great Brittain I omitted to beg the Government's leav to go out of that Kingdom, which renders me obnoxious to be persecuted by the Ministry of Great Brittain'. Gordon to Lord Golovin, 5/11/1740, NAS Abercairney GD 24/1/855, f.88.

9 Thomas Saunders to Campion, 10/5/1718, BL Stowe 232, ff.96,96v.

10 George Home of Whytfield to Earl of Mar, Paris, 27/9//1717, *Calendar of the Stuart Papers Belonging to His Majesty the King, Preserved at Windsor Castle*, 7 vols. (London, 1902–1923), 5, p.79.

11 The main financial resources of the exiled court were the pension of 50,000 livres a month from the French Court to the Queen, and 5,000 Roman crowns a quarter from the Pope. The total annual income was therefore 683,000 French livres, the equivalent of between 42,000 and 43,000 English pounds. The pension from France was not regularly paid, so Jacobites lacking other sources of income often found themselves in debt. *HMC Stuart*, 5, pp.xx,xxi; Cardinal de Noailles to James III, 24/1/1718, Ibid., p.404.

the second month running in arrear'. There were only two courses of action. Either they '. . . transport themselves home, where they may have bread, or to some other place, where they may have service'.[12] James III attempted to counteract this by seeking employment for those who had served him immediately after the failure of the 1715 Rising. Already by 1716, the Court at Avignon was seen as a place of stagnation. Mar wrote to Sir Hugh Paterson of the hopelessness and insecurity facing exiles there,

> . . . There's little appearance of any service being got for them elsewhere and none, if they come from here. They are apt to take it ill and think themselves slighted if they are not allowed to come here, and by their coming they spend any little they have and it will keep them from being employed elsewhere'.[13]

It was the financial plight of many of the Jacobite community, as much as any thought of promoting the Cause, which motivated the Jacobite leadership to recommend them for employment elsewhere. In addition, it was desirable to relieve the exiled court of responsibility for them until such time as the men could be of service again. This concept of temporary foreign employment was stressed in Mar's plea to Dr Erskine, written on behalf of a brother of Aytoun of Inchdarnie's in Fife for recommendation to the Russian army. He referred to other Jacobites in France,

> . . . worthy honest gentlemen, your countrymen, who have lost their all by endeavouring to do their duty in serving their rightful king and country, who would gladly enter the service of some foreign prince, till their own has occasion for them. If your master thought fit to employ some of them, I am sure he could not be better served . . .[14]

Many 'foreign princes' were approached in this way, including Spain, Sweden,[15] Sicily and Russia, military service being the obvious employment for men whose exile was a consequence of armed rebellion. Although other outlets could be found, those without military skills were often bound by penury to the exiled court. John, eighth Master of Sinclair, for example, who had no naval experience, wrote in despair to Thomas Gordon, '. . . its a great misfortune to have nothing to doe, would to God I had followed your trade . . .'[16] Relatively young men with military skills and fit for active service were at an obvious advantage in the search for mercenary employment.

The 'Jacobite exile' is not, therefore, easily categorised, either in terms of social origin or of level of political dissidency. The very varied composition of the diaspora in Russia was illustrative of this, and defies any but the most

12 Thomas Bruce to Lt.Gen. Dillon, 17/5/1718, *HMC Stuart* 6, p.440.
13 Earl of Mar to Sir Hugh Paterson, Avignon, 3/8/1716, *HMC Stuart* 2, p.323.
14 Mar to Dr Erskine, Avignon, 3/8/1716, *HMC Stuart* 2, p.323.
15 In 1716, the British Ambassador in Paris, Lord Stair, learned that the Swedish envoy in Paris, Sparre, was accepting Jacobites into Swedish service. L.A.Nikoforov, *Russko-angliiskie otnosheniya pri Petre I* (Moscow, 1950), p.134.
16 John Sinclair to Thomas Gordon, 8/5/1724, NAS Abercairney GD 24/1/856, ff.182–183.

general description of a body of men who, to a greater or lesser extent, shared a preference for a Stuart over a Hanoverian monarchy, and were disaffected both to George I and to his government.

Russia's Reputation and Reality: 'Nothing at heart but the welfare of his subjects . . . ?'[17]

Peter I's efforts to attract foreign talent in order to build Russia into a world power gained it recognition as a country in which merit was rewarded by promotion, and career opportunities for foreigners were limitless.[18] His reputation abroad stemmed principally from his first European tour in 1697–98, when he had recruited hundreds of foreign specialists from Hamburg.[19] The *Atlas Geographus*, published in London in 1711, observed that the Russians, '. . . make use of a great many Scots and German officers, who instruct them in all the warlike exercises that are practised by other European nations'.[20] In April 1702, Peter had issued an edict to attract to Russia, '. . . foreigners of all nations who understood military affairs and had served some time'.[21] This was also known as the 'Tolerance Manifesto', because, besides a safe passage and a special legal dispensation to be tried by Roman, rather than Russian law,[22] it promised foreigners freedom of confession.[23] In terms of attracting Jacobites, this situation compared favourably with that in Spain, where, as James Keith and Captain Carse discovered, non-Catholics were debarred from promotion.[24] Contemporaries therefore regarded Peter I as an enlightened monarch, who had brought civilisation to Russia. The Jacobite John Menzies, writing to Thomas Gordon, described him as '. . . a Great

17 William Cooper to Thomas Gordon, 24/5/1721, NAS Abercairney GD 24/1/856, f.159.
18 Foreigners had served in Russian armies for centuries, and the practice of foreign recruitment had actually reached its peak under Peter I's father, Alexei Fyodorovich, when about eighty per cent of commanders were non-Russian. However, Peter's superior military and political prominence has reaped him much of the credit for the import of Western talent. See R.Hellie, 'The Petrine Army: Continuity, Change and Impact', *CASS* 8 (1974), p.242.
19 Erik Amburger, 'Aus dem Leben und Wirken von Hamburgern in Russland', in *Fremde und Einheimische im Wirtschafts- und Kulturleben des Neuzeitlichen Russland* (Wiesbaden, 1982), p.293.
20 *Atlas Geographus*, 5 vols. (London, 1711–1717), 1, pp.159–160.
21 A.Gordon, *The History of Peter the Great . . . 2 vols.* (Aberdeen, 1755), p.165.
22 S.M.Solov'ev, *Istoriya Rossii s drevneishikh vremen*, 3rd ed., 29 vols. and index, (St.Petersburg, 1911), 15, p.1344.
23 The manifesto was formulated by a Livonian, von Patkühl, in terms which were enlightened for their time: '. . . dasz wir, bey der Uns von dem Allerhöchsten verliehenen Gewalt, Uns keines Zwanges über die Gewissen der Menschen anmassen, und gerne zulassen, dasz ein jeder Christ, auff seine eigene Verantwortung sich die Sorge seiner Seligkeit lass angelegen seyn'. Quoted in H.Nolte, 'Verständnis und Bedeutung der Religiösen Toleranz in Russland, 1600–1725', *JGO* NF 17,3 (1969), p.513.
24 Religious intolerance in Spain encouraged Keith to go to Russia, J. Keith, *A Fragment of a memoir of Field-marshal James Keith written by himself 1714–1734* (repr. Edinburgh, 1843), p.68; Carse (also Kerse), had returned to Scotland from a Scottish regiment in Finland to fight in the 1715 Rising, was promoted by James III to captain, and, like Keith, was debarred from serving as an officer at the siege of Gibraltar. Eventually his cousin, Father Clark, confessor to the Spanish King, recommended him to the Russian ambassador, for Russian service. Report of I. Shcherbatov, 3/14 June, 1728, AVPR F9 o1 ll.3–3v.

Emperor . . . he has, as it were, Created his Country and Greatness out of Nothing. Has bred and Civiliz'd and Aggrandize'd a People that seem'd not onely unfit, but unwilling for such a happiness'.[25] One recruit, William Cooper, viewed Russia as a welcome escape from the Hanoverian regime, writing that, '. . . My pleasure is in exchange of this Mortgaged Nation, I am going to a Prince, who has nothing at heart but the welfare of his subjects'.[26] He had no difficulty in finding other recruits who shared this view, and were willing to try their fortunes in Russia, '. . . having heard how Gracious a Monarch the Czar is, and how likely merit is to succeed'.[27] Kenneth, Lord Duffus, whose Jacobitism had deprived him of a captaincy in the British Navy, turned to Russia to pursue a naval career, '. . . The Czar being the only prince at present I find gives any encouragement to men of my profession'.[28] James Paterson of Prestonhall, the nephew of John, Master of Sinclair, and brother to the great Jacobite Sir Hugh Paterson, applied to enter the Russian navy because it promised better promotion prospects than that of Italy.[29] Thomas Gordon, to whom these applications were addressed, did nothing for his part to dispel their optimism, but made it known that he was,

> . . . very pleas'd with the countrey and the people, and so is every person that has work and does his duty, you may in my name assure any gentleman that you intend to engage that the service is as agreable and easy here as anywhere.[30]

Contrary to Peter I's reputation, however, during the last fifteen years of his reign, he was in fact attempting to replace the foreign officers in his armed forces with native talent by cutting the incentives previously offered to foreigners. By 1709, land officers could no longer expect immediate promotion, but were being accepted at the same rank as they had held at home.[31] In November 1720 a decree was issued by the War College, forbidding recruitment of all

25 John Menzies to Thomas Gordon, 2/1/1722, NAS Abercairney GD 24/1/856, f.164.
26 William Cooper to Thomas Gordon, 24/5/1721, NAS Abercairney GD 24/1/856, f.159.
27 William Cooper to Thomas Gordon, 14/3/1720/21 o.s., NAS Abercairney GD 24/1/856, f.150.
28 H.Tayler, ed., _Jacobite Epilogue, A Further Selection of Letters from Jacobites among the Stuart Papers at Windsor_ (Edinburgh, 1941), pp.xv,xvi.
29 He had left the British navy, then served as a lieutenant in 'the King of Sicily's service' after a period of exile in France, (Theophilus Oglethorpe to Mar, 22/1/1718, _HMC Stuart_ 5, p.402.) In April 1724, however, he wrote to Thomas Gordon in Russia, under whom he had served in the British Navy, complaining that Spain's annexation of Sicily and Sardinia in 1718 and 1719 had decimated the navy and ruined his career prospects. Although he had sufficient to live on, sixty pounds a year, the service did not offer the career advancement he felt his position deserved and he found 'this way of serving is very disagreable espetially to those who have been bred up otherwise'. He viewed the Russian fleet, by contrast, as offering superior career opportunities, as 'a fleet where there is prospect of advancement'. J.Paterson to T.Gordon, 4/4/1724, NAS Abercairney GD 24/1/856, f.154.
30 Thomas Gordon to William Cooper, n.d.1720, NAS Abercairney GD 24/1/859, f.271.
31 M.D.Rabinovich, 'Sotsialnoe proiskhozhdenie i imushchestvennoe polozhenie ofitserov reguliarnoi russkoi armii v kontse Severnoi voiny', in Pavlenko, ed., _Rossiya v period reform Petra I_ (Moscow, 1973), p.157.

foreign officers but those from the Baltic area.[32] At the end of the Northern War in 1721, foreign sailors were dismissed and sent home by Imperial decree.[33] The same year commissioned ranks in the artillery were restricted to Russians only.[34] In 1722, foreign officers entering Russian service were ordered to remain in their former rank for at least one year, and were to be accepted at ranks lower than their Russian counterparts.[35] In the following year, an attempt was made to deprive the newly-conquered Balts of their superior 'foreign' status by engaging them on the same terms as Russians.[36] According to statistics of naval servicemen for 1721, foreign officers filled only an eighth of officer ranks, as opposed to the proportion of a third foreigners to two-thirds native officers laid down in the 1711 military 'establishment'.[37] If one is to judge by this legislative trend, Russia appears not to have been as welcoming to foreign mercenaries as is commonly believed.

Career Opportunities for Naval Jacobites

In the light of the measures described, one would expect career prospects for foreign officers to have decreased sharply over Peter's reign, and there is indeed some evidence of this. The Jacobite Adam Urquhart, for example, complained to Admiral Apraksin in 1719 that he had been promised the rank of captain lieutenant when he was recruited in 1717, but had to serve as a lieutenant due to a lack of vacancies.[38] Likewise, in 1723, four Britons recruited by Van den Burg in Amsterdam were appointed to the same ranks they had held in Britain.[39] Evidence suggests, however, that rather than being determined by Imperial directives, as historians have tended to conclude, career prospects for foreigners fluctuated in response to current requirements.[40] By contrast with this apparent downward trend in recruitment and promotion for foreigners in general, the Jacobites, and particularly those from the Royal Navy, were often favoured with immediate promotion and, in fact, rose higher than would have been possible in Britain.

Many Jacobites appear to have benefited from preferential prospects extended to ex-Royal Navy officers, the result of Peter I's admiration of the Royal Navy. Thomas Gordon, a relative of Patrick Gordon of Auchleuchries, who had served as a captain in the Scots Navy and the Royal Navy since 1703, was accepted into Russian service in 1717 as a captain commodore. Within two years he was already a 'shautbenakht'.[41] In two more years he was a

32 Apraksin to von Lieven, 7/11/1720, RGAVMF F233 o1 d257 ll.543–544.
33 Note from Admiralty College, 7/3/1722, RGAVMF F212 o11 d54 ll.104–5.
34 L.G.Beskrovny, 'Reforma armii i sozdanie voennomorskogo flota', in B.B.Kafengauz *et al.*, eds., *Ocherki istorii SSSR period feodalizma, Rossiya vo pervoi chetverti XVIIIv.* (Moscow, 1954), p.359; Rabinovich 'Sotsialnoe proiskhozhdenie' pp.154, 170–171, P.Dukes, *The Making of Russian Absolutism 1613–1801* (New York, 1982), p.72.
35 Imperial decree, 28/2/1722, *PSZ* 3913.
36 Imperial decree, 23/9/1723, *PSZ* 4309.
37 Rabinovich, p.154; *PSZ* 5, 2319.
38 Urquhart to Apraksin, 12/3/1719, RGAVMF F233 o1 d177, l.401.
39 RGAVMF F212 o11 d34/189 ll.81,103,116,132.
40 October, November 1723, RGAVMF F212 o11 d34/189.
41 'Shautbenakht' is the earlier term, borrowed from Dutch, for the rank of rear-admiral.

vice-admiral, and in 1727 admiral of the fleet. Thomas Saunders was likewise recruited as captain commodore in May 1717 [42] after serving as a captain in Britain, and was 'shautbenakht' by 1721. Kenneth, Lord Duffus, as John Deane recorded, arrived in St Petersburg in 1722 and, '. . . soon had the character of rear admiral conferred on him', although he had only been a captain in the British Navy.[43] Robert Little was recruited in Amsterdam in summer 1717 as a second rank captain. In November 1718, after his arrival, his request for promotion to first rank captain[44] was apparently granted, for Deane noted that, '. . . one Mr Little made a captain by the Tsar soon after his landing'.[45] Contrary to the trend of legislation designed to restrict foreign careers discussed above, prospects for naval promotion were particularly favourable in early 1721. Thomas Gordon, writing to William Cooper with reference to a Captain Thomas Rue, who had left the Russian Navy in 1717 after three years,[46] promised that if Rue returned, he would probably receive a commandership soon, '. . . for it is upon another footing than it was in his time'.[47] Even at the end of the Northern War, when foreign officers in Russia were being sent home, naval career opportunities remained. Men like Thomas Wisheart were not only re-recruited, but were actually promoted. In November 1722 the number of captain lieutenants was found to be four short of the established quota of twenty-seven and there were as many as twenty vacant positions for lieutenants.[48] Foreigners who happened to apply for entry to Russian service while there were vacancies, like James Innes, who had served as a lieutenant for only a short time, were able to take advantage of the situation and find employment despite a minimum of experience.[49] Although measures to restrict the promotion of foreign recruits were in force, there was evidently some disparity between legislation and practice, particularly in the recruitment of ex-Royal Navy applicants.

The successful recruitment of these Jacobite naval men does not necessarily imply that Peter I favoured Jacobites above other foreigners. Certain Jacobites did, of course, travel to Russia specifically to serve the Stuart cause, and this issue will be dealt with in detail at a later stage. The true reason for the success of naval officers suggests a more subtle correlation between recruitment and political disaffection. A large proportion of those entering Russian service from the Royal Navy at this time were Britons disenchanted with the Hanoverian

---

42 Memorial Saunders to Apraksin, June 1718, RGAVMF F233 o1 d163 l.546.
43 J.Deane, *History of the Russian Fleet during the Reign of Peter the Great by a Contemporary Englishman* (1724), ed. by Vice Admiral Cyprian A.G.Bridge, Navy Records Society, 15, (London, 1899), p.120; Duffus arrived 22 July 1722 (RGAVMF F212 o11 d3/157 l.888.) He was made rear-admiral 4 June 1723, (RGAVMF F212 o1 vyazka 55 ll.65,68).
44 Robert Little to Apraksin, 7/11/1718, RGAVMF F233 o1 d163 ll.41–42.
45 Deane, p.58.
46 R.C.Anderson, 'British and American Officers in the Russian Navy, *Mariner's Mirror*, 33, p.25.
47 Thomas Gordon to William Cooper, 5/1/1721, NAS Abercairney GD 24/1/859, ff.271–272.
48 Report by kanzeliarist Krymskoi, RGAVMF F212 o11 d34/189, f.10.
49 James Innes to Peter I, 16/11/1722, St Petersburg, RGAVMF F212 o1 d34, f.8.

monarchy and attracted by career prospects in Russia. Their swift promotion was due to the Tsar's high opinion of British naval expertise rather than to his sympathy for their political affiliations. A combination of poor Anglo-Russian relations, which restricted the possibilities for open recruitment of British officers, Russia's acute shortage of naval officers, and Peter I's great admiration for the Royal Navy, encouraged the Tsar to take measures to exploit unrest within Britain to Russia's advantage.

Throughout Peter I's reign, and indeed long afterwards, Russia's need for competent naval officers was compounded by the poor quality of native servicemen. John Deane observed in 1724 that, 'There are some men of capacity amongst the Russians, but as to the generality of these, in quality of lieutenants, foreigners ever desire to leave 'em ashore'.[50] Friedrich Christian Weber, the Hanoverian representative in Russia, commented in 1718 on a chronic lack of experience in the navy,

> . . . the old Complaint still continued, that the Sailors were not yet skilled in their business, for though there had been about two thousand German sailors distributed among the Fleet, yet many of the old ones being gone off, there were not able Hands enough for working the Ships in an Engagement.[51]

After visiting Britain in 1698, Peter I had come, '. . . by degrees entirely to dislike the Dutch building and masters, and discharged them as he could procure English'.[52] British shipbuilders for their part, '. . . used their utmost endeavours to put the Tsar out of conceit with all ships but such as are built by themselves or the Russ builders at St Petersburg', thereby promoting a monopoly of ex-members of the Royal Navy in the industry.[53] Peter's preference was also manifest in the officer ranks. A contemporary witness recounted a disagreement between Rear Admiral Thomas Gordon and Rear Admiral Sievers, a Dane of great experience who was also Gordon's senior officer and superior flag, in which Peter supported Gordon with the comment that he '. . . was a brave officer, and had served long in a better regulated navy than ever Sievers did'.[54] In 1722 Peter gave Gordon a command superior to that of Sievers, on the grounds that he had '. . . conceived a good opinion' of him '. . . from his long serving in the British, justly esteemed by the Tsar the best regulated navy in the world'.[55]

Britain's own naval requirements during the period after 1716, when Anglo-

50 Deane, p.114.
51 F.C.Weber, *The Present State of Russia* . . ., 2 vols. (London, 1723), 1, pp.231–232.
52 C.Whitworth, *An Account of Russia as it was in the Year 1710* (Strawberry Hill, 1758), p.112. Perhaps the most significant naval recruits early in the century were British shipbuilders such as Richard Cousins, John Deane, Brown, Ramsey, Joseph Ney, Hadley, Johnston, Davenport, Gardiner and Webb, who constructed the most successful early vessels, Deane, p.5.
53 Deane, p.118.
54 'Digression on the Relations between Admirals Gordon and Sievers', written in a contemporary hand, but one different from John Deane's manuscript, Deane, p.86.
55 Deane, p.90.

Russian relations were rapidly deteriorating, prompted measures to prevent its seamen from leaving the Royal Navy for foreign service. In June 1716 a proclamation was issued '. . . forbidding all officers and seamen to enter into the marine service of any foreign prince or state under severe penalties'.[56] The Tsar, however, was prepared to act in the face of British Government prohibitions to obtain the officers he needed by covert means. In 1717 he commissioned Thomas Gordon to write to his ex-colleagues in the Royal Navy and persuade them to leave the service for Russia. Several of them did so. In 1720 Gordon was involved in further illegal recruitment from the Royal Navy when, '. . . by the Tsar's order',[57] he enlisted William Cooper to recruit eight officers and carpenters. The enterprise was a particularly sensitive one because Britain itself was in great need of men for the Baltic fleet, which was, among other things, safeguarding British and Hanoverian interests from a possible Russian threat.[58] Cooper's letters betray his fear of '. . . being detected and incurring the Penalties of the Law',[59] a fate which he only avoided by using two addresses and three different names. The risks involved in such defection were considerable, and William Sutherland, a ship-builder, rejected Gordon's offer because '. . . the penalties alloted here, not only for the persons attempting to leave their country, but also such as promotes it, mightily discourages persons to attempt it'. Among his concerns was that he would lose his good 'character', his indispensable letter of recommendation, and thus destroy his career prospects elsewhere. Nevertheless, a lack of opportunity at home combined with the promise of advancement in Peter's navy, presented a real temptation. Sutherland described his predicament, that, '. . . altho' I am in no capacity to exert and shew my skill here, yet am bounded and confined from shewing it elsewhere'.[60]

A sufficient number of disaffected Britons went to Russia to cause James Jefferyes, Britain's representative in Russia, to comment with irony on the military implications of this drain of talent. He posed the question to Stanhope, the Secretary of State,

> . . . whether it will be for the interest of Great Britain to be a spectator of so growing a power as this, especially at sea, and brought about by her own subjects . . . ?[61]

When it was discovered where British officers were going, the Russia Company, based in London, demanded that Peter I's 'enticement' of British seamen into Russian service be stopped.[62]

---

56 Menzies to Inese, 11/6/1716, *HMC Stuart* 2, p.228.
57 Deane, p.120.
58 William Cooper to Thomas Gordon, 14/3/1720/21, NAS Abercairney GD 24/1/856, f.150.
59 William Cooper to Thomas Gordon, 31/1/1720, NAS Abercairney GD 24/1/856, f.148.
60 William Sutherland to Thomas Gordon, London, 26/3/1720, NAS Abercairney GD 24/1/856, f.152.
61 Jefferyes to Stanhope, St Petersburg, 3/4/1719, *SIRIO* 61, p.515.
62 D.K.Reading, *The Anglo-Russian Commercial Treaty of 1734* (New Haven, Conn., 1938), p.58.

British attempts to discourage its sailors from leaving the Royal Navy have given rise to the assumption that poor Anglo-Russian relations greatly reduced the number of Britons entering Russian service in the later years of Peter I's reign.[63] The situation probably did discourage those loyal to the Hanoverian monarchy, and certainly prompted some to leave Russia. Captain Thomas Stokes, for example, demanded his discharge while in service in Finland in 1720, following news that Britain had made a separate treaty with Sweden against Russia, '. . . because he heard of the alliance of the English King with the Swedish Queen, and it was unfitting so to act against one's own King'.[64] By the same token, however, the growing hostility between George I and Peter I directly benefited the recruitment into Russian service of those dissatisfied with Britain. Rather than stemming the flow of Britons, therefore, the situation tended instead to encourage the influx of Jacobites.

The Jacobites: A Select Elite

It is worthy of note that many of the Jacobites in Russian service, not only during the reign of Peter I, but also subsequently, enjoyed great success in terms of their military careers. Peter Lacy, James Keith, Thomas Gordon, George Brown, Kenneth Sutherland and Robert Fullarton were among those who reached the very top of the military hierarchy. One possible reason for this remarkable success rate was that Jacobites who entered Russian service tended to meet the requirements of an extremely selective recruitment system, designed to benefit Russia's military status at a minimum cost to the country.

By contrast with many countries which made extensive use of mercenaries at this period, Russia had an unlimited supply of men to fill the lower ranks of its armed forces. In previous centuries, foreign mercenary regiments in Russia had been entities largely independent of the native population. Peter I, however, employed foreign officers with experience and military expertise in the capacity of trainers and organisers of native manpower. Foreigners were not generally accepted unless they carried a written agreement from their government or monarch, and documents proving their eligibility to serve as officers. Those who had no such documentation could only serve as unpaid volunteers.[65] Peter I insisted on being personally involved in the recruitment of senior officers; whereas junior officers could be enlisted abroad by ambassadors and Russian commanding officers, staff officers[66] were to be engaged only with Imperial approval.[67] Military experience was a prerequisite for acceptance, and superseded personal ties. Asked by Lord Balmerino to engage a

---

63 M.S. Anderson, 'Great Britain and the Growth of the Russian Navy in the Eighteenth Century', *Mariner's Mirror* 42 (1956), p.136.

64 Report 1720, RGAVMF, F233 o1 d257.

65 Rabinovich, 'Sotsialnoe proiskhozhdenie', pp.157–158.

66 The land ranks covered by the term 'Shtab ofitser' are from major to colonel inclusive and lie between the 'general' ranks (major general and above, ranks one to four in the 1722 Table of Ranks), and the 'ober ofitser' ranks (lieutenant and below, ranks nine to fourteen in the Table of Ranks). Brockhaus-Efron, 'Tabel o rangakh'.

67 Rabinovich, p.157.

mutual acquaintance in 1720, for example, Thomas Gordon replied with regret that, '. . . it is not in my power to serv people that are not bred to sea and experienc'd officers'.[68]

As might be expected, this stringent recruitment procedure affected the distribution of foreigners among the higher ranks of the armed forces. In his classic study of the social origins of officers in the regular land army in 1720–1721, based on career accounts of those years, Rabinovich has calculated that, of data available for 2245 officers in 1721, 281 (12.6%) were foreign. They occupied 219 of 2049 (10.69%)[69] ober officer ranks (captain and below), and 62 of 196 (31.63%) staff officer ranks (majors to colonels inclusive). In the rank of colonel, as many as 21 of 46 officers were foreigners, that is 45.65%.[70] Rabinovich does not take into account the 'general' ranks, where the proportion of foreigners was equally high. In 1722, of a total of 28 general officers, 12 (42.8%), were foreign.[71]

Likewise in the navy, lists of seamen for the years between 1723 and 1742, which include details of the lowest ranks, reveal no foreign sailors at all. As in the case of the land forces, the proportion of foreigners in the navy was greatest in the higher ranks. In 1723, of the first four ranks, corresponding to the 'general' ranks in the land forces, 55.56% of officers were of foreign origin. Of the 'stab' officers, 66.67% were foreign, so that, of the first eight naval ranks, as many as 64.3% of officers were non-native.[72] The recruitment of tradesmen to the armed forces was equally selective. Peter decreed that,

> . . . those masters accepted from other states should demonstrate without
> delay whether they know their trade; if they do not know it, they should
> be released immediately without ill feeling; if they are useful, they should
> be retained at their pleasure.[73]

No recruitment policy could be completely failsafe, however. One remarkable case of deception was that of William Cooper, who came on Thomas Gordon's recommendation in February 1722. He claimed to have been trained by his father in Portsmouth in various naval and accounting skills, and is described by Deane as '. . . formerly storekeeper in His Majesty's yard at Portsmouth'.[74] He was employed in a similar capacity in St Petersburg with a salary of 2000 roubles a year, and in 1726 was put in charge of all naval stores, docks and dockworkers. However, his accounting turned out to be defective and he fell into severe debt. Eventually he was recognised as a 'trickster without a conscience' and sent from St Petersburg. He then proceeded to pull off a

68 Thomas Gordon to Lord Balmerino, 26/9/1720, NAS Abercairney GD 24/1/859 f.269.
69 This figure corrects a computational error in Rabinovich, p.139.
70 Rabinovich, pp.154–155.
71 List of 'generalitet' and colonels, 11/1/1722, *SIRIO*, 11, 440–443.
72 These ranks are calculated according to the 1722 Table of Ranks. Statistics from 'spisok
   lichnogo sostava voenogo morskogo flota' for 1723, RGAVMF, F212 ol d13.
73 (My translation), 1722, Solov'ev, 18, p.738.
74 Deane, p.120.

similar deception in Moscow, before being expelled from Russia by the Admiralty on 12 April 1731.[75]

In general, however, foreigners recruited to Russia were of good quality, either experienced military officers or skilled tradesmen, whose talents could be employed to Russia's advantage. The Russian policy of selectivity, which continued to apply during subsequent reigns, had a number of implications for the recruitment of Jacobites. Firstly, it tended to favour Jacobite exiles who had had military experience fighting for the Stuart cause. Secondly, the Jacobites who entered Russian service were encouraged to do so by their monarch, James III, who was prepared to provide them with the required letters of recommendation. Although Russia's preference for officers meant that it employed proportionally fewer foreigners and thus fewer Jacobites than elsewhere in Europe, the high recruitment standard meant that these few dozen Jacobites were a select élite, who reached the top of their professions, and whose power and influence far outweighed their numbers.

Pay and Exploitation

An examination of the financial rewards offered to foreigners in Russia reveals a correlation between pay and the recruitment of exiles. It was a long established practice in Russia to pay foreign mercenaries at a higher rate than native servicemen in order to attract them into Russian service. In the mid-seventeenth century, foreigners were being paid about sixty per cent more than their native counterparts.[76] Servicemen were categorised into three groups according to the length of time they had been in Russia, and each group paid to a different wage scale. This was still the case in 1715, when Peter Henry Bruce[77] remarked that

> . . . officers of equal rank, and in the same regiment, have three different pays; for instance, a captain who is a foreigner, has eighteen rubles a month; a captain of foreign parents, born in Russia, has fifteen rubles; and a native Russian has only twelve rubles.[78]

According to the salary scale of the military establishment of 1711, which remained in force until the 1760's, foreign general officers in the land forces were paid between fifteen and sixty six per cent more than Russians.[79] In the

75 Admiralty report on the behaviour of William Cooper, RGAVMF F212 o11 d45.

76 R.Hellie, *Enserfment and Military Change in Muscovy* (Chicago, 1971), p.84.

77 Peter Henry Bruce, of the Bruces of Airth, near Stirling, was a kinsman of General Count James Daniel Bruce, Peter I's chief artillerist and master general of the ordnance and his brother Robert, who was commandant of St Petersburg. His memoirs of his mercenary service in Prussia, Russia and Britain were published in 1782. He was born in 1692, was a captain in the Russian army between 1711 and 1724, and returned home to fight against the Jacobites in the 1745 Rising, although kinsmen, the Bruces of Clackmannan, were on the Jacobite side. P.H.Bruce, *Memoirs of Peter Henry Bruce, Esq* . . . (London, 1782); NAS Abercairney, GD 24/1/450; *The Prisoners of the '45* SHS 1, p.81.

78 P.H.Bruce, *Memoirs,* p.140.

79 Foreign generals were paid 3600 roubles p.a., Russians 3120 roubles; foreign lt. generals 2160 roubles, Russians 1800 roubles; foreign major generals 1800 roubles, Russians 1080 roubles. *PSZ* 43, pts. 1,2; 44, pts. 1,2. These pay scales applied with little alteration in 1728. See *SIRIO,* 79, pp.369–372.

navy, foreign commissioned officers received salaries for a year calculated as thirteen months, while Russians were paid for only twelve.[80] The Admiralty College naval list drawn up in 1723[81] made a distinction within each rank between Russian and non-Russian servicemen, the latter commonly receiving about a third less per month.

It might be expected that this disparity between Russian and non-Russian salaries would serve the purpose of offering foreigners competitive rates of pay as an incentive for entering Russian service. The experiences of individual recruits indicate, however, that by the latter half of Peter's reign salaries for mercenary officers in the Russian armed forces were far from competitive. When George Paddon wrote to the Jacobite captain William Hay in June 1717 to persuade him to enter the Russian Navy, he mentioned that the salary offered was low. 'I am afraid the pay will not seem much to you because a first rank captain is only given forty roubles a month . . .'[82] In 1695, when, according to Charles Whitworth, the rouble was worth ten shillings,[83] this salary of forty roubles or twenty English pounds a month would have been £260 a year (a naval year was traditionally calculated as thirteen months), that is £13. 15s. less than the basic pay of a First Rate captain of the English Navy in 1690.[84] Twenty years later, however, the rouble had been devalued by half, to five shillings. In 1717 a captain of British first rate was paid £42 per month plus £7 4s. allowance for eight servants.[85] The equivalent captain in Russia was allowed four servants (not three as claimed by Cyprian Bridge).[86] Nevertheless, his salary of forty roubles was now worth only ten pounds. When Thomas Saunders and Captain Geddes proposed to enter Russian service as captain-commodores in 1718, they initially demanded a salary of £500 per year. After fifteen years in the British Navy, six of these as a lieutenant being paid about £100 per annum, nine as a captain with a top salary of £504 per annum not including servants allowance,[87] Saunders felt that his demands were not unreasonable.[88] However, Peter ordered that they be offered a maximum of 70 roubles a month or 910 roubles for a thirteen month year. If the value of the rouble is taken as five shillings, this was equivalent to only £227. 10s. per year. Captain Robert Little was likewise offered 30 roubles a month (£97. 10s. per year) as a second rank captain, when his British counterpart would have received about £396 a year

80 Deane, p.97.
81 'Spisok lichnogo sostava flota', 20/5/1723, RGAVMF F212 o1 d13.
82 George Paddon to William Hay, 9/6/1717, RGAVMF F233 o1 d163 1.545.
83 Whitworth, pp.75–76.
84 'Pay of the English Navy in the Age of Peter the Great', by Cyprian Bridge, in Deane, p.149.
85 'The Three Establishments Concerning the Pay of the Sea Officers, London, 1705', printed in Deane, p.153.
86 William Hay and Robert Little, both first rank captains in Russia, were allowed four servants. RGAVMF F212 o1 d13.
87 Figures taken from 'The Three Establishments Concerning the Pay of the Sea Officers, London, 1705', in Deane, p.153.
88 Saunders' proposed terms of service, 12/8/1718, RGVIA F495 o1 d104 ll.2–2v.

not including servants allowance.[89] Lieutenant Adam Urquhart would have been paid about £100 at home. In Russia he received 260 roubles a year, or £65. Perhaps the most conclusive evidence that Russia did not offer real financial incentives to foreign seamen can be found in Dr Erskine's report to Peter on the results of his recruitment campaign of 1717. It appears that the only men prepared to accept such low salaries were Jacobite exiles. Even one of their number, Captain Geddes, returned home on being offered only 70 roubles a month. As for the others, Erskine reports that, '. . . the rest of the naval officers who presented themselves for recruitment in Holland refused to serve at that wage and returned home'.[90]

These relatively low rates of pay for officers also applied to the lower ranks of the navy. Prior to the devaluation of the rouble, the income of foreigners of lieutenant's rank and below, calculated for a thirteen month year, would have been higher than in Britain. In the last ten years of Peter's reign, however, this was not the case. A Russian boatswain, for example, was paid 130 roubles (£32 10s.) per year,[91] whilst the top salary for a British boatswain was £48.[92] The situation for foreign naval officers was further undermined after the end of the Northern War in 1721 by the abolition of the thirteen month financial year.[93]

The only naval mercenaries still to benefit financially after the fall of the rouble were the shipbuilders. John Deane recorded that Cousins, Ney and Brown received a basic wage of 1000 roubles a year, Ramsay 800 roubles and Hadley 600 roubles. When these salaries were established they were higher than those of their British counterparts.[94] Peter demonstrated his favour towards them by granting them an additional allowance to compensate for the weakness of the rouble.[95] In 1719, their salaries were still around double what they would have been in Britain.[96] This favouritism for the men most literally responsible for the creation of the navy is indicative of Peter's priorities. Similarly, when Thomas Gordon was ordered to recruit carpenters from the Royal Navy in 1720, it was ensured that the incentives offered exceeded all possible competition. As Gordon himself commented to his agent, Cooper, '. . . the Carpenters can't make such conditions any where in the world as what I offered you'.[97] Peter was obviously well aware of the financial incentives required to attract the experts he required and was prepared to augment them according to need.

The land branch of Peter the Great's armed forces, contrary to what might be expected, did not suffer to quite this extent. Although John Deane, writing

89 Saunders' proposed terms of service, 12/8/1718, RGVIA F495 o1 d104 11.2-2v.
90 Report by Dr Robert Erskine to Peter I, 1718, RGAVMF F233 o1 d165 ll.162–163.
91 Deane, p.97.
92 *Ibid.*, p.153.
93 *Ibid.*, p.99.
94 *Ibid.*, p.100.
95 *Ibid.*, p.100.
96 Jefferyes to Craggs, 7/11/1719, PRO SP 91/9, f.345.
97 Thomas Gordon to William Cooper, 6/6/1720, NAS Abercairney GD 24/1/859, f.267.

in about 1724, commented that '. . . the pay of the foreign officers in the land service is much inferior to those at sea; except in the artillery branch',[98] a comparison of equivalent ranks, as defined by the 'Table of Ranks' issued by Peter in 1722, indicates the reverse. Lieutenant General Peter Lacy was receiving 175 roubles a month in 1721,[99] whereas his equivalent rank in the navy, Vice-Admiral Gordon, was being paid only 100 roubles.[100] Major General Douglas, according to the establishments of 1711 and 1720, was paid 150 roubles a month,[101] while Rear-Admiral Saunders in the navy received, like Gordon, only 100 roubles.[102] A foreign army colonel, likewise, had a monthly salary of 50 roubles;[103] his naval equivalent, Captain William Hay, receiving only 40 roubles. This was a significantly lower yearly salary, even before the abolition of the thirteen month financial year for foreign naval officers. Nevertheless, officers' salaries in the land forces in Russia compared very unfavourably to their equivalents in Britain. In the early eighteenth century a British general was earning six pounds a day, £2190 a year,[104] whereas even a foreign general in Russia had a yearly salary of 3600 roubles or £900.[105] A British major general received £730 a year,[106] a foreign major general in Russia the equivalent of £450. A British dragoon colonel could earn as much as £738 a year,[107] but in Russia the yearly salary for foreign colonels was only 588 roubles or £147.[108]

The salaries of foreign mercenaries in Russia were not only generally lower than those of the British armed forces, but they were very irregularly paid. For many new recruits, the salaries promised to them on recruitment simply did not materialise. In March 1719 eighteen months after his contract was drawn up, Lieutenant Adam Urquhart had neither been granted the rank nor the pay promised to him.[109] Captain Robert Little, likewise, protested to Admiral Apraksin in 1718, over a year after his entry into Russian service, that he had not been paid from the date agreed in his contract, and had received no money at all for much of the current year.[110] Even Thomas Gordon, who was a vice-admiral by 1721, and enjoyed the favour of the Tsar, frequently complained in his correspondence of the inadequacy of his salary. In March 1722 he had not been paid since the previous October, yet he was expected to

98 Deane, p.101.
99 Career account of Peter Lacy, 'Ofitserkie skazki', RGVIA F490 o2 d50.
100 'Spisok lichnogo sostava flota' 20/5/1723, RGAVMF, F212 o1 d13.
101 Table of officers' pay, 2/1/1728, based on establishments of 1712 and 1720, *SIRIO*, 79, pp.369–372.
102 RGAVMF F212 o1 d13.
103 *SIRIO* 79, pp.369–372.
104 Major R.E.Scouller, *The Armies of Queen Anne* (Oxford, 1966), p.127; Colonel Clifford Walton, *The British Standing Army, AD 1660–1700* (London, 1894), p.649.
105 *SIRIO* 79, pp.369–372. In all cases the exchange value for one rouble is calculated as 5 shillings.
106 Walton, p.649.
107 Walton, p.646.
108 Rabinovich, p.156.
109 Adam Urquhart to Admiral Apraksin, 12/3/1719, RGAVMF F233 o1 d177 l.401.
110 Robert Little to Admiral Apraksin, RGAVMF F233 o1 d163 ll.41–42.

entertain lavishly.[111] A year later the situation had worsened. '. . . I am not in a condition at present to help my own children', he wrote, '. . . for the sallary allow'd me is small, the Charges of having to support my Character and dearness of living at this place payments very backward straitn's me so that I am not able to do anything for my familly'.[112] Despite Gordon's high rank, and the fact that, as he wrote, '. . . in this great Empire there is 20 can sitt above me', his financial situation was much poorer than he had anticipated when he came to Moscow.[113]

John Deane maintained that the financial straits suffered by foreigners in Russian service were the result of a deliberate policy of exploitation, only one of '. . . various stratagems . . . used to impoverish 'em in their fortunes'. He emphasises this point by concluding that '. . . No one maxim obtains more generally than this; and now, if I am not misinformed, prevails more than ever from the highest to the lowest degree'.[114] Despite the fact that Peter I rewarded skill and experience with promotion, this benefit was overshadowed, except in the case of his shipbuilders, by very poor material prospects for foreign mercenaries. This factor acted as a disincentive to some potential recruits, but for exiles in need of a military career, was of secondary importance. Peter was fortunate, therefore, in being in a position to take advantage of the political divisions and general discontent within Britain by recruiting the talent he required at a cheap rate. His need for foreign expertise coincided opportunely with the exodus of impoverished Jacobite exiles and unemployed naval officers in the years after 1715. Once these men were in Russian service, he was able to use their skills at little cost. The conclusion reached by James Jefferyes on this question in a report to Stanhope in April 1719 was in many ways an accurate one. With reference to Thomas Gordon's financial straits he wrote,

> . . . I think these people disaffected to their king and country are used here according to their demerit, for this court knowing that they dare not return home, obliges them to serve on what conditions they think fit, which makes their case little better than the slaves of the country.[115]

Viewed from this perspective, the Jacobites emerge as a group self-selected by the need for employment and vulnerable to exploitation. Whatever advantages Russian service offered them in terms of career opportunity, this was offset by the frustrations of chronic material insufficiency.

111 Thomas Gordon to John Gordon, 16/3/1722, NAS Abercairney GD 24/1/859, f.279.
112 Thomas Gordon to Adam Strachan, 29/4/1723, NAS Abercairney GD 24/1/859 f.284.
113 Thomas Gordon to John Gordon, 16/3/1722, NAS Abercairney GD 24/1/859 f.279.
114 Deane, p.101.
115 Jefferyes to Stanhope, 24/4/1719, *SIRIO* 61, p.528.

The Growth of the Jacobite Community in Russia and the Breakdown of Anglo-Russian Relations, 1715–1719

The Jacobite Tradition in Russia

Although the low rates of pay offered to mercenaries in Russia probably acted as a disincentive to men in less extreme financial straits than the exiles, the recruitment of Jacobites to Russian service after 1715 was by no means due solely to negative selection. There is evidence that Jacobite loyalty played a greater role in attracting the disaffected than has hitherto been recognised, and that the Jacobite identity of exiles was preserved in political activity after they had settled in Russia.

Russia's contact with Jacobites and the Stuart cause far predated the 1715 Rising. Peter the Great's father had been so shocked by the execution of Charles I that he had expelled English merchants from Moscow to Archangel.[1] In this case the sympathy of one royal house for the other was perhaps also a shared belief in the divine right of monarchs. It has been recorded that the Russian archives hold '. . . numerous notices of the friendly feeling which the Czar displayed in different ways towards King Charles II during his exile from England'.[2] Numbers of Scots refugees fled domestic turmoil in the mid-seventeenth century for Russian service.[3] Others, like the Irish Peter Lacy, whose service to Russia spanned fifty years, left Ireland after the surrender of Limerick in 1691 and, after five years in French service, was recruited in 1700 to take part in Russia's Northern War against Sweden. James VI and I had mediated between Russia and Sweden for the transfer of Ingria, which, according to Alexander Gordon, elicited from Peter I the comment that he was, '. . . more obliged to the predecessors of the Chevalier de St George, than to all the monarchs of the world'.[4]

One ardent Jacobite to whom Peter I was greatly obliged, and who exerted a considerable influence on him during the early years of his reign, was General Patrick Gordon. Gordon entered Russian service in 1661, and it was to him that Peter owed, in a large measure, the modernisation and success of his armed forces. In addition, according to recent research on Gordon's life, this Scot is known to have, '. . . established and nurtured a Jacobite community' in Russia

1 A.Gordon, *The History of Peter the Great*, 1, p.62.
2 J.W.Barnhill and P.Dukes, 'North-east Scots in Muscovy in the Seventeenth Century', *Northern Scotland*, 1 (1972), pp.53–54.
3 Ibid., pp.54–63.
4 A. Gordon, 1, p.54.

between 1688 and his death in 1699, to, '. . . ensure that the Russian court remained pro-Jacobite and anti "the Pretender King Wiliam"'.[5] In 1691, he sent home to Scotland for '. . . any bookes or papers set out in favour of King James or anything impartiall relating to the tymes'.[6] Not only was he a Jacobite propagandist, but it is possible that he may have debated or discussed Jacobite issues with the Tsar himself, to whom he had daily access.[7]

It would, however, be fanciful to conclude that Russia's past association with the cause of the Stuart monarchy exerted a direct influence on Peter I's leadership. Whatever personal sympathy Peter might have felt for individual Jacobites, decisions of national importance were directed solely by his ambitions for his country and were as changeable as the winds of European politics. Indeed, in 1711, when it was rumoured that Queen Anne would cede her crown to her brother, the Tsar was prepared to support the House of Hanover in the hope of gaining British aid for the war against Sweden.[8]

Jacobitism and Political Expediency

The period following the 1715 Rising was unique in Jacobite-Russian history for the very reason that Peter I's political interests began to diverge from those of the new King of Great Britain and Elector of Hanover, George I, and thus to converge with those of the Jacobites. As a result, Jacobite hopes were fuelled that Peter would provide military aid for the restoration of James III. Jacobite contact with Russia, which included the influx of a wave of Jacobites into Russian service and a high level of Jacobite intrigue in Russia itself, played a significant role in the deterioration of Anglo-Russian relations, which culminated in 1719 in the total collapse of diplomatic links between Britain and Russia. This breach was not repaired until the early 1730's.

An attempt to assess the importance of Jacobite activity for the three principal parties concerned, the Jacobites, Britain-Hanover and Russia, however, inevitably draws attention to the extent to which the Jacobite threat was subject to exploitation for purposes of diplomacy. In the course of discussion, a number of questions must be addressed. Firstly, was Britain, with its powerful navy and sophisticated intelligence network, ever seriously concerned by the possibility of a Russian attack at home, or did it merely use accusations of Jacobite involvement to veil or justify defence of its Hanoverian possessions? Indeed, was it ever within Russia's capabilities or even its interests to support an invasion of Britain, or did it merely extend an undefined threat to intimidate George I? Was the damage inflicted by Jacobites to British diplomatic interests nevertheless serious enough to constitute a political, if not a direct military threat? While the question of how close Jacobite plans came to realisation is

5 Graeme P.Herd, 'General Patrick Gordon of Auchleuchries – A Scot in Seventeenth Century Russia', Unpubl. Ph.D thesis (Aberdeen University, 1994).
6 Diary of Patrick Gordon, Letter 'Loveing Cousin', signed 'Yor affectionate Kinsman', 16/2/1691, RGVIA, F15 o5(2), l.131.
7 Graeme P.Herd, 'General Patrick Gordon'.
8 Golovkin to Kurakin, 21/12/1711, *Arkhiv Knyyazya F.A.Kurakina*, 10 vols. (St Petersburg, 1890–1901), 5, p.182.

obviously a central one, it is important to take account of the fact that it was the British perception of a threat at a given time, not a retrospective analysis of Jacobite support, which was the determining factor in British foreign policy. These considerations apply not only to the reign of Peter I, but to the whole period of over fifty years during which Jacobitism continued to exert an influence on international diplomacy.

Anglo-Russian Relations, 1715–1717

The rift which was soon to widen between George I and Peter I was not immediately apparent in 1714. George I's accession to the British throne prompted from Peter I a demonstration of friendly intentions towards the new monarchy. The British resident in St Petersburg, George MacKenzie, reported that Peter had '. . . signified his best dispositions to do everything that may be either useful to our nation or agreable to His Majesty', and had even drunk publickly to renewed Anglo-Russian friendship.[9] Indeed, initially, Jacobite activity actually had a temporary beneficial effect on Anglo-Russian relations. By 1715, Swedish privateers were impeding British trade in the Baltic, in addition to which, in June and July of that year, Britain learned of Jacobite attempts to co-ordinate a joint French, Swedish and Spanish expedition to overthrow George I.[10] Peter I immediately saw an opportunity to exploit Anglo-Swedish hostility in order to get British naval support in his continuing war with Sweden.

The Jacobite Rising in Scotland, which began in September 1715, naturally gave the British government reason to maintain amicable links with Russia in case preventative military action against Sweden became necessary.[11] However, with the failure of the Rising, and James III's flight from Scotland in February 1716, the Swedish threat was lifted, and instead of lending Peter I military support against Sweden, more conciliatory measures were taken to secure Anglo-Swedish co-operation.[12] In May 1716, Admiral John Norris was sent with a British squadron to the Baltic with instructions to request Sweden not only to cease its attacks on British shipping but to refuse any assistance to the Jacobites. When these demands were ignored, inciting considerable British anger, it appeared that Russia had at last gained the anti-Swedish military coalition it sought. In mid-August 1716, a united Russian, British, Dutch and Danish fleet under the chief command of Peter I left Copenhagen, ready to drive the Swedish fleet back to port and to attack southern Sweden. Uncertainty of victory, and the late season, however, caused the Tsar to abort the attack at

---

9 MacKenzie to W.Bromley, 17/9/1714, MacKenzie to G.Tilson, 22/11/1714, *SIRIO* 61, pp.273, 313.
10 McLynn, *The Jacobites*, p.28; Gøran Behre, 'Gothenburg in Stuart War Strategy 1649–1760', in G.Simpson, ed., *Scotland and Scandinavia* (Edinburgh, 1990), p.110.
11 George I also hoped, with Russian help, to acquire the duchies of Bremen and Verden for Hanover, and signed a treaty with Russia as Elector of Hanover in October 1715. Dukes, *Russian Absolutism*, p.73.
12 The division of the former Swedish empire left George I in October 1715 in possession of the duchies of Bremen and Verden, a claim which he sought to confirm through an Anglo-Swedish alliance. Nikoforov, *Russko-angliiskie otnosheniya pri Petre I*, p.143.

short notice, a move which irritated Britain, and cut short any further co-operation with Russia. Friction between Peter I and George I was further increased by the presence of Russian troops in Mecklenburg, threatening George's electorate of Hanover.

The sharp decline in Anglo-Russian relations which accompanied these developments in late 1716 has been attributed solely to the concern of George I and of his chief Hanoverian minister, Baron Bernstorff, over the security of Hanover.[13] British mistrust of Russia was, however, seriously increased by the efforts of Jacobite agents in the Hague in the autumn of 1716 to engineer a Russo-Swedish peace, thus freeing both Sweden and Russia to overthrow the Hanoverian monarchy. The extent to which Britain exploited evidence of Russo-Jacobite co-operation to safeguard Hanover is a matter for debate. What is undisputed, however, is that the apparent complicity of Peter I's chief physician, Dr Robert Erskine in this affair, inflicted considerable damage on Anglo-Russian relations.

Dr Robert Erskine and Russo-Jacobite Diplomacy, 1716–1717

While the failure of the unaided 1715 Rising prompted James III to regard foreign assistance as a prerequisite for all subsequent restoration attempts, there was inevitably a fine divide between patronage of the cause and exploitation of the Jacobites as political victims of Britain's enemies. In the Swedish-Jacobite plot which became known as the 'Gyllenborg conspiracy', both the Jacobites and Russia found themselves to be pawns in a larger diplomatic game. Apart from the damage it dealt to relations between Peter I and George I, the significance for the Jacobites of Russia's involvement in this affair lay principally in the firm establishment of Russia as a potential Jacobite ally, and in the encouragement this gave to the growth of a Jacobite community there.

When the Jacobites turned towards Sweden and Russia, in the hope of bringing about a peace between the warring nations and uniting with them against Britain, the Earl of Mar, who had commanded the Jacobite army in the 1715 Rising, proposed that this would give them '. . . an admirable opportunity of revenging themselves on Kenrick [George I], whom they have reason to look on as their common enemy'.[14] At the same time, the first minister to the King of Sweden and ambassador at the Hague, Baron Görtz, was travelling Europe in an attempt to procure financial support for Sweden's expensive war with Russia. In September 1716, when both Holland and France had proved unforthcoming, Görtz, as a last resort, promised the Jacobites military assistance in exchange for money, a proposal which was met with great enthusiasm.[15] As well as obtaining money for ships, the Swedes hoped that an opportunity would arise to obtain the restitution of the duchies of Bremen and

13 D. McKay, 'The Struggle for Control of George I's Northern Policy, 1718–19', *JMH*, 45 (1973), p.368.

14 Mar to General Dillon, 23/10/1716, *HMC Stuart* 3, p.136.

15 Dillon to James III, 26/9/1716, *HMC Stuart* 2, p.477.

Verden from George I. Görtz, with Count Gyllenborg and Baron Sparre, the
Swedish ministers in London and Paris, became deeply involved in this
intrigue, and, although it later appeared that the King of Sweden had not
been party to such a promise, went as far as to agree to supply armed troops for
a descent on Britain on 20 April 1717.[16] These frenzied negotiations in the
autumn of 1716 and early 1717 coincided with the sojourn of Peter I,
accompanied by Dr Robert Erskine, in Copenhagen, Amsterdam and the
Hague, part of the Tsar's extended tour of Europe between February 1716 and
October 1717. It was in the interests of both the Jacobites and of Sweden to seek
a favorable peace with Russia, and Dr Erskine, as Peter's principal confidant,
immediately became the focus of their attempts to negotiate with the Tsar.
Suddenly, from being a passive and rather lazy Jacobite sympathiser, Robert
Erskine was thrown onto centre stage, and found himself in a position to play a
pivotal role in Jacobite intrigue.

Robert Erskine had left for Moscow in 1704, after being elected Fellow of
the Royal Society and Freeman of the Russia Company, and had taken
advantage of the development of medical science under Peter the Great to
make a highly successful career as the Tsar's personal physician.[17] In 1706 he
was created the first 'Arkhiator', head of the newly founded Medical Chancellery, on a salary of fifteen hundred ducats.[18] In 1716, he was described as
'. . . in as great prosperity as such service can afford'.[19] He was by no means
an impoverished exile, but rather an exemplary immigrant who had achieved
not only the pinnacle of his career with the concomitant financial reward,
but also the confidence of the Tsar and thus a considerable influence at
court.

Having made such a successful career, Erskine had no vested interest in a
Jacobite restoration. There is no indication that he corresponded with the
Jacobites on his own initiative until after the 1715 Rising; indeed, for many
years he did not write even to his relatives.[20] In 1715, when the British fleet was
defending its interests against Sweden in the Baltic, he had acted as an
intermediary between the Tsar and Admiral Norris, who later wrote that
Erskine had been, '. . . by his influence of great service to the British'.[21] After

16 Mar to Jerningham, *HMC Stuart* 3, p.481.
17 J.Appleby, 'James Spilman F.R.S. (1680–1763) and Anglo-Russian Commerce', *Notes and
    Records of the Royal Society, London,* 48, 1, (1994), p.18; 'British Doctors in Russia, 1657–
    1807', Ph.D. thesis, (University of East Anglia, 1979), pp.32–45.
18 F.G. Clemow, 'Medicine Past and Present, in Russia', supplement to *The Lancet,* 7/8/1897,
    pp.355,358.
19 Henry Stirling to John Erskine, 22/9/1716, *SHS Misc.* 2, p.418.
20 Robert Erskine to John Erskine, 12/2/1710, *SHS Misc.* 2, pp.400–401. Also Mar to James
    III, 4/5/1718: '. . . he has not wrote to his mother these ten years and been designing to
    do it every post'. *HMC Stuart* 6, p.402. The Earl of Mar had difficulty in obtaining any
    response to his approaches, through the British resident, George MacKenzie, in 1714.
    G.MacKenzie to Mar, 8/10/1714, 29/10/1714, *SHS* Misc. 2, pp.404–411. These letters
    followed the snub from George I which caused Mar to make overtures to James III, but
    they contained no direct reference to Jacobitism. F.McLynn, *The Jacobites,* p.97.
21 Norris to Aylmer, 22/8/1715, in J.F.Chance, *George I and the Northern War* (London, 1909),
    p.93.

the Rising, in 1716, when his cousin, the Earl of Mar[22] and his brothers had all been in some way involved in Jacobite activity, he was presumed to have Stuart sympathies. As Mar commented, any Erskine must support the restoration, '. . . if they do not, they are unworthy to be come of that family'.[23] During his first ten years in Russian service, however, Dr Erskine's political sympathies remained at best passive.

Historians have speculated for some time both on the extent of Robert Erskine's active involvement in Jacobite intrigues with Russia, and on whether the Tsar was in any way party to them. There is particular uncertainty as to Erskine's role in the 'Gyllenborg conspiracy', which was abruptly curtailed by the British government in February 1717.[24] It appears that Dr Erskine's contemporaries too lacked the documentary evidence to form a reliable opinion. Alexander Gordon of Auchintoul, himself a Jacobite general, simply commented that,

> . . . The doctor was supposed in latter years of his life to have kept a correspondence with the Chevalier de St. George's agents; whatever be of that, he was an agreeable, open-hearted, fine gentleman.[25]

John Mottley, the biographer of Peter I and a staunch Hanoverian, accused Erskine of taking 'the first step' in promoting Görtz's plans in Russia, but extended no proof of this.[26] Since that time the publication of a selection of the Erskine papers by Reverend Robert Paul for the Scottish History Society, and of Jacobite correspondence by the Historical Manuscripts Commission has made more detailed evidence available. Nevertheless, the editor of the Erskine papers, wrote that, '. . . with regard to Dr.Erskine's conduct in this business, it is exceedingly difficult to come to any certain determination. Any positive proof of his actual complicity in the plot is wanting indeed'.[27] Russian historians have tended to discount any Jacobite involvement. Solov'ev maintained that '. . . it never occurred to the Tsar to help the Pretender and all that was in the Swedish ministers' letters was a blatant lie', and that '. . . as far as Erskine is concerned, there is to this day no direct incriminating evidence'.[28] Nikoforov was more equivocal; '. . . the extent to which Peter I was prepared to help James III to win the English throne remains unclear'.[29]

When the conspiracy was uncovered, and the scandal broke in early 1717, both Erskine and Peter the Great vehemently denied any involvement with the

22 Robert Erskine was the grandson of Sir Charles Erskine of Alva, whose brother had been third Earl of Mar, the sixth Earl's great grandfather. Sir Malcolm Innes of Edingight, 'Ceremonial in Edinburgh: The Heralds and the Jacobite Risings', *The Book of the old Edinburgh Club*, new series 1 (Edinburgh, 1991), p.1.
23 Mar to Robert Erskine and Henry Stirling, 21/10/1716, *HMC Stuart* 3, pp.115–117.
24 F.Clemow, for example, referred to the charges against Erskine but did not discuss their veracity. Clemow, 'Medicine Past and Present in Russia', p.358.
25 A. Gordon, 2, pp.170–71.
26 J.Mottley, *The History of the life of Peter I, Emperor of Russia* (London, 1740), 3, pp.170–1.
27 *SHS Misc.* 2, pp.386–7.
28 Solov'ev, *Istoriya Rossii*, 17, p.357.
29 (My translation), Nikoforov, *Russko-angliiskie otnosheniya*, p.128n.

Jacobites. In the memorial sent to Secretary Stanhope by the Russian resident, Veselovsky, answering British charges of Russian collaboration in Jacobite intrigues, Erskine was represented as quite innocent;

> . . . His Majesty's Surprize in that Respect, was the greater in that his Enemies, to give some colour to their malicious Insinuations, have been so daring, as to mention in their Letters, that Mr. Areskine, Physician to the Czar my Master, had held a Correspondence with the Earl of Mar . . .he protested that he was entirely innocent of this whole Plot; the rather, because he never received Orders from his Czarish Majesty to enter into such affairs . . . and he afterwards declar'd, upon Oath, and on the forfeiture of his Life, that he never wrote such letters, either to the Earl of Mar, or any other . . .[30]

Robert Erskine himself wrote a letter to Stanhope, stating that he never corresponded with the Earl of Mar to the detriment of the King.[31]

In the interests of minimising the diplomatic damage to Russia of the ensuing scandal, Peter I and his physician had, of course, no choice but to deny all charges. An examination of the evidence available, however, leaves no doubt of a closer involvement than these denials suggest. Dr Erskine's individual role in manipulating the course of Russo-Jacobite relations during the period following the 1715 Rising is worthy of more detailed attention.

Robert Erskine's first known correspondence from Russia on Jacobite affairs was of a personal rather than an overtly political nature. In the autumn of 1716, his brother Sir John Erskine, attainted for his part in the 1715 Rising, was endeavouring, with the help of his nephew, Sir Henry Stirling of Ardoch, to obtain a pardon from the British Government by promising a tenth of the ore recovered from his silver mine in Alva, near Stirling, to the Treasury. To add weight to his case, he proposed that Robert seek the intercession of the Tsar on his behalf, and to this end intended to meet him while he was with Peter in Copenhagen.[32] However, both Sir John and Sir Henry were at the same time acting as Jacobite agents, and were concerned in efforts to solicit Swedish and Russian support for their cause. In Dr Erskine's reply to his brother's letter he invited him to Copenhagen in order that '. . . we can more freely talke about our Domestick affaires, and perhaps do some business'[33] Erskine's reference to 'business' in this context strongly suggests that he was prepared at least to discuss the demands of the Jacobites with his brother.

The Jacobites responsible for attempting to engineer a liaison between Russia and Sweden became convinced of Dr Erskine's loyalty as a result of two letters written by Sir Henry Stirling after a meeting with him at Copenhagen. He wrote,

30 Extract from the memorial sent by order of Tsar Peter to Secretary Stanhope, 12/3/1717, *SHS Misc.* 2, pp.422–3.
31 Nikoforov, *Russko-angliiskie otnosheniya,* pp.152–153.
32 John Erskine to Mar, 29/8/1716, *HMC Stuart* 2, pp.388–389.
33 Robert Erskine to John Erskine, 1/9/1716, *SHS Misc.* 2, pp.417–418.

. . . Immediately after my coming I saw your friend Murphy [Robert Erskine] who has for Brumfield [Mar] and Meinard [John Erskine] all the respect and friendship you can desire. I can tell you with great pleasure that Davys [Tsar] and he both have all the desire in the world to do the utmost services to Truman [James III] and that with great reason they have such bad impressions of Haly [George I] that they heartily wish him at the d[evi]l.[34]

On the same day he wrote, again to John Erskine, that Dr Erskine had interceded on his brother's behalf with Peter I, and that '. . . the Czar has by his means promised and undertaken to gett your affair done, if the t'other way should faill'.[35]

If Stirling's reports were accurate, they indicate a number of important points. Firstly, they confirm Dr Erskine's proximity to the Tsar and his influence on decisions regarding foreign policy. Secondly, they suggest decidedly pro-Jacobite sentiments on the part of the Tsar and of his physician. Stirling's reference to 'the t'other way' can also be taken as evidence for Erskine's and the Tsar's complicity in Görtz's, Gyllenborg's and Sparre's Swedish-Jacobite plot, which had been initiated by a meeting of Sparre and the Jacobite General Dillon in Paris on 7 September.[36] It was not unusual, however, for optimistic Jacobites to over-state the strength of their case, and Stirling's second-hand accounts on their own are insufficient evidence on which to base an assessment of Erskine's role.

An examination of Jacobite correspondence in autumn and winter 1716 gives some insight into the extent to which Erskine was actually involved in the Gyllenborg plot. It was not until November 1716, when Peter I and Robert Erskine were expected to arrive in Holland, that Baron Görtz decided to gain access to the Tsar through his physician in order to facilitate a peace agreement with Russia. He wrote to Sparre that,

. . . par le Canal du Medecin Confidant l'on pourroit cultiver les bonnes Dispositions du Czar . . . En cas que le Czar vint icy et qu'il y eut moyen d'avoir un entretien avec le confidant, nous menerions certainement loin les choses, suppose comme j'ay dit que ce que le confidant ecrit se trouvoit bien fonde.[37]

Although it is apparent that Dr Erskine had had no direct correspondence at this stage with any of the Swedish ministers, Görtz's letter implies that information sent to the Jacobites by Erskine was reaching him through Jacobite channels. Indeed, in a letter to his brother, Gustav Gyllenborg reported at the same time that Erskine had sent Mar 'des Lettres fort amples' to the effect that,

34 Henry Stirling to John Erskine, 22/9/1716, *HMC Stuart* 2, p.495.
35 Henry Stirling to John Erskine, 22/9/1716, *SHS Misc.* 2, p.418.
36 *SHS Misc.* 2, p.418n.
37 Görtz to Sparre, 12/11/1716, *SHS Misc.* 2, p.419; *HMC Stuart* 3, pp.562–563.

. . . le Czar n'entreprendra d'avantage contre le Roy de Suede, qu'il se brouille avec ses allies, qu'il ne pourra jamais s'accommoder avec le Roy George, qu'il le hait mortellement qu'il connoit la juste Cause du Pretendant, qu'il ne souhaite rien plus qu'une Conjoncture pour le pouvoir retablir dans ses Royaumes'.[38]

If Dr Erskine did indeed send 'full and explicit letters' to Mar describing Peter I's hatred for George I and support for the Jacobites, this would at least indicate his complicity in Jacobite efforts to secure a Northern peace, although he may not have been apprised of Görtz's plans for a united descent on Britain. It appears from Mar's intention in October to set up correspondence with Dr Erskine,[39] however, and from his first letter to the doctor,[40] that the only information he had received of the Tsar's sentiments had come from Sir Henry Stirling, and stemmed almost certainly from Stirling's letter of 22 September, quoted above. The Swedish ministers seem, therefore, to have based their opinion of Dr Erskine's and his master's inclinations on one possibly exaggerated third-hand account, rather than, as they were led to believe, from the hand of 'le Confidant' himself. Although Gyllenborg's letter cannot necessarily be accepted at face value as evidence of Russian support, it is nevertheless important to note that it was an alleged statement of Dr Erskine's which first prompted the Swedish ministers to make contact with Russia as a preliminary to peace negotiations.

There is, however, more concrete evidence which would suggest that the Jacobites' hopes in Robert Erskine were in fact well-founded, and that he was party to the Swedish-Jacobite peace negotiations and perhaps even to the projected restoration attempt. On 17 November, Dr Erskine wrote to Mar in response to Mar's letter of 21 October, in which he had suggested a triple Russo-Swedish-Jacobite alliance and military aid for a restoration. Erskine confirmed that, '. . . Mr Davys [Tsar] is willing to do as much for Trueman [James] as lies in his power and only wants an occasion to show it'. He described his own efforts, '. . . to create new differences twixt Mr Davys [Tsar] and Haly [George I], which can't be easily accommodated'. However, Sweden's refusal to accept Russia's high peace demands rendered the Tsar unable to offer practical support. This letter to Mar clearly contradicted Dr Erskine's subsequent disclaimers that he had ever carried on correspondence with the Jacobites, and casts doubt on the remaining denials made in the official letters to the British government in 1717. Additional evidence of the depth of Erskine's involvement was contained in a letter to Dr Erskine (not to Thomas Gordon as is mistakenly claimed in *HMC Eglinton* etc. pp.168–170), from the Earl of Mar. In this Mar described how the doctor should behave while in Holland with the Tsar. He saw the necessity of informing the King of Sweden through his agents that the Tsar was favourably inclined towards the Jacobites.

38 Gustav Gyllenborg to Count Gyllenborg, 17/11/1716, *SHS Misc.* 2, p.419.
39 Mar to Charles Erskine, 21/10/1716, *HMC Stuart* 3, p.113.
40 Mar to Robert Erskine or Henry Stirling, 21/10/1716, *HMC Stuart* 3, pp.115–7.

'Hanlon's [Sweden's] friends', the agents he referred to, were without doubt Görtz, Gyllenborg and Sparre. He wrote,

> . . . It must be Mr.Duddel's [Dr Erskine's] part to keep Buckly [Tsar] up in his good intentions and not to let him too soon dispair of Hanlon's [Sweden's] coming to reason . . . We are told that Buckly intends a visit to his old acquentance (sic) Nealan [Holland] and I doubt not but Mr.Duddel [Erskine] will be with him. There is one of Hanlon's [Sweden's] friends I mention above and a chife one with that gentleman, he knows of Duddels [Erskine's] inclinations and if they chance to meet I am confident they wou'd get things concerted to Buckly's [Tsar's] satisfaction.[41]

This letter was clearly an attempt to bring Dr Erskine directly into Swedish-Jacobite negotiations through a meeting with a Swedish minister, probably with Görtz or Sparre, rather than relying on a Jacobite intermediary.

The time for a Russo-Swedish peace seemed ideal; Russia's suspicion of Britain had grown following rumours that George I was hoping to settle a separate peace with Sweden, and the Tsar and Erskine were accessible in Holland. The Tsar had even offered to include the Emperor in an alliance against George I.[42] In mid-December, Count Gyllenborg wrote promising Baron Görtz a letter of introduction to Dr Erskine.[43] On 27 December, Mar wrote to the Jacobite agent, Jerningham, that Görtz very much wanted an interview with Dr Erskine, and it was proposed that Erskine persuade the Tsar to treat directly with Görtz for a Russo-Swedish agreement.[44] It appears that there may even have been direct correspondence between Erskine and the Swedish ministers at this time, for, in a letter to Görtz of 29 December, Count Gyllenborg made reference to, '. . . les Lettres prêtes pour le Medecin que Je n'ose pas hazarder par la Poste'.[45] Dr Erskine was clearly very much involved in attempts to secure the Tsar's support for the Jacobites and bring Russia into a union with Sweden, and appears to have been instrumental in the success of the former. As the Jacobite agent, Sir Hugh Paterson wrote, 'Murphy [Robert Erskine], has brought matters as great a length with Mr Blunt [Tsar] as could be wished, and that matter now depends entirely on Saxby [King of Sweden]'.[46]

The planned Swedish-backed descent on Scotland was a much more closely-kept secret than the Jacobite peace project. By 12 January, over 30,000 livres had been collected for Sweden, but the Swedish King demanded over twice that amount before he would provide military backing.[47] On 27 January, Mar sent

41 Mar to Robert Erskine, 13/11/1716, *Reports on the Manuscripts of the Earl of Eglinton, Sir John Stirling-Maxwell, C.S.H.Home Drummond Moray* . . . Publications of the Historical Manuscripts Commission (London, 1885), pp.160–170; *HMC Stuart* 3, p.212.
42 Charles Erskine to Mar, 24/12/1716, *HMC Stuart* 3, p.346.
43 Count Gyllenborg to Görtz, 11/12 or 12/12/1716, *SHS Misc.* 2, p.421.
44 Mar to Jerningham, 27/12/1716, *HMC Stuart* 3, p.483.
45 Count Gyllenborg to Görtz, 29/12/1716, *SHS Misc.* 2, p.421.
46 Hugh Paterson to Mar, 29/12/1716, *HMC Stuart* 3, p.371.
47 James III to Mr Rigg (Francis Atterbury, Bishop of Rochester), 26/1/1717, *HMC Stuart* 3, p.475.

Jerningham powers to treat with Görtz. In his letter, he emphasised that, although many Jacobites knew of the money being collected in England, the plan for a descent was to be kept secret even from the Jacobites in the Netherlands, Dr Erskine, Charles Erskine and Sir Henry Stirling.[48] It is possible therefore, that Dr Erskine was entirely ignorant of the invasion plot right up to the moment when the British government, which had been intercepting Jacobite letters for some time, arrested those involved. By February, the planned Swedish descent on Britain was apparently very close to being put into execution. James III believed, as he wrote to the Jacobite Bishop of Rochester, that the King of Sweden was ready to attack Britain without waiting for the Jacobite leaders to join him.[49] Baron Görtz was actually arrested on 19 February, just in time to foil the project. Gyllenborg and several other conspirators were also taken.

Despite the secrecy surrounding the plot, Dr Erskine might well have been informed of it. During the final weeks before the arrests, Erskine's contact with the Swedish ministers was very close. In January, Gyllenborg had acquired a letter of introduction from Robert's brother William Erskine as a preliminary for meeting him,[50] and Görtz had arranged for an interpreter so that he too could speak with the doctor.[51] Most importantly of all, Dr Erskine and George Jerningham, one of the agents most actively negotiating the planned invasion, were meeting together with Görtz in Amsterdam when the latter learned that he was about to be seized. Jerningham described to Mar that when Görtz received this news, '. . . having first spoken with Murphy [Dr Erskine], he decamped from his inn to a private lodging'.[52] There is no extant record of what Görtz told Dr Erskine just before his arrest. Given Erskine's influential role as the Tsar's confidant and principal Russo-Jacobite intermediary, as well as his close relationship with Mar and encounter with Jerningham, it is not improbable that he had some knowledge of Sweden's plans.

What is certain, however, is that the accusations levelled against both the Tsar and Dr Erskine by Britain in February 1717, were completely justified. The Tsar had had knowledge of, and had approved of Jacobite attempts to secure peace with Sweden at Britain's expense. Robert Erskine had, after all, had the Tsar's confirmation that he was '. . . willing to make up matters with Hanlon [King of Sweden] and that with the same breath both of them should join stocks with Mr Brown [James III]'.[53] Dr Erskine had '. . . held a Correspondence with the Earl of Mar', and had also corresponded with his Jacobite relatives, despite the Tsar's claims to the contrary. Although the arrests of the main protagonists put an end to the Gyllenborg conspiracy, the British government was right to view Dr Erskine as a key figure in Russo-Jacobite relations, and was reconfirmed in its suspicions of Peter I as posing a direct threat to British interests.

48 Mar to Jerningham, 27/1/1716, *HMC Stuart* 3, pp.479–481.
49 James III to Francis Atterbury, 15/2/1717, *HMC Stuart* 3, p.525.
50 Gyllenborg to Görtz, 18/1/1717, *SHS Misc.* 2, p.421.
51 Görtz to secretary Mambke, 31/1/1717, *SHS Misc.* 2, p.422.
52 Jerningham to Mar, 22/2/1717, *HMC Stuart* 3, pp.532–533.
53 Charles Erskine to Mar, 24/12/1716, *HMC Stuart* 3, p.345.

The public disclosure of the Gyllenborg conspiracy provided George I with an opportunity to exploit the defusing of a Jacobite threat for political ends. Leading ministers had been informed of Jacobite intrigues since the summer of 1716, and had only awaited the most profitable moment to curtail them. In doing so, James Stanhope, who effectively directed British foreign policy from the beginning of 1717 until his death in 1721, not only rallied domestic support for the Whig party, but bound Britain's allies, notably the Dutch Republic, to support Electoral policy against Sweden and Russia.[54] Russia's apparent complicity in the affair provided the Elector with a convenient pretext to send a British fleet to the Baltic for principally Hanoverian purposes.[55] At the same time, however, George I's success in polarising Britain and Russia in order to pursue his electoral policy was to prove a hollow victory for his British Kingdoms. It served as open encouragement for the intensification of Russo-Jacobite relations to the point where they presented a serious threat to Britain.

Dr Robert Erskine, Peter I and Jacobite Recruitment

The scandal surrounding Russian involvement in the Gyllenborg conspiracy brought to British public attention the threat posed by the growth of a Jacobite community in Russia. A contemporary wrote that, '. . . It appeared publickly . . . that the Czar gave all manner of Protection and Encouragement to a great Number of his Majesty's Rebel Subjects'.[56] Although, as discussed, there were career incentives offered to foreigners in the Russian armed forces which attracted disaffected British servicemen to Russia, evidence suggests that the increase in the number of Jacobites was not simply a matter of professional opportunism. Nor was it entirely the result of a process of natural accretion. Rather, there was a strong element of calculated effort on the part of Jacobites already established in Russia to encourage the recruitment of fellow 'rebels'.

In the aftermath of the Gyllenborg affair, Dr Erskine was undoubtedly the most influential Jacobite at the Russian court, with close access to the Tsar, and a decisive role in political, as well as medical affairs. In his 'Observations on Russia', a visitor, M.le Brun commented that, 'Dr Areskin . . . had Power of Life and Death over those that were under him'.[57] His influence in matters of politics was publicly acknowledged during his visit to Europe with Peter I from 1716 to 1717, when diplomats of all parties made use of him as the primary channel to the monarch's ear. De La Vie, the French envoy, attempted through

---

54 Townshend and Robert Walpole, who did not share George I's and the Hanoverian minister Bernstorff's fear of Russia, being more concerned to secure Britain against a Swedish-Jacobite invasion, had been dropped from the ministry at the beginning of 1717 in favour of Stanhope and Sunderland. On the 'Whig split', see R.Hatton, *George I: Elector and King* (London, 1978), p.193.

55 D.McKay, 'The Struggle for Control of George I's Northern Policy, 1718–19', *JMH*, 45 (1973), p.372.

56 John Mottley, *The History of the Life of Peter I, Emperor of Russia*, 3 vols. (London, 1740), 3, p.187.

57 'Observations on Russia', in Weber, 2, p.428.

Erskine to establish a Franco-Russian commercial treaty.[58] Meanwhile, Admiral John Norris, the British envoy sent to the Tsar in Paris, proposed '. . . in a private way, by means of the physician', to have Russian troops removed from Mecklenburg.[59]

British attempts to use Erskine's influence over the Tsar were, however, hopelessly at odds with Erskine's own Jacobite allegiance, which had been brought to the surface by the atmosphere of growing Anglo-Russian hostility. De La Vie reported that '. . . Ce docteur n'a pu s'empêcher de glisser quelques mots dans son discours, qui me font croire qu'il est zèle Jacobite'.[60] Rather than making any concession to British requests, Erskine became actively involved in attracting Jacobites into Russian service.

One of the first and most prominent Jacobites already to have settled in Russia as a direct result of Dr Erskine's influential position was his nephew, Sir Henry Stirling of Ardoch, the family seat in Perthshire. Having arrived in 1716 on a mission to arrange a government pardon for his other uncle, Sir John Erskine, through the intercession of Dr Erskine and the Tsar, his second employment, as a Jacobite agent, involved him so heavily in Jacobite politics in Russia that he remained there. In 1726, he married the daughter of the Admiral and fellow agent, Thomas Gordon, and added another family to the Jacobite community.[61]

The most intense period of Jacobite recruitment, however, took place in 1717, during the Russian monarch's visit to France and Holland. Large numbers of prominent Jacobites converged on Paris, following rumours on the 'Jacobite grapevine', which operated through a complex system of letter bearers, loyal merchants, codes and spies, that Peter I had arrived there. The prevailing atmosphere was one of anticipation and excitement. The Earl of Mar had written to Robert Erskine's brother Charles in March, suggesting that the Tsar might persuade the King of Prussia to join an alliance with Scotland and Sweden against Denmark and England, and many hoped that the treaty could be concluded while Peter was in Paris.[62] Peter I actually requested an audience with the Earl of Mar, but the Regent forbade it, fearing that it could prejudice a potential defensive treaty between France, Holland and Britain.[63] Instead, the Tsar communicated with Mar by correspondence, and there was a general optimism that Russia would soon take action to restore the Stuart king. Thomas Crawfurd reported from Paris in May to Lord Polwarth, the British plenipotentiary in Copenhagen, that '. . . All the Jacobites flock about his [Peter I's] house and pretend to have great credit in it. Dr Erskine is their

---

58 De La Vie to Dubois, 6/17 May 1717, *SIRIO* 34, p.214.
59 Sir John Norris to Sunderland, 26/7/1717 o.s., *SIRIO* 61, p.393.
60 De La Vie to Dubois, 3/6/1718, *SIRIO* 34, pp.344–5.
61 Henry Stirling married Ann Gordon on 21/12/1726, 'A Register Book of all the Christenings, Marriages and Burials in the English Congregation at St Petersburg', Guildhall Library, Ms. 11,192B, f.13.
62 *HMC Stuart* 4, pp.xx–xxvii.
63 Mar to [John Hay], 10/5/1717, *HMC Stuart* 4, pp.233–234; Mar to James III, 17/5/1717, *HMC Stuart* 4, p.249.

patron'.[64] This activity aroused the suspicions of British agents, who had been prewarned by,

> . . . certain advice that upon the arrival of the Paris courier at Pezzaro, where the Pretender is, the Dukes of Ormond and Perth, the Earl Marischal and others set out at once for France, which makes one think that the Jacobites are concocting something.[65]

In addition to the recent scandal over the activities of Görtz and Gyllenborg, Britain's mistrust of Peter I had been heightened by his refusal, allegedly due to sudden illness, to have an audience with George I as he passed through Holland on his way back from Hanover. Although Peter had later sent Kurakin and Tolstoy in his stead, rough weather had hindered their passage to Britain, where it was commonly believed that, '. . . this was a trick to avoid the meeting, because of various political disputes and disagreements'.[66] There was considerable anxiety that such behaviour on the Tsar's part might signify that he was in league with the supporters of James III.

British concern was justified to the extent that Peter I put Dr Erskine in charge of recruiting skilled foreign officers and tradesmen from France and Holland. Inevitably, the abundance of willing candidates, unemployed exiles seeking a means to combine a career with service to James III, in conjunction Erskine's own political sympathies, resulted in the recruitment of a number of loyal Jacobites into Russian service. John Deane, a captain in Peter I's navy, described in a contemporary account how Peter brought seven new officers back from Europe; Captain Commodores Gordon and Saunders, Captain Hay, Captain Lieutenants Urquhart and Serocold and '. . . these with two land officers, all Britons'.[67] The identity of the two land officers is unknown, although it is possible that one was Duncan Robertson of Struan, whose elder brother Alexander had been attainted for his part in the 1715 Rising, and who came to Russia at around this time.[68] Of the remainder, all without exception were active Jacobites.

In terms both of his military achievements and in his active commitment to Jacobite politics during his service in Russia, Thomas Gordon was the most remarkable of these recruits. Dr Erskine gave an account in a memorial to Admiral Apraksin of being personally responsible for engaging 'Captain-commandore Mr Gordon' while Peter the Great was in Paris, that is, sometime in May or June 1717. It is evident from the letters of various Jacobites written on Gordon's behalf that he first went to France in February 1717, and that he held recommendations from 'Mr Caesar' to the Earl of Oxford, and from Menzies 'to them all'.[69] Although Gordon had not himself been involved in the 1715

64 Thomas Crawfurd to Lord Polwarth, Paris, 6/17 May 1717, *HMC Polwarth* 1, p.233.
65 J.Robethon to Lord Polwarth, St.James, 24/5 o.s. 4/6 n.s. 1717, *HMC Polwarth* 1 p.248.
66 Yazykov, *Prebyvanie Petra Velikago v Sardame i Amsterdame v 1697 i 1717 godakh* (Berlin, 1872), p.58.
67 Deane p.56.
68 R.Douglas, *The Baronage of Scotland, containing an historical and genealogical account of the gentry of that kingdom* (Edinburgh, 1798), p.409. Duncan was made a colonel and died in 1718. D. Fedosov, *The Caledonian Connection* (Aberdeen, 1996), p99.
69 Captain Ogilvie to 'Duke' of Mar, Dunkirk, 13/4/1717, *HMC Stuart* 4, p.189.

Rising, his political allegiance was well known to the Jacobite leadership, for the Earl of Mar reported to James III in April that Gordon,

> . . . is to come over from yr f[r]iends either to go to k.5 [King of Sweden] or to attend k.1 [James] when he has occasion that way himself, which it is presumed he will soon. He was directed to go to m.13 [Mar], who they believed to be about d.13 [Dunkirk]. Le Brun [Ogilvie] met with him and advised him to go to p.19 [Paris], where he would hear of m.13 [Mar], and this minute, as I am a writing, he is come in to me . . . In my opinion it is now past time for him to go to k.5 [the King of Sweden], for in all appearance he would come too late and so be lost, therefore I think it is better for him to remain with p.19 [Paris] until we see further and if k.1 [James] have occasion for him, but I shall hear tomorrow what they think, and we shall do what's for the best.[70]

While in Paris, Gordon travelled incognito, probably because he was a recognised Jacobite and had left the Royal Navy without permission. Like many exiles, he was granted a secret audience with James III's mother, Queen Mary of Modena.[71]

The efforts made by the Earl of Mar and other prominent Jacobites to extend Gordon every possible support, and to place him in a manner and position profitable to the Stuart cause, were evidence of the cohesion and influence of the exiled community. The backing of influential acquaintances and the possession of letters of recommendation from men of standing, which were vital prerequisites at that time to furtherment of any kind, were automatically obtainable through the Jacobite support system. Gordon's recruitment into Russian service as a captain commodore in June 1717, and perhaps also his swift promotion on arrival, were to a great extent due to the assistance he received from this network, of which Dr Robert Erskine was equally a part.

As soon as he was accepted into Russian service, Gordon himself became an active member of this Jacobite 'clientele structure'. In May, 1717, at the time of his recruitment, the Tsar ordered him to '. . . write to England and summon naval officers to his Imperial Majesty's service'.[72] Naturally, the men he wrote to were Jacobites. One of them, Thomas Saunders described how, on receipt of Gordon's letter, he travelled directly to Flanders and had an audience with the Tsar himself in Maestricht, before being sent to Dr Erskine in Amsterdam for the drawing up of his contract as a captain commodore.[73] Erskine reported to the Russian Admiralty that Saunders was accompanied by a Captain Geddes, who was, however, discouraged from joining the Russian navy by the low rate of

---

70 Mar to James III, 8/4/1717, *HMC Stuart* 4, p.170.
71 L.Inese to Mar, 9/4/1717, *HMC Stuart* 4, p.176; Thomas Gordon to Lord Golovin, 5/11/1740, NAS Abercairney, GD 24/1/855, f.88; Queen Mary had received James Keith, the future Russian general, a few months before. Keith, *A Fragment*, p.34.
72 Memorial of Thomas Saunders to Admiral Apraksin, June 1718, RGAVMF F233 o1 d163 l.546.
73 Ibid. The rank of 'captain commodore' lay fifth in the 1722 Table of Ranks, one rank above a 1st rank captain.

pay.[74] Robert Little probably came by the same summons. He had served with Gordon in the Royal Navy, and came to the Netherlands at the same time as Saunders. In a report to Admiral Apraksin, he wrote that he had already been to the Netherlands twice in the hope of entering Russian service. On 17 July, 1717, he too had an audience with the Tsar in Maestricht, was ordered to Amsterdam to be vetted by Dr Erskine, and was accepted as a captain.[75] Lieutenant Adam Urquhart, the third son of John Urquhart of Newhall, and 'an ardent Jacobite', was recruited by Erskine in the Netherlands in August.[76]

The reluctance of other applicants to accept the low Russian salary complicated Erskine's task of meeting the Tsar's demand for, '. . . two further captain-commodores and other naval officers' besides Captain Commodore Gordon.[77] This fact ensured that Saunders, Little and Urquhart would probably have been accepted with alacrity regardless of political considerations. The Jacobite 'clientele structure' which helped them find employment was also open to use by Jacobites who had no further interest in the Stuart cause. There is convincing evidence from Jacobite correspondence, however, that the naval officers who were recruited in 1717–1718, came for political as much as for professional reasons. Sir Hugh Paterson of Bannockburn wrote to Mar in April 1718 with the news that the Tsar had ordered Thomas Gordon to send for sailors,

> . . . on which some are going, and I expect to see them here as they pass. They are all such as the King [James] may depend on whenever he has any occasion to employ them, and their ships were taken from them on account of their inclination that way [ie Jacobite sympathies]. Their being to be disposed of this way may, I hope, be for the King's service, and I am sure they will follow whatever orders he thinks fit to give them.[78]

In a further letter to Mar, Paterson re-confirmed the pro-Jacobite sentiment of the recruits, referring to

74 This was very probably the same Jacobite [Sandy] Geddes who, with the future Russian rear-admiral, Lord Duffus, was, '. . . ingaged in the french service by Mr Law's friendship' in November 1719, Jacob Johnston to Thomas Gordon, 24/11/1719, NAS Abercairney GD 24/1/856, f.147. Geddes also went to Austria, where he was interrogated by the British minister in Vienna, Lord Forbes, on suspicion of Jacobite involvement, but managed to convince him of his innocence. Forbes to Delafaye, 19/3/1719, PRO SP 35/15, f.106, Tilson to Leathes, 23/6/1721, PRO SP 35/27, f.34.

75 Robert Little's memorial to Admiral Apraksin, 7/11/1718, RGAVMF F233 o1 d163 ll.41–42.

76 Henrietta Tayler recorded that, 'In the Stuart Papers at Windsor under date April 25, 1718, there is a letter from Captain Ogilvie in which he alludes to "the brother of Captain Urquhart MP, who was in a man-of-war under Queen Anne, but will not serve George, and so is now seeking service under the Czar of Russia."', *History of the Family of Urquhart* (Aberdeen, 1946), p.247. Tayler had no record of his christian name, but in Russian documents he appears as 'Edmond' or 'Adam'. RGAVMF F233 o1 d177, f.272/401. He was killed in 1719 trying to save his ship which had run aground. D Fedosov, *The Caledonian Connection*, p.116.

77 'O prinyatie v sluzhbu inozemtsev' (Recruitment of foreigners), Erskine to Apraksin, RGAVMF F233 o1 d165, ll.162–163.

78 Hugh Paterson to Mar, 21/4/1718, *HMC Stuart* 6, p.344.

. . . those three persons I told you in my last were to pass that way for Petersburg in order to enter into the Czar's service, and who went there only on the view of being useful to the King.[79]

Although the Jacobites in question were not named for reasons of confidentiality, they were almost certainly those recruited by Erskine and Gordon.

Several other Jacobites followed this movement into Russian service during Peter I's reign, encouraged by those already there. Captain William Hay arrived in 1718 on the recommendation of Admiral George Paddon, a New Englander who had just himself left the Royal Navy for Russia. Although no reference was made to politics in Paddon's invitation to Hay to join him, Paddon mentioned the imminent arrival of Thomas Saunders.[80] Hay was, however, a committed Jacobite, and later became an important Jacobite agent. Henry Bruce, nephew of the Laird of Clackmannan, came to Russia with two James Bruces in 1720.[81] The Bruces of Clackmannan were Jacobites. James Keith, who had accompanied his brother the Earl Marischal to Paris in 1717, at the news of Peter I's visit, attempted to enter Russian service in June but failed at his first attempt, as he later wrote, '. . . perhaps because I did not take the right measures in it'. In 1722, Kenneth Sutherland, third Lord Duffus, who had been released from the Tower of London in 1716 after attainder as a result of his part in the 1715 Rising, and had subsequently '. . . lost his money in Mr Law's misfortune', approached Prince Kurakin, then Russian ambassador to the Netherlands, for employment in the Russian Navy, largely for financial reasons. His report to the Jacobite leadership of his plans, however, indicated that his Jacobite sympathies remained paramount,

. . . Prince Kourakin has received me most favourable and I having showed him that I besides my little skill as a Commander I have apply'd myself particularly to the knowledge of the whole Economics of the Navy through all its Offices, Establishments and Regulations; I have given him a copy of the Index of my Collections, which he has sent to his Master, and promised me his friendship in the affair, but till I know the King my Masters Pleasure I shall keep myself from being intirely engadged [sic], . . . I flatter myself his Majesty will not deny his recommendation whereby I might subsist and keep my poor ffamily [sic] from starving, till such time as I have the honour of his further Commands, which shall ever be sacred to me.[82]

Duffus arrived in Russia on 22 July 1722 and was made a 'shautbenakht' or rear-admiral.[83]

There were also other Britons who may have been Jacobite, but whose politics are unconfirmed. James Innes, who described himself as, '. . . of the Scots nobility', was recruited from the Royal Navy through the offices of Prince Kurakin, and boarded a Russian ship under the captaincy of James Lawrence at

79 Hugh Paterson to Mar, 20/5/1718, *HMC Stuart*, 6, p.451.
80 Paddon to Hay, 9/6/1717, Hay to Apraksin, 3/6/1718, RGAVMF F233 o1 d163, ll.544,545.
81 Keith, *A Fragment*, p.34; D. Fedosov, *The Caledonian Connection*, p.14.
82 H.Tayler, *Jacobite Epilogue* (Edinburgh, 1941), pp.xv,xvi.
83 Duffus to Admiralty, RGAVMF F212 o11 d3/157, f.459/888; F212 o1 vyazka 55, ll.65, 68.

Ostend. On his arrival in Cronstadt, Thomas Gordon, who was already a vice-admiral, appointed him as a lieutenant to the Svyatoi Alexandr.[84] James Kennedy, an Irishman, entered Russian service as a sub-lieutenant at the time of the accession of George I in 1714, and proved so excellent an officer and was so frequently promoted, that he was made a vice-admiral in 1757.[85] Thomas Wisheart was recruited by Thomas Saunders on 20 October 1718 when he arrived at the port of Reval (Tallin) seeking service as an under-steersman.[86] William Cooper, who was certainly not loyal to the British government, came to Russia on the recommendation of Thomas Gordon in early 1722, having illegally recruited a number of tradesmen from the Royal Navy, including William Naki[87] and Captain Stobs, and was employed as the chief accountant to the Admiralty until his expulsion for fraud in April 1731.[88] Numerous other names which might have belonged to Jacobites appear in military lists, including David Cook, John Logan,[89] and James Ferguson.[90]

Although there were a few Jacobites in Russia prior to the 1715 Rising, and Jacobites continued to enter Russian service over the course of subsequent reigns, the period of worsening Anglo-Russian relations towards the end of the reign of Peter I was a high point in Jacobite recruitment. Political disaffection in the aftermath of the Hanoverian succession and the 1715 Rising, resulting in a sharp increase in the number of unemployed military servicemen, was uniquely combined with Anglo-Russian hostility, with Peter I's European visit and his recruitment campaign. The wave of Jacobites entering Russian service at this time laid the foundations of the Jacobite 'clientele structure' which continued to operate after Peter I's death. Although this Jacobite network functioned to some extent on the level of pure nepotism, there is no doubt that many Jacobites chose their careers in Russia with the Stuart cause in mind. While it is not always possible to assess the extent of individual loyalties, and there is a temptation to generalise from the evidence available, one can to some extent regard the diaspora in Russia as a cohesive group, distinguished from the mass of foreign mercenaries by a shared allegiance to a monarch and a political goal. As such, it played an important role in opposing British interests within Russia, contributing to the political alienation which led to diplomatic rupture in 1719.

84 James Innes to Admiralty College, 16/11/1722, RGAVMF F212 o11 d34/189, l.8; James Lawrence to Admiralty College, 10/7/1722, Ibid.,l.9. This may have been the Captain Innes referred to as 'honest Innes', in a letter from the Jacobite merchant John Ochternlony to Thomas Gordon, which would suggest a Jacobite connection, 5/12/1730, NAS Abercairney GD 24/1/856, f.202.

85 V.N.Berkh, *Zhisneopisaniya pervykh rossiiskikh admiralov*, 4 vols. (St Petersburg, 1831–1836) 3, p.244; R.C.Anderson, *Mariners' Mirror* 33, p.23.

86 Thomas Wisheart to Admiralty College, 26/2/1722, 27/2/1722, RGAVMF F212 o11 d18, ll.88–91.

87 Report to Admiralty College, 18/8/1722, RGAVMF F212 o11 d3/157, l.212/137.

88 The case of William Cooper, RGAVMF F212 o11 d45.

89 Logan, a steersman, was granted an amnesty on the occasion of the peace with Sweden in 1721 from a sentence of forced labour at Schlüsselburg 'for certain crimes', Memorial of Admiralty College, 14/12/1721, RGAVMF F212 o11 d18, l.23.

90 'Spisok lichnogo sostava flota', 1723 RGAVMF F212 o1 d13.

The Jacobites and the Anglo-Russian Diplomatic Rupture of 1719

George I's use of the Gyllenborg conspiracy to justify sending a British fleet to the Baltic to protect his Hanoverian possessions against Russia and Sweden had the serious implication for Britain that it encouraged communication between the Jacobites and Peter I, and heralded one of the most dynamic chapters in Russo-Jacobite politics. The recruitment of disaffected Britons into the Russian armed forces in spring 1717, one aspect of this, greatly benefited Russo-Jacobite diplomacy in that it established a body of Jacobite agents in addition to Robert Erskine and his nephew, Sir Henry Stirling. The most active of these were Thomas Gordon and William Hay, but Thomas Saunders, Kenneth Sutherland, Lord Duffus and Peter Lacy were also acknowledged by the exiled court as political representatives of the Jacobite community in Russia. It was these men who co-ordinated Jacobite policy in Russia not only in subsequent years but in subsequent reigns.

In June 1717, when hope of independent support from Sweden was fading, the Duke of Ormonde was invited on the Tsar's suggestion to Spa, where, in July, he was received both by Dr Erskine and the Tsar himself.[91] Peter I, who was prepared to contemplate any means of opposing George I, '. . . professe[d] great inclinations to serve James'.[92] The Earl of Mar had had several meetings with Dr Erskine in May to discuss the benefits of a Russo-Swedish peace, and remained in close contact with him throughout the summer, despite the fact that the Regent's disapproval of Russo-Jacobite relations restricted public contact with Jacobites in France.[93] At the same time, Russian ministers in Amsterdam and the Hague, including Erskine, were excluding Britain from negotiations with representatives from France, Prussia and Sweden in order to end the Northern war to Russia's advantage, and in August, Russia signed a defensive agreement with Prussia and France, directed against Britain.[94] To Britain's displeasure, Peter I also provided Baron Görtz, who had come to Holland after his release from British custody, with a passport to return to Sweden and arrange a peace congress on the Aland islands for the following year.[95]

Peter I's encouragement of the Jacobites was more than a mere symbol of political hostility towards George I. They represented one element of a larger body of opposition to Britain which could procure him an advantageous peace with Sweden, as well as weakening his rival in the Electorate and at sea. The

91 News that Charles XII had rejected both Peter I's peace proposals and George I's offers of mediation arrived at the end of May. Mar to James III, 4/6/1717, Mar to R.Erskine, 31/5/1717, *HMC Stuart* 4, pp.291–294, 313–315; Ormonde was invited to Spa by the Tsar in order to, '. . . be more at liberty to speak fully to him of affairs', Mar to James III, 7/6/1717, *Ibid.*, p.325, Dillon to Mar, 14/7/1717, *Ibid.*, pp.450–451.
92 Ormonde to James III, 13/7/1717, *HMC Stuart* 4, pp.446–447.
93 Mar to Erskine, 14/5, 22/5, 31/5, 1/7, 27/7, 29/8/1717, *HMC Stuart* 4, pp.242–3, 265–6, 291–4, 473–5, 543; 15/9/1717, *HMC Stuart* 5, p.46. Mar to James III, 17/5/1717, *Ibid.*, p.249.
94 Treaty signed 4/8/1717 o.s., Solov'ev, *Istoriya Rossii*, 17, p.365, 366.
95 Chance, *George I and the Northern War*, p.236.

efforts of the British Secretary of State, Stanhope, to curtail the territorial ambitions of Philip V of Spain, had encouraged the Spanish chief minister, Cardinal Alberoni, and the head of the pro-Spanish party in France, D'Uxelles, to work together with Jacobite agents for a separate Prusso-Russian peace with Sweden. The Jacobites, through Dr Erskine, encouraged the Tsar's interest by offering to mediate between Russia and Sweden[96] and Peter I granted them three months to free General Rank, the plenipotentiary minister empowered by Sweden to negotiate, who had unfortunately been detained in Denmark. In August the agent George Jerningham's letters from James III were 'well received' by Prince Dolgoruky.[97] Jerningham, Charles Wogan and Daniel O'Brien, followed by Ormonde himself, travelled to Danzig to remain in contact with both Charles XII and Peter I, who was on his return journey to Russia.[98] At the end of September, the Tsar spent two nights in Danzig, and ordered Ormonde to follow him to Riga and to await an answer to Jacobite negotiations in Sweden. While at Danzig, Ormonde met with Dr Erskine, who recommended that his nephew, Sir Henry Stirling, be present at the Russo-Swedish peace congress planned to take place on the Aland islands. In October, while at Mittau in Courland expecting instructions to proceed to Russia, Ormonde received confirmation through Dr Erskine that the Tsar was giving Jacobite proposals serious consideration. Erskine wrote,

> . . . I spoke with the Czar of your affairs, and he is of the opinion you should send as soon as possible to Sweden to know their resolution, and if they will not undertake the affair out of hand, you should think of proposing it to Marechal d'Uxelles and those of his party, that they might oblige the Regent to make a descent on that side, and, if we can have a peace with S[weden], I engage that the Czar will send 20,000 men to Rostock to enter into the country to oblige King George to return and hinder Holland from giving any succour . . . The Czar offers his daughter in marriage to the King and wishes that this affair of the descent may be concluded this winter . . .[99]

At this stage, Peter I viewed his own role in any concerted effort against George I to consist in threatening Hanover. Nevertheless, his response to the Jacobites, and particularly his unprompted proposal to marry his daughter, Anna Petrovna, to James III, confirmed that he was not only well aware of their aspirations, but that he acknowledged them as an important political force which could serve as a useful weapon in his own conflict with George I. Both the Tsar's and his physician's close contact with them also clearly belied the disclaimers they had offered to the British government earlier in the year.

The extent to which Jacobite involvement in northern politics concerned

96 Mar to Erskine, 31/5/1717, *HMC Stuart* 4, pp.291–297.
97 Jerningham to H.Paterson, 25/8/1717, *HMC Stuart* 4, pp.532–533.
98 Dillon to James III, 4/9/1717, *HMC Stuart* 5, pp.4–5; Inese to Mar, 5/9/1717, *Ibid.*, pp.11–13; H.Paterson to Mar, 18,19/10/1717, *Ibid.*, p.145.
99 R.Erskine to Ormonde, 29/9 o.s., 10/10/1717 n.s., *HMC Stuart* 5, p.154.

not only Hanoverian but also British ministers was demonstrated in 1718 by demands that Peter I cease his contacts with Jacobite agents. In February 1718, Sir Henry Stirling received news from Dr Erskine that, '. . . the Czar has complaints made him from England that the Duke of Ormonde is protected in this country'.[100] In early March, Stirling wrote to Ormonde in Mittau, warning him of the Tsar's, '. . . letters from England, which demand either that he will remove the Duke of Ormonde or that they will look on it as an open breach and that they would act accordingly'.[101] It also transpired that the Hanoverian minister in Russia, Weber, had taken the initiative, without the King's orders, to write a memorial in the name of King George applying for the removal from Russia of certain known Jacobite agents. In the words of Sir Henry Stirling, Weber was '. . . pretending that, while the Czar entertained such servants in his family, it could not be wondered that the English minister's master and he were not good friends'.[102] Stirling was named in the memorial, and he believed the second man referred to by Weber to be Thomas Gordon. De la Vie, however, reporting the news to France, was of the opinion that it was Dr Erskine himself.[103]

Jacobite and British-Hanoverian representatives gave widely differing versions of Peter I's intentions. In May, Stirling reported to Sir Hugh Paterson, that '. . . It's false what the English ministry gives out that the Czar had promised to remove Ormonde, for he always affirmed that he knew nothing of the matter and that their information was false. The same is as little true as to Sir H. Stirling'.[104] De la Vie was first informed by Weber that the contents of the memorial meant that the Jacobites would be expelled, '. . . comme rebelles et intentionnes de tramer en cette cour quelque intrigue en faveur du chevalier de S-t Georges', and that Dr Erskine was to send his nephew home and was forbidden '. . . sous peine de son indignation, de favoriser aucun emissaire ou partisan du Chevalier de S.G'. This rumour was also reported by the Dutch secretary, Baron de Bie, who claimed not only that the Tsar had promised to expel Henry Stirling, but that he had even offered to break off the Aland congress to appease George I.[105] However, Erskine and other British subjects were of the opinion that Weber, a foreigner, had involved himself in English matters without the King's orders, rendering his demands not only invalid, but against British law. Moreover, Peter, '. . . qui aime fort le docteur Areskeen', was apparently intending to demand Weber's recall.[106]

It was British and Hanoverian vulnerability to hostility in the north which had prompted this reaction against Jacobite support within Russia. In April, the Tsar had threatened Britain with armed retaliation if it should make a

100 Henry Stirling to Duke of Ormonde, 10/21 February 1718, *HMC Stuart* 5, p.499.
101 Henry Stirling to Duke of Ormonde, 3/14 March 1718, *HMC Stuart* 6, p.147.
102 Henry Stirling to Sir Hugh Paterson, 12/23 May 1718, *HMC Stuart* 6, p.466.
103 De la Vie to Dubois, 3/6/1718, *SIRIO* 34, p.344.
104 Sir Henry Stirling to Sir Hugh Paterson, 12/23 May 1718, *HMC Stuart* 6, p.466.
105 Report of Baron de Bie, 23/5 o.s., 3/6/1718 n.s., Elagin, *Materialy* 4, pp.158–159.
106 De la Vie to Dubois, 3/6/1718, *SIRIO* 34, p.344.

separate peace with Sweden.[107] The opening of the Aland congress in May, in which all parties interested in Russo-Swedish peace had included plans for Jacobite support should negotiations succeed, posed a risk to both Britain and Hanover which could not be estimated. This risk was augmented by the threat of conflict with, or even an invasion from Spain, which meant that Stanhope and the English ministers had to restrict the number of vessels they could send to safeguard the Baltic. Despite the supreme confidence of Jean de Robethon, the Count Bernstorff's private secretary, that Admiral Norris and his squadron of twelve ships sent to the Baltic could prevent a union of the Swedish and Russian fleets,[108] it soon became obvious that the Russian fleet was stronger than anticipated.[109] Norris himself reported with concern that, '. . . if Sweden drop in and joynes the Czarr . . . our aperance hear is a very ill figure'.[110]

Peter I's response to British demands that he refuse to harbour Jacobites took the form of a compromise which, on the surface, propitiated Britain, while keeping his options open to support James III should it benefit him to do so. In May 1718, to the disappointment of the Jacobites, he '. . . ordered the English Jacobites at the Court of the Duchess of Courland to withdraw',[111] and in public, consistently denied any involvement in Jacobite intrigue. The presence of the British squadron, and his concern not to give George I 'any handle' or encouragement to conclude a separate Anglo-Swedish peace, made him reluctant to make the Jacobites firm promises which might prove compromising, and he took care to emphasise that the Jacobite marriage proposal was conditional on a Russian peace with Sweden.[112]

Nevertheless, Sir Henry Stirling, Thomas Gordon and other active Jacobite agents were permitted to remain in Russia, and Peter did not turn away the Jacobites recruited during his visit to Europe who were just arriving in his kingdom. Although the Tsar was unwilling to risk open hostility with Britain by public support of the Jacobite cause, this by no means meant that he was prepared to sacrifice some of his best officers to the demands of a rival power. Moreover, he refused to lose touch with a cause which might encourage other powers to lend their support against George I, support which would certainly further Russian territorial interests.

Despite Peter I's superficial concessions to British demands, he continued, in secret, to pursue his plan to offer Charles XII Hanoverian possessions in exchange for Livonia and Estonia, and instructed Osterman to assure Görtz, the Swedish negotiator on the Aland islands, that he would consider aid to the

107 Peter I to Veselovsky, 25/4/1718, *Arkhiv Kurakina* 3, p.60.
108 He wrote, '. . . The Czar cannot hurt us . . . His fleet is ruined'. 27/3 or 7/4/1718, Robethon to Polwarth, *HMC Polwarth* 1, p.471.
109 This was, to a large extent, the result of the work of British shipbuilders. Weber to Polwarth, 16/27 June, *HMC Polwarth*, pp.518–520.
110 Norris to Polwarth, *HMC Polwarth* 1.
111 M.Stiernhock to Earl of Mar, 21/5/1718, *HMC Stuart* 6, p.459.
112 Ormonde to James III, 30/3/1718, Ormonde to H.Stirling, 30/3/1718,; H.Paterson to Dillon, 20/5/1718, *HMC Stuart* 6, pp.225, 226, 452.

Jacobites to achieve this.[113] Meanwhile, the Jacobite agent, George Jerningham, who had travelled to St Petersburg in May, having met with Görtz in
Sweden, received assurances from Shafirov that, '. . . the Tsar's support might
firmly be relied upon, that there was little doubt that he would be allowed to go
to the Aland congress, and his master admitted as a principal in the expected
treaty'.[114] By late summer, Spanish-Jacobite plans were also reaching fruition.
In August, Spain had responded to the conclusion of the Quadruple Alliance
between Britain, France and Austria,[115] which was directed against Spain in the
south, and Russia, Sweden and Prussia in the north, by offering Russia a joint
Russo-Spanish-Swedish alliance, which was to involve a Jacobite restoration
attempt.[116] The destruction of the Spanish fleet at Cape Passaro the following
month redoubled Spain's determination to have its revenge on George I, and,
Patrick Lawless, an Irish Jacobite agent in Spain, travelled to Sweden to
engineer a Russo-Swedish peace and arrange the invasion of Britain by Russian,
Swedish and Spanish ships for the following spring. Peter I, through Prince
Kurakin and the Spanish ambassador at the Hague, Marquis de Beretti Landi,
conducted a detailed investigation into the Spanish project, having secretly
requested Spain not to make any concessions to its enemies until Russia had
concluded its peace with Sweden.[117] He even met personally with Lawless at
Reval to discuss Spanish-Jacobite preparations.[118] If this plan were successfully
executed, it would deprive Britain not only of Bremen and Verden, which
would go to Charles XII, but would damage British trade in the Baltic and
overthrow the British government and monarchy.

By late 1718 Russia's involvement with the Jacobites, although principally
motivated by Peter I's own territorial interests in Mecklenburg and on the Baltic,
and thus endangering Hanover more directly than Britain, had become a direct
threat to British security. The foreign policy of Bernstorff, which had alienated
Russia in an effort to safeguard Hanover, had created ideal conditions for the
Jacobites to promote a northern alliance in conjunction with Britain's enemies in
the south. In autumn 1718 Bernstorff was negotiating an alliance with Austria
and Saxony without the knowledge of British ministers,[119] which would secure
Hanover against Russia, but could also antagonise Peter I into naval action
against Britain at a time when its coasts were at risk from Spain.

113 During the Aland congress (May 1718–Sept. 1719) Görtz and Count Osterman concerted
     plans to the effect that '. . . if Great Britain interfered in retaking Bremen and Verden,
     that they would, with their joint fleets and forces, make a descent on Britain with the
     pretender, and place him on the throne', P.H.Bruce, pp.190–191, Solov'ev, *Istoriya Rossii*
     17, p.499.
114 5/6/1718, Chance, *George I and the Northern War,* p.269; Shafirov to Osterman, 9/6/1718,
     Solov'ev, *Istoriya Rossii,* 17, p.500.
115 It was intended that the Dutch Republic also accede to this.
116 Solov'ev, *Istoriya Rossii,* 17, p.564–566.
117 Instructions to Campredon, *Recueil des Instructions données aux Ambassadeurs et Ministres de
     France* . . ., ed. by A.Rambaud, 8 Russie, p.198; Peter I to Kurakin, 19/9/1718, Solov'ev
     Istoriya Rossii, 17, pp.564–565.
118 *Recueil,* 8 Russie, p.199.
119 McKay, 'George I's Northern Policy', pp.376,377.

The yearly presence of a British squadron in the Baltic and the conclusion of the Quadruple Alliance in August 1718 were evidence of the level of British concern over Russia. In September, Stanhope, fearing the possible outcome of Spanish-Russian co-operation, made a formal protest to the Russian ambassador, Veselovsky, accusing Peter I of continued involvement with Jacobite agents. Veselovsky's response, which claimed,

> . . . que nous n'avons jamais eu connaissance icy d'aucuns Emissaires du Prétendant, et que Personne de sa part n'a pas paru directement devant nous, et que Nous n'avons accepté aucunes Propositions de luy, ni qu'aucun des Emissaires n'a été admis auprès de nos Ministres . . .[120]

was, at best, a distortion of the truth. He countered the complaint that Peter I had failed to expel Sir Henry Stirling with the excuse that Stirling had remained due to Dr Erskine's illness, and that, '. . . comme trop jeune homme, il n'estoit capable d'entrer en aucune affaire serieuse'.[121] Britain was justifiedly unconvinced by Russian disclaimers, being in any case well aware through intercepted correspondence of Stirling's very active Jacobite role.[122] In a final effort to counteract the Russian threat, the ministry decided to send Admiral Norris and James Jefferyes to St Petersburg to negotiate a peace agreement with the Tsar.[123] Their instructions, '. . . modestly to complain of the good reception the Jacobites still find at the Czar's Court', confirmed that Britain perceived the presence of Jacobites as an important sign of Peter I's hostility towards George I and thus as an obstacle to any rapprochement.[124]

Fortunately for Britain, by the time Jefferyes arrived in Russia in January, without Norris, two events had occurred which effectively banished the government's nightmare of an anti-British northern alliance with Spanish and Jacobite support. Firstly, the shooting of Charles XII at Frederikshald on 12 December 1718, put a sudden end to Spanish negotiations with Sweden, and thus also with Russia.[125] In the same month, Dr Erskine died at Olonetz, and with him the Jacobites lost their most important channel of access to the Tsar.

Peter I's regret at the death of Charles XII stemmed from the loss of an opportunity to win part of the Baltic littoral. Charles's successor, lacking his traditional enmity for Britain, might, by means of a separate Swedish peace with George I, deprive Peter I altogether of his coveted territory. His regret at Erskine's death was more personal. At the funeral, in January 1719, Peter took

120 Veselovsky to Stanhope, 3/10/1718 o.s., PRO SP 100/52, ff.5,6.
121 Ibid.
122 Whitworth wrote, '. . . I should rather fancy Weselowski, whilst he endeavours to amuse the ministers, may be underhand tampering with the Jacobites, there is a strong leven in that Court which will not be removed as long as Areskin has credit, and the Czar dares not part with him'. Whitworth to Tilson, 21/10/1718, in Chance, *George I and the Northern War*, p.286. For Stirling's intercepted correspondence see BL Stowe 232.
123 Stanhope to Norris, 5/10/1718 o.s., Chance, *George I and the Northern War*, pp.283–284.
124 Instructions to James Jefferyes, 14/10/1718, *SIRIO* 61, p.451.
125 Spain had been on the point of giving Charles XII ships, arms and money for the invasion when he was killed. Stair to Robethon, 14/1/1719, BL Stowe 231, f.261.

part in the procession, carrying a lighted candle.[126] Weber, the Hanoverian resident, described how, after the ceremony, '. . . His Majesty . . . gave some Marks of the Esteem he had had for the deceased'.[127] During the course of the funeral Peter was also very gracious towards other Jacobites present, and, '. . . shewed particular Favour towards his (Dr Erskine's) Relation Sir Harry Stirling, who was come to Russia under the Czar's protection . . .'[128] Peter I's strong territorial motive for support of the joint Jacobite offensive on Britain, combined with his close relationship with individual Jacobites, encourage speculation that he would have participated in a Jacobite rising, had circumstances permitted it.

It is tempting to conclude that the deaths of Charles XII and Robert Erskine marked the end of Peter I's involvement with the Jacobites for some time after 1718. Maurice Bruce, in an article on 'Jacobite Relations with Peter the Great' limited himself to the final five years of Peter's reign on the assumption that his relations with the Jacobites, '. . . ceased abruptly at the end of 1718 . . . it was not until after the Peace of Nystad . . . that the Jacobites again took a place in Peter's policies'.[129] Although the removal of Sweden from plans for a northern coalition against George I eliminated any territorial benefit the Tsar could derive from collaboration with the Jacobites, his continued contact with them in the course of 1719 did, in fact, contribute directly to the diplomatic rupture with Britain at the end of that year.

Britain's perception of a threat from Russia was by no means banished by Charles XII's death. Indeed, there was every reason to fear that the Tsar would seize the opportunity to make good his territorial ambitions, and rumours continued to abound that he was still in league with Spain. In January the Hanoverian minister Jean de Robethon wrote to Lord Polwarth, the British plenipotentiary in Copenhagen, with news of a rumour of Jacobite plans to set Holstein on the Swedish throne, and then '. . . in concert with the Czar, set on foot the old projects for a descent on Scotland, even though Dr Erskine is dead'.[130] Soon after this he confirmed that

> . . . We have recently received new proofs of the intelligence maintained by Baron Görtz with the emissaries of the Pretender . . . having full assurance from Görtz that, if peace is concluded with the Czar they then will consider the re-establishing of the Pretender and a descent on Scotland.[131]

In February, Stanhope made a searing reply to a further claim by Veselovsky that the Tsar was ignorant of Jacobite activity, by recounting, point by point, the evidence to the contrary as revealed by British espionage. Not only did he refer to

126 Mottley, 3, p.134.
127 Weber, 1, p.246.
128 *Ibid.*
129 M.W. Bruce, 'Jacobite Relations with Peter the Great', *SEER* 14 (1936), p.344.
130 Robethon to Polwarth, 2/13 January 1719, *HMC Polwarth* 2, p.17.
131 J.Robethon to Lord Polwarth, 6/17 January 1719, *HMC Polwarth* 2, p.21.

the Tsar's implication in the Gyllenborg conspiracy, but to the fact that subsequent Russian disclaimers had been proven false by Peter's audiences with Jacobites in Holland, by the negotiations of Ormonde from Mittau and of Stirling and Jerningham at Petersburg, by his failure to hinder Görtz's Jacobite invasion plans at the Aland congress, and finally, by, '. . . les propositions que le Czar a fait faire plus d'une fois à la Cour d'Espagne pour la faire entrer dans une Alliance offensive en faveur du Prétendant'.[132] Stanhope's letter clearly indicates the extent to which Peter I's contacts with the Jacobites became a symbol of a more general hostility towards George I, quite independently of whether or not these contacts were supported by concrete promises of assistance.

There was no reason for the ministry to feign its concern over the Jacobite threat, as was amply demonstrated by the Spanish-backed Jacobite rising which took place in Scotland that spring. Although this was easily defeated in June by government forces at Glenshiel, in the Western Highlands, Russia's favourable response to news of the affair increased Britain's suspicions of the Tsar, and of Jacobite activity in Russia. Jefferyes reported to Stanhope that the Spanish invasion, '. . . makes no little noise in these parts of the world; this court hears it with pleasure and will no doubt make the best advantage of it for compassing their designs'.[133]

The ministry's fear of Peter I stemmed principally from the strength of the Russian navy, particularly between 1718 and 1720, when British involvement in war with Spain in the Mediterranean drained its naval resources from the Baltic and left its own coasts vulnerable. Jefferyes noted with concern the lack of ships for the Baltic, and wrote, '. . . we shall have great occasion for [our ships] both for the preservation of our trade, and for inforcing a peace with Sweden'.[134]

There was no doubt that Russia had an intimidating naval capacity, much more powerful than that sent to Scotland by Spain in April, and physically capable of carrying out an invasion of Britain, let alone attacking Hanoverian duchies. By 1718 the navy which the Tsar had been steadily expanding since his first visit to Europe in 1697–8, with the assistance of several leading British shipbuilders, had twenty-seven ships-of-the-line on patrol in the Baltic alone.[135] Admiral Norris reported that

> . . . The improvements he [Peter] has made, by the help of English builders, are such as a seaman would think almost impossible for a nation so lately used to the sea. They have built three sixty-gun ships, which are in every way equal to the best of that rank in our country.[136]

In July 1719, Jefferyes described the Russian fleet as consisting of '. . . upwards of 30 sail, whereof 27 or 28 are ships of the line . . . these are looked upon to be

132 11/2/1719 o.s., Stanhope's reponse to Veselovsky's memorial of 14/12/1718 o.s., PRO SP 100/52 unfol.
133 Jefferyes to Stanhope, 10/4/1719 o.s., *SIRIO* 61, p.522.
134 Ibid.
135 Deane, p.60.
136 J.Barrow, *Memoir of the Life of Peter the Great*, 3rd edn. (London, 1839), p.239n.

ships as good and as well built as any Europe can afford'.[137] By the end of Peter I's reign, it comprised forty-eight ships-of-the-line, 787 galleys and other vessels, and was manned by around 28,000 men.[138]

Britain's fear of Russian naval power found expression in an Act of Parliament of 1719 to prevent British tradesmen from entering foreign service, and in subsequent attempts by Jefferyes to persuade British shipbuilders in Russia to return home, despite the fact that they would suffer a fifty per cent drop in salary. It was feared that

> . . . if they remain, they may by bringing the moscovites into a good method, and by teaching their people the way of building do more damage to Great Britain than what a yearly expence of 20 times as much as the Czar allows them will amount to.[139]

In August it was resolved at Whitehall to pay the six shipbuilders identified by Jefferyes as most useful to Peter I, as much as he offered them to leave Russian service, but to ensure, '. . . that he do this with all possible secrecy'.[140] Of even greater concern was news that Thomas Gordon, a known Jacobite, had been ordered to engage further British sailors into the Russian Navy.[141]

British mistrust of Russia was fuelled directly by the influence of disaffected Britons in Peter I's navy, and by information implying the extent of the Tsar's past Jacobite involvements. In addition to this, however, in 1719, it appears that there was a deliberate attempt on the part of certain Jacobites to exacerbate Anglo-Russian hostility by carrying on politically disruptive correspondence in order to drive the two powers apart. The unlikelihood that Peter would actually support a Jacobite restoration at this point was expressed in a letter from Veselovsky to Peter I complaining at the injustice of the rumours reaching Britain. He wrote,

> . . . I am very much afraid that there must be some liar among the Jacobites living in Russia who, on the strength of a bribe, or out of malice, is informing this court of something which his friends are perhaps not doing; but it is true that the British Ministry is taking this affair as the highest insult, which justifies all the hostilities of the Hanoverian court towards us. The whole population . . . is convinced that your Majesty is in

137 Jefferyes to Craggs, 16/7/1719, *SIRIO* 61, p.561. The British Baltic fleet in this year was composed of eighteen ships-of-the-line. Chance, *The Northern War*, p.361.
138 Solov'ev, 18, p.776.
139 Jefferyes to Craggs, 16/7/1719, *SIRIO* 61, pp.561–567. See also Jefferyes to Stanhope,15/5/1719, *Ibid.*, p.536; Jefferyes to Craggs, 29/5/1719, Ibid., pp.537–8.; Jefferyes to Craggs, 8/6/1719, *Ibid.*, p.550.
140 Minutes of Whitehall, 13/8/1719, PRO SP 44/280. However, although these men were apparently '. . . all good subjects and well affected to His Majesty's government', by November only three of them, Ney, Cousins and Devenport, had agreed to return home, while Brown and Ramsey refused to accept the lower salary. Jefferyes to Craggs, 16/7/1719, *SIRIO* 61, p.565; Hadley, in Kazan, had not replied to the offer. Jefferyes to Craggs, 7/11/1719, PRO SP 91/9, f.345.
141 Jefferyes to Stanhope, 20/2/1719, *SIRIO* 61, p.496.

league with Spain and intends to make a descent on England at the first opportunity.[142]

However, documents discovered in the Archive of Ancient Acts in Moscow (RGADA) confirm that Vice-Admiral Thomas Gordon was involved in passing both British naval intelligence and information of Jacobite projects to the Tsar, thereby not only arousing Peter's hostility towards Britain, but also laying him open to British accusations of Jacobite collusion. When, in June, Gordon received a letter from England informing him of ministerial intentions to oppose the Russian fleet, he immediately '. . . wrote to each of [his] people in England, in order to discover all the British government's intentions and actions relating to the Czar'.[143] He then had his secretary translate two of the replies in strict confidence, and forwarded them to Peter, offering to continue this information service if it proved useful. Several of these translated letters have been preserved in Moscow, so Gordon's proposal to act as an informant to the Tsar was probably accepted. Of those replies received before the diplomatic rupture, two are in the Archive of Ancient Acts in Moscow and are of 17 and 21 July 1719. One more reply, of 28 July, is in the St Petersburg Naval Archive. All three were probably from the same Jacobite, James Johnstone, the great uncle of John Hay, later Earl of Inverness. The first letter reported that orders had been issued repeatedly from Hanover to send reinforcements to Admiral Norris's squadron at the entrance to the Baltic under Admiral Miles '. . . with orders to sink or destroy'.[144] On 21 July the correspondent informed Gordon from London of Britain's alarm at the Tsar's naval preparations, and of plans to send six war ships to aid Norris, who had been ordered to take the offensive in the Baltic. In addition to this, many transport ships had assembled ready to embark on a secret mission, possibly to carry between 4,000 and 6,000 French troops to Spain.[145] Johnstone reported on George I's efforts at that time to secure the alliance of Prussia by means of a bribe of £295,000.[146]

By the act of forwarding this information of George I's precautions against Russia to the Tsar, Gordon was, from a Russian perspective, damaging Anglo-Russian relations as directly as rumours of Jacobite conspiracy had unsettled Britain. In addition to naval intelligence, the letters also contained plans for Russian support for a restoration attempt, of which Peter I may well have been aware. That of 21 July claimed that the British people '. . . groan and curse the day when [they] were put under a foreign yoke', and suggested that the Tsar send '. . . only six or seven thousand military men', to be joined with an equal number of Spaniards. The correspondent maintained that '. . . seven or eight

142 (My translation), Veselovsky to Peter I, c.May 1719, Solov'ev, *Istoriya Rossii,* 17, p.572.
143 T.Gordon to Peter I, 31/8/1719, RGADA F35 o1 pt.2 d481, ll.1,1v.
144 [J.Johnstone] to T.Gordon, 17/7/1719, RGADA F35 o1 pt.2 d481 ll.2,2v; Norris had received secret orders to destroy the fleet if necessary: '. . . Every Englishman will be obliged to you, if you can destroy the Czar's fleet', 19/21 August 1719, Chance, *The Northern War,* p.361.
145 [James Johnstone] to T.Gordon, 21/7/1719, Ibid. l.3.
146 James Johnstone to Thomas Gordon, 28/7/1719. Elagin, *Materialy po istorii russkago flota,* 4, pp.175–6.

thousand military men can set up a revolution here in ten days'.[147] In another letter, Johnstone suggested that the Tsar avenge himself on George I; '. . . all His Czarish Majesty has to do is to send a few of his troops here as soon as possible, and I assure His Majesty that he will achieve his intentions in ten days'.[148] Jacobite hopes of Russian assistance persisted, for the Jacobite agent George Jerningham mentioned in a letter to James that he had written to Henry Stirling on the matter,[149] and in August actually claimed that '. . . the Czar [was] resolved to help the King of Spain to restore'.[150] There was little support for this statement, particularly at this juncture, in the wake of the defeat of the 1719 Rising. It is possible, however, that it was generated not by naive Jacobite over-optimism, but by the calculated exploitation of rumour as a political tool to undermine Anglo-Russian relations. The ministry's suspicions of continuing Jacobite communication with Russia certainly remained strong. In August, Jefferyes reported the visit to the Tsar of a man thought to be De Baraillon, a Russian spy from Switzerland, who had been in Sweden and was now travelling to the Hague to report to the Spanish ambassador involved in the Spanish-Jacobite rising, Marquis de Beretti Landi.[151]

This mutual mistrust, manifested in disputes over Jacobite support, which doomed to failure any hope of Anglo-Russian peace in 1719, was reflected in the precautions taken by Britain to limit Russian power. In February, Britain and Hanover were planning a peace with Sweden which would deprive the Tsar of the Baltic provinces, and ensure Swedish support against the Russian fleet. Peter I declared angrily that he would regard a separate Anglo-Swedish peace as, '. . . a declaration of war on Russia',[152] which heightened the general alarm in Britain in July that the Russian fleet was preparing an offensive, which could lead to open war.[153] Once again a squadron under Admiral Norris was sent to the Baltic, and Hanoverian and British ministers redoubled their diplomatic efforts to weaken the Tsar. In August, after the overthrow of Bernstorff by British ministers, George I signed a defensive treaty with Prussia on behalf both of Britain and Hanover, and in July and November, treaties were concluded between Sweden, and Britain and Hanover respectively.[154] Britain's 'anti-Russian' coalition proved of little value to its new ally, however, for Peter I was so incensed by the prospect of losing the Baltic states that he invaded Sweden. This was the final blow to Anglo-Russian relations, and George I immediately ordered his representatives in St Petersburg, Jefferyes and Weber, to retire to Danzig.[155]

147 [James Johnstone] to Thomas Gordon, 21/7/1719, RGADA F35 ol ed.kh.481, l.3.
148 James Johnstone to T.Gordon, Elagin, *Materialy* 4, pp.175–6.
149 Jerningham to James III, RA Stuart 44/29.
150 Jerningham to James III, 11/8/1719, RA Stuart 44/35.
151 Jefferyes to Craggs, 6/8/1719, *SIRIO* 61, p.573.
152 Solov'ev, *Istoriya Rossii*, 17, p.571.
153 [James Johnstone] to Thomas Gordon, 21/7/1719, RGADA F35 ol ed.kh.481,l3.
154 McKay, *George I's Northern Policy*, p.384.
155 Jefferyes to Stanhope, 16/10/1719, *SIRIO* 61, p.586. They left on 4/10/1719 o.s., Chance, *The Northern War*, p.398.

Britain's awareness of Peter I's encouragement of disaffected Britons in his armed forces, and his receptivity to Jacobite projects as a means of achieving territorial aims in direct conflict with British and Hanoverian interests, played an important role in increasing Anglo-Russian tension. In 1718, in particular, the possibility of a northern alliance involving Jacobite support greatly concerned both British and Hanoverian ministers, and directed subsequent foreign policy towards isolating and containing the power of Peter I. By 1719, the mere presence of Jacobites in Russia had become a symbol of the Tsar's hostility, and the Jacobites themselves exploited this fully, to the lasting detriment of Anglo-Russian relations.

THREE

The Climax of
Russo-Jacobite Diplomacy, 1720–1725

1720, A Year of Change

The rift which had opened between Peter I and George I in 1719 did not immediately improve Russia's relations with the House of Stuart. This was primarily due to the success of moves by foreign minister Stanhope both to isolate Peter I and to insulate British possessions. As well as concluding alliances with Prussia and Sweden in 1719 to protect north Germany, Britain brought Spain into the Quadruple Alliance in January 1720, ending a two year conflict.[1] Sweden reinforced its position against Russia by signing treaties with Poland in January, Prussia in February and Denmark in June.[2]

Although the diplomatic rupture raised Jacobite hopes of Peter I's support,[3] viewed from within Russia, the state of affairs was less optimistic. In a letter to James III in January 1720, Sir Henry Stirling reported Jacobite prospects as being, '. . . in a very indifferent situation'. Although Stirling assured James that the Tsar was, according to those close to him, '. . . ready to embark in your quarrel', and recommended that negotiations be initiated through Prince Boris Kurakin at the Hague,[4] any assistance from Russia would have been unthinkable, particularly while Peter I was preoccupied with the continuing war in Sweden. In addition to this, Jacobite correspondence to and from Russia in 1720 went missing, probably falling victim to British interception. This included a letter from James III to Stirling containing instructions and a full empowerment for him to carry on negotiations which, '. . . by some evil misfortune, never reached [his] hands'.[5] For the present, therefore, Britain's lack of diplomatic representation in St Petersburg was unimportant. Jefferyes and Weber, safe in Danzig, felt cocksure enough to taunt the Tsar's minister for favouring Britain's enemies, and wrote to Stanhope,

> . . . we begged leave to ask him [Shafirov] what they had gained by their intrigues with the disaffected party in France, what their correspondence

1 W.Michael, *England under George I*, 2, *The Quadruple Alliance* (London, 1939), p.125.
2 Swedish-Polish treaty, 7/18 January 1720; Swedish-Prussian treaty, 21/1 or 1/2/1720; Swedish-Danish treaty, 3/14 June 1720, Michael, 2, p.266.
3 Thomas Gordon's correspondent in London was convinced that if Peter sent 8–10,000 troops for a descent in March or April 1720, George would be powerless to defend himself, [James Johnstone] to Thomas Gordon, 31/10/1719, RGADA F35 o1 ed.kh.481, ll.5–6.
4 H.Stirling to James III, 25/1/1720, RA Stuart 46/11.
5 H. Stirling to Peter I, 8/12/1721 o.s., AVPR F35, o1 d505.

with the spanish ambassadors and with the emissaries of the pretender had availed them.[6]

Fortunately for the Jacobites, British complacency was temporary, for 1720 also saw the gradual disintegration of Stanhope's 'anti-Russian' coalition, and demonstrated Britain's ultimate inability to force Peter I to peace with Sweden. Anglo-Austrian friction increased over Britain's growing amity with Prussia, its support for the Protestant faction in religious confrontations in the Empire, and over Vienna's consequent refusal to oppose Russia.[7] Peter I exploited this by sending Paul Iaguzhinsky to Vienna at the end of April, and the envoy found common ground in support expressed both by the Russian and the Catholic monarch for the House of Stuart against the Hanoverian monarchy.[8] By June, Anglo-Austrian relations had virtually collapsed.

In April Norris was again in the Baltic, this time with a strong fleet specifically intended to prevent a Russian attack on Sweden, to which he gave orders that, '. . . at all times when you shall come up with any Russian ships you shall do your utmost to take, sink, burn or otherwise destroy them'.[9] However, when neither Austria, Prussia nor France would assist British efforts to impose peace terms on Russia, and Peter I proved hostile to any but the most advantageous agreement, Stanhope, realising Britain's impotence, advised Sweden to make its own peace with Peter I.[10] The hostility of Norris's fleet was regarded by Russia as the final straw, and on 17 October 1720, the Russian resident in London, Count Mikhail Bestuzhev-Riumin, in a twenty page letter to George I, expressed the Tsar's anger at each successive measure taken by Britain to frustrate his ambitions. Echoing Veselovsky's memorials of the previous year, he denied, albeit only half-truthfully, accusations of Jacobite support and alleged plans for a Russian alliance with Spain, sharply criticising Britain's treatment of Russia.[11] So strongly-worded was the letter that Bestuzhev was ordered to leave the following month, thus completing the formal breakdown of diplomatic links between Britain and Russia. These were the first steps in a process which destroyed Britain's attempts to isolate Peter I, injected new energy into Anglo-Russian rivalry, and encouraged Russian contact with the Jacobites.

The Tables Turn: Russia and the Atterbury Plot, 1721–1722

By early 1721 Britain's position at home and abroad was alarmingly weak. Not only had it lost the support of Austria and Sweden, but the country was in a state of political upheaval following the collapse, in August 1720, of a huge invest-

---

6 Jefferyes to Stanhope, 14/11/1719, *SIRIO* 61, pp.589, 590.
7 McKay, 'George I's Northern Policy', pp.385–386.
8 Solov'ev, *Istoriya Rossii* 17, p.532.
9 The squadron comprised twenty-one ships-of-the-line and ten frigates and other vessels. Chance, *George I and the Northern War*, pp.423–424. See also Norris's Journal, BL Add.Ms. 28129.
10 B.Williams, *Stanhope* (Oxford, 1932), p.427; Chance, *George I and the Northern War*, p.445; Chance, *Diplomatic Instructions*, 1 Sweden, pp.146–150.
11 Bestuzhev-Riumin to George I, 17/10/1720, PRO SP 100/52, unfol.

ment venture by the government in the South Sea Company. Although originally planned to alleviate the National Debt, the fiasco financially ruined thousands of investors, and directed a wave of anger against the Whig ministry.[12] The scandal shook the foundations of the government and provided the Jacobites with what has been described as, '. . . the most favourable opportunity to rally support for their cause since the death of Queen Anne'.[13] The aftermath of the 'South Sea Bubble' reverberated throughout the country for over a year, giving the Jacobites time to formulate a plan for a Rising to take place in Britain during the Spring elections of 1722. Named the 'Atterbury plot' after the official Jacobite resident in England, Francis Atterbury, Bishop of Rochester, this was to be a primarily domestic insurrection, involving a number of Tory MPs and culminating in the capture of London and the rising of many counties in England and Wales.

Although the Earl of Sunderland, who had pretended Jacobite sympathy, was partially privy to these plans from an early stage, and the plot was defused in April 1722, actually serving to salvage Walpole's reputation after the South Sea fiasco, it could have caused considerable damage.[14] Luke Schaub reported from Paris that the Regent Orleans had been informed, that, '. . . l'enterprise est si bien concertée et conduite par des personnes si sages et si capables, que si le secret est observé comme on se le propose elle est infaillible'.[15]

Historians have concentrated on the domestic aspect of this conspiracy, probably because it was initiated by English Jacobite proposals to exploit the domestic turmoil of the South Sea Bubble, even if foreign assistance could not be co-ordinated in time. James III and other leading English Jacobites hoped in these circumstances that a purely English Rising would be sufficient.[16] This by no means implied, however, that foreign support was not sought. In fact, there was considerable international preparation for an invasion, and a strong body of Jacobite opinion on the Continent felt foreign aid to be essential to the success of the enterprise. Nor were plans restricted to England; General Dillon was to raise the Scottish people, and the Irish were also to participate.[17] Both

---

12 For details of this, J.Carswell, *The South Sea Bubble* (London, 1909).

13 P.Fritz, *The English Ministers and Jacobitism between the Rebellions of 1715 and 1745* (Toronto, 1975), p.67. This was also believed by contemporaries, as a spy reported, '. . . they never had such an opportunity since Queen Anne's Death'. Information of Lodowick Anderson, 11/4/1722, in Delafaye, 13/6/1722, PRO SP 35/71, f.136.

14 Incriminating papers in Sunderland's possession were seized at his death on 19 April 1722, and the Regent betrayed Jacobite plans at the same time. Fritz, *The English Ministers*, p.82.

15 L.Schaub to J.Carteret, 19/30 April 1722, BL Add Ms. 33005, ff.375–377.

16 James wrote, 'I cannot but think that if those concerned considered well their own strenth & power they would find it practicable to do by themselves what has been thought hitherto not to be compassed without the help of forreign partners', James III to Mar, 22/11/1721, RA Stuart 55/134. For a discussion of the domestic politics surrounding the plot, see B.W.Hill, *Sir Robert Walpole* (London, 1989), p.119.

17 15/10/1721,'Considerations by some of the King's Friends . . .', RA Stuart 65/18. The spy Lodovick Anderson was apparently told by James Keith that Sir Alexander Cameron, Alasdair Ban MacDonald, nephew of Glengarry, and MacGregor of Glengill [sic] (Glengyle) had all gathered in Paris to prepare for a Scottish rising. Report of Delafaye, 13/6/1722, PRO SP 35/71, f.136.

France and Spain were approached for arms, a request was made to the Regent for troops,[18] and James ordered Dillon, who was in Paris, to gather Jacobite officers serving abroad and send them across the Channel.[19]

Very little has been written on the importance of Russia in Jacobite plans at this time. Maurice Bruce, the only historian of Russo-Jacobite relations during this period, did not link Jacobite activities in Russia with the Atterbury plot, instead maintaining that the Jacobites,

> . . . concentrating upon those endeavours to bring about an unaided rising in England that led to the "Atterbury" and "Layer" "plots" in the summer of 1722, suspended their efforts to gain the assistance of foreign Powers.[20]

Similarly, he underplayed James III's interest in Russian assistance, claiming that he was too preoccupied with the English Rising to give Russia serious consideration.

Although the organisation of the domestic insurrection inevitably took first place, both James III and many of his adherents placed their greatest hopes in the Tsar as the only foreign monarch independent, strong, and disaffected enough towards George I to lend them military assistance. A British spy who later reported details of the plot from the mouth of James Keith, confirmed that, '. . . the Pretender . . . was to be assisted from Spain, Muscovy and France'.[21] Far from being distinct from the Atterbury affair, negotiations with Peter I were intensified in the hope of co-ordinating the English rising with Russian military assistance. While Spain did promise arms, both France and Spain were allied with Britain, and French dependence on this alliance precluded public co-operation with James III, and indeed caused the Regent to betray details of the plot to the ministry. Russia, by contrast, was, '. . . the only Power who appears at present not in measures with George'.[22] Moreover, Peter I was at the zenith of his power, having won from Sweden much of the Baltic littoral and with it the prospect of Baltic supremacy, at the Peace of Nystad in 1721.[23] In St Petersburg, two months later, he had been proclaimed, 'Father of the Fatherland, Peter the Great, and Emperor of All Russia'. The import of his victory was reflected in the efforts of virtually every major European power to court his favour.

---

18 For details of the Atterbury plot see E.Cruickshanks, 'Lord North, Christopher Layer and the Atterbury Plot: 1720–23', in E.Cruickshanks and J.Black, *The Jacobite Challenge*, pp.92–116; Fritz, *The English Ministers*, pp.67–80; also 'A Scheme for a General Rising in England', RA Stuart 65/60.

19 James III to Dillon, 1722 (he also wrote to seven other Jacobite generals and lieutenant-generals in France at the same time), RA Stuart 58/66.

20 Maurice Bruce, 'Jacobite Relations with Peter the Great' *SEER* 14 (1936), p.346.

21 Information of Lodowick Anderson of 11/4/1722, and of 'MacIntosh', in Delafaye to ministry, 13/6/1722, PRO SP 35/71, f.136.

22 'Considerations by some of the King's Friends in France upon the present state of affairs and what has been lately proposed to his Majesty from England', 15/10/1721, RA Stuart 65/18.

23 Peace concluded 31/8 or 11/9/1721, Chance, *George I and the Northern War*, p.482. George I failed to gain inclusion in this treaty. Chance, 'George I and Peter the Great after the Peace of Nystad', *EHR* 26 (1911), p.278.

Peter I's principal political interest in becoming involved with the Jacobites was to obtain an alliance with France, which, according to his minister at Paris, Baron Schleinitz, would give him joint control of Poland, power over the election of a new emperor should Charles VI fail to produce an heir, and consequent influence in the disposal of Austrian territories.[24] It would also enable him to consolidate his position in north Germany without British hindrance. In addition to this, Peter had ambitions to marry his daughter into the French royal family, by offering to assist the bridegroom to the Polish throne.[25] In the Baltic, he sought exemption for his Swedish acquisitions from paying Sound duties. Most importantly, he supported the Duke of Holstein-Gottorp in his efforts to obtain restitution for the loss of Schleswig from Britain's ally, Denmark, and proposed to strengthen his own hand in Sweden by raising him to the Swedish throne.[26] France was very eager to conclude a Russian alliance to prevent Peter from approaching Austria, as he had done in 1720. There was, however, a fundamental divergence between French and Russian objectives; whereas Dubois sought, through the negotiations of Campredon at St Petersburg, to reconcile Russia within the Anglo-French alliance, Peter I preferred, for his own ends, a treaty from which George I was excluded, a treaty which Jacobite negotiation might procure.

Russian assistance was considered in one of the earliest plans for a rising in 1722, drawn up by a group of Jacobites in France, who wrote off the proposal for an unaided rising as doomed from the outset, and decided that success would hinge on '. . . endeavours . . . to get the Czar . . . to give the assistance of some of his troops from Archangel the beginning of next summer'.[27] James, far from restricting his attention to a domestic rising, welcomed this initiative, and in November composed a long letter to Thomas Gordon, then Peter's vice-admiral, asking him to approach the Tsar on his behalf.[28]

James hoped to capitalise on the aftermath of the Peace of Nystad; not only had Peter '. . . made so advantageous a bargain', but '. . . he [would] have I suppose at present many idle workmen on his hands and a great quantity of materials of all kinds'. James was also well aware of the coincidence of Tsar's new stability and power with Britain's turmoil, and emphasised, '. . . how ripe matters are at present . . . that at a smal [sic] trouble he could make a sure game of it'.[29] There was an immediacy in the tone of the letter which suggests that James wanted to exploit this fortunate coincidence of energies and

24 Schleinitz to Peter I, 28/9/1721, *Recueil*, 8 Russie, p.247.
25 In January 1722, Schleinitz approached the Duke of Chartres as a possible husband for one of Peter's daughters, 'Projet de m. de Schleinitz', 10/1/1722, *SIRIO* 49, p.4; see also further negotiations by Kurakin with Duke of Bourbon, Solov'ev, *Istoriya Rossii*, 18, p.745.
26 Britain expected conflict with the Tsar on this point, fearing that, '. . . he may soon find a handle to quarrel, and help the Duke of Holstein that way'. Tilson to W.Leathes (resident at Brussels), PRO SP 35/28, f.74a.
27 'Considerations by some of the King's Friends in France upon the present state of affairs and what has been lately proposed to his Majesty from England', 15/10/1721, RA Stuart 65/18.
28 James III to Thomas Gordon, 17/11/1721, RA Stuart 55/122.
29 James III to Thomas Gordon, 17/11/1721, RA Stuart 55/122.

interests without delay, and Gordon was instructed to make his proposals to the Tsar as soon as possible.

The Jacobites in Russia were swift to react, being as aware as James was of the necessity for speed. The evidence of this is preserved in the Archive of Foreign Affairs in Moscow in the form of a long and very detailed memorandum of 8 December, presented to the Tsar by Sir Henry Stirling.[30] This memorandum was not simply a request for military aid, it was a logical and thorough presentation of the reasons why Peter had much to gain and little to lose by supporting the Jacobites, followed by an assessment of Jacobite chances of success. In tone and style it was far from the outpourings of a Jacobite '. . . blinded . . . by the fervent optimism bred by exile'.[31] Stirling viewed the Tsar's interests quite dispassionately; Peter could avenge himself on George I for consistently supporting Sweden and he would gain a Stuart ally in Britain whose fleet could be united with his own to improve trade, and who would grant him training facilities and other privileges. In case of failure his men would simply be sent home as the Spaniards had been in 1719. Any lost ships would be reimbursed, and there would be no damage to Anglo-Russian trade because Britain depended on it. Stirling also emphasised that England was ready to stage an insurrection, that Britain was in a state of turmoil, and that the spring would bring easterly winds to favour a Russian marine attack. It was estimated that 8,000 to 10,000 troops accompanied by ships and transports would be sufficient to ensure the success of the venture.[32] Although the opportunity for a Russo-French alliance was not mentioned, this well-reasoned memorandum must have created the impression that the Jacobites were a force to be taken seriously, certainly not idealistic exiles clutching at straws, as the pejorative image of Jacobitism promoted by the British government would have one believe.

On 26 December General Dillon, who was James III's chief representative in France, and one of the principal advisors on the proposed English rising, wrote to Thomas Gordon on James's orders to reinforce Stirling's plea to the Tsar. In his proposal, he decreased the number of troops requested to '. . . five or six thousand men with arms and ammunition for twenty thousand' in the hope that this would make it more acceptable. It was apparent from his reference to the current turmoil in England, that, '. . . not only the King's but the peoples hopes are fixed upon his Imperial Majesty's good and generous intentions', that the requested support was to form part of the 1722 restoration attempt. He also offered, if necessary, '. . . to give [the Tsar] authentick lights from the King

---

30 James's letter from Italy to Gordon was dated 17 November New Style, and Stirling's memorial was dated 8 December according to the Old Style calendar still current in Russia (19 December New Style), so Stirling's memorandum was almost certainly, as internal evidence confirms, 'a result of particular instructions directed to me', by James III. For details of the 11-day difference between the Old Style calendar, used in England and Russia, and the New Style, used on the Continent, see Note on Dates, also G.H.Jones, *The Mainstream of Jacobitism* (Cambridge, Mass., 1954), pp.vii, viii.
31 M.Bruce, 'Jacobite Relations with Peter the Great', p.345.
32 Henry Stirling to Peter I, 8/12/1721, AVPR F35 o1 d505.

and the British nation as will give entire satisfaction'.[33] Gordon ensured that the Tsar read Dillon's request by forwarding it to him together with another of his own on 23 February.[34] On 2 April, Gordon sent yet another proposal to the Tsar, which elaborated on Dillon's plan, including an estimation of the naval resources required to transport the requested 6,000 troops, and the measures to be taken to avoid attack by the Danish or British fleets on the voyage over. Although there was no direct reference in Gordon's letter to the English plot, he emphasised that, '. . . all the news from England', indicated the strength of domestic support. Most importantly, enclosed in this proposal, although unfortunately not preserved, was '. . . a letter by that King [James] himself'. If this was indeed a recent message, as must be assumed, it would undermine Bruce's claim that James was too 'fully occupied' to continue to take an active part in courting Peter's support.[35]

These efforts were reinforced by frequent meetings between Jacobites and the Tsar's Ambassador in Paris, Prince Vasilii Dolgoruky, in late 1721 and in the spring of 1722. In a letter to James III in Rome, the Jacobite agent John Menzies reported that he had written to Thomas Gordon, and that he had met

> . . . one that's a great friend of his and lately come from those parts, very particularly employ'd and trusted [Dolgoruky] . . . I am often with him by his own desire . . . I am very glade to perceive some aggreeable Rays from one whom I find to be intirely Trusted by our Cousin Dragee [Tsar].[36]

James III's response to Menzies's letter in January 1722 was evidence that James III both knew and approved of Jacobite negotiations with Dolgoruky. He wrote, '. . . I am glad of what you say in relation to the Czar, whose friendship must be cultivated by all means possible'.[37] Contact with proceedings in Russia was one element in the drive for foreign support which was taking place simultaneously in France and Spain.

Dolgoruky was on his way to Spain in December 1721, on a mission from the Tsar to visit the Duke of Ormonde, the principal Jacobite there. Although there is no conclusive evidence that this had any connection with Jacobite approaches to Peter I, one Jacobite informant, '84', reported that

> . . . a friend of his who was concern'd in the last transactions with the Czar some years ago had undertaken to renew that Correspondence and thinks he may succeed in it by something that has fallen from Prince Dolhorouki in a Discourse of which an acquaintance of his in France has just now informed him. The Czar he thinks having his hands now free may be persuaded to enter upon such a glorious attempt by the way of Scotland, and may propose to himself great advantages, if he succeeds . . .[38]

33 Dillon to T.Gordon, 26/12/1721, *HMC Eglinton* etc. pp.171–172.
34 T.Gordon to Peter I, 2/4/1722, RGADA F9 o5 ed.kh.1 ll.147–8.
35 T.Gordon to Peter I, 2/4/1722, RGADA F9 o5 ed.kh.1 ll.147–8.
36 J.Menzies to James III, 8/12/1721, RA Stuart 56/32.
37 James III to J.Menzies, 11/1/1722, RA Stuart 57/31.
38 Anon. 12/2/1722, enclosed in letter from 'W.F.', 31/3/1722, PRO SP 35/71, f.20.

If Ormonde, who had met the Tsar in 1717, and been sent to Russia the following year, was the 'friend' referred to here, Dolgoruky's visit to Spain perhaps had a more overtly political motive than simply to recruit Jacobites into Russian service.[39] The fact that Dolgoruky had orders to meet Ormonde, who was the main co-ordinator of Spanish arms and officers for the planned rising, encourages speculation that Peter I might have been gauging the level of Spanish hostility towards Britain. In any case, the meeting was at least evidence of Peter I's personal involvement with leading Jacobites abroad.

At the same time as Menzies's conferences with the Russian minister, General Dillon, who had instructed that Jacobite correspondence from Russia be sent to him, '. . . by Prince Dolhoroukys channell',[40] was intending to meet him on his return from Spain. Bruce has concluded that Dillon did not have this audience until May or June 1722,[41] that is, after Atterbury had informed James in mid-April that the opportunity for a rising had been missed, and that the English affair was at an end.[42] In fact, a coded letter from Dillon to Thomas Gordon of 5th April, New Style, (which Bruce has not considered), included a description of a meeting with Dolgoruky in March. He wrote,

> . . . I thought it convenient to benefit of an occasion offer'd me by the return of a well dispos'd and understanding Factor of Kemps [Dolgoruky] who has managed some affairs of his here for a time.[43]

Dillon, who was at this time involved in purchasing French arms for the Rising, clearly intended his letter to reach Gordon while there was still time for Russian participation in it, and emphasised that, '. . . as the time is precious and the remoteness great I think proper to lose no time in giving you an account of matters . . .'[44] At the meeting with Dolgoruky, Dillon had proposed a joint invasion attempt to be made from Sweden by 'Coalman and Kemp' [Sweden and Russia], and, at Dolgoruky's request, had written a memorial to be presented to the Tsar, which included details of his plan to send 6,000 men, '. . . disposed on the coast at or about Gottembourgh and to be rendered at his choice to Mrs Euans [England] or Mrs Story [Scotland]'.[45] Dillon was particularly encouraged by Dolgoruky's hostility towards the Hanoverian monarchy, and his conclusion that, '. . . his master's [Peter's] concerns seem'd to require the removal of Herne [George I] out of Euan farme [England]'. Although Dolgoruky made it clear that Peter I would probably be reluctant to give military support independent of Sweden, Dillon informed Gordon that he

39 George Camocke, a Jacobite naval officer who was later an informer for Britain, was offered the position of Admiral in early 1722, William Stanhope to Carteret, February 1723, PRO SP 74/92; Camocke to James III, 6/9/1723, RA Stuart 68/55.
40 Dillon to T.Gordon, 26/12/1721, *HMC Eglinton* etc., p.172.
41 M.Bruce, 'Jacobite Relations', p.347.
42 Fritz, *The English Ministers,* p.79.
43 A.Dillon to T.Gordon, 26/3 or 5/4/1722, *HMC Eglinton* etc., pp.172–173.
44 A.Dillon to T.Gordon, 26/3 or 5/4/1722, *HMC Eglinton* etc., pp.172–173.
45 Bruce was unaware of the contents of the memorial. M.Bruce, p.346.

would continue to negotiate with him.[46] A letter from Henry Stirling to James III on the subject of Dillon's efforts, written some time later, '. . . that the Czar had the most sincere inclinations in your favour and had given orders to his Minister at Paris to confer with M.Dillon and only waited his answer to come to a resolution', suggested that Peter I had both supported Dolgoruky's contact with the Jacobites and encouraged Dillon's proposals.[47]

Russian negotiations with the Jacobites did not have time to reach conclusion, before the examination of Sunderland's papers, and Luke Schaub's report from the Regent Orléans of Jacobite intentions, led to the public disclosure of the plot in May 1722.[48] In response to these discoveries, Robert Walpole, the new First Lord of the Treasury, launched a full-scale investigation into the affair, one so merciless that it has been referred to as, '. . . one of the largest "witch hunts" of British history'.[49] Its ruthlessness was not a direct reflection of government fears, but was primarily an effective means of redeeming the public face of the Whig ministry in the aftermath of the South Sea Bubble. It was a characteristic of this campaign to draw attention to past dangers while emphasising present ministerial control, and Walpole ensured the permanency of this control by greatly expanding British information-gathering networks both at home and abroad.[50]

Walpole's intelligence network notwithstanding, the lack of British representation in Russia after 1719, which forced Walpole to depend for information on the letters of the French minister Jacques Campredon, suggests that the ministry was poorly informed of the extent of Jacobite communication with Peter I. The consequent scarcity of sources, and the fact that the Jacobites never achieved their aim, has bred a retrospective tendency to disregard their negotiations in Russia as of less import than those in France or Spain.

In fact, there were those within the ministry who expressed serious concern that Peter I might assist the Jacobites. In autumn and winter 1721, the presence of Russian shipping near Ostend had caused the British Under-Secretary George Tilson to complain that

> . . . before we are aware we may hear of a Russ squadron in the British ocean ready to take part with our enemies. You may imagine we can't be much in favour with the Czar; our fleet is his only curb in the Baltic . . . we may find how his pulse is, either for the King, or as his private practices have been, for the Pretender . . . he may prove a terror to us all here, and make us all repent of our easiness in fostering such a serpent in our bosoms . . .[51]

46 Ibid.
47 H.Stirling to James III, 15/2/1723, RA Stuart 60/31.
48 L.Schaub to J.Carteret, 19/4 or 30/4/1722, BL Add Ms. 33005, ff.375–377.
49 Fritz, *The English Ministers*, p.82.
50 Walpole's anti-Jacobite intelligence network involved the copying of Jacobite letters passing through the post offices of Danzig, Brussels, Louvain, Leyden, Antwerp, Calais and Hamburg, P.Fritz, 'The Anti-Jacobite Intelligence System of the English Ministers, 1715–1745' *HJ* 16,2 (1973), p.273.
51 Tilson to Leathes, 21/8/1721, PRO SP 35/28, f.23. See also 20/10/1721, *Ibid.*, f.84.

Although Peter I did not do what ministers feared he might at this stage, the extent of Russo-Jacobite negotiations suggest that certain assumptions regarding the Atterbury plot are in need of some reappraisal. Firstly, the Jacobites did not '. . . suspend their efforts to gain the assistance of foreign powers'.[52] Russian assistance was sought from the inception of the plot, and continued after it was terminated by the British government in spring 1722. Nor were attempts to win the favour of Peter I regarded as independent of the Atterbury plot; it was those organising the English Rising, particularly Dillon, who approached Russia to lend military reinforcement to domestic efforts. Moreover, James III's active, and according to the evidence, uninterrupted, support for negotiations with Peter I throughout the period of preparation for the Rising indicated the store he placed in Russia. Most importantly, despite the fact that the Tsar, now the 'Emperor', did not meet Jacobite demands, his close contact with them, both at home and abroad, was much more than a demonstration of his opposition to George I, an unnecessary gesture from one so powerful. Rather it was based on the prospect that the wide net of Jacobite influence in Europe could, in suitable political circumstances, facilitate his own ambitions at the Hanoverian monarchy's expense. It was in this spirit, despite Walpole's counter-espionage and deciphering operations, and the failure of the Atterbury plot, that the Jacobite campaign in Russia in 1721–1722 served only as a foundation for further, and more promising Russo-Jacobite co-operation.

Daniel O'Brien: The First Envoy Extraordinary and Minister Plenipotentiary from King James III to Emperor Peter I, 1722–24

In 1724 Walpole dismissed his spy François Jaupain, the postmaster at Brussels and controller of 31 post offices throughout Europe, for failing to report anything of significance since 1723. According to Paul Fritz, this was due to '. . . the simple fact that little seemed to be happening in the Jacobite camp between 1723 and 1725'.[53] A brief glance at the frenzied correspondence passing between 'the Jacobite camp' and Jacobites in Russia throughout this period, would have sufficed to convince him otherwise.

In the summer of 1722, when the Atterbury plot had been ruthlessly terminated, the negotiations of the Jacobites with Prince Dolgoruky in Paris were, conversely, just beginning to bear fruit, and contact with Russia was pursued with renewed energy. The ministry was kept well-informed on Russo-Jacobite contacts in France. In June, Schaub reported to Carteret that '. . . il se tient de frequentes conferences de Jacobites chez O'Bryan, et qu' outre Lord Lansdown et Dillon, le Prince Dolhoroucki s'y trouve souvent'. Rumours of Russian military support for the Jacobites also persisted; '. . . On me rapporte qu'il s'y parle des vaisseaux que le Czar équippe à Archangel, et que les Jacobites y sont estat'.[54]

52 Maurice Bruce, 'Jacobite Relations with Peter the Great', *SEER* 14 (1936), p.346.
53 Fritz, *The English Ministers,* p.116.
54 Schaub to Carteret, 3/6/1722 n.s., BL Add.Ms.33005, ff.395–6.

However, Walpole's dependence on Campredon's dispatches as his only diplomatic source from Russia after 1719 proved a severe limitation on Britain's intelligence of Jacobite activity there.[55] In 1725, Walpole proposed to bribe an employee of Henry Stirling at St Petersburg to obtain copies of his letters.[56] Thomas Consett, the chaplain to the English factory in St Petersburg since 1717, acted as an informer on Jacobite activities in Russia, but he was suspected by the Jacobite community and relieved of his position in 1727.[57] Walpole's efforts apparently enjoyed some success, for James III complained to Stirling in October 1719 and Dillon in December 1721 that nothing had been received from him for several months, and that letters addressed to him appeared not to have arrived.[58] In January 1722 James commented that '. . . it is very unlucky that correspondence with that part of the World should be subject to so many accidents, for I have found out of late that many letters of Sr Hary Stirlings have miscarried from thence'.[59]

Nevertheless, the limits of this success were betrayed by the British government's apparent ignorance of what was, for the Jacobites, one of the most remarkable and promising events of Peter's reign, the official embassy to the Russian court in 1723, at Peter I's invitation, of a Jacobite plenipotentiary minister.[60] Campredon's dispatches did not mention this envoy, Daniel O'Brien, probably because the French minister was housebound during his visit.[61] In addition, O'Brien's efforts to travel incognito, under the name Daniel Perin, and his refusal to make a public appearance at the Russian court aided his concealment. His apparent success in evading mention in contemporary dispatches is demonstrated by his absence even from the most thorough account of the diplomatic correspondence of the period by J.F.Chance.[62] Chance makes passing reference to O'Brien's presence in Russia in 1724, but with the aid of a Russian, not a British source.[63]

The weakness of Walpole's espionage and deciphering network in Russia, potentially Britain's most dangerous enemy, had a dual effect. Firstly, it allowed Russo-Jacobite intrigue to reach alarming proportions by the end of Peter I's

55 In 1721 the Danzig post office had come under the control of Walpole's anti-Jacobite information system through the efforts of a British spy, Joshua Kenworthy, who sent copies of Campredon's dispatches to the ministry. D.B. Horn, *The British Diplomatic Service, 1689–1789* (Oxford, 1961), pp.277–278.
56 Fritz, *The English Ministers*, p.133.
57 Consett did not leave Russia in 1725 as Fritz claims in *The English Ministers*, p.130n., but on 25/7/1727, J.Cracraft, ed., *For God and Peter the Great* (New York, 1982); A.G.Cross, 'Chaplains to the British Factory in St.Petersburg,' 1723–1813, *ESR* 2 (1972), p.108.
58 James III to H.Stirling, 1/10/1719, RA Stuart 45/18; Dillon to T.Gordon, 26/12/1721, *HMC Eglinton* etc., p.172.
59 James III to John Menzies, 11/1/1722, RA Stuart 57/31.
60 This startling fact was first noted by M.Bruce, 'Jacobite Relations', p.353. The first indication of the mission in British diplomatic correspondence was apparently an anonymous letter of 8/6/1744, PRO SP 35/50, ff.18–18v.
61 Campredon's dispatches are printed in *SIRIO* 40, 49, 102.
62 For this period, Chance, 'George I and Peter the Great after the Peace of Nystad', *EHR* 26 (1911), pp.278–309.
63 Chance referred to a letter of Peter I to B.I.Kurakin, 16/2/1724, *Arkhiv Kurakina* 1, p.34; 'George I and Peter the Great', p.308n.

reign, posing a threat to Britain of which even Walpole was not fully cognisant. Secondly, however, it heightened ministerial sensitivity to the possibility of Russian hostility, eliciting serious concern, even panic, at the slightest sign of activity from the Russian camp. Never was the perceived threat from Russia so real, nor George I and Peter I so directly at loggerheads, as during this period.

Paradoxically, it was probably the success of Walpole's anti-Jacobite intelligence network in France and Spain after the Atterbury affair which encouraged Jacobite activity beyond his reach in Russia. James was also anxious to build on the encouragement from Russia which had been a positive outcome of the negotiations of the previous two years.[64] Thus the Atterbury plot, by virtue of its failure, directly benefited Russo-Jacobite relations.

In May 1722, encouraged by news of Thomas Gordon's correspondence with Peter I, James III sent Dillon two blank full powers to enable Henry Stirling and another suitable person to negotiate both with the Tsar and the King of Sweden, as Dillon had proposed in March.[65] On 15 June, James wrote directly to Peter I, thanking him for his continued encouragement, which had been demonstrated by his orders to Dolgoruky to conduct negotiations with Jacobites in Paris.[66] With the letter, he enclosed a memorial containing an invasion plan, to be presented to the Tsar by Dolgoruky, who was about to return to Russia.

The original of this letter, which is preserved in the Archive of Foreign Affairs in Moscow, unlike the copy in the Stuart Papers at Windsor, included this detailed plan. Dillon, the author, requested the provision of 6,000 infantry and 2,000 cavalry for a landing to be made on the undefended coast between the Firth of Forth and the Humber estuary. Meanwhile, 10,000 Lowlanders and English would march on London under the Duke of Ormonde, while the same number of Highlanders prepared to join the Russians, and a diversionary force was sent to Ireland. Dillon emphasised that Spain and France would not oppose the rising. Moreover, the fact that only 14 English ships patrolled the coast would greatly improve the chances of invasion from the east rather than the Channel. It was also proposed that the troops be sent to the Baltic or Archangel under the command of Thomas Gordon as a cover, prior to crossing the North Sea.[67]

Bruce has suggested that Dillon's memorial had probably been hurriedly written just prior to Dolgoruky's departure from Paris, that there was therefore no time to submit it for James's approval, thereby explaining the absence both of the memorial, and of James's comments on it, in the Stuart Papers.[68] Solov'ev refers only briefly to the memorial, describing it as, '. . . an extension

---

64 Cf. James's comment, 'considering the present favourable disposition of the nation [Russia], and the importance of profiting of so [illeg.] a juncture all possible measures ought to be pursued', James III to Lord Orrery, 15/6/1722, RA Stuart 60/23.
65 Dillon to T.Gordon, 5/4/1722, *HMC Eglinton* etc., pp.172–173; James III to Dillon, 1/5/1722, RA Stuart 59/77; 9/5/1722, RA Stuart 59/98.
66 James III to Peter I, 15/6/1722, AVPR F35 o1 d506, ll.1–2. Also RA Stuart 60/38 (without memorial).
67 James III to Peter I, 15/6/1722, AVPR F35 d506, ll.4–5v.
68 M.Bruce, pp.347–8.

of the plan drawn up in Gordon's letter' (of April 2 1722).[69] Bruce is unaware, however, that Dillon's original memorial for Dolgoruky, containing a invasion plan, had been drawn up as early as March.[70] Although the version given to Dolgoruky in June differed slightly from the earlier one in that it requested an additional 2,000 cavalry and was much more thoroughly calculated, James would have had ample opportunity to approve its general outlines. It was, after all, not an expansion of Gordon's proposal of 2 April at all, but based on the invasion plan formulated by Dillon the previous December.[71]

In the Archive of Foreign Affairs the memorial is followed by a commentary on it written by a Jacobite, probably also Dillon, drawing attention to the number of Jacobites in Russian service who would join the invasion, particularly, '. . . le vice admiral gordon . . . qui cognoit en perfection les costes de la grande Bretagne' and '. . . le général Lacy, d'une famille distingué'. The Jacobite case was further substantiated by an appended account of the British national debt, with the suggestion that Britain was incapable of sustaining a war against Russia.[72] James III was in close contact with Dillon's progress, and wrote personally to Dolgoruky to thank him for offering to present his case to the Tsar.[73]

The intensity of these efforts was a reflection of James III's conviction, in the aftermath of the Atterbury plot and France's unreliability, that, '. . . we cannot take too much pains to engage the Czar to be favourable to us'.[74] Although the Jacobites have often, and with some justification, been accused of hopeless idealism, the proposals to Russia were striking for their thoroughness and detail, evidence of military professionalism. It was a measure of this that Peter I never failed to give the Jacobite case serious consideration, even when it was not in his immediate interest to assist them.

The Jacobites did not wait long for Peter I's response. In fact, they received two responses from Russia to their earlier proposals, before Dolgoruky could convey Dillon's most recent plans to Russia in October. The first was detailed in a letter from Sir Henry Stirling, written in June, but not received until the autumn, and forwarded to Dillon in September. On one hand, it confirmed that Gordon had discussed Jacobite affairs with Peter I, and that the Tsar had considered his proposals. Stirling wrote,

> . . . it is but now [on] Captain Gordon's arrival that I can acquaint you of the Czar's real thoughts and Intentions in that affair & by his own command [tell you] that he wisheth for nothing more than an opportunity to serve you.[75]

69 (My translation) Solov'ev, *Istoriya Rossii* 18, p.749.
70 See above, Chapter 2, Dillon to T.Gordon, 5/4/1722, *HMC Eglinton* etc., pp.172–173.
71 Dillon to T.Gordon, 26/12/1721, *HMC Eglinton* etc., pp.171–172.
72 Anon., 1722, AVPR F35 o1 d506, l.6; 'Un court Etat des Dettes Publiques d'Angleterre et des Resources qu'elle a pour soutenir une Guerre', Ibid., l.7.
73 James III to Dolgoruky, 12/9/1722, AVPR F35 o1 d507; Dillon to James III, 17/8/1722, RA Stuart 61; James III to Dillon, 12/9/1722, RA Stuart 62/31.
74 James III to Lord Orrery, 15/6/1722, RA Stuart 60/23; James III to Dillon, 12/9/1722, RA Stuart 62/31.
75 H.Stirling to James III, 15/6/1722, RA Stuart 60/31.

However, the inevitable requirement that Jacobite demands be married with Russian political interests was not so easily satisfied. Stirling reported that the Tsar was reluctant to sail his fleet through the Danish Sound for fear of attack by Denmark, '. . . which would He thinks render an Expedition in your favour fruitless'. However, Peter was willing to pursue his own territorial interests in north Germany within a Jacobite coalition

> . . . to satisfy you of the sincerity of his intentions he is willing the King makes use of his name and interest. Induce either France or Spain to undertake an expedition in your favour he engages to march an Army of 60 or 100,000 men through Poland into Germany to hinder any troops going from Hanover or the neighbourhood into England.[76]

As far as James III was concerned, this indication that the Tsar had attempted to make constructive use of Jacobite plans for his own ends was a positive development. However, the unrealistic size of the force offered, given Russia's commitments to a war with Turkey on its southern border, suggests either exaggeration on the part of Gordon or Stirling, or an attempt by Peter to appease the Jacobites with an impressive offer he knew he would never be held to. This was characteristic; Campredon once commented that Petrine policy consisted in listening to all propositions with a view to accepting the most advantageous.[77]

Peter I's response cannot, however, be disregarded on these grounds. The fact that he did not reject Jacobite proposals out of hand suggests, at the very least, that he considered them sufficiently significant to encourage further efforts. In the past, the exiles had, after all, been a useful source of intelligence on British foreign policy. It would be an oversimplification to conclude that he was using them merely to flaunt George I, in the interests of forcing some form of restitution for the Duke of Holstein. What is more likely, as events in 1723 and 1724 would confirm, was that, as Campredon had observed, he preferred to keep his options open, and retained the support of the Jacobites in the belief that they could benefit him at a future stage. What is certain is that Peter's territorial interests remained in direct conflict with those of George I and that the Jacobites were thus well within the sphere of his political sympathies.[78]

The second Russian initiative which encouraged James III in autumn 1722, apart from that described in Henry Stirling's report, was Prince Dolgoruky's proposal, on the eve of his own departure for Danzig, that a Jacobite envoy be sent after him to his destination to be available for negotiation with the Tsar.[79] This positive response from Russia was, naturally, welcomed by the Jacobite camp with great enthusiasm, particularly because Dolgoruky had chosen

---

76 H.Stirling to James III, 15/6/1722, RA Stuart 60/31.
77 Campredon to Dubois, 15, 16/1/1722, *SIRIO* 49, p.18.
78 Chance, 'George I and Peter the Great', p.291.
79 Dillon reported Dolgoruky's suggestion to James on 21 and 28 September. Although these letters have not been traced, their contents can be deduced from James's reply of 19/10/1722, RA Stuart 62/98.

Daniel O'Brien for the post himself, and had '. . . invited [him] in a most pressing manner to visit [Russia]'.[80] James immediately approved the choice, for Colonel Daniel O'Brien had not only been well received by Dolgoruky in conferences with him in Paris, but had already been to Mittau in 1718 with Ormonde. He was also most suitable for the job, '. . . on account of the particular knowledge he hath of my English affairs at this time'.[81] However, James was unable to give him detailed instructions by post, for fear of falling foul of Walpole's growing interception network, and so wrote simply,

> . . . nothing ought to be refused to a Prince who undertakes my restoration except in cases where ane absolute impossibility or a manifest detriment to ye interest of my dominions should appear, in the granting of what may be demanded, as to the plan of ane expedition and the demands you are to make in that respect, the memoire which Prince Dolhorouky is to carry with him must be your rule.[82]

Daniel O'Brien's invitation was, by any standards, of considerable political significance. Although James was perhaps overconfident in his declaration to Henry Stirling in October that, '. . . my chief confidence & perfect hopes are now placed in the Czar,' there was, at least, promise of negotiation.[83]

Daniel O'Brien's Mission, 1723–1724

Daniel O'Brien wrote to James on 15 December 1722 that he intended to leave for Danzig at the end of the month, so that his arrival would coincide with Peter I's return from his campaign on the Caspian in January.[84] For reasons beyond his control, perhaps due to bad weather, he was unable to leave until March, although he and Dolgoruky corresponded in the interim. He eventually arrived incognito in Danzig on 12 May 1723 to find that his disguise was a very necessary precaution to avoid the suspicions of the many Whigs in the town. It was dangerous even to speak to Jacobites in public, and he concealed his true mission by posing as a mercenary on his way to seek service in Russia.[85]

Meanwhile, James had attempted to prepare the way for O'Brien's reception by the Tsar by addressing letters of recommendation both to Peter, and to his wife, Catherine, in January.[86] Dolgoruky had delivered the

---

80 Dillon to T.Gordon, n/d., *HMC Eglinton* etc., p.173. This letter, though undated, clearly refers to this event, and suggests that Dolgoruky had a greater personal involvement than is evident from James III's correspondence.

81 James III to H.Stirling, 9/10/1722, RA Stuart 62/81.

82 James III to O'Brien, 9/10/1722, RA Stuart 62.

83 James III to H.Stirling, 9/10/1722, RA Stuart 62/81.

84 O'Brien to James III, 15/12/1722, RA Stuart 64/1.

85 There appears to have been a Jacobite/Whig split in Danzig; O'Brien was offered the services of a Jacobite merchant, Lesly, but they were unable to meet in public. O'Brien to James III, 12/5/1723, RA Stuart 67/20.

86 James III to Peter I, 18/1/1723, N.N.Bantysh-Kamenskii, *Obzor vneshnykh snoshenii Rossii po 1800 god*, 1 (Moscow, 1894), p.131; James III to Catherine, n.d.,1723, RGADA F4 o1 d50, ll.1,1v.

Jacobite proposals to the Tsar as soon as he arrived in St Petersburg in April.[87]

Further delays awaited O'Brien. In a letter of 24 April, Dolgoruky informed him that an illness had prevented him from travelling from Moscow to inform the Tsar at St Petersburg of the envoy's arrival, but that he was now on his way.[88] This news did not reach O'Brien until 28 May, by which time he had become concerned at Dolgoruky's silence. A letter from James, written in March, had only arrived on 1 June, so O'Brien was feeling understandably isolated. On receiving Dolgoruky's letter, he wrote immediately to ask him for permission to travel on to Riga, in order to be in closer touch with proceedings. Once there, he waited another month before he received further news from Dolgoruky, and for a time it appeared that his great embassy had failed before it had really begun. Dolgoruky reported from St Petersburg, but was still ill in bed and unable to approach the Tsar. Not only that, but Peter was now preoccupied by the alarming news that the Turks had taken Georgia and were threatening Derbent, and had no time for other matters.[89] O'Brien was advised to abandon his mission because, '. . . il est inutile de presser puisque le temps n'est pas propre'.[90] It seemed that circumstances were conspiring to thwart Jacobite hopes once again. Fortunately for James III, however, his envoy decided to remain in Riga.

O'Brien was in frequent contact throughout these months with both Thomas Gordon and James III. Gordon met Dolgoruky himself in early August 1723, but could tell O'Brien little but that a court ceremony was presently interfering with all official business.[91] James received O'Brien's pessimistic news at the beginning of September, but he approved of his decision to wait in Riga, and instructed him to remain there all winter to await developments or fresh orders. Realising that problems of communication over such great distances could jeopardise the mission, he demanded that O'Brien both write to him at least once a fortnight, and maintain regular correspondence with Thomas Gordon.[92] Ironically, the very communication delay which James was attempting to minimise meant that his advice was already irrelevant.

By the time James's letter arrived in Riga in October, the situation had altered dramatically. On 23 August, Dolgoruky had written to O'Brien, formally inviting him to St Petersburg, and had sent orders to Prince Repnin, Governor of Riga, to supply him with passports.[93] On 27 August Gordon confirmed this good news.[94] O'Brien must have received these invitations in a very short time, for he wrote to inform James on 1 September that he was on his

87 Dolgoruky to O'Brien, 24/4/1723, RA Stuart 67/6; Dillon to T.Gordon, 15/5/1723, *HMC Eglinton* etc., p.174.
88 Dolgoruky to O'Brien, 24/4/1723, RA Stuart 67/6.
89 Chance, 'George I and Peter the Great', p.303.
90 Dolgoruky to O'Brien, 30/6/1723, RA Stuart 67/127.
91 T.Gordon to O'Brien, 9/8/1723, RA Stuart 68/56.
92 James III to O'Brien, 4/9/1723, RA Stuart 68/142.
93 Dolgoruky to O'Brien, 23/8/1723, RA Stuart 67.
94 T.Gordon to O'Brien, 16/27 August 1723, RA Stuart 68/67.

way to the capital, and left the very next day.[95] In exactly a week, on 9 September, Daniel O'Brien, the first Jacobite Minister Plenipotentiary and Envoy Extraordinary to the Emperor Peter I, arrived in St Petersburg. At a time when Russia would tolerate no British diplomatic representation, this formal gesture of welcome from the Emperor of one of the most powerful nations of Europe to an envoy of the hereditary King of Great Britain was a momentous event in the course of Russo-Jacobite relations.

As soon as O'Brien arrived in St Petersburg the frequency of his dispatches increased as events began to gather pace. On 12 September he wrote two long reports to James III, between which the situation had time to change again. In the first O'Brien described a conference with Henry Stirling and Thomas Gordon two days previously, but they had received no new information. Gordon had tried to tell Dolgoruky of O'Brien's arrival, but he was still ill and not receiving visitors. Not only that, but Gordon informed O'Brien that the fleet had already been disarmed for the year, and would not be able to provide assistance in 1723. There were, however, grounds for optimism. Firstly, Russia's tense relations with Sweden and Turkey appeared to have been temporarily resolved, therefore he wrote that, '. . . il y a tout lieu d'ésperer qu'il donnera toute son attention a celle d'Angleterre'. In addition, Dolgoruky was obviously in favour with the Tsar, for he had just been created senator, and would thus be in a better position to promote Jacobite affairs.[96]

The second report was written in a mood of great excitement. Just after finishing his first letter to James, O'Brien had received a note from Dolgoruky, inviting him for an interview at six the same evening. O'Brien spoke with the senator for four hours on Jacobite affairs. Dolgoruky assured him, first of all, that there was nothing that the Russian monarch would not do for James, promised to arrange an audience with Peter as soon as possible, and advised O'Brien on how to present his case. Most importantly, he conveyed a message from the Tsar that, '. . . n'ayant rien a faire avec l'Elector de Hannover, il [O'Brien] pouroit paroistre publiquement a sa cour, si il le vouloit'.[97] Peter I's invitation to O'Brien to be publicly received as a Jacobite minister at the Russian court was, at one level, a sign that the Tsar would treat him on the same terms as the envoy of any other monarch, thus, it would appear, implying that he accepted James's right to the British throne.

At the same time, however, good will on both sides had ultimately to manifest itself in a mutual fulfilment of demands. In terms of Petrine 'Realpolitik', O'Brien's public appearance at court would have served as a demonstration of Russia's independence of George I's continuing attempts, through Campredon, to attract the Tsar into the Anglo-French alliance. Cardinal Dubois and Lord Carteret, as Secretary of State for the Southern Department, had been

95 O'Brien to James III, 12/9/1723, RA Stuart 69/17.
96 O'Brien to James III 12/9/1723, RA Stuart 69/17.
97 O'Brien was told to state his case 'avec fermite . . . de ne pas attendre qu'il me questione sur chaque article du proces de Lewiston [James III], mais de luy bien expliquer tout'. O'Brien to James III, 12/9/1723, RA Stuart 69/12.

under the mistaken assumption that Peter I would welcome a triple alliance to guarantee his treaty with Sweden, and both had pursued it since 1720, principally to avert the possibility of an Austro-Russian treaty.[98] At the end of 1722, Prince Boris Kurakin had met Dubois, and the benefits of a separate Russo-French alliance had been referred to, but Dubois would not contemplate any breach with Britain.[99] However, on 10 August, Dubois had died, leaving the Regent Orleans as first minister. In view of this, the timing of Dolgoruky's audience with O'Brien may not have been fortuitous, an impression which was confirmed by his repeated questions on the subject of the Regent's political sympathies and reliability. From the Jacobite side, O'Brien assured Dolgoruky of Spanish support, and extended the possibility of French assistance now that Dubois was dead.[100]

The conference with Dolgoruky was constructive in that it clarified both the sentiments and the requirements of each side. It was not a case of a Jacobite plea for help. The Jacobite plenipotentiary minister was treated with respect, as a diplomat on an equal footing with the negotiating representative of any other European power. This stemmed from the prospect that Russo-Jacobite co-operation could be of mutual benefit.

After the meeting O'Brien waited in anticipation for a week, during which time Thomas Gordon encouraged him further with details of his plan to avoid confrontation between the Russian and Danish fleets during the voyage through the Danish Sound.[101] Meanwhile, James III, hopelessly out of touch with the progress made, was writing his envoy a letter of condolence, which O'Brien was not to receive in any case until the end of October![102]

At last, on 21 September, O'Brien was delivered the long-awaited news from Dolgoruky that the Tsar was expecting him at four the same afternoon.[103] It is unfortunate that O'Brien's account of this crucial audience is missing from the Stuart Papers, as are his letters numbered 27 and 28 to James III, but other Jacobite correspondence provides a good indication of what took place.[104] According to a letter to James III from Henry Stirling of 24 October, O'Brien had requested ten thousand men for an invasion of Britain. Presumably, he also presented Gordon's plan to provide sixty-eight transport ships for the troops at Reval on the Baltic, with a convoy of three or four war ships to take the fleet past the Danish Sound before they could be attacked.[105] The Tsar

98 For a discussion of this, see Chance, 'George I and Peter the Great', pp.280–282.
99 Dubois to Campredon, 15/1/1723, *SIRIO* 102, p.5; Solov'ev, *Istoriya Rossii*, 18, p.746; Dubois to Campredon, 2/4/1723, *SIRIO* 102, p.48.
100 O'Brien to James III, 12/9/1723, RA Stuart 69/12.
101 O'Brien to James III, 19/9/1723, RA Stuart 69/34.
102 James III to O'Brien, 25/9/1723, RA Stuart 69/61; O'Brien to James III, 31/10/1723, RA Stuart 69/151.
103 Dolgoruky to O'Brien, 10/9/1723 o.s., RA Stuart 70.
104 Historians have failed to note that O'Brien also had at least one more Imperial audience before his next extant letter of 21 October, for he refers to a letter to James of 10 October in which he reported an audience of the previous Wednesday, that is of 6 October. His demands at each were consistent, according to other correspondence.
105 O'Brien to James III, 19/9/1723, RA Stuart 69/34.

renewed his proposal to provide a diversion in Germany, while France and Spain, who would benefit from a Russian alliance against Britain and Austria, supported the main Rising. The conference concluded with his agreement, in principle, to provide the military support requested, and O'Brien wrote optimistically to James on 21 October that, '. . . il n'attend que les derniers ordres de Czar pour prendre des arrangemens fixé avec D.O'Brien autant que l'état des choses le permettent.[106]

There was, however, the inevitable problem of France. As Dolgoruky had hinted, the Tsar refused to promise anything, '. . . jusqu'a ce que l'on sache si M. le Regent St denys [Orleans] veut entrer dans quelque accomodemt'. Nevertheless, O'Brien remained optimistic. Firstly, Peter I had approved his suggestion to send an envoy to France to negotiate a Russo-French agreement.[107] Secondly, even if the Tsar's support consisted of an attack in Germany, co-operation between Russia, French and Spain would serve the interests of all three.[108] In fact Jacobite optimism was by no means without foundation; throughout the autumn of 1723, and particularly after the death of Dubois, the British ministry was desperately opposing a French change of policy in favour of a separate alliance with Russia.[109]

Britain's efforts to counter a separate Russo-French alliance culminated in October in a Treaty concluded between Britain and Prussia at Charlottenburg, which had mixed implications for Jacobite hopes of Russia. On one hand it strengthened the Anglo-French alliance, making it unlikely that Orleans would break with George I. On the other, however, the rumours which subsequently reached Peter I that Britain was seeking the support of Prussia, Poland and Denmark for a defensive league against him, prompted him to ask Boris Kurakin at the Hague to discover Orleans's sentiments towards Russia and assess the possibility of a treaty with France.[110] On 19 December O'Brien reported to James III the good news from Dolgoruky that

> . . . le Czar avait dejà fait expedier un ordre pour son Ministre en Hollande tel que Dan. O'Brien l'avoit demandé et qu'il ne doutait pas que l'on ne le remit en main propre a ce dernier pour le présenter luy mesme.[111]

The Tsar himself continued to give O'Brien encouragement, asking him through Dolgoruky for details of the arms and ammunition he required. According to Dolgoruky, he was even prepared to write personally to James III, assuring him that if France would support the Stuart restoration, Russia

---

106 O'Brien to James III, 21/10/1723, RA Stuart 69/119.
107 O'Brien to James III, 19/12/1723, RA Stuart 71/65.
108 O'Brien to James III, 31/10/1723, RA Stuart 69/151.
109 Dubois had actually proposed this just before his death, allegedly as a preliminary to British inclusion, but Britain was strongly hostile to the suggestion, fearing for its French alliance. Chance, 'George I and Peter the Great', pp.302–306.
110 O'Brien to James III, 14/11/1723, RA Stuart 70/39.
111 O'Brien to James III, 19/12/1723, RA Stuart 71/65.

would participate.[112] In the meantime, however, negotiations with the Regent Orleans had already assured British ministers that France would do nothing to damage the Anglo-French alliance.[113]

Suddenly, at the end of December, before Kurakin could be sent to Paris, some news reached Russia which completely altered the situation in the Jacobites' favour. On 2 December the Regent Orleans had died suddenly, and was replaced as first minister by the Duke of Bourbon, who was known to sympathise with the Stuart cause and to have little enthusiasm for the Anglo-French policies of his predecessors. The timing of the Regent's death, just as Peter I was preparing for negotiations with France, could not have been more propitious, and the Tsar's reaction to it was overwhelmingly positive. According to O'Brien, on hearing the news, Peter immediately went to Thomas Gordon's house, where a gathering was taking place, and ordered wine for a celebration, '. . . ne pouvant contenir sa joye'. During the ensuing party he called Gordon into an adjoining room and they discussed the implications of Orleans' death. Peter is alleged to have said to Gordon, '. . . voicy . . . le vray tems de pousser les affaires du Roy en France et il peut toujours compter sur tout ce que dependera de moy'. Although Peter's mood of 'gayete suprenante' was undoubtedly elicited more by the prospect of a Russo-French alliance than by the upturn of Jacobite fortunes, the fact that his first response was to share his news with the leading Jacobite in Russia was significant.[114] It implied a recognition of mutual interests, and Peter probably anticipated that the Jacobites could facilitate Russian negotiations at the French court. The Regent's death had an immediate effect both on the Tsar's French policy and on his readiness to co-operate with the Jacobites. He had intended to leave St Petersburg at the end of the year, but decided instead to remain there during January, presumably to take advantage of O'Brien's presence.[115] O'Brien had been recalled from Russia by James as early as November,[116] and in December was instructed to travel directly to Paris to report on the outcome of his mission.[117] Before his departure, however, he requested, as a guarantee of Russian commitment to James III, that Peter both send a Russian envoy to France to confer with Bourbon, and give O'Brien a written declaration, promising his assistance in a Jacobite Rising, conditional on French support.[118] This documentary proof from Russia was expected to influence Bourbon in their favour. At O'Brien's request, he was granted another audience with the Tsar on 15 January, in order to make these demands.[119]

112 O'Brien to James III, 19/12/1723, RA Stuart 71/65; O'Brien to James III, 11/1/1724, RA 72/38.
113 Chance, 'George I and Peter the Great', p.306.
114 O'Brien to James III, 30/12/1723, RA Stuart 71/70.
115 O'Brien to James III, 19/12/1723, RA Stuart 71/65.
116 Bruce mistakenly maintained that this letter is missing from the Stuart Papers. James III to O'Brien, 19/11/1723, RA Stuart 70/71.
117 James III to O'Brien, 21/12/1723, RA Stuart 71/68.
118 O'Brien to James III, 11/1/1723, RA Stuart 72/38.
119 O'Brien's account of this audience is also absent from the Stuart Papers, but, again, subsequent letters reconstruct the discussion.

Peter's response was immediate; whereas he had previously been reluctant to entrust a possibly compromising letter to James to the post, he was now eager to have O'Brien convey letters to Paris.[120] On the day directly following the audience the Tsar wrote the requested letter to James, together with an Imperial ukase to Kurakin in the Hague, instructing him to support O'Brien and the Jacobite negotiations in Paris. In the interests of confidentiality, however, his letter to James was in Russian and avoided any risk of detailed reference to the negotiations. He wrote,

> . . . The bearer of this visited us, and we discussed the matter with which you entrusted him several times. He can give you a thorough report of this, and can bear witness to the fact that our side has done as much as possible, and will continue to do so if the other side will come into this affair.[121]

Peter was careful not to specify what was meant by '. . . doing as much as possible', and avoided a promise of commitment to the Jacobites, although he did write and sign the letter himself. The only condition stated clearly was that the 'other side', the French, enter into negotiations.

An examination of Peter's instructions to Kurakin, which are contained in the published Kurakin archives, is reassuring, in that they reveal a more explicit commitment to the Jacobite cause. They are reproduced here in translation, as primary evidence of the extent of Peter's support;

> . . . The bearer of this letter will speak to you. Take as much part in his affair as you can, especially to assist Mr Perin [Daniel O'Brien] in every way possible to achieve his ends. We are also sending a separate account of their [Jacobite] affairs in another place, and if one of them writes to you or asks you to do the same [give assistance] that will be the same bearer.[122]

Having procured the letters he needed for negotiations with the French court, O'Brien left for Paris in February.[123] His mission in Russia had lasted longer and been more eventful than anyone had expected. Thanks largely to the conjunction of Russian and Jacobite interests, and to the timely death of the Duke of Orleans, it had also enjoyed an unexpectedly large measure of success. In addition to the fact that a Jacobite Plenipotentiary Minister had been invited to appear at the Russian court, and that James's case had received serious consideration, O'Brien left Russia not with empty promises, but with concrete evidence of the Tsar's support. Peter's interests certainly lay primarily in securing a treaty with France, but there was every possibility that having achieved this goal, the Hanoverian monarchy would be vulnerable to attack from a number of areas. By February 1724 O'Brien and the Jacobites in Russia

120 O'Brien to James III, 19/12/1723, RA Stuart 71/65.
121 Peter I to James III, 5/1/1724 o.s., RA Stuart 72/35.
122 Peter I to Boris Kurakin, 5/1/1724 o.s., *Arkhiv Kurakina* 1, p.31.
123 H.Stirling to James III, 17/2/1724, RA Stuart 66/51.

had done everything within their power. The success or failure of the enterprise now lay with France.

Aftermath: Kurakin and the Jacobites in France, 1724

Kurakin was in Paris in early March, and was reporting to the Tsar before O'Brien arrived in April. These dispatches, some of which are published, some preserved in the Archive of Ancient Acts in Moscow, provide a Russian perspective on the role the Jacobites played in Petrine policy.

Kurakin's letters immediately reveal that the Tsar's primary interest was to secure an alliance with France. Britain's inclusion in this agreement might be a compromise which Russia would be forced to make; thus Jacobite demands were only a subsidiary consideration. In his dispatch of 13 March, Kurakin reported that he had given Lords Townshend and Carteret a cold reception when they had approached him to suggest an Anglo-Russian alliance. He observed however, that, since his arrival, hostility between the courts of France and Spain had made France '. . . so closely bound to England that it is impossible to be more so'. He nevertheless wrote secretly to the Duke of Bourbon, without the knowledge of the French ministry, to try to effect a Russo-French alliance independent of reconciliation with Britain.[124]

James had written to Kurakin in March to instruct him to communicate with Dillon in Paris.[125] On 21 April, having sounded Bourbon and Cardinal Fleury, the young King's preceptor, on the Jacobite question, Kurakin wrote an illuminating and, in part, encouraging, dispatch back to the Tsar. He discovered that '. . . this court is fundamentally a friend to the Pretender, but they hide it if possible', in order not to antagonise Britain. Bourbon had told Kurakin that the French alliance with Britain was purely 'pro forma' and emphasised that France would support James III as soon as the opportunity arose to break from Britain without risk to its own security. Following his advice, Kurakin reported to Peter that Russia could, likewise, be superficially reconciled with Britain, '. . . by complete dissimulation', and thus be free to pursue his own ends. A rising against George I could then be staged in three years time, when the French King was older; meanwhile, it was necessary to retain the favour of the Jacobites, so that '. . . the Tory and the Pretender's party in Britain do not weaken in support of your Imperial Majesty'.[126]

There was no doubt that Bourbon was not alone in France in his preference for the Catholic Stuarts above the House of Hanover, but political efficacy dictated a passive, non-committal stance. On 5 May, after Kurakin had sent the above report to the Tsar, General Dillon and Colonel O'Brien gave him the Tsar's hand-written instructions. According to Dillon, Kurakin appeared willing to comply with the Tsar's order to promote the Jacobite cause, and later wrote to James in the warmest terms, spoke further with Bourbon, and met with

124 B.Kurakin to Peter I, 2/13 March, 1724, *Arkhiv Kurakina*, 3, pp.247–248.
125 James III to B.Kurakin, 6/3/1724, RGADA F4 o1 d50, ll.4,4v.
126 Kurakin to Peter I, 21/4/1724, RGADA F9 o5 d1pt.1, ll.496–499.

Dillon, O'Brien and Francis Atterbury throughout the summer.[127] It was already obvious, however, that it was not in Bourbon's power, '. . . without an open breach of the Quadruple Alliance to enter into any a strict association with the Czar untill differences were at last seemingly adjoosted between him and D. of Hanover'.[128] Although Bourbon promised Kurakin in June that France would join Russia in James's favour if Anglo-French relations deterio- rated, it was clear that even an initiative from the Tsar could do nothing to remove the fundamental obstacle of the Anglo-French alliance.[129] However willing Peter I had been to support them, Jacobite hopes appeared once more to have foundered on the rock of power politics.

The Death of Peter I

Although Kurakin remained in correspondence with Jacobite leaders in Paris during the remainder of 1724,[130] Jacobite hopes were further undermined by Campredon's apparent success in negotiating an Anglo-Russian reconciliation. James reported to Dillon in November that '. . . the Czar & George I are on terms of accommodation'.[131] Townshend, likewise, wrote to Stephen Poyntz, the British envoy in Paris,

> . . . the scene of affairs is intirely changed with relation to the Czar . . . the King having all the reason in the world to think his reconciliation with that prince as good as concluded.[132]

Negotiations had reached the stage of a draft defensive treaty between France, Britain and Russia, drawn up in October.[133]

In early 1725, however, mistrust between the negotiating parties, caused by Prussian advances to Russia, and Peter I's continued efforts to procure an exclusively Franco-Russian agreement, led to the suspension of Campredon's negotiations. Kurakin reported this development to O'Brien in January, and within a month, James III had already sent a second Jacobite envoy, Captain William Hay (not Thomas, as Bruce mistakenly referred to him), to Russia.[134] By the time of his departure in February, however, he was already too late, for Peter I had died on 8 February after a short illness.

The effect of the Tsar's death on Jacobite hopes was severe. James received the news with great regret; he referred to Peter I as 'le principal object de mes

---

127 Kurakin to James III, 8/5/1724, RA Stuart 74/48; Kurakin to Peter I, 16/27 May 1724, RGADA F9 o5 d1 pt.1, l.513.
128 Dillon to James III, 8/5/1724, RA Stuart 74/52.
129 Kurakin to Peter I, 22/5 or 2/6/1724, RGADA F9 o5 d1 pt.1, l.518.
130 James III to Kurakin, 22/10/1724; 31/10/1724, RGADA F9 o5 d1 pt.1, ll.527,528.
131 James III to Dillon, 12/11/1724, RA Stuart 77/169.
132 Townshend to S.Poyntz, 9/10/1724 o.s., Chance, 'Northern Affairs in 1724', *EHR* 27 (1912), p.506.
133 Chance, 'Northern Affairs in 1724', p.506.
134 O'Brien to James III, 29/1/1725, RA Stuart 79/90; William Hay to T.Gordon, 17/2/1725, RA Stuart 80/54. This was the same William Hay who had served as a captain in the Russian navy from 1718–24.

ésperances'[135] The fate of the Jacobites was, of course, contingent on the state of international affairs, not the whim of a single monarch, but in Peter personal contact and political interest had been combined in their favour, and the loss of such support was great indeed. Nevertheless, by the time of Peter I's death, the Jacobites had established their political identity in Russia, not as a group of exiled dissidents, but as representatives of a King whose rights and demands were to be taken seriously.

Conclusion

Daniel O'Brien's embassy marked the climax of Russo-Jacobite co-operation during Peter I's reign due to a happy coincidence of political interests. What emerged most forcibly from it, however, was that, although it did not succeed, its failure was not a foregone conclusion.

O'Brien's achievements were numerous. Not only was he personally invited to Russia, and conducted successful negotiations with the Tsar himself which prompted secret Russo-French talks in Paris, but he did all without discovery by British intelligence. The secrecy of his mission, which Peter I could easily have publicised, undermines the contention that the Tsar was using the Jacobites merely to show public defiance for George I.[136] Although it foundered on the strength of the Anglo-French alliance, it also drew attention to Britain's dependence on France, and its extreme vulnerability should the alliance fail. Had French policy-makers been less inclined to back George I, particularly before the Anglo-Prussian treaty, and had Bourbon relations been better, the outcome for Britain could have been very different indeed.

British fear of Russia has often been defined principally as a reflection of '. . . George I's Hanoverian anxieties rather than British ministerial fears about Russian support for Jacobitism'.[137] Chance maintained that,

> . . . The danger apprehended from Russia was not to Great Britain . . .
> But for the King's Hanoverian interests, the rise of Peter the Great's
> power might have been regarded with comparative indifference. [138]

The great ministerial scare aroused in July 1723 by news that Russia was about to attack Sweden gives a dual angle on this. Britain's immediate fear of Russian control in Sweden, should the Duke of Holstein demand restitution for Schleswig or become King, was the threat to north Germany, secondly to Baltic trade. While George I, Townshend and Carteret, then in Hanover, favoured a subsidy to Sweden to enable it to defend itself, Walpole, in England, did not condone securing Hanover at British expense. Their

---

135 James III to Catherine I, 26/3/1725, RA Stuart 81/31.
136 '[The Tsar] delighted in needling George I, for example by flaunting a public trust in his
    chief physician Robert Erskine . . . his employment of Scotsmen . . . such as the naval
    captain Thomas Gordon, was primarily out of respect for their experience and a
    consciousness of Russia's past links with Scotland . . .', David Aldridge, 'Jacobitism and the
    Scottish Seas, 1689–1719', in T.C.Smout, ed., *Scotland and the Sea* (Edinburgh, 1992), p.84.
137 J.Black, *British Foreign Policy in the Age of Walpole*, p.143.
138 Chance, 'George I and Peter the Great', p.283.

correspondence, however, had a double level of meaning. Townshend wrote secretly to Walpole that if Russia controlled Sweden, '. . . we might in a short time see Swedish and Muscovite squadrons in conjunction at Gottenburgh, able to terrify and distress all the coasts of Great Britain,' and proposed that he sanction a large, secret donation to Sweden and Denmark.[139] The following week Walpole addressed the problem to Newcastle. Should the Tsar win power over Sweden, he wrote,

> . . . this must naturally make the Czar Master of the Baltick, which is so near Scotland, that it will not be a difficult matter for him Enterprising as he is [to cause] a very great disturbance . . . I doubt when he has turnd out one King He will think of doing the same to another. Especially the only one that can thwart his designs in that part of the world.

However, Walpole used this, conversely, as a ground to refuse the Swedish subsidy, claiming that it would antagonise Russia and '. . . certainly give new life to the Jacobites'.[140] By August, this 'Storm of the Czar' had in any case passed, and no financial assistance was necessary.[141] While this was clearly a case in which an ostensible Jacobite threat from Russia was used to cover decisions of Hanoverian policy, a trivialisation of the Jacobite threat on these grounds would be inaccurate.

Although the news of an imminent Russian attack proved unfounded, the government panic which met it demonstrated well the ministry's ignorance of current Russian political and military affairs, and likewise the potential threat posed by Russia. Walpole complained bitterly to Newcastle,

> . . . Sure we have been but very ill serv'd by Mr Finch in Sweden, and also by the King's German Ministers at Hannover, who cou'd get no sort of Intelligence of the Czar's designs till they were just ready to be put in Execution, and God knows whether all we can doe can in any measure prevent the ill consequences . . .[142]

Britain's fear of Russia was indeed, principally directed towards Germany and the Baltic, but its lack of awareness of O'Brien's secret embassy, which, after all, would have threatened both British and Hanoverian interests by the conclusion of a separate Russo-French alliance, suggests that this was, in part, due to ignorance of Russian affairs. In this case too, it is inaccurate to make a sharp distinction between, 'Hanoverian anxieties' and 'Russian support for Jacobitism'; one of the plans O'Brien considered, and certainly that most likely to have been executed, was that Peter I provide a diversion in Hanover, while the assault on Britain be launched from France and/or Spain.

The period between the Atterbury plot and the First Treaty of Vienna

139 Townshend to R.Walpole, 16/7/1723, in W.Coxe *Memoirs of the Life and Administration of Robert Walpole,* 3 vols., (London, 1798), 2, pp.253–4.
140 Walpole to Newcastle, 26/7/1723, BL Add.Ms.32686, ff.286–287v.
141 Newcastle to Townshend, 11/8/1723, BL Add.Ms. 32686, ff.304–305v.
142 Walpole to Newcastle, 26/7/1723, BL Add.Ms.32686, ff.286–287v.

(1725), has been referred to as a 'relatively calm period' in British politics.[143] Fritz described England in mid-1724 as enjoying '. . . an uninterrupted tranquillity abroad, and a period of calm and stability the like of which had not been seen since George I's accession'.[144] Townshend's letter to George I of April 1724, from which these words are taken, however, continued in a different vein with a warning that

> . . . the jacobite party is still very strong . . . the foreign ministers who are best acquainted with this country . . . constantly represent the present tranquility of this nation, as owing more to the despair of giving your majesty any disturbance from abroad, than to any real change of submission wrought in the minds of the pretender's adherents.[145]

Townshend emphasised that, should Spain or France support the Jacobites, '. . . the sparks of resentment, which now lye smother'd, would break out into as fierce a flame as ever'.[146]

These years were indeed stable when placed in the context of the Jacobite risings and multiple government controversies which had characterised the first ten years of George I's reign. As Walpole freely admitted, however, Jacobitism was, '. . . a danger we shall always be more or less exposed to'.[147] The failure of Russo-Jacobite co-operation under Peter I was due not to a lack of political will on the part of Russia, but to Britain's consistent policy of securing its bond with France, which proved on each occasion to be its most effective weapon against Jacobitism.

143 J.Black, *British Foreign Policy*, p.144.
144 Fritz, *The English Ministers*, pp.106–107.
145 Townshend to George I, April 1724, in W.Coxe, *Sir Robert Walpole*, 2, pp.297–8.
146 *Ibid.*
147 Cobbett, *Parliamentary History*, 10, p.401.

PART TWO

The Reign of Catherine I, 1725–1727

FOUR

Agents and Intrigue

One of the great misconceptions which surrounds the role of Jacobitism in Russia is that, after reaching a climax under Peter I, it virtually ceased on his death. Bruce maintained that 'The death of Peter the Great closed a chapter in Jacobite relations with Russia and in the story of Jacobite designs in general',[1] and the Jacobite historian Frank McLynn, likewise, assumes that when '. . . Peter the Great died . . . Jacobite hopes of Russian support died with him'.[2] These conclusions are, in fact, unfounded. Although little has been written on the reign of Peter's wife and successor, Catherine I, and nothing specifically on Jacobite activity in Russia at that time, her determined espousal of the Holstein cause and hostility for George I made Russia a breeding ground for Jacobite conspiracy. Until her own death in May 1727, political changes in Europe enabled Russia to keep Britain, Hanover, its possessions and allies in a state of intermittent panic, which escalated at the mere rumour of military preparations or Jacobite intrigue, revealing for the first time to a shocked British government the size and power of the Jacobite community.

Threats from North and South

George I's relief at the death of his arch-enemy, Peter I, in February 1725, was accompanied by the pleasant anticipation that Britain's influence in Europe would now increase at Russia's expense, and that the threat to north Germany would wane. Newcastle optimistically foresaw '. . . a very good opportunity of securing the several powers in the north to the interest of England and France'.[3] However, a series of events in the first months of 1725 not only undermined these hopes, but greatly weakened Britain's position in Europe. France's rejection of the Spanish infanta as a bride for Louis XV brought about a Franco-Spanish rupture, which seriously threatened Britain when Spain sought an alliance with Austria. It soon became apparent that the secret negotiations in Vienna conducted by the Queen of Spain's agent, Jan Willem Ripperda, if successful, might encourage the Emperor to consolidate his power by seeking alliances with Russia, Sweden and other northern states. Britain immediately instructed Campredon, the French envoy in St Petersburg, to continue his efforts to bring Russia into alliance with France and Britain, but Campredon's disastrous first audience with Catherine I, on 19 April, opened a hornet's nest. Not only did she declare that her strong support for the Duke of Holstein, her future son-in-law, was irreconcilable with Britain's refusal to cede

1 M.Bruce, 'Jacobite Relations', p.361.
2 F.McLynn, *The Jacobites*, p.43.
3 Newcastle to R.Walpole, 22/2/1725 o.s., BL Add.Ms. 33199, f.275.

Schleswig, but she even threatened to launch an attack on Denmark.[4] George I, for whom Russian support for Holstein's ambitions in Sweden and north Germany represented a nightmare scenario, made desperate attempts to counter it. Stephen Poyntz, the Hanoverian envoy in Stockholm, conveyed large subsidies to the opposing party in Sweden, hoping to quash the Holstein faction and secure a Swedish alliance. Meanwhile, Frederick Wilhelm of Prussia, tempted by the offer of Swedish Pomerania, should he assist Holstein to the Swedish throne, was drawn to support Catherine I. Ministerial suspicions that Holstein's case was also favoured at Vienna intensified British fears, so when Ripperda's negotiations in Vienna came to fruition on 30 April 1725 with the conclusion of a public treaty of peace and a private one of defensive alliance between Spain and Austria, Britain and its allies, France and Denmark, found themselves vulnerable from both north and south.

The Return of William Hay

The Jacobite envoy, Captain William Hay, was already on his way to St Petersburg by the time news reached James III in late March of the death of Peter I. Fortunately for the Jacobites, he was not recalled. Instead, he was instructed '. . . to pursue the same measures [he] would have done had the Czar lived'.[5] Hay had been chosen because he was '. . . well acquainted with the country',[6] having served in the Russian navy from 1718 until his voluntary retirement in February 1724,[7] and his return to Russia had been prompted by news of the Duke of Holstein's engagement to Peter's daughter,[8] and by the breakdown of negotiations for an Anglo-Russian reconciliation. Besides his instructions and full powers of negotiation, he carried letters for the Tsar, the Duke of Holstein, Admiral Thomas Gordon, Rear Admiral Thomas Saunders,[9] and a message for General Peter Lacy.[10]

Hay's written instructions were limited to a general order to obey Thomas Gordon, or, in his absence, Thomas Saunders, '. . . doing nothing without his advice and counsel,' and to assure Peter I that France would support the Jacobites as soon as it could throw off its alliance with Britain. The details of a more specific plan, communicated orally to him for reasons of security, can be reconstructed from other correspondence. James III referred to 'the proposed

4 Karl Friedrich, the dispossessed Duke of Holstein, had become engaged to Peter I's daughter Anna in December 1724 and married her the following June. The Holstein question had proved fatal to French efforts to have Britain included in a Franco-Russian treaty. J.F.Chance, *The Alliance of Hanover* (London, 1923), p.77.

5 James III to T.Gordon, 26/3/1725, RA Stuart 81/30.

6 Instructions to Captain William Hay, 29/2/1725, RA Stuart 80/82.

7 NAS Abercairney GD 24/1/859, ff.286,287; MM 33, p.23; *Obshchii morskoi spisok*, 1, p.94.

8 James III to Daniel O'Brien, 6/2/1725, RA Stuart 80/5.

9 Saunders was a 'shautbenakht' (rear-admiral) in 1725, and was promoted to vice-admiral in 1727 (died 1733). *Obshii morskoi spisok*, 1, pp.332–333.

10 Instructions to Captain William Hay, 29/2/1725, RA Stuart 80/85; Blank Powers of Plenipotentiary, 24/2/1725, *HMC Eglinton* etc., p.161; James III to Peter I, 20/2/1725, RGADA F4 o1 d50 ll.6–9v; James III to Saunders, 19/2/1725, RA Stuart 80/58; James III to Gordon, 19/2/1725, RA Stuart 80/60.

project' in the letter Hay carried to Gordon, adding that Hay '. . . is apprised of the whole affair which is of such a nature as requires the most universal secrecy'.[11] James's secretary, John Hay of Inverness, couched an accompanying letter in deliberately ambiguous terms, to the effect that Gordon was to deliver James's letter to the Tsar and to negotiate with him for ships, troops and arms for fifteen or twenty thousand, to be paid for with an advance of 25,000 Spanish pistoles. It was suggested that the Duke of Holstein, under the aegis of Peter I in Sweden, might command the troops and preface the invasion of Britain with the conquest of Norway. The place of embarkation was to be Archangel, and the plan to be executed the following summer.[12]

Although the proposed Jacobite co-operation for the mutual benefit of Holstein and Stuart would, in principal, have met with Catherine's approval, the Empress had not yet established her own throne when Hay arrived, much less that of another monarch. Moreover, the close personal acquaintance which Gordon had enjoyed with Peter I was now lacking, and, despite his initial optimism, he complained in April that he had had '. . . frequent opportunitys of access to his Imperiall person, but now it is very difficult to talke of private affaires with the Empress'.[13] Despite these initial drawbacks, however, Hay's arrival at St Petersburg in mid-May[14] meant that, unlike Britain, the Jacobites were now fully prepared for the commencement of diplomatic relations with the new monarch.

Britain's Need for a Spy

In early 1725, and still under the illusion that the Russian threat had diminished, the British government disregarded intelligence of Jacobite activity. Writing to Horatio Walpole in March, Newcastle described an intercepted letter by Daniel O'Brien as, '. . . in every article so flattering and so contrary to truth, that there is very little attention to be given to it'. He maintained that

> . . . there never was . . . so universal a satisfaction and tranquility throughout the nation as there is at present; so it is hardly to be imagined that the Jacobites can be mad enough to think of making any disturbance at this time.[15]

There is no evidence at this point that the government was aware that William Hay was on his way to Russia; it would, at this point, probably have aroused little concern.

In the course of the next months, however, as Catherine I was seen to establish herself with all the authority of her late husband, the ministry realised its increasing need for reliable information on Russian affairs. In May

11 James III to T.Gordon, 26/3/1725, RA Stuart 81/30.

12 John Hay to T.Gordon, 24/2/1725, RA Stuart 80/78,80.

13 T.Gordon to James III, 2/2/1725, reference in James III to Gordon, 26/3/1725, RA Stuart 81/30;17/4/1725, T.Gordon to R.Arbuthnot, NAS Abercairney GD 24/1/859, f.290.

14 Campredon to Morville, 19/5/1725, *SIRIO* 58, p.325.

15 Newcastle to H.Walpole, 11/3/1725 o.s., BL Add.Ms. 33199, f.281.

there came news that Frederick Wilhelm of Prussia was negotiating the provision of Russian troops for possible deployment in Germany.[16] At the same time, Stephen Poyntz, the Hanoverian envoy in Sweden, reported that Catherine I had threatened war on Denmark in support of the Duke of Holstein.[17] Thomas Robinson in Paris informed Townshend that Menshikov and Apraksin were to have the Russian army and navy ready for action by mid-May,[18] and in June, Poyntz received a report of 20,000 Russian and 4,000 Swedish troops about to disembark at Kiel.[19] Meanwhile, the arrival of William Hay, '. . . on the Pretender's business', was noted by a member of the British Factory in St Petersburg, and Campredon, likewise, reported the mysterious arrival of 'le Sieur Hay', whose frequent nocturnal conferences with known Jacobites led him to suspect '. . . que cet homme est chargé de quelque commission secrete pour traverser l'alliance projetée entre le roi, le roi d'Angleterre et la Russie'.[20] This intelligence corresponded disturbingly with rumours spread by Ripperda that the Treaty of Vienna had included a secret clause for the restoration of James III.[21] Although these rumours were initially disregarded, Britain was convinced of the existence of a secret treaty and sought to discover whether it could be detrimental to British interests.[22] As the situation worsened, the sparse information on Russian affairs being gleaned by British diplomats and their spies elsewhere, particularly Stephen Poyntz and Robert Jackson at Stockholm,[23] Edward Finch at Dresden and Saint-Saphorin at Vienna, was no longer sufficient. Even Walpole's access to Jacques Campredon's dispatches from St Petersburg was unsatisfactory; by 1725, doubts were beginning to circulate regarding Campredon's integrity.[24] The decision by the British government to send a spy to St Petersburg in May 1725 was indication of its need for more detailed first-hand information to combat its growing unease at rumours of possible Russian hostility.

---

16 Du Bourgay to Townshend, 13/24 May 1725, PRO SP 90/19, unfol.
17 Catherine first threatened this in a harangue against Campredon in April, referred to in Coxe, *Memoirs of Sir Robert Walpole*, 1, p.243. Poyntz reported it to Townshend, 14/5/1725 o.s., Chance, *The Alliance of Hanover*, p.42.
18 Robinson to Townshend, 18/6/1725, BL Add.Ms.32743, f.280.
19 Baron Söhlenthal to Poyntz, 8/19 June 1725, PRO SP 95/37, f.188.
20 Correspondent to Jackson (Stockholm), 7/5/1725, 28/5/1725, PRO SP 95/41, ff.61, 73–73v; Campredon to Morville, 19/5/1725, 22/5/1725, *SIRIO* 58, pp.311, 325, 333.
21 Saint-Saphorin to Townshend, 26/5/1725, PRO SP 80/55, unfol.
22 H.Walpole to Newcastle, 15/5/1725 n.s., BL Add.Ms.32743, ff.189–190.
23 Both Poyntz and Jackson had paid correspondents at St Petersburg at this period, one a member of the British Factory, then later a Swedish officer. Poyntz refused to send a Briton following Deane's experiences. Poyntz to Townshend, 6/7/1725 o.s., PRO SP 95/38, f.15.
24 'At present they [the French] can have no intelligence but from M.Campredon, whose behaviour has been all along such as has given the greatest dissatisfaction to the King', Newcastle to H.Walpole, 22/2/1725, BL Add.Ms.33199, f.275; also Poyntz to Walpole, 2/2/1725 o.s., PRO 95/36, ff.37,38. Campredon altered letters meant for the British government to conceal exclusively French issues. Chance, 'George I and Peter the Great', p.299.

John Deane's Mission to St Petersburg

Captain John Deane received the official commission of consul to the British government,[25] but his real mission was, as Townshend informed Poyntz, '. . . to transmit hither what intelligence he may be able to get for his Majesty's service'[26] in the light of rumours of Russian naval preparations. Chance has maintained that he had been appointed consul once before in 1721, but this appears not to have been the case.[27] He was, however, particularly suited to the task of informant, having served in the Russian navy for eleven years until his dismissal in 1722 for laying down his commission at Britain's demand.[28] He spoke good Russian, was loyal to the Hanoverian monarchy and was well informed on Russian naval affairs.[29]

Captain Deane landed at Cronstadt on 2 June, travelled to St Petersburg, and departed for home on 21 June. The short duration of his mission was, however, quite disproportionate to its significance. Firstly, the record of his visit, preserved in his dispatches and in a detailed account of his experiences, provides a unique insight into the size and influence of the Jacobite community in Russia. Secondly, the information which he gathered concerning Jacobite activities proved of crucial importance both to Jacobite fortunes and to the course of Anglo-Russian relations in the ensuing months.

One fact which Deane's visit brought into sharp relief was the existence of opposing factions, both within the British community and the Russian nobility. The general point of division in both cases was support for, or hostility towards, the Hanoverian monarchy. For the Britons this was a Jacobite/Hanoverian split; the Russians appear to have divided into those in favour of the Duke of Holstein and against alliance with Britain and France, and those with opposing

25 Deane's commission was dated 11/5/1725 o.s., Chance, *The Alliance of Hanover*, p.84.

26 Townshend to Poyntz, 7/7/1725, PRO SP 95/37, ff.211–215v.

27 Chance, in *The Alliance of Hanover*, p.84, cited a letter dated 27/7/1721 o.s. in which the governor of the Russia Company, Nathaniel Gould, protested at the appointment of Deane to the post of consul because he was 'very obnoxious to the Russian government'. Chance apparently mistook the date of this letter; Deane was still in Russian service in 1721 and had not yet been disgraced; the letter referred to is PRO SP 91/107, dated 2/7/1725; this is corroborated by the Minutes of the Russia Company for 2/7/1725 in the Guildhall Library Ms.11741/5, f.187 in which it is resolved that Gould write a letter of protest to Townshend at Deane's appointment. D.B.Horn repeated this error in *British Diplomatic Representatives, 1689–1789*, Camden Society, third series, 46 (London, 1932), p.112.

28 The reason for Deane's expulsion from Russia in 1722, not mentioned in his own account, but Russia's principal objection to him in 1725, has been a mystery. However, another contemporary, Peter Henry Bruce, wrote, '. . . I could not then presume to insist further on my discharge, for fear of sharing the fate of captain Dean of the fleet, who was sent into banishment for laying down his commission, upon a proclamation by king George the First, forbidding all British subjects to serve in Russia; a copy of which proclamation was given captain Dean, by Mr Jefferies, the British minister. The captain was released some time after, and returning to England, was sent consul to Ostend.' P.H.Bruce, *Memoirs of Peter Henry Bruce*, 1882 edn., p.210.

29 Deane was the author of the very informative *History of the Russian Fleet during the Reign of Peter the Great by a Contemporary Englishman* (1724), since edited by Vice Admiral Cyprian A.G.Bridge for the Navy Records Society 15 (London, 1899).

views. Campredon had complained in April that the alliance between Britain, France and Russia was being delayed by the body of opposition within the Russian nobility. He named those for the union as the President of the War College, Menshikov, President of the Admiralty College, Apraksin, Vice-President of the College of Foreign Affairs, Osterman, and Senators Golitsyn and Tolstoi. Those against alliance with Britain were the President of the College of Foreign Affairs, Golovkin, Ministers Vasilii Dolgoruky and Repnin, and Senator Iaguzhinsky.[30] The issue of Deane's fate prompted a conflict between these camps, and his expulsion from Russia after only nineteen days marked a clear victory for the enemies of Hanover.

Deane's reception was a foretaste of what was to come. When he was confronted on arrival by the Jacobite Rear-Admiral Thomas Saunders, he initially pretended to have come on commercial business, but was soon forced to produce his commission as British consul. His arrival in an official capacity without credentials and without prior notification could be seen to constitute a contravention of diplomatic custom, and Saunders was quick to object to this. From the outset, Deane realised that

> . . . I should stand in need of friends to support my Cause against the united force of the Holsteiners and the Jacobites, which were caballing and studying all ways to frustrate my Designs.[31]

His fate, he knew, depended on whether he could find a sufficient number of friends to overcome this opposition.

A solid body of support for Deane's visit did exist, for he reported that '. . . Upon my arrival in the Country his Majesty's ffreinds rejoiced, believing it might facilitate the Reconciliation and be a check to the insolency of ye Jacobites, which is at this time intolerable'.[32] He sought support from Count Apraksin, the high admiral of the fleet, whose anti-Jacobite sympathies were well known to him from his previous service in the Russian navy.[33] They discussed the possibility of an Anglo-Russian reconciliation, and Apraksin arranged audiences for him with the President of the College of Foreign Affairs, Gavril Golovkin, and with Senator Petr Tolstoi. Tolstoi could be expected to favour Deane's mission; the visit to the hostile Golovkin was obligatory for a foreign representative. Deane also sought out Britons loyal to Hanover. He lodged with the ship-builder Joseph Ney, and was accompanied to his ship, despite Jacobite heckling, by the Welsh engineer, Edward Lane and the ship-builder Richard Brown. One of the most active Hanoverians, who provided Townshend with information on Russian affairs was the chaplain to

---

30 Report by Campredon, April 1725, Solov'ev, *Istoriya Rossii* 19, p.959.
31 John Deane's account of his mission to Russia, PRO SP 91/107, f.2.
32 PRO SP 91/107, f.12.
33 In Deane's *History of the Russian Fleet under Peter the Great*, Apraksin is reported, in 1721, to have 'looked on Gordon [the Jacobite Thomas Gordon] and his associates as men of turbulent dispositions and malevolent principles; that having set their native country in a flame without finding their account in it some of them were forced to fly from justice, and were now caballing to foment divisions in Russia.' Navy Records Society 15, pp.85,86.

the British Factory of the London Russia Company at St Petersburg, Dr Thomas Consett. He reported to Townshend on the strong support of certain Russian bishops for reconciliation with Britain.[34] However, it appears from Consett's own treatment at the hands of the Jacobites that supporters of George I in the British Factory were in the minority. Deane reported of him that

> . . . for his zeal he lives a miserable life amongst that set of men, who abuse him for naming his Majesty in his publick prayers, at the mention of which some are observed constantly to spit & one of the ffactory threatened to cane him for having taken the oaths [to King George] and 'tis really believed that they will next year turn him out and send him home.[35]

In fact, Consett was effectively dismissed from his post through the influence of his enemies in July 1727, and left Russia soon afterwards.[36] Although loyal subjects of George I were in evidence, they appear to have had neither organisation nor influence.

The Jacobites, on the other hand, formed a more or less cohesive group organised against a common enemy. In this case their victim was Deane. They had had the benefit of advance warning of his arrival, apparently from a recently arrived Irish Jacobite,[37] and they were well aware that he had come as a government agent. Their leading members, Thomas Gordon and Henry Stirling, had just received instructions from James III via William Hay. Hay had arrived two weeks previously and was now sharing a house with Stirling while he co-ordinated Russian support. Apart from the many Jacobite naval officers, the Jacobite community appears to have been concentrated primarily in the British Factory.[38] This official body provided the Jacobites with a

---

34 T.Consett to Townshend, 30/6/1725, PRO SP 91/9, f.396.

35 PRO SP 91/107, f.17.

36 There has been some confusion regarding Consett's departure. Fritz dated it erroneously as autumn 1725, *English Ministers*, p.130n; A.G.Cross, in his 'Chaplains to the British Factory in St Petersburg', regards the reason for it as a mystery, but cited William Tooke p.108, that he was dismissed by a resolution of 10/7[1727], *ESR* 2 (1972), 126–8. In November 1725, Consett wrote, 'The Factory has shown me their resentment by withdrawing my services as chaplain from May next, with no reason', Consett to Townshend, 16/11/1725, PRO SP 91/9, f.413; Townshend reported to Walpole, '. . . I am persuaded that the disaffected there . . . have got him turned out for those reasons [as a spy], and because he was a friend of Capt. Deane's', 15/26 Oct.1725, CUL CH 1250. However, he was reconciled with the Factory in March 1726, Cracraft, *For God and Peter the Great*, p.19. His ultimate dismissal was probably closely linked, as he himself suspected, to rumours '. . . that I am a spy for His Majesty', Consett to J.Deane, 9/?/1725, PRO SP 91/9, f.411.

37 O'Connor probably brought this news. PRO SP 91/107, f.16. According to Jackson's spy, however, the imminent visit of a British minister was 'universally talked about' and shrouded in rumour and speculation as early as April. Correspondent to Jackson, 9/20 April 1725, PRO SP 95/41, ff.41–42v.

38 Horn has commented on the '. . . strong admixture of Roman Catholic Irish and Scottish Jacobites' in British trade Factories at this time. An English merchant at Riga in the 1720s complained that '. . . the minister [of religion] when I was there was . . . an open bigoted Jacobite, with whom were joined about half-a-dozen more'. D.B.Horn, *The British Diplomatic Service*, p.248.

platform from which to organise and execute their attack on Deane. More importantly, the Russia Company in London, which it represented, served as an influential channel through which the protests of Factory members could find a hearing in Parliament.[39]

The superior organisation of the Jacobites was in evidence as soon as Deane arrived. They were able to put him under constant observation, effectively preventing him from carrying out his mission. Deane reported that

> . . . The Disaffected both in the Russian Service as well as those in the Factory . . . had their meetings every Day and several things were proposed to get me away.[40]

They had a number of means of having him expelled without divulging their true motivation. If the Russian court did not insist on the banishment order which had accompanied Deane's dismissal three years before, they could present a memorial to the Russia Company, which in any case disliked ministerial intrusion into its affairs, claiming that Russian hostility towards Deane was damaging trade. If that failed, they planned to send the government a list of the objections raised against him in 1722 and to present a Bill to Parliament in protest.[41]

In the event, it was the Jacobites who swung the balance. The Russia Company's complaint to Townshend demanding Deane's recall was not made until after his departure.[42] Russian ministers were prepared to grant him two months in which to produce credentials before reaching a decision on his fate. It appears that the swiftness of his expulsion was a direct result of Jacobite pressure, and, more specifically, of the influence of certain individuals on prominent Russian statesmen. Deane himself suspected '. . . one Morly an Enemy of mine for some Years, who is very intimate with Iagozinsky, and I believe contributed more to my being sent away than any of the rest'.[43] Iaguzhinsky was one of those appointed to decide Deane's case, and known to favour the Jacobite faction.[44] When Deane received his extradition order on 18 June, Iaguzhinsky left for the country with four members of the Factory, including Morley, to celebrate the victory. In addition, Deane suspected Count Nikolai Golovin, of whom he wrote,

39 For details of the Company, although little on the Jacobite element, see D.S.MacMillan, 'The Russia Company of London in the Eighteenth Century . . .', *Guildhall Miscellany* 4 (1973), pp.222–236.

40 PRO SP 91/107, f.6.

41 PRO SP 91/107, f.6.

42 Minutes of the Russia Company, 2/7/1725, Guildhall L. 11741/5, f.187; Nathaniel Gould to Townshend, 2/7/1725, PRO SP 91/107. The memorial was, however, drawn up by 'most of the factory', Correspondent to Jackson, 11/22 June 1725, PRO SP 95/41, f.83.

43 PRO SP 91/107, f.7. This may have been George Morley, who was an assistant to the Russia Company in 1710. Minute Book of the Russia Company, 1710, Guildhall L. 11741/4, f.70. The names George and Francis Morley appear in 'The Names of all the persons of the English Congregation in Mosco Anno domini 1706', Guildhall L. 11192b, unfol.

44 Deane recounted that Iaguzhinsky had renamed a member of the Factory, Randolph Mainwaring, whose father's name was George, Randolph 'Jakovlev', or 'son of James', saying he preferred James to George. PRO SP 91/107, f.8.

. . . he has for several years been a tool of the Jacobites & served to represent their affairs at Court . . . his Company at Petersburg was ever with the Jacobites, both those in the Service and those of the ffactory, Morley and Vigor lodging in his House.[45]

Powerful and organised as the Jacobites proved themselves to be, their ultimate success was due to the prevailing anti-Hanoverian climate at the Russian court, which accompanied the ascendancy of the Holstein faction.[46] Deane was assured of '. . . how impotent their Endeavours would have proved, had they not been supported in their insolence by some men in Power'.[47] The speed with which Deane's case was concluded to the detriment of British interests, however, augured well for the support which Jacobites could hope to elicit from Russia in other areas.

The overwhelming impression created by Deane's account is of an expatriate British community in which one set of political beliefs easily prevailed, reversing the domestic British power balance. Deane attributed this excess of zeal to the lack of '. . . the Eyes of a watchful Ministry', and commented,

. . . to a person upon the Spot, who observes that one Party is caressed upon all occasions whilst the other is forced to bow and cringe at a distance, if not insolently used, it is easy to perceive that the friends of the Government want support, and that they insensibly decrease, this has also an ill effect upon fforeigners, who, forming their Ideas of us from what they see & finding in Russia at least three to one that don't stick either publickly to declare, or at least insinuate their disaffection; from hence naturally conclude that his Majesty being possessed rather maintains himself on the Throne by something like artful force, than any Interest or Esteem in the Hearts of his people.[48]

This account was clearly an attempt to alert the ministry to the fact that such a strong Jacobite body could represent a real danger to British diplomatic interests even without a resort to arms.

Deane's preoccupation with the prominence of the Jacobite faction in Russia does not appear at this point, however, to have been shared by the British government. The hostility he had twice experienced in St Petersburg was evidence of the strength of anti-British sentiment amongst a certain number of the dissident foreign community and native nobility. In the short term his expulsion certainly represented a victory for the Jacobites, and provided some indication of the influence exerted by the Holstein faction at the Russian court. Britain's failure to respond to this evidence with anything more than mild concern was undoubtedly due to the reassurance Deane was able to give regarding the state of military preparedness of the Russian fleet. By the

45 PRO SP 91/107, f.16.
46 Deane reported on the power enjoyed by the court of the Duke of Holstein through Catherine's support. PRO SP 91/107, f.13.
47 PRO SP 91/107, f.11.
48 *Ibid.*, f.20.

summer British fears of the rumoured offensive in favour of Holstein were greatly alleviated by reports that the Russians had abandoned their expedition.[49] British bribes to the anti-Holstein party in Sweden were having an effect. Deane's conclusion that a lack of provisions would, in any case, prevent the launching of a Russian fleet that summer, clearly eliminated the Russian threat even in the light of the most determined support either for Holstein or the Jacobites.[50] Townshend wrote confidently in June to Poyntz in Sweden that there was no longer any danger of naval action from Russia that season.[51]

The Aftermath of Deane's Mission: Spies and Jacobite Letters

The most important impact of Deane's mission, which was not felt until some time after his departure, was not to reassure, but to undermine ministerial confidence that the Russian threat had been averted. Despite the short duration of his visit and the constantly inhibiting presence of Jacobite spies, Deane had succeeded in securing the services of a number of informants, whose reports proved critical to Britain's awareness of Jacobite activities in Russia. He employed a former seaman named Trescod, who owned a tavern and had '. . . a very good account of the real state of Maritime affairs', as well as one un-named non-Jacobite member of the British Factory.[52] There was a particular irony in the fact that by far his most important source of information was a Jacobite, probably the very man who had warned the exiles in St Petersburg of his arrival. Moreover, this double agent, Edmund O'Connor, was a relative of one of Russia's greatest generals, the Jacobite Peter Lacy, and he had earlier brought secret dispatches from Spain for the conspirators in Russia.[53]

Just after Deane's arrival in Cronstadt rumours began to reach British spies that twelve Russian ships were preparing to sail, possibly to join Sweden, '. . . upon some Extraordinary Expedition'.[54] O'Connor heightened Deane's suspicions when he reported that William Hay's business in Russia was to buy twelve ships of war, ostensibly for the Mississippi Company, but in fact for the Jacobites, using Spanish and Papal money.[55] Deane had himself sighted three

49 Poyntz to Townshend, 6/17 July 1725, PRO SP 95/38, f.10v.
50 PRO SP 91/107, f.13.
51 Townshend to Poyntz, 29/6/1725, PRO 95/37, ff.217–218.
52 PRO SP 91/107, f.18. This may have been the same man who informed for Robert Jackson in Stockholm, PRO SP 95/41, f.40.
53 Deane described O'Connor as having been an active Jacobite for some years. He was apparently a relative of James III's former minister in Madrid, Tobie du Burg, and had worked as a spy in Spain, but had also had contact with Stanhope there. Stanhope to Townshend 6/11/1725, PRO SP 94/93 unfol. He had been in Russia five months, having come with a recommendation to a lieutenancy in the Russian service, but disliked Russia and wished to return to Britain. He demanded a pardon to enable him to do so as a condition for providing information (granted by Townshend with £100 reward, Townshend to Newcastle, 4/10/1725, Coxe, *Walpole*, 2, p.180). See also Deane, PRO SP 91/107, ff.14–15.
54 Correspondent to Jackson 25/6/1725, encl. in Jackson to Tilson, 21/7/1725, PRO SP 95/41, ff.87–89v.
55 PRO SP 91/107, ff.15,16.

Russian men-of-war sailing through the Sound for Cadiz as he neared Russia.[56] In June Poyntz reported the celebrations of the Holstein faction at news that the ships had passed the Sound, and linked this with the arrival from Britain of a French Jacobite, and the journey to Stockholm of a suspected Jacobite and 'Scotchman', Samuel St Leger. Soon afterwards, he learned that the ships had '. . . landed their Arms in the North of Scotland'.[57] These rumours fuelled government suspicions that a Jacobite/Holstein conspiracy was being co-ordinated between Russia, Sweden, Spain and possibly Austria, but concern did not escalate to panic until O'Connor provided the ministry with a number of Jacobite letters which appeared to confirm its worst fears. Having deceived the Jacobites in Russia into believing he was travelling to Spain, he had been entrusted with secret dispatches for Spain and France, but went instead to Amsterdam, from whence he had sent everything to Townshend. Consett later reported that the Jacobites in St Petersburg had suspected him of treachery, but had been too late to prevent his departure.[58] O'Connor probably retained the original letters, for Townshend offered him a rich reward to deliver them and intercept the answers.

The letters in question, which were all dated 25 July and reached Townshend in late September or early October, were signed by Sir Henry Stirling, Thomas Gordon and William Hease, a member of the British Factory, and were addressed to Messrs. Butler and Kelly, merchants in Madrid, and to Messrs. Hease and William Waters, Paris bankers. Stirling's letter to Madrid, the most detailed, referred to three ships laden with 'goods' from Russia, which he hoped had arrived safely in Spain. He promised that an additional three would be sent by the end of the month, and assured the recipient of '. . . the unalterable good wishes of this factory, who are as desirous to contribute to establish your trade as may be'. He demanded that someone reliable be sent immediately to Stockholm to meet a '. . . sure friend of ours there, sent by this factory', and that this envoy be given at least £20,000, presumably to pay for the 'goods'. He added that William Hease was about to leave for Stockholm to inspect what was there, and that he hoped that '. . . our goods may pass free from any treacherous designs'. He also mentioned that Princes Dolgoruky and Kurakin had been instructed, '. . . to close with such as you appoint to treat with them'.[59]

Hease's letter to Paris was concerned with the same ships. He mentioned that since the 28 June, '. . . the factory of this place condescended to let us have five more'. Three of these were almost ready; the remainder would follow. He added that, '. . . We have all the assurances that can be had of a secure

56 Deane to Townshend, 26/5/1725 o.s., PRO SP 91/9, f.387.
57 Poyntz to Townshend, reference to letter 9/6/1725 o.s. in 6/7/1725 o.s., PRO SP 95/37, ff.9–15v.
58 Townshend learned from O'Connor himself that '. . . a Whore he kept company with' had discovered his treachery and informed the Jacobites; Townshend to R.Walpole, 15/26 October 1725, CUL CH 1250; Townshend to Newcastle, 4/10/1725, in Coxe, *Robert Walpole*, 2, p.480.
59 PRO SP 91/107; also printed in Coxe, *Robert Walpole*, 2, p.480.

commerce with this factory, of which you shall know more at large by the middle of October', and concluded, '. . . tis expected that you make all preparations to begin along with the company next season'. Like Stirling, Hease also appeared concerned for the secrecy of these plans. He observed that '. . . We are all very timorous of the treachery of our Enemies in Obstructing the present, but as they have no Friend of Significance here; We are in hopes they are not better acquainted than what the Suspicions of a Guilty conscience can produce.'[60]

Ministerial Panic and Political Dissimulation

By the time Townshend, who had accompanied George I to Hanover, received the letters, the three ships seen by Deane were reported to have landed in Cadiz after stopping in Ireland and Scotland, apparently laden with arms and naval stores for the Spanish government.[61] His alarmed response was immediate. Believing that the situation, '. . . might not only have been dangerous, but even fatal, if it had not been discovered in time,' Townshend wrote to Newcastle of what he was sure was a Jacobite/Holstein plot. He understood Stirling's reference to 'goods' to denote arms provided by the 'factory', or the court of St Petersburg, for '. . . an attempt upon us next spring', in which not only Russia, but also Spain and Austria were involved, according to the rumoured secret Jacobite article included in the Treaty of Vienna. The collaboration of the Duke of Holstein in the conspiracy appeared to be confirmed by recent intelligence sent to Walpole from the letters of Swedish and Holstein ministers.[62]

Townshend's proposed course of action was comprehensive. Firstly, he ordered Newcastle to maintain absolute secrecy after he had informed Walpole; the ministry would then have the advantage of surprise and six months left, '. . . for defeating the wicked intentions of our enemies'. Secondly, he pressed for Britain to do its utmost to strengthen its diplomatic position by bringing Sweden, Holland and Hesse into the Alliance of Hanover, concluded between Britain, France and Prussia in September.[63] Newcastle was ordered to send General Wade to carry out 'the strictest search' of the Highlands for the arms left by the Russian ships, to ensure that Fort Augustus and Inverness be fortified against attack. In addition, George I was in favour of sending naval reinforcements to the West Indies to obstruct financial assistance from Spanish colonies, and of capturing the next two Russian ships as they left the Baltic.[64]

Walpole, on the other hand, was reluctant to send ships to the West Indies; not only would such a move trigger domestic and parliamentary alarm, but it would weaken Britain's defence of its own coasts. He was also reluctant to risk war by seizing the Russian ships sailing to Spain on the basis of rumour,[65] but a

---

60 Hease to Messrs Butler and Kelly Marchmont, Copy, PRO SP 91/107.
61 Holzendorf (Stanhope's secretary) to Tilson, 11/9/1725, PRO SP 94/93, unfol.
62 Townshend to Newcastle, 23/9 or 4/10/1725, in Coxe, *Robert Walpole*, 2, pp.480–484.
63 Chance, *Alliance of Hanover*, p.72.
64 *Ibid.*
65 Walpole to Townshend, 2/13 October 1725, Coxe, *Robert Walpole*, 2, pp.485–6.

report that the Russian fleet was arming at Reval forced him to promise that 10,000 seamen and 30 or 40 ships of the line would be discreetly prepared for war early the following year.[66] The threat he claimed to anticipate was not an attack on north Germany, but a three-pronged invasion of Britain. He wrote,

> . . . I must confess the apprehensions of some design next spring, obtain so much with me, that I think it deserves the greatest attention . . . the design at present appears to me in this light: the difficulty that Spain is under to furnish ships or to equip them, has made it necessary for Russia to supply the ships . . . the movements . . . in the Russian fleet, has the appearance of a fleet's being designed to come early from thence, and to sail at the same time with the embarkation design'ed from Spain, one probably for Scotland, the other for the west of England; and if the emperor engages in the design, the land forces, that must have the greatest share in the execution of this project, must be had for Flanders, by way of Ostend.[67]

His solution was simply to rely on the Royal Navy, confident that '. . . a sufficient fleet, sent early enough to the Baltick, and another to be employed in our own seas, as occurrences shall direct, and to guard our own coast, may probably defeat the project'.[68]

That this was a Jacobite scare, rather than a cover for the defence of Hanover, is beyond question. General Wade's search of the Highlands and particularly the island of Lewis, where the ships had landed,[69] Robert Walpole's interception of letters arriving in Paris, Hamburg and Leyden for Jacobite bankers and merchants, and the examination of the packet boats of the Jacobite merchant Croagh at Amsterdam, were all measures specifically directed against Jacobite intrigue.[70] Likewise, the decision to retain the bulk of the Royal Navy on British coasts acknowledged the possibility of a Jacobite invasion. At home, rioting in Scotland in June following the introduction of the controversial malt tax, had prompted parliamentary legislation to disarm the Highland clans.[71] British ministers in Europe were put on their guard against Jacobite conspirators, of which there were many. Robinson in Paris reported the young Swedish representative there, Cederhielm, to be pro-Jacobite.[72] This redoubled Townshend's concern at the sending of Count Golovin, '. . . one of the most noted jacobites of all Russia', as ambassador to Stockholm.[73] News of the embassy of the Jacobite Duke of Wharton to Vienna

66 R.Walpole to Townshend, 12/21 October 1725, Coxe, *Robert Walpole*, 2, pp.487–488.
67 R.Walpole to Townshend, 12/21 October 1725, Coxe, *Robert Walpole*, 2, pp.487–488.
68 R.Walpole to Townshend, 12/21 October 1725, Coxe, *Robert Walpole*, 2, pp.487–488.
69 Townshend to Newcastle, 4/10/1725 n.s., in Coxe, *Robert Walpole*, 2, pp.485–6.
70 The Hamburg post master checked the mail of the banker Drusina; the post office at Leyden did the same to the mail of a Rotterdam merchant, John Archdeacon. Townshend to R.Walpole, 15/26 October 1725, CUL CH 1250.
71 Cobbett, *Parliamentary History*, 8, p.483.
72 Robinson to Townshend, 8/19 July 1725, BL Add.Ms. 32743, ff.479–481.
73 Townshend to Newcastle, 4/10/1725 n.s., Coxe, *Robert Walpole*, 2, p.481.

in July aroused fears that he was facilitating an alliance between Austria, Russia and Sweden.[74] From St Petersburg Campredon sent information that Tolstoi, Menshikov and the Holstein minister Bassewitz were winning support for the Holstein faction, which was co-operating with the Jacobites.[75] In September news came that Austria was sending the Livonian Löwenwold, a friend of the Jacobite Duke of Wharton, to St Petersburg to negotiate an Austro-Russian alliance.[76] Meanwhile frequent accounts of Ripperda's support for the Jacobites at Vienna reached Britain from the informant there, Petküm.[77] At the same time Britain learned of Spanish plans to send General Seissan, a suspected Jacobite, as ambassador to Russia for imminent negotiations.[78] The ministry was disturbed by the favour the Jacobite Duke of Ormonde enjoyed at the Spanish court, and was informed that Spain had paid four million crowns into a bank in Amsterdam, possibly for Jacobite use.[79]

Of course it is difficult to isolate the 'anti-Jacobite' element within what was a government response to a more comprehensive threat. Just as the phantom of invasion was lent substance by the Jacobites' involvement in every European quarrel which could be detrimental to Britain, so the threat created by Jacobite intrigue was not confined to a Jacobite restoration attempt alone. Wherever ministers turned Jacobites were plotting against them. British concern at the presence of Jacobite agents in Vienna, Stockholm, St Petersburg or Madrid was inevitably and inextricably linked with its concern over the Holstein question, the security of Hanover, Baltic trade, Spanish claims on Gibraltar and Port Mahon, and every other source of political and territorial rivalry. The conclusion in September of the Treaty of Hanover between France, Britain and Prussia was a direct reaction to Britain's crisis in north and south, to which Jacobitism had made a significant contribution.

To complicate matters, there is also evidence that the ministry actually used the Jacobite threat for its own ends once it had allayed its initial fears over the danger posed by the ships. It has been observed that '. . . one of the chief sources of Sir Robert Walpole's strength in opposing the allies of Vienna was the support given, or supposed to be given, by them to the Pretender'.[80] Walpole also wrote to Townshend rather ambiguously at the height of the Jacobite alarm of 1725 that

> . . . If we are to be engaged in a war . . . tis to be wished that this nation may think an invasion, the support of the Pretender, and the cause of the protestant succession are the chief and principal motives that obliged us to part with that peace . . . which we now enjoy.[81]

74 Newcastle to Walpole, 6/8/1725 o.s., BL Add.Ms. 33199, ff.323–4.
75 Campredon to Morville, 18/8/1725, *SIRIO* 58, pp.501–506.
76 Carrard (Vienna) to Townshend, 29/9/1725, PRO SP 80/56, ff.64–5; Count Rabutin was in fact sent in his place.
77 Petküm to [Townshend], 22/9/1725, PRO SP 80/56, ff.56–58.
78 Walpole to Townshend, 16/9/1725, BL Add.Ms. 32744, f.257.
79 Townshend to Newcastle, 4/10/1725 n.s., Coxe, *Robert Walpole*, 2, p.483.
80 B.Williams, 'The Foreign Policy of England under Walpole', *EHR* 15 (1900), p.669.
81 Walpole to Townshend, 2/13 October 1725, Coxe, *Robert Walpole*, 2, p.486.

The mystery of the origin and true purpose of the ships was not resolved, but secret investigations ordered by Townshend and Newcastle not only in Russia, but in France,[82] Prussia,[83] Spain,[84] Sweden[85] and Hamburg,[86] into the source and mission of the Jacobite ships proved inconclusive. Cyril Wich in Hamburg discovered nothing.[87] Horatio Walpole in Paris received information that Campredon was conveying Jacobite letters from Petersburg and had failed to inform the Duke of Bourbon at all of the three suspect ships.[88] Townshend informed Poyntz in Sweden of the imminence of a Russo-Austrian alliance, warning that if Sweden then sided with Russia, '. . . you will see that the Jacobites' scheme is not so ill laid, and you will find that that kingdom will soon be made too hot for you'.[89] Nevertheless, Poyntz could only discover that Captain St Leger was attempting to procure a ship and some 'miserably old and unfit' weapons from the Swedish government. He concluded that '. . . affairs in Russia tend so fast to confusion that his Majesty may be perfectly easy from that quarter'.[90] He did hear of a Russian ship near Gothenburg, whose commander, the Jacobite John Serocold, was trying unsuccessfully to enlist navigators for a Russian expedition in the spring, but it returned to Russia, not to Spain. Nor was there any information regarding the arrival of William Hease in Sweden.[91] In response to rumours of a Russian-assisted Jacobite attack from Spain,[92] Stanhope, after lengthy inquiry, reported that the three Russian ships had landed at Cadiz on 28 August in order to trade with Spain, having been forced by storms to shelter in Scotland. The Russian minister in Spain, he wrote, had no information of any Russo-Spanish conspiracy, and ridiculed the idea as contrary to Russian interests.[93]

Stanhope's memorial appeared to find confirmation in the account of James Young, a sailor on one of the ships. Interviewed by John Deane two years after the event, he maintained that the ships had been laden with naval stores, and carried only a few small arms and cannon, that they had stopped on the island of Lewis only to mend a leak, and in Ireland to refit a mast. He denied that they had unloaded any arms, although they had received visitors on board.[94] They had wintered at

82 Newcastle to Walpole, 5/10/1725, BL Add.Ms.33199, f.336.
83 Townshend to King Frederick Wilhelm, 24/9 or 5/10/1725, PRO SP 102/46 unfol; Du Bourgay to Townshend, 13/10/1725, PRO SP 43/7, ff.251–253v.
84 Townshend to Stanhope, 19/10/1725, PRO SP 43/7, ff.292–295.
85 Poyntz to Townshend, 5/10/1725 o.s., PRO SP 95/39, ff.2–9v.
86 Wich to Townshend, 24/10/1725, PRO 82/42, ff.271–273v.
87 Wich, 24/10 to 17/11/1725, PRO 82/42.
88 H.Walpole to Townshend, 6/17 October, 1725, BL Add.Ms.32744 ff.362–376.
89 Townshend to Poyntz, 25/10 or 5/11/1725, Chance, *Diplomatic Instructions*, 1 Sweden, p.199.
90 Poyntz to Townshend, 5/10/1725 o.s., PRO SP 95/39, ff.2–9v; 14/10/1725, PRO SP 43/8, ff.7–13v.
91 Townshend to R.Walpole, 15/26 October 1725, CUL CH 1250.
92 Walpole to Townshend, 30/11/1725, BL Add.Ms.32744, f.384.
93 Memorial by Stanhope on the Russian ships, 24/11 or 5/12/1725, BL Add.Ms.32744, ff.559–564.
94 Account of an interview with James Young written by John Deane, 14/11/1727, PRO SP 100/52, unfol.

Santander and returned to Reval in May 1726. Deane, acting as interpreter with the British squadron in the Baltic at that time, learned from the Russian minister, who had visited the ships, that they contained nothing of significance.[95] It appeared that the government, after all, had had no serious grounds for concern.

Rather than responding favourably to these encouraging accounts, however, Townshend continued to give the impression that he viewed the Jacobite threat as serious. He advocated having the three ships seized and searched as secretly as possible.[96] He dismissed the rumour that Spain was arming to regain Gibraltar, maintaining that its real intention was '. . . towards supporting the Jacobite scheme concerted between the Courts of Madrid and Peters-burg'.[97] He even went as far as to attempt to incite Turkish hostilities against Russia allegedly to avert the Jacobite threat. By his own account he intended

> . . . to create Troubles in her [Catherine's] Dominions in order to render her less able to carry on the Jacobite Scheme, and give his Majesty Disturbance in his own Kingdoms.[98]

Townshend's motives for exaggerating the Jacobite threat probably had more to do with countering a more general vulnerability generated by Britain's poor diplomatic position. By demonstrating that Britain was '. . . not at all prepared against any rupture',[99] he persuaded Walpole to support the inclusion in the King's speech to parliament for 1726 of a clause for the immediate arming of a large fleet, ostensibly '. . . to defeat attempts upon Great Britain'.[100] In fact, he intended to remove the Russian threat both to Britain and Hanover at source by using a British fleet in the Baltic to encourage Sweden to accede to the Treaty of Hanover. As he had told Poyntz after the discovery of the Jacobite letters, '. . . bringing about the accession of Sweden to this treaty is the most acceptable and most important service you can do the King at this juncture'.[101] Naturally, the threat of a Jacobite invasion in Britain was a more acceptable justification for the expense of a Baltic squadron than the need to defend Sweden, a non-ally, for what were partly Electoral interests.

The fact that British ministers used the Jacobite menace for wider political ends should not, however, detract from evidence of the government's genuine fear both of Jacobite invasion, and of the influence of Jacobite agents on international diplomacy. Townshend was sincere when he wrote that '. . . too great precaution cannot be used in hindering the least spark of rebellion's being kindled . . .'[102] Any risk to Britain's domestic stability or its position within Europe at such a critical time could not be taken lightly.

95 John Deane to Townshend, *Torbay* in Copenhagen roads, 26/4/1726 o.s., PRO SP 42/77 unfol.
96 Townshend to Newcastle, 4/11 or 15/11/1725, in Coxe *Robert Walpole*, 2, pp.490–1.
97 Townshend to Newcastle, 27/11/1725, PRO SP 43/8, ff.77–81v.
98 Townshend to Stanyan, 8/19 November 1725, PRO SP 43/8, f.98.
99 Townshend to Newcastle, 27/11/1725, PRO SP 43/8, f.80v.
100 Townshend to Walpole, 27/11/1725, Coxe, *Robert Walpole*, 2, pp.492–494.
101 Townshend to Poyntz, Chance, *Diplomatic Instructions*, 1 Sweden, pp.197–8.
102 Townshend to Newcastle, 27/11/1725, PRO SP 43/8, ff.77–81v.

'The Pretender and his Tools'[103]

While the British ministry was preoccupied with investigations into the mysterious ships, the Jacobites were once again stepping up their approaches to Catherine I. The true extent of Jacobite success in negotiations with Russia in the summer of 1725 has been obscured by the mixture of rumour and speculation in British reports. Thomas Gordon was granted an audience with the Empress on 10 July, at which he almost certainly delivered the letters brought by William Hay, and presented the plan for Russian military support. He was assured that '. . . Kent [Catherine] had the same sentiments for le Gendre [James III] as Gumley [Peter I] had', and that the Empress would give her support once her domestic affairs were more stable.[104] By August, the Empress had informed the Duke of Holstein of Jacobite plans, which she considered, 'neither too difficult nor impracticable', and Gordon himself had had several audiences with both Holstein and his minister Bassewitz, who professed their support.[105] The most promising assurance Gordon received was that Campredon's efforts to ally Russia with France, Britain and Denmark were '. . . by the means of the Duke of Holstein, to be rejected', because '. . . an Arly [negotiation] is begun between Potter [the Emperor], Kent [Catherine] and Martin [Sweden].[106] William Hay left Russia on 18 August, carrying favourable Russian replies to James III's letters.[107] Throughout the remainder of the year, Gordon continued to report optimistically on Russia's readiness to co-operate with Austria, Spain and Sweden, and on Holstein's promise to assist the Jacobites.[108]

Curiously, although Gordon corresponded regularly with James III throughout this period, and was in contact with William Hay, he made no reference to the ships which, according to the intercepted letters, Hay and Stirling were sending to Spain. It seems difficult to believe, given the prospect of support from Spain, and the fact that Hay had been sent to solicit Russian military assistance, that Stirling and Hay were merely involved in an innocent trading venture. This view is supported by certain phrases in the letters, particularly the assurance that, '. . . Prince Dolgoruky and prince Kourakin have instructions to close with such as you appoint to treat with them'. Also, as Townshend noted, Stirling referred to O'Connor's desire to go to Spain '. . . to be near your [the recipient's] favours', suggesting that his letter was written not to a banker, but to a leading Jacobite in Spain, possibly the Duke of Ormonde.[109] Ormonde, the Duke of Liria and the Duke of Wharton, were

103 Poyntz to Townshend, 13/11/1725, PRO SP 95/39, f.148.
104 T.Gordon to le Gendre [James III], 17/7/1725, NAS Abercairney GD 24/1/859, f.290.
105 T.Gordon to James III, 18/8/1725, RA Stuart 85/61,62; NAS Abercairney GD 24/1/859, f.291; T.Gordon to Edwards [John Hay], 18/8/1725, RA Stuart 85/118.
106 T.Gordon to James III, August 1725, RA Stuart 85/117.
107 T.Gordon to James III, 21/8/1725, NAS Abercairney GD 24/1/859, f.292.
108 T.Gordon to James III, 18/9/1725, NAS Abercairney GD 24/1/859, f.292; T.Gordon to John Hay, 13/11/1725, Ibid., f.294; T.Gordon to James III, 13/11/1725, RA Stuart 87/72.
109 H.Stirling to [Ormonde], 25/7/1725, Coxe, *Robert Walpole*, 2, pp.484–485.

all at that time involved in Jacobite negotiations at Madrid and Vienna. The existence of the Russian ships, their landing in Scotland and Ireland, and efforts by Jacobites in Sweden to obtain arms and ships there, were corroborated in Poyntz's reports.[110] A letter from John Serocold to Golovin in Sweden, who supported both Holstein and the Jacobites, indicated that the recruitment of pilots was linked to '. . . a design of attacking Sleswik next Spring',[111] and subsequent interception of Golovin's letters linked these plans exclusively with Jacobites in the Russian navy. Gordon and Saunders had signed the orders, Duffus was to pay Golovin '332 Reichtaler, 23 slyvers'(sic), for his assistance, and the 17 pilots were '. . . to have done long voyages', particularly 'in the north East navigation', that is, near the British coasts.[112]

Exactly what the enterprise was that involved so many Jacobite supporters and aroused so much ministerial suspicion remains a mystery. Whatever the truth of the matter, it remains a strong possibility that some form of intrigue against Britain was involved, with Jacobitism as the motivating force. Although Poyntz himself, when his investigations proved inconclusive, wrote that '. . . one would almost suspect the letters from Petersburg to be a fiction,'[113] he later assured Townshend that, despite this, he '. . . never made the least doubt but the Pretender and his Tools were capable of it'.[114] What emerges is not that British ministers exaggerated or falsified their information; the Jacobites were indeed involved in a wide range of activity directed against George I, and Russia was rightly called '. . . Muscovy, the very nest of the most desperate Jacobites that are abroad'.[115] Unfortunately for the Jacobites, despite the initial, and possibly well-founded fears of the British government, their efforts appear to have lacked the unity and co-ordination which might have made them effective.

British Confidence Undermined, 1726

In the aftermath of the Treaties of Vienna and Hanover, despite the political rift in Europe, there was an air of ministerial confidence in Britain that a strong fleet sent to the Baltic in early spring would be adequate defence against the northern threat, and would '. . . render all [Jacobite] . . . projects vain and abortive'.[116] Concerted efforts, particularly in Sweden, to increase the membership of the Hanover alliance, and a secret conspiracy to incite Turkish hostility towards Russia,[117] were con-

110 Poyntz to Newcastle, 7/7/1725, PRO 95/30, ff.31–32v., Poyntz to Townshend, 5/10/1725, PRO SP 95/39, ff.2–9v., Poyntz to Townshend, 13/11/1725, PRO SP 95/39, ff.136–147.
111 Poyntz to Townshend, 20/10/1725, PRO 95/39, ff.83–85.
112 Copy of translation of Golovin's letters to the Empress, 27/11/1725, 12/2/1726, 4/3/1726, PRO SP 95/47, ff.88–89.
113 Poyntz to Townshend, 14/10/1725 o.s., PRO SP 43/8, f.12.
114 Poyntz to Townshend, 13/11/1725, PRO SP 95/39, f.148.
115 Robinson to Newcastle, 20/4/1726, BL Add.Ms.32745, f.450.
116 George I's Address to Parliament, January 1726, Cobbett, *Parliamentary History*, 8, p.491.
117 Townshend's instructions to Abraham Stanyan in Constantinople, 19/11/1725, PRO SP 43/8, ff.97–101.

sidered sufficient to counter even the reportedly imminent Russian invasion of north Germany.[118] The shattering of this confidence owed much to the hostility of Spain and Austria, but it was in fact Russia which posed the greatest threat. The conclusion that Jacobite hopes of Russian military aid '. . . were minor compared to those of Austrian and Spanish assistance'[119] does not take full account either of Catherine I's sentiments or of the contact between Russia, Sweden and the allies of Vienna, which the Jacobites helped to promote.

The Jacobites' principal aim in 1726 remained to engineer an alliance between Russia, Sweden and the allies of Vienna. Sir John Graeme, James III's minister in Vienna, described

> . . . the Conclusion of the Alliances as the first great step towards a restoration, a declaration of War the next, and then I think it will be in a fairer way than ever it has been since the usurpation.[120]

There was, therefore, keen Jacobite support for Russia's desire to have Austria included in the Treaty of Stockholm, concluded with Sweden in 1724, and when Vienna agreed to send an envoy, Count Rabutin, to St Petersburg, Thomas Gordon was sent full powers to treat with him to promote the alliance, and ensured that he was '. . . fully instructed in the King's affairs'.[121]

In January the Duke of Wharton wrote to Gordon from Vienna on James III's orders to request Russian assistance, both in providing military aid, and in persuading the Emperor to do so. He proposed that 6,000 men, landed from Ostend, would be sufficient to overthrow the monarchy.[122] At the same time, Gordon was in correspondence with Count Nikolai Golovin, the Russian envoy in Stockholm, who was under specific orders to foil Poyntz's attempts to win Sweden to the Hanover Alliance. Golovin was actively furthering both Jacobite and Holstein interests there, and he reported to Gordon that '. . . a good project is forming in favour of Mr Williams trade [James III]'.[123] On 6 February, Gordon met with Bassowitz, the Duke of Holstein's minister, to discuss Wharton's letter.[124] Subsequently, Holstein himself had a conference with the Empress on the matter, and Gordon reported back to Wharton, to Graeme, and to James III's secretary in Rome that both Catherine and Osterman, her first minister, had promised Russian support, on the condition that Austria would do the same.[125]

In March 1726 the promised British squadron of 24 ships under the

---

118 Campredon reported from St Petersburg that a large-scale Russian invasion of Bremen with Danish and Imperial assistance was intended for the summer, and that Austria, Denmark, Spain and Sweden were already negotiating against the allies of Hanover. Campredon to Louis XV, 3/1/1726, *SIRIO* 64, pp.172–199.
119 J.Black, *British Foreign Policy in the Age of Walpole*, p.146.
120 Graeme to John Hay, 20/4/1726, RA Stuart 93/6.
121 T.Gordon to [ ], 13/11/1725, RA Stuart 87/72.
122 Wharton to T.Gordon, 19/1/1726, NAS Abercairney GD 24/1/859, RA Stuart 89/114.
123 T.Gordon to John Hay, 11/1/1726, NAS Abercairney, GD 24/1/859.
124 T.Gordon to John Hay, NAS Abercairney, GD 24/1/859 f.297.
125 T.Gordon to Hay, Graeme, Wharton, RA Stuart 90/116, 117.

command of Vice-Admiral Sir Charles Wager was sent to the Baltic, confident that it could intimidate Russia. Britain's official justification for this potentially hostile presence on the Russian coast placed great emphasis on Russia's alleged encouragement of the Jacobites as a ground for enmity. It was written into Wager's instructions that the ministry had, '. . . received undoubted intelligence of the court of Petersburg having entered into measures in favour of the Pretender and his adherents', and that the squadron was necessary to protect '. . . the peace and security of this Our Kingdom'. Wager was given a free rein to take offensive action against the Russian fleet, and even to destroy it should it attempt to leave port.[126] He also conveyed a letter from George I to Catherine I, which maintained that the Russians had '. . . without the least provocation on our part', taken '. . . measures in favour of the Pretender to Our Crown' and given '. . . great Encouragement to his adherents'.[127]

Catherine responded directly and explosively to these accusations, expressing outrage that Britain had not had the courtesy to explain itself prior to sending a fleet and blaming it for the break-down of reconciliation attempts. She protested that

> . . . as they could find out nothing else, so this old stuff and false accusation must be again produced, and as it has been a covering to all former unfriendly proceedings against us, so tis now to this extraordinary one.[128]

Just as her husband had done, she accused the ministry of inventing Russo-Jacobite conspiracy, maintaining that it was not in Russia's interest to risk British hostility by such activities.[129]

Although there is a case for accepting Britain's allegations of Jacobite intrigue as the principal motive for sending a Baltic fleet,[130] Wager's instructions suggest that Jacobitism was once more being used to veil more sensitive aims. These were, namely, to avert a Russian attack on Sweden and Denmark, to encourage Sweden to accede to the Alliance of Hanover,[131] and to safeguard British Baltic trade.[132] Townshend actually admitted that he was concealing from parliament, '. . . the real motives of sending this squadron', which Poyntz termed '. . . the two grand aims', Sweden's accession and its defence.[133]

---

126 Instructions to Sir Charles Wager, Chance, *Diplomatic Instructions*, 1 Sweden, p.207.
127 George I to Catherine I, PRO SP 102/50 ff.11–16.
128 15/6/1725 o.s., English translation from original German of Catherine I's reply to George I's letter of 11/4/1725, PRO SP 102/50 ff.17–19.
129 *Ibid.*
130 Ilse Jacob maintained in her work on Russo-Turkish relations that Wager's squadron was sent with the primary purpose of forestalling a Jacobite invasion, *Russland und die Turkei*, pp.103–4.
131 Townshend to Poyntz, 25/10/1725, Chance, *Diplomatic Instructions*, 1 Sweden, pp.197–8. Having been promised by the anti-Holstein minister Count Horn that a British fleet would secure Sweden's accession, Townshend had taken the calculated risk of promising British assistance, believing that '. . . after making so great an expense for the protection of Sweden surely the King might in return expect to have the accession finished all at one stroke'. Townshend to Poyntz, 22/3/1726 o.s., PRO SP 95/42, ff.192–202.
132 Instructions to Sir Charles Wager, Chance, *Diplomatic Instructions*, 1 Sweden, p.207; PRO SP 44/65.
133 Poyntz to Townshend, 27/5/1726, PRO SP 95/43, ff.85–93v.

Catherine I's response, likewise, focused on Jacobitism as a means of avoiding the central controversy over the Duke of Holstein and Austro-Russian negotiations.

Between Wager's departure from Britain and his arrival outside Reval on 8 June, however, several momentous events changed the face of European politics, making Britain aware that the Jacobite threat from the north had become a more serious one. Whatever Britain's motives had been for sending a squadron to the Baltic, the decision to do so was vindicated by a new, potentially dangerous international situation.

Firstly, on 16 and 17 April, to the great dismay of the ministry and shock of Poyntz in Sweden, Austria acceded to the Treaty of Stockholm, formally aligning itself with Russia and Sweden. The arrival of Rabutin in St Petersburg soon afterwards was welcomed by the Jacobites as a preliminary to Swedish and Russian accession to the Alliance of Vienna, which would be '. . . a mortal stroke to the family of Hanover'.[134] Britain's alarm coincided with rumours that Catherine I had invited Friedrich Wilhelm of Prussia to defect from the Alliance of Hanover, and that he '. . . pressed the execution of the Russes wild projects with greater heat than any of the duke of Holstein's ministers, or most devoted friends'.[135]

Secondly, in the same month, the actions of Baron Ripperda, the Queen of Spain's agent, confirmed British suspicions that Catherine I was involved in the web of Jacobite intrigue stretching between Vienna, Madrid and St Petersburg. His triumphant return to Madrid in December 1725 after concluding the Treaty of Vienna had been followed by his promotion to Secretary of State, with control of foreign affairs. Very soon, however, his efforts to provide Austria with subsidies according to the treaty agreement had left his administration in critical financial difficulties, which he had attempted to remedy by sending for revenue from the West Indies. While awaiting its arrival, he had distracted Britain by spreading rumours to the effect that the Treaty of Vienna had contained clauses for the restoration of James III, for the seizure of Gibraltar from Britain, and for the support of the Ostend Company's trade in the East Indies. His claims had been reinforced by his attempts to undermine the Anglo-French alliance, and his frequent contact with the Duke of Wharton, both in Vienna in autumn 1725, and when Wharton came to Madrid in April 1726. It was in April that Stanhope and the Dutch minister Van der Meer received information of two plans for the restoration of James III, one by the Duke of Liria, the son of the Duke of Berwick, the other by Wharton himself.[136] In May, when Spain was nearing financial ruin, Ripperda, to the shock and disgust of the Jacobites, took refuge in Stanhope's house, gave him an account of the alleged secret clauses in the Treaty of Vienna and showed Stanhope and Benjamin Keene the two Jacobite projects.

134 Graeme to J.Hay 20/4/1726, RA Stuart 93/6.
135 Du Bourgay to Townshend, 19/30 April 1726, PRO SP 90/20 unfol.
136 Stanhope to Newcastle, 22/4/1726, PRO SP 94/94, ff.110–119.

According to Keene's report, Liria, in February, had proposed a Spanish naval expedition from Navarre with the assistance of 6,000 imperial troops embarking at Ostend, all under the command of the Duke of Ormonde and the Earl Marischal.[137] Wharton's plan, meanwhile, depended for its execution on Russian naval assistance. It was proposed that the Empress send to Scotland 10,000 troops with arms and transports to come under the command of the Earl Marischal, and to act as an encouragement to raise support in the Highlands. The King of Spain was to embark 8,000 men from Galicia under the Duke of Ormonde, while the Emperor gathered 6,000 at Ostend and ensured that the Dutch could not assist Britain. Wharton included elements of Liria's naval plan, for which the King of Spain was expected to advance 60,000 piastres. In addition, the Jacobites in France and England had, according to Wharton, £2,000,000 and 20,000 arms in France. The success of the enterprise, however, depended on the Russian naval attack occurring while the British navy was away from port. Spain's reward, should the plan succeed, was to be the restoration of Gibraltar and Port Mahon, and the granting of trade privileges. The Emperor would be guaranteed the right of the Ostend Company to trade in the East Indies, hitherto challenged by Britain. Russian gains, although not mentioned, would presumably have favoured the Duke of Holstein. James III himself was to finalise the project in Vienna and St Petersburg and then embark for Britain from Archangel.[138]

The authenticity of Wharton's plan has not been questioned,[139] despite the fact that Benjamin Keene's report of Ripperda's confession was the only detailed account of it.[140] According to Ripperda and Keene, Wharton had been sent by the Emperor to communicate the plan to the Spanish court. Ripperda had apparently shown Stanhope the plans of both Liria and Wharton in their own handwriting, at the very time when the authors were demanding through his wife that he return them.[141] However, Wharton's plan, which had been formulated prior to his arrival at Madrid in April to discuss its contents, had not been communicated either to Graeme in Vienna or to Gordon in St Petersburg. Wharton's letter to Thomas Gordon of January 1726 leaves no doubt that he hoped for Catherine I's support in persuading the Emperor to provide 6,000 men at Ostend, but at this stage he had not planned Russian military assistance in detail.[142] Wharton did leave Vienna for Madrid in February 1726 on '. . . a commission of his King', and did meet with the

---

137 Stanhope to Newcastle, 30/7/1726, Coxe *Robert Walpole*, 2, p.612. 'Substance d'un projet qui fut donne au ministre le mois de Janvier dernier par Monsr L.D.L. [Le Duc de Liria] contenant ce qui suit', encl. in Finch to Townshend, 7/5/1726 n.s., PRO SP 84/290, ff.59–60.

138 Benjamin Keene to Newcastle, Coxe, *Robert Walpole*, 2, pp.606,608.

139 B.Williams, *EHR* 15, p.671; Chance, *The Alliance of Hanover*, pp.241,242.

140 Benjamin Keene to Newcastle, 15/6/1726, Coxe, *Robert Walpole*, 2, pp.606, 608.

141 *Ibid.*

142 This was the letter which Gordon had presented to the Russian court, and probably the one Graeme reported showing to Sinzendorf in March. Sinzendorf had expressed doubt that James III could go to Ostend, which implies that the letter he read was Wharton's letter of January, rather than the plan. Graeme to John Hay, 23/3/1726, RA Stuart 92/23.

Russian minister there.[143] However, prior to April their correspondence concerned only what was contained in Wharton's January letter. If Wharton's plan existed in the form Keene, Stanhope and Ripperda claimed, then it remained at the negotiating stage in Spain, and did not reach Russia itself.

Regardless of the veracity of Ripperda's account, however, the plan, coupled with intelligence that a French Jacobite, Lambilly, carrying 80,000 Spanish pistoles and a commission to buy Russian ships, was travelling to St Petersburg at Ripperda's request, convinced the ministry of Russian involvement in Jacobite conspiracy. This was further confirmed by news that the Russian ambassador at Madrid, Golitsyn, had been ordered by his mistress, Catherine, to send an account of Spanish military strength.[144] A report that James III had left Rome on a mysterious journey was sufficient to arouse a minor panic in the ministry. Although he returned after a week, Newcastle suspected that

> . . . he is, in concert with the court of Vienna, gone to some private place, there to remain till the scheme shall be more compleat, and the Emperor shall think fit openly to avow and espouse him; and as the discourse of the Jacobites, as well as the advices both from Petersburg and Berlin give reason to suspect that some disturbance will soon be endeavoured from the north.[145]

By the time Vice-Admiral Wager with his squadron arrived near Reval, therefore, British confidence had been replaced with anxiety, and concerted efforts were being made to counter what was now regarded as a serious Russian threat. The ministry had had Campredon recalled from St Petersburg on suspicion that he was involved with Holstein and the Jacobites,[146] and financial incentives had been distributed in Stockholm,[147] Vienna[148] and St Petersburg[149] to try to increase support for the allies of Hanover. Realising Wharton's dangerous influence, George I sent him a personal letter, commanding him to return home, which he ignored.[150] Preparations were also made for the formation of a large army to safeguard northern Germany against a possible Russian invasion.

Quelling the Jacobite Threat?

While it is true that the Jacobite threat from Russia was, for five months in 1726, effectively '. . . quelled by the British naval movement to Baltic waters',[151] this

143 Wharton to Sinzendorf, 2/3/1726, RA Stuart 91/43; John Hay to T.Gordon, 18/5/1726, RA Stuart 94/5.
144 Stanhope to Stanyan, 29/4/1726 n.s., PRO SP 94/94, f.134, Stanhope to Newcastle, 6/5/1726, PRO SP 94/94, ff.138–145v.
145 Newcastle to H.Walpole, 17/5/1726, Legg, *Diplomatic Instructions*, 4 France, p.158; BL Add.Ms.32746, f.73v.
146 Newcastle to Robinson, 4/4/1726 o.s., BL Add.Ms. 32745, ff.411–420.
147 Townshend to Poyntz, 13/7/1726, Chance, *Diplomatic Instructions*, 1 Sweden, p.226.
148 Graeme to John Hay, 4/5/1726, RA Stuart 93/74.
149 Campredon is reported to have spent 60,000 ducats to this end in Russia. Solov'ev, *Istoriya Rossii*, 19, p.960.
150 George I to Wharton, 4/5/1726, RA Stuart 94/84.
151 J.Black, *British Foreign Policy in the Age of Walpole*, p.146.

does not mean that the gravity of the threat should be underestimated, nor that the success of Wager's mission should be overestimated. Wager, in fact, enjoyed only mixed success. Between May and September, while the squadron was in the Baltic, the threat of a European war and with it a Jacobite invasion had loomed nearer, and Townshend was rightly sceptical of Catherine I's disclaimers of Jacobite involvement:

> . . . We know not in what sense they understand engagements, but we are certain that his agents are countenanced and caressed at Petersburg, that there have been plans projects and intrigues in his favour jointly with other princes, and that his adherents have placed great hopes in the assistance of the Muscovites.[152]

When Wager arrived on the Russian coast, he received a report from Cronstadt that twenty ships-of-the-line and two bomb vessels, fully prepared with six weeks provisions, and an additional seven unrigged war ships and twelve galleys were at Catherine's immediate disposal, and that Cronstadt itself was very strongly fortified. There were a further hundred galleys at St Petersburg, and 26,000 men to man the fleet.[153] This confirmed British suspicions that Russia had been on the point of launching a naval expedition.[154] The strength of the Russian fleet was greater than Wager had expected, and he expressed his relief at having decided to remain at Reval,

> . . . for if I had gone near Cronslot they would have seen, in two or three days, that we could do them no hurt, whereas now they are still in fear that we have some design upon them.[155]

British naval superiority was marginal, and the outcome of a confrontation was by no means the foregone conclusion which might, with hindsight, be assumed.

Although the physical presence of a British squadron in Russian waters eliminated the immediate Jacobite threat, assessed in terms of its original purpose, to procure the accession of Sweden, it failed badly. Rumours in Stockholm that Britain sought to force Sweden into the Hanover Alliance, rather than discouraging the Holstein and Russian party, actually prompted many Swedes to approach Golovin for Russian assistance. In July, Poyntz's negotiations in Sweden suffered a set-back when Horn unexpectedly postponed further discussion of the accession until the Rikstag in September. Most importantly, Wager's presence failed to prevent Russia's accession to the Treaty of Vienna on 6 August, which, to Britain's horror, included a pledge by the Emperor to take arms to satisfy the demands of the Duke of Holstein, if he had not received compensation within a year.[156] Scarcely two weeks later, in St

---

152 Townshend to Wager, 26/7/1726 o.s., PRO SP 42/77, unfol.
153 Lt Barnett to Wager, 5/6/1726, PRO SP 42/77, unfol.
154 '. . . the Numbers of Gallies and Troops make it, I think, very plain that some Enterprise was intended . . .', Wager to Townshend, 9/6/1726 o.s., PRO SP 42/77, unfol.
155 Wager to Townshend, 26/6/1726, PRO SP 42/77, unfol.
156 Saint Saphorin to Townshend, 14/8/1726, PRO SP 80/58, unfol.

Petersburg on 21 August, Prussia seceded from the Alliance of Hanover and allied with Russia. In September it was reported that Catherine was marching 14,000 men towards Riga, to be reinforced by 40,000 more Russians, 16,000 Imperial troops and possibly also Prussians ready for an attack on France. This would almost certainly discourage Sweden from taking the side of Britain and France at a time when they most needed its support.[157] Although Wager was ordered to restrain the Russian fleet until the Swedish Rikstag in September, it was apparent that the British presence could not exert the necessary political influence, and he was forced to return to Britain without securing a Swedish alliance.[158] He had not held Jacobite intrigue at bay, and at his departure Britain's vulnerability to the Jacobite threat from Russia was not diminished, but increased.

Jacobitism and International Hostility

Although the British squadron did eliminate the immediate possibility of Russian assistance until September 1726, Russia's accession to the Alliance of Vienna in August introduced a prospect of war against George I which would certainly benefit the Jacobites. Townshend wrote in despair that '. . . The appearances of a War grow now stronger than ever and . . . an attempt may be made even before winter to bring a Body of Russian troops into the Empire'.[159] Francis Atterbury, meanwhile, described it as '. . . the greatest occasion that ever presented itself'.[160] In Russia, correspondence between Jacobites and Russian ministers flagrantly belied Catherine's public denials of involvement with the Jacobite cause. In August James wrote to the favourite, Menshikov, who sat on the Supreme Privy Council, to the Duke of Holstein, and to his minister, Bassowitz, thanking them for their support, and asking them to negotiate with Thomas Gordon.[161] In October, Gordon was invited to a private audience, at which he delivered these letters. The Russian historian, Bantysh-Kamensky, not finding documentary evidence of a Russian response to James's letters, has concluded that there was none.[162] It is certain, however, that all three men met with Gordon to discuss the possibility of a restoration attempt, and that Menshikov declared his intention to write to James III in February.[163] Soon after the letters had been delivered, Gordon reported that '. . . Mulberry [Menshikov] express'd in strong terms his inclinations to Maxton [Jacobite restoration]', that Osterman had promised his support, and that Holstein '. . . is convinced that a Jacobite restoration is the only means for his satisfaction'. Gordon, who had full powers to negotiate with Russian and Imperial ministers, proposed to Osterman that orders be sent to Russian ministers in Vienna and Madrid to approach those courts in favour of James III, and that

157 H.Walpole to Newcastle, 3/9/1726, BL Add.Ms.32747, f.232v.
158 Townshend to Poyntz, 12/8/1726, PRO SP 95/43, ff.323–327v.
159 Townshend to Poyntz, 19/8/1726, PRO SP 95/46, f.366v.
160 Atterbury to James Keith, 8/7/1726, *HMC Eglinton* etc., p.218.
161 James III to Menshikov, Bassowitz, Holstein, RA Stuart 96/10.
162 N.N.Bantysh-Kamensky, *Obzor vneshnykh snoshenii Rossii*, p.131.
163 T.Gordon to John Hay, 14/2/1727, NAS Abercairney GD 24/1/859, f.307.

Kurakin in Paris be empowered to do the same in the hope that France would leave the Hanover Alliance.[164] Bassowitz and Osterman complied and sent proposals for joint Jacobite assistance to the Imperial minister Rabutin, to Kurakin and to the other courts, as promised.[165]

The Jacobite plan for military aid from Russia centred on the embarkation of a number of Russian ships from Archangel, presumably with the co-operation of troops and naval assistance from Russia's allies. This plan received the serious consideration of Russian ministers; in December, Osterman discussed with the Jacobites how the necessary ships could be provided, and Gordon was told that they, '. . . would not be wanting', as soon as Catherine was ready to act on the Jacobites' behalf.[166] In January 1727, however, when it was reported that Catherine intended to provide the Emperor with 30,000 men under the Jacobite General Peter Lacy for an attack on Hanover, Gordon was prepared to abandon the Archangel scheme in preference for a plan to occupy Hanover with the support of the Vienna allies.[167]

On an international level, Russia's accession to the Treaty of Vienna was of particular importance for the Jacobites in that it gave Spain both the impulse and the courage to make war on Britain. The sources of Anglo-Spanish hostility, Ripperda's alleged agreement with Austria to recover Gibraltar by force, and the consequent British naval presence both off Gibraltar and in the West Indies, cutting off revenue needed for armaments, had prompted Stanhope, on George I's instructions, to present a caustic memorial to the Spanish court in September. One of the main justifications given for British naval action was evidence of Russo-Spanish co-operation in favour of the Jacobites,[168] and Stanhope reported that the Spanish court was '. . . too much elevated and even intoxicated with their fancied irresistible power, upon their new additional strength from the Czarina's accession'.[169] Indeed, in late 1726, Spanish military preparations in Andalusia and all Stanhope's intelligence from Spain, suggested that an attack on Gibraltar was inevitable, and that this would be accompanied by a restoration attempt.[170] Newcastle was informed by one agent that 8–10,000 troops would be carried to Britain in fishing boats in one night, and that, with the assistance of Catherine I and the Emperor, '. . . it would not be in the power of his Majesty's ships to hinder their landing'.[171]

George I's address at the opening of Parliament in 1727, which had the support of Townshend and Walpole, presented the threat of Jacobite invasion in as serious a light as possible, drawing on every piece of information gleaned by

---

164 T.Gordon to John Hay, 29/10/1726, SRO Abercairney GD 24/1/859 f.305.
165 T.Gordon to John Hay, 21/1/1727, SRO Abercairney GD 24/1/859 ff.305–6; Gordon to Hay, 28/1/1727, *Ibid.* f.307.
166 T.Gordon to [ ], 3/12/1726, RA Stuart 99/122.
167 T.Gordon to John Hay, 28/1/1727, SRO Abercairney GD 24/1/859 f.307.
168 Stanhope to De la Paz, 25/9/1726 n.s., PRO SP 94/95, ff.33–35; Stanhope to Newcastle, 4/10/1726, PRO SP 94/95, ff.39–49v.
169 Stanhope to Newcastle, 18/9/1726, PRO SP 94/95, ff.7–7v.
170 Stanhope to Newcastle, 21/12/1726, PRO SP 94/95, ff.222–233.
171 William Windsor to Newcastle, 18/29 December 1726, PRO SP 94/214 unfol.

foreign ministers, including Ripperda's confession, to implicate Spain, Russia and the Empire in a conspiracy to invade Britain.[172] Although a primary motive for emphasising the Jacobite threat was to justify the expense of the three squadrons sent to sea in 1726, and to rally support for military preparations to defend Gibraltar,[173] the speech had the effect, not of intimidating the Allies of Vienna, but of antagonising them further. The Spanish minister in London, Pozobueno, had already written Stanhope on 1 January a refutation of British accusations of Jacobite involvement which virtually amounted to a declaration of war, and the King's speech only hastened the opening of the siege of Gibraltar in February.[174] The Emperor reacted so violently against Britain that the Imperial minister was expelled from London in March,[175] and Catherine I had her ministers Kurakin and Golovkin declare once more on her behalf that she had never been involved in any agreement with James III.[176] O'Brien who, like other Jacobites, was 'charmed' by the divisive effect of British allegations, observed with insight that, even were the ministry attempting to instil fear into the British people to exert '. . . un pouvoir despotique', the address to Parliament was counterproductive in that it fuelled public belief in the inevitability of foreign support, and thus encouraged the foreign powers in question.[177]

The Flame in the North

Britain's war with Spain redoubled the threat of Russia, its new ally, and Townshend warned, '. . . tho the fire begins so farr off as Gibraltar, yet the train is so laid that the flame would soon reach the north'.[178] Indeed, in December 1726, while Pozobueno was publicly declaring Spain's innocence of any Jacobite involvement, Philip V of Spain was vindicating British suspicions by appointing a Jacobite, James Fitzjames, Duke of Liria and grandson to James II through the illegitimate Duke of Berwick, to the post of Spanish ambassador in St Petersburg. Among Liria's instructions was the secret order to exert all his influence on the Empress to send a strong Russian fleet to Archangel, in order to overthrow the Hanoverian monarchy and restore James III with Spanish assistance.[179] He was simultaneously under secret orders to the same effect

172 George I's address to Parliament, 17/1/1727, Cobbett, 8, pp.523–5, 532–3, 535–42.
173 Assisted by evidence of Jacobite intrigue, the motion for military spending was carried by an overwhelming majority of 251 to 81. *Ibid.*
174 The siege of Gibraltar itself attracted large numbers of Jacobites, including James Keith, whose motive for participating was a '. . . meer necessity to be revenged on the English'. Keith, *A Fragment,* p.68.
175 Chance, *The Alliance of Hanover,* p.620.
176 Kurakin declared on Catherine I's orders '. . . qu'elle n'a jamais contracté aucun engagement avec le prétendant, et qu'elle regarde ces nouvelles débitées par les Ministres Englois pour des Veritables et pures Calomnies.' O'Brien to John Hay, 10/2/1727, RA Stuart 103/64,65; Robinson to Delafaye, 8/2/1727, PRO SP 75/185, f.13; printed declaration 4/2/1727, encl. in Dayrolle to Townshend, 21/2/1727, PRO SP 84/295, ff.48–49v.
177 Daniel O'Brien to John Hay, 10/2/1727, RA Stuart 103/66.
178 Townshend to Glenorchy, 23/12/1726 o.s., PRO SP 75/49, f.385
179 Philip V's creditive and secret instructions for Liria, 22/1/1727, 'Pis'ma o Rossii v Ispaniyu Duka de Liria', in Bartenev, *Osmnadsatyi vek istoricheskii sbornik* (Moscow, 1869), 2, p.11.

from James III, but concealed this fact from Philip V to avoid the possible interference of power politics in his Jacobite mission. His plan of negotiation, unlike his proposals to Ripperda the previous year, was to convince the Duke of Holstein and hence Catherine I, that he would only be free to achieve his ends after the removal of George I and the British Navy.[180]

Russia's accession to the Vienna Alliance and Britain's war with Spain greatly increased the Jacobites' prospects of foreign assistance from at least one of the allies. From Russia, although Catherine I never actually pledged military assistance, they had received verbal promises of support not only from the Empress, but from Osterman, Menshikov, Holstein and Bassowitz, reinforced by written proposals in their favour from these ministers to other European courts. Chancellor Sinzendorf had made it clear that Austria would not rule out Jacobite assistance in case of war, although it was reluctant to commit itself unilaterally.[181] Russian and Spanish disclaimers of Jacobite involvement, following the accusations levelled against them in George I's address, were true only in the narrowest sense. While Pozobueno's vehement memorial was robbed of all credibility by the embassy of Liria, so Kurakin, who had presented Catherine's official rejection of the allegations, was simultaneously receiving orders to lobby at Paris '. . . in favor of Williams [James III]'.[182]

The Flame Extinguished

Despite these promising circumstances, no amount of Jacobite negotiation, or of Russian receptivity to Jacobite proposals, could remove a number of serious obstacles to their ambitions, which eventually proved insurmountable. Firstly, despite the Anglo-Austrian rupture, Austria would not support the Jacobites unless it were involved in a war, and it was reluctant to commit itself to that. Throughout the spring of 1727, Britain repeatedly received intelligence that the Emperor, with Russian and Prussian aid, was poised for an invasion of George I's German dominions. However, Britain responded to these rumours by ensuring adequate military support from France, Sardinia, Holland and Denmark to deter Austria from taking the initiative. At the same time, despite mutual mistrust, Britain succeeded in drawing Austria into negotiations to avert war. Although Russian ministers approached Rabutin, the Imperial minister, on behalf of the Jacobites, he failed to respond to their requests.[183] By April it was apparent to the Jacobites that there was no assistance to be had from the Imperial quarter, and Liria confirmed on his arrival in Vienna in May that Austria was not to be trusted.[184] On 28 May the news finally arrived from Vienna that the terms of the allies of Hanover for an Anglo-Austrian agreement

180 His methods were less conventional; he intended to gain Holstein's confidence by '. . . the varietys of my wines', believing that '. . . in that part of the world all affairs are concluded on a bottle'. Liria to James III, March 1727, RA Stuart 104/71.
181 Sinzendorf to Palm, 21/12/1726, Coxe, *Robert Walpole*, 2, p.511.
182 T.Gordon to John Hay, 28/1/1727, NAS Abercairney GD 24/1/859, f.307.
183 Rabutin made the excuse that Chancellor Sinzendorf was ill. T.Gordon to John Hay, 21/1/1727, NAS Abercairney GD 24/1/859 ff.305–6.
184 Liria, 'Pis'ma o Rossii', in Bartenev, 2, p.11.

had been accepted, and to Britain's great 'joy and surprize' and the despair of the Jacobites, peace preliminaries were signed in Paris at the end of the month.[185] With this event, Jacobite hopes of joint Russian and Austrian support for a restoration came to an end.

Secondly, concerted British efforts in Sweden to defeat the Austro-Russian agreement in favour of the Duke of Holstein had a marked effect on Jacobite prospects. In October 1726 Britain had had its bitterest opponent at Stockholm, Count Vellingk, arrested on a pretext of misconduct. The repercussions of this were felt in Russia the following year, and proved a serious set-back to the Holstein party.[186] The final blow was struck in March, when Sweden was finally persuaded, at considerable financial cost to Britain, to accede to the Alliance of Hanover. This was a great victory for the government, and fatal for the Holstein and consequently the Jacobite movement in Russia. Gordon recorded the shock with which Holstein received the news, and observed that '. . . it seems to have this effect that Mulberry [Menshikov] is all'.[187] Although Menshikov had been prepared to declare his support for the Jacobites, he was deeply hostile towards the Duke of Holstein and his assumption of power effectively sounded the death knell for Jacobite support from the Holstein party.

The rather distant hope of support from France was also quashed. Kurakin approached the French court on the Jacobites' behalf, but reported back to Osterman that nothing would be forthcoming unless the Hanover Alliance were destroyed, a highly unlikely eventuality.[188]

British naval supremacy and Spanish military inadequacy doomed from the outset Spain's pretensions to Gibraltar. Liria's mission, although promising in its inception, was rendered ineffective by poor timing. He did not reach St Petersburg until February 1728, by which stage Jacobite fortunes in Russia had already deteriorated.

The final stroke of Jacobite ill-fortune, however, came with the death of Catherine I on 17 May 1727. Just prior to this, Magnan, the French representative at St Petersburg, had warned that Sweden's unexpected accession to the Alliance of Hanover had finally prompted the Empress to send a strong fleet to sea to contend the issue.[189] Britain, not wishing to jeopardise its new alliance, and not underestimating the Russian navy, immediately dispatched Admiral Norris with a strong force of 22 ships to the Baltic. At last it appeared that the two enemies would come into conflict. It was typical of Jacobite fortunes that the death of their principal source of hope should occur at such a juncture. However, it should be borne in mind that, unaided by its allies, Russian chances of success against the British fleet would in any case have been slim. Catherine's death removed the prospect of hostilities by marking the end

185 Townshend to Poyntz, 26/5/1727 o.s., PRO SP 95/47, ff.153–156.
186 T.Gordon to John Hay, 21/1/1727, NAS Abercairney GD 24/1/859, f.305.
187 T.Gordon to John Hay, 11/4/1727, NAS Abercairney GD 24/1/859 f.312.
188 T.Gordon to John Hay, 14/2/1727, NAS Abercairney GD 24/1/859 f.307.
189 Magnan to Morville, 26/4/1727, *SIRIO* 64, pp.551–556.

of Russian support for the Duke of Holstein and thus of a principal cause of the Anglo-Russian conflict which had encouraged the Jacobites.

It was, therefore, the death of Catherine I, not of Peter I, which turned the tide of Jacobite hopes of assistance from Russia. Between 1725 and 1727 the Jacobites had regarded Russia as the lynch pin of their projects, connecting their interest in the Duke of Holstein's fate in the north with their negotiations with Spain and Austria in the south. Their failure to translate European conflicts into military opposition to the Hanoverian monarchy was never inevitable; indeed, only astute naval precautions and the unceasing activity of Britain's representatives abroad diverted the Russian threat from its possessions. During the two years of Catherine I's reign, the threat to Britain from the Jacobite lobby in Russia was as serious as it had ever been during the reign of her husband.

PART THREE

The Reign of Peter II, 1727–1730

The Embassy of the Duke of Liria, 1727–1730

Bleak Prospects and Divided Loyalties

The year 1727 marked a downturn in Jacobite fortunes throughout Europe. The blow dealt to Jacobitism by the death of Catherine I and the subsequent departure of the Duke of Holstein from Russia was reinforced by the un-opposed accession of George II on his father's sudden death in June.[1] Initial Jacobite hopes for a national revolt involving the overthrow of Walpole quickly evaporated.[2] The international situation gave little prospect of assistance. In Russia the fleet was again confined to harbour by the presence of a British squadron at Copenhagen. It soon became clear to the Jacobites that there would be no opportunity for negotiation during the young Emperor Peter II's minority.[3] Most importantly, the removal of the Holstein threat brought a discernible relaxation of Anglo-Russian relations. In 1728 Britain sent a consul, Thomas Ward, and his secretary Claudius Rondeau to investigate the possibility of rapprochement with Russia.[4] This marked the first stage of a process of reconciliation which culminated in the renewal of Anglo-Russian diplomatic relations in 1731. Meanwhile, the realignment of British and Russian interests generated inevitable problems for Jacobites in Russia, who regarded George II with as much hostility as they had his father. They were confronted with a situation in which any activity on behalf of James III would inevitably conflict with their service to the Russian monarch. This dichotomy between personal allegiance and professional obligation became increasingly difficult to recon-cile as Britain and Russia drew closer together.

The problem of divided loyalties affected individual Jacobites to varying degrees according to their professional obligations. For some, despite a history of Jacobite activity, career considerations were allowed to take precedence. In many cases the very fact that Jacobite prospects of Russian assistance were poor to some extent eased the source of conflict. James Keith, for example, was one of several Jacobites who had been encouraged to enter Russian service by the promise of Russian support during Catherine I's reign.[5] Although he had been

---

1 He died on the night of 10/11 or 21/22 June 1727, PRO SP 35/64, f.143.
2 Secret intelligence from Paris, 24/9/1727, Coxe, *Robert Walpole*, 1, p.290.
3 T.Gordon to James III, 28/10/1727, NAS Abercairney GD 24/1/859 f.319.
4 Rondeau reported that 'M-r Ward was received with much more civility than could be well expected, both by the english factory and Count Munich'., Rondeau to [Townshend], 7/8/1728, *SIRIO* 66, p.2.
5 Keith's was only one of a number of applications for Russian service. Captain Carse had served as a volunteer in a Scots regiment in Dutch service before leaving to join the Jacobites at the battle of Preston and eventually escaping to Spain. A non-Catholic, like Keith, he was a volunteer at the siege of Gibraltar, before applying to Russia. *(cont'd)/*

a volunteer on the Spanish side at the siege of Gibraltar, even the recommendation of Father Clark, Philip V's Jacobite confessor, was insufficient to permit him, as an Episcopalian, to serve permanently in Catholic Spain.[6] The cease-fire at Gibraltar in June 1727, coupled with the news that his friend, the Duke of Liria, was to be sent as Spanish ambassador to St Petersburg, prompted him to go to Russia. Jacobite loyalty was his primary motive; he wrote to James III that he was willing to go wherever '. . . I can be of more use to your service'.[7] Liria's recommendation on Keith's behalf proved so successful that Keith was accepted into Russian service at the rank of major general in January 1728.[8] However, by the time Keith arrived in Russia, Catherine was dead and Jacobite prospects had reached a low ebb. He, like many other Jacobites already in Russia, turned his attention from political activity to matters of career, and was able to some extent to avoid a conflict of interests by allowing his Jacobite sympathies to lie fallow.

While Russia's distance from European conflicts allowed many Jacobites, like Keith, to concentrate on military careers there without risk of compromising their loyalty to James III, those with a higher political profile, like the Duke of Liria, were in a more vulnerable position. He discovered, when he came to Russia with both a Spanish and a Jacobite commission, that a duality arose between personal loyalty and professional responsibility which could not easily be reconciled.

Liria's Mission

James Fitzjames, Duke of Liria, was appointed the first Spanish ambassador to Russia in January 1727, at a time when Spain was openly hostile to Britain, and Spanish and Jacobite interests coincided. His confidential instructions from Philip V combined both: to arrange defensive and commercial treaties with Russia, to favour the Treaty of Vienna, and, in addition, to engineer Russian military support for the Jacobites against Britain.[9] At the same time he promised James III, as his official representative in Russia, that '. . . it shall be my chief endeavour in Muscovy to obey [your commands] with fidelity and care'.[10]

cont'd George Keith to James III, 17/2/1728, RA Stuart 114/43; Report of Ivan Shcherbatov, 3/14 June 1728, AVPR F9 o1 d3, l.3. In 1727, Thomas Gordon was also approached to assist a 'Brigadier Mr Campbell' (a Campbell entered the army in 1731 RGVIA F489 o1 d7340.), and 'one Captain Willobey from the north of Ireland . . . that is come hither to serve in the troops', NAS Abercairney GD 24/1/859, ff.309,310.

6 J.Hay to J.Keith, 18/2/1727, RA Stuart 103/137; J.Keith to James III, 3/1/1728, RA Stuart 113/15.

7 J.Keith to James III, 3/1/1728, RA Stuart 113/15.

8 James Keith, *A Fragment*, pp.74–76; Liria to James III 9/20 May 1728, RA Stuart 116/56; Liria also applied on behalf of Keith's brother, the Earl Marischal, to have him enter Russian service as a lieutenant general, but George Keith never followed up the request. Report by Ivan Shcherbatov, 27/5 o.s. 7/6/1728 n.s., AVPR F9 o1 d3, l.1; Report on Liria's memorial of 7/7/1728, *Ibid.*, l.2.

9 Liria, 'Pis'ma o Rossii', Bartenev 2, p.11.

10 Liria to James III, March 1727, RA Stuart 104/71.

During the term of Liria's commission to Spain, however, the international situation altered dramatically. The Treaty of Seville, concluded in 1729 between Spain, Britain and France, split the Vienna Alliance, alienating Spain from Russia and Austria.[11] On his return from Russia in 1731, Liria then became involved in the accession of Spain to a new Treaty of Vienna between Spain, Britain, Austria and Holland. In the space of three years, therefore, Spanish and Jacobite affairs had diverged, and Spain, joined later by Russia, aligned itself with Britain. Inevitably, in executing his orders from Spain, Liria was forced against the current of Jacobite interests. His correspondence reveals the extent to which he led a dual existence, and it is at times difficult to ascertain where his true loyalties lay.

Initially, Liria's efforts on behalf of Spain coincided conveniently with his Jacobite commission in that they were directed against Britain. Philip V sent him to Russia via Italy with instructions to reconcile James III with his estranged wife, Clementina Sobieska, a mission which was conducted successfully.[12] He travelled on to Vienna and Dresden to assess the level of anti-British sentiment there, arrived in St Petersburg on 23 November 1727 and had his first audience with the young Emperor on 30 December.[13] Once there, his main concerns were to foil what he perceived to be Britain's ambitions; to hinder Anglo-Russian reconciliation by obstructing British attempts to entice Russia away from the Vienna Alliance, and to return the Russian court from Moscow to St Petersburg to ensure that Russia remained a military threat to Britain.[14] In addition, as instructed, he sought to conclude defensive and commercial treaties between Spain and Russia.

Liria enjoyed a sphere of influence which made him invaluable as a diplomat both to the Jacobites and to Spain. His freedom with money was reported to have '. . . gained him great credit with the Czar and the affections of the common people'.[15] He himself boasted that he enjoyed the confidence of both Osterman and Ivan Dolgoruky, who represented opposing factions at the Russian court.[16] In June 1728, he suspected the Duke of Wolfenbüttel's envoy of receiving money from Britain to split Russia from the Vienna Alliance, and had a spy monitor his movements.[17] When Britain sent consul Thomas Ward to Russia in July 1728, Liria was able to use his influence to elicit from Prince Dolgoruky a promise of support against Britain's attempts to secure a Russian alliance.[18] He also attempted to dissuade Russia from resuming relations with Britain by warning Count Osterman that Britain was providing Turkey with financial encouragement

11 W.Coxe, *Memoirs of the Kings of Spain of the House of Bourbon, 1700–1788* (London, 1813), 2, p.425.
12 Liria, 'Pis'ma o Rossii', Bartenev 2, p.11.
13 Liria to De la Paz, 25/11/1727, Liria, 'Pis'ma o Rossii', Bartenev 2, pp. 25, 26, 29.
14 Liria to De la Paz, 19/7/1728, *Ibid.*, 2, p.87.
15 Rondeau to Townshend, 10/2/1729, *SIRIO*, 66, p.36.
16 Liria to De la Paz, 10/5/1728, 'Pis'ma o Rossii', Bartenev, *op.cit.*, 2, p.69.
17 Liria to De la Paz, 7/6/1728, *Ibid.*, 2, p.73.
18 Liria to De la Paz, 13/9/1728, *Ibid.*, 2, p.101.

to make war on Russia.[19] To some extent, therefore, it was possible simultaneously to serve two masters.

Jacobite Secrets

From the outset, Liria made it clear to James III, his uncle, that he would keep his Jacobite activities strictly secret from Philip V, and wrote that '. . . a discovery would not only blast my endeavours, but eternally ruin me with the King of Spain, who is naturally jealous of those he employs'.[20] James, likewise, believed that the secrecy of Liria's mission would better serve Jacobite ends, '. . . since the less you appear to be directly employed by me, the more useful I think you may be to me in those parts'.[21]

As well as serving those interests common to both Spain and the Jacobites, Liria was also secretly involved in exclusively Jacobite matters, remaining in close correspondence with James III and carrying out his orders independently. While in Dresden on his way to Russia he attempted, albeit unsuccessfully, to rouse support for the Jacobites. At Mittau he met with the Polish Prince Radziwil to try to arrange that James be included in the will of his father-in-law Prince James Sobieski.[22] On his arrival in St Petersburg, he even suggested to Osterman that one of James III's sons be supported to succeed to the throne of Poland. This proposal was badly received by Russia, Prussia and Poland, and Liria was quick to ascribe it to personal initiative in order not to compromise his relations with the King of Spain. It is possible, however, that his suggestion had been prompted by James III's instructions.[23] Liria became James III's principal agent at the Russian court when Thomas Gordon was sent to command the fleet in Spring 1728 and was sent full powers to negotiate on James III's behalf should the occasion arise.[24] In May 1727, under pretext of congratulating Emperor Peter II on his recent coronation, James sent him a letter under Liria's cover to recommend to him the Jacobite agents in Russia.[25] In a further letter to Liria, James enclosed a memorial addressed to Peter II, detailing the benefits which would accrue to Russia should it support the Jacobite cause.[26] After consultation with Thomas Gordon, Liria delivered James's first letter to Peter II via Osterman in August.[27] and the memorial in December, when the court returned from the country.[28] His ease of access to Russian ministers made him the undisputed principal Jacobite representative in Russia, and James relied on his discretion to ensure that this correspondence reached the proper recipients. Liria remained in contact with the exiled

19 Liria to De la Paz, 19/2/1728, *Ibid.*, 2, p.44.
20 Liria to James III, March 1727, RA Stuart 104/71.
21 James III to Liria, 22/5/1728, RA Stuart 116/65.
22 Liria to James III, 2/12/1727 o.s., RA Stuart 112/85A.
23 Rondeau to Townshend, 25/8/1729 o.s., PRO SP 91/10, f.152.
24 Liria to T.Gordon, 25/3/1728, *HMC Eglinton* etc., p.166.
25 James III to Liria, 22/5/1728, RA Stuart 116/165.
26 'Memoire pour l'Empereur de Russie', 5/6/1728, RA Stuart 116/165, in James III to Liria, 9/6/1728, RA Stuart 116/169.
27 Liria to James III, 30/8/1728, RA Stuart 119/137.
28 Liria to James III, 13/12/1728, RA Stuart 122/84.

Jacobite court throughout the term of his embassy, notwithstanding the changing political situation.

On a personal level, Liria was on close terms with the Jacobite community in Russia, and exerted his influence in favour of fellow-Jacobites seeking careers there, including James Keith, James Hewitt and Captain Carse. In his letters to Thomas Gordon he addressed him as 'dear father', sending his greetings to mutual Jacobite friends, including Henry Stirling, 'Jemmy' Keith, Lord Duffus and Captain Robert Little.[29] Every year of his employment in Russia he invited a large party of Jacobites to celebrate James III's birthday on 10 June, and openly referred to him as the 'King of England'.[30] This display of Jacobitism, although public, does not appear to have met with significant Russian or Spanish disapproval.

Although Liria's personal political affiliations were well-known, it appears that he successfully concealed the extent of his Jacobite correspondence. Rondeau and Ward observed him closely, but were unable to discover evidence that he was actively in Jacobite service. In June 1729, Claudius Rondeau assured Townshend that Liria and the Imperial minister, Count Vratislav, spent their time with the favourite, Prince Ivan Dolgoruky, '. . . who has nothing to do with foreign affairs', rather than approaching Counts Osterman or Golovkin, and concluded that Liria had '. . . nothing to negotiate'.[31] Rondeau was obviously unaware of the approaches Liria had made to Osterman on James's behalf since the arrival of the British representatives the previous year. Count Osterman and Prince Vasilii Lukich Dolgoruky were the ministers who had shown favour to the Jacobites in the past, and Thomas Gordon maintained that they were '. . . the only persons that know of my correspondence with the King'.[32] After the death of Catherine I, however, when Gordon found it more difficult to gain access to Osterman,[33] Liria became the Jacobite best positioned to make contact with the Russian court, and, unknown to Rondeau, his efforts actually enjoyed a measure of success, despite the unfavourable international situation. Osterman's response to the Jacobite lobby was overwhelmingly positive, although he regretted that Russia was not at that time in a position to lend assistance.[34] Thus the impression given by Rondeau that Liria was concerned solely '. . . to pass [his] time in the the agreablest way [he] can', was unjustified, the product of British ignorance.[35]

Taking Risks

Liria's embassy in Russia was beset by difficulty, not least as a result of alterations in the political climate. Firstly, his instructions from Spain to negotiate treaties with Russia proved impracticable. Soon after his arrival he

29 Liria to T.Gordon, 16/11/1730, *HMC Eglinton* etc., p.168.
30 Liria to De la Paz, 27/6/1729, 'Pis'ma o Rossii', Bartenev, 2, pp.169–170.
31 Rondeau to Townshend, 26/6/1729, PRO SP 91/10, f.108; *SIRIO* 66, p.53.
32 T.Gordon to Liria, 15/7/1728, NAS Abercairney GD 24/1/859, f.321.
33 T.Gordon to James III, 19/8/1727, NAS Abercairney GD 24/1/859, f.316.
34 Liria to James III, 27/9/1728, RA Stuart 120/141.
35 Rondeau to Townshend, 26/6/1729, PRO SP 91/10, f.108; *SIRIO* 66, p.53.

expressed his misgivings that a Russo-Spanish defensive alliance was either possible or desirable.[36] He continued, however, to press for a commercial treaty which would be detrimental to British trade.[37] Nevertheless, Rondeau reported that Russia and Spain lacked sufficient common interest to unite, and it was believed that Liria's efforts in that direction were hopeless.[38] Liria concentrated, therefore, on preventing Russia from sending troops to assist the Emperor, who was intent on blocking Spanish territorial ambitions in Italy.

In addition, he encountered hostility from within the Russian court, which he found to be deeply divided into two opposing factions. One, headed by Osterman, favoured foreigners and supported the Vienna Alliance. The other, which included Princes Dolgoruky and Golitsyn, resented the foreign influence in Russia and desired Osterman's fall. The most reactionary of the latter, which exerted considerable influence, wanted to return the capital to Moscow, dispense with the involvement of foreigners in Russian affairs and '. . . return to their old way of living'.[39] Liria, who initially sought the support of Osterman against Britain, was met with a hostile reception from his enemies, who perceived the Spanish ambassador as a foreigner who sought to involve Russia in European affairs, and who, siding with Osterman, presented an obstacle to their ambitions. Moreover Spain was known to sympathise with the discredited Holstein faction[40] and to be the enemy of Britain, with whom Russia was now anxious to resume commercial relations. Liria's enemies may well have been reluctant to show support for a known Jacobite in case they jeopardised Anglo-Russian rapprochement. Indeed, Liria's Jacobitism was probably one reason why Thomas Gordon was effectively exiled from the capital at this time. He complained to James III soon after his arrival that

> . . . I am positive that they sent away Admiral Gordon only because he came to meet [me] out of town and shewed himself so publicly [my] friend this is in two words the situation of this Court & mine it is not very comforting for your Majesty.[41]

Although there is no direct evidence that Liria's Jacobite connections played a part in this, it is likely that the powerful Dolgoruky family, who had a great influence over the young Tsar, were concerned to avert the threat to their interests which the Jacobites and other foreigners could now pose.

Liria was certainly suspected of Jacobite activity by foreign ministers representing powers hostile to the Vienna Alliance. In autumn 1728 it was rumoured that he was buying Russian ships for use against Britain, although Rondeau's

---

36 Liria to De la Paz, 30/1/1728, 'Pis'ma o Rossii', Bartenev, 2, p.41.
37 Liria's project of Russo-Spanish trade, presented by Liria and Count Vratislav to the Russian court 31/5/1728, referred to in Rondeau to Townshend, 31/12/1728, *SIRIO* 66, p.31.
38 Rondeau to Townshend, 30/5/1729, PRO SP 91/10, f.104.
39 Liria to James III, 16/12/1727, RA Stuart 112/112.
40 For the opposition of the Dolgorukys towards the Duke of Holstein, see Rondeau to Townshend, 29/12/1729, *SIRIO* 66, p.117.
41 Rondeau to Townshend, 29/12/1729, *SIRIO* 66, p.117.

investigations into the rumours were inconclusive. He reported, '. . . I cannot hear that the Duke of Liria has bought any ships or ammunition here unless it be those two which it is thought are gone to Spain'.[42] In August of the following year Rondeau noted that Liria had approached the Russian court to have two ships belonging to St Malo merchants sent to the East Indies under Russian colours but had met with no response. The ministry suspected that these probably belonged to the Ostend Company.[43] In February 1729, however, following allegations by Count Vratislavsky that he was involved in Jacobite affairs in Russia and had been instructed by James III to buy ships for Jacobite use, Liria denied any Jacobite involvement, ascribing Count Vratislavsky's accusations to an envy of his good relations with both Osterman and Ivan Dolgoruky, the favourite.[44] In May, he answered in the negative a similar charge that he had purchased ships. This time he observed,

> . . . it is a very curious thing, that obstinacy with which not only the British, the Dutch and the French, but even the Danes, who have the gates to this place in their hands, persist in the belief that I have bought ships here for the King our Master.[45]

Spain's history of support for the Jacobites against the allies of Hanover was well known, and Liria, as Spanish ambassador and Jacobite opposing British interests in Russia, was a prime target for suspicion. Liria's Jacobite correspondence, however, contains no indication that he was involved in purchasing ships for military purposes. It is more likely, given the poor state of Jacobite affairs, that he was pursuing a commercial concern.

It is nevertheless important to note that, despite the impotence of the Jacobite threat, accusations of Jacobite involvement could still serve as a damaging diplomatic weapon. Liria was at pains to deny any Jacobite activity, despite the fact that he was the principal Jacobite envoy at the Russian court, and had recently presented James's memorial to Count Osterman, detailing Jacobite demands. The nature of these accusations was evidence that Liria's Jacobite loyalty involved an element of risk to his diplomatic career even before the conclusion of the Treaty of Seville altered the pattern of European alliances.

The Treaty of Seville

By late 1729, Austro-Spanish relations had deteriorated badly. The death of Charles VI's youngest daughter the previous year had provided him with a pretext to call off the marriage of his remaining daughters to Spanish princes, and he was reluctant to concur with Spanish claims on contested duchies in Italy. Spain became impatient; in March 1729 it broke off relations with Austria, and on 9 November 1729, concluded the Treaty of Seville with Britain, France

42 Rondeau to Townshend, 26/8/1728, *SIRIO* 66, p.10.
43 Rondeau to Townshend, 25/8/1729, *SIRIO* 66, pp.69–70.
44 Liria to De la Paz, 7/2/1729, 'Pis'ma o Rossii', Bartenev, 2, p.143.
45 Liria to De la Paz, 2/5/1729, 'Pis'ma o Rossii', Bartenev, 2, p.161.

and Holland in exchange for support for Prince Don Carlos's control of the duchies.

The abrupt end of the Alliance of Vienna meant that Liria in Russia was suddenly expected to side with the allies of Hanover against those with whom he had hitherto been involved, including the Viennese minister Count Vratislavsky and Count Osterman. In January 1729, he received orders from Spain to work closely in support of the British, French and Dutch ministers in Moscow.[46] Read in isolation, his diplomatic correspondence suggests that his transfer of loyalty to Britain, and necessarily against the Jacobites, was automatic and wholehearted. He wrote to Rondeau on receipt of his new orders that '. . . I am just going on to bed and with a large glass in my hand to drink to the continuation of our alliance'.[47] Three days later he claimed, '. . . I am now overjoyed that, obeying my masters' orders, I can follow my own inclinations'.[48] Rondeau reported that Liria '. . . seems at present entirely devoted to the interest of England'.[49] He regarded him as a great asset to Britain, '. . . because he has such a universal acquaintance with the russ nobility that he may be of great service to our new alliance', and because his efforts represented '. . . a step towards a good understanding between us and Russia'.[50] Liria's efforts to split Russia from its alliance with Austria were very much in Britain's interests. At one point Liria was even forced to borrow money from the British consul to enable him to continue his work.[51] It is difficult to believe that such a committed Jacobite should become so assiduous in the service of the Hanoverian monarchy. A closer examination of Liria's diplomatic activity and personal correspondence, however, reveals the extent of his allegiance to Spain, Britain and the Jacobite cause, and suggests that he managed to maintain his position without serious compromise on any front.

Liria certainly fulfilled his duty to Spain. In his role as Spanish ambassador, Liria welcomed the Treaty of Seville because Spain now had support in its efforts to unite with Russia and prevent Russian troops assisting Austria. Whereas before he had opposed Anglo-Russian rapprochement as prejudicial to Spanish commercial interests, he now presented Rondeau with a detailed plan to promote it in order to increase opposition to Vienna. The incentive offered to Britain was the prospect of making '. . . the russ blindly do whatever the king of Great Britain pleases'.[52] Throughout the remainder of his embassy he worked very hard to procure Russia's accession to the Treaty of Seville and split it from Austria. When, on 25 July 1730, he finally received the recall he had desired almost since his arrival, having found the xenophobia and general confusion in Russia too much '. . . for a man used to living in less barbaric

46 Liria to Rondeau, 12/1/1730, PRO SP 91/11, f.11.
47 *Ibid.*
48 Liria to Rondeau, 12/1/1730, *SIRIO* 66, p.127.
49 Rondeau to Tilson, 29/12/1729, *SIRIO* 66, p.118.
50 Rondeau to Townshend, 2/2/1730, 16/2/1730, PRO SP 91/11, ff.21, 27.
51 Liria to De la Paz, 3/4/1730, 'Pis'ma o Rossii', Bartenev 3, pp.60, 61.
52 Rondeau to Townshend, 12/1/1730, *SIRIO* 66, p.120.

lands',[53] he withheld the news, so concerned was he to see his plans completed before his departure.[54] He was prepared to conceal his schemes from Osterman, and took the risk of negotiating secretly with the latter's enemies, Iaguzhinsky and Cherkassky. One of his plans for limiting the Austrian threat even included the suggestion that the Spanish king's second son accede to the Polish throne.[55] During this period he remained in close contact with Rondeau, with the result that the British government was kept informed of the details of his confidential negotiations. This was important for Britain because the diplomatic necessity of maintaining good relations with Osterman prevented Rondeau himself from becoming involved. Liria's efforts were evidence of a real commitment to Spanish interests.

Liria and Britain

Although Liria worked closely with French and British ministers to prevent Russian military support for Austria, however, this was not in itself indicative of a transfer of loyalty. Indeed, there is evidence that he was prepared to work in the interest of Britain only in as far as it coincided with that of Spain. Although he was aware that British ministers welcomed his negotiations as a means of achieving reconciliation with Russia, he nevertheless stopped short of directly promoting Britain's objectives. In March 1730 orders were in fact sent from Spain that he should actively assist British negotiations for a treaty with Russia, but he, fortunately, did not receive them until late July, when they arrived together with his letter of recall.[56] Prior to this, he had already protested to de la Paz that, despite British wishes, he would refuse to become involved in Anglo-Russian rapprochement. He gave as his ground for this Osterman's alleged deep opposition to an Anglo-Russian agreement, borne of George I's insulting behaviour towards his late master, Peter I,[57] and maintained that Russian hatred for Britain rendered him powerless to benefit such a negotiation.[58]

There is evidence, however, that Liria's negative response to Spanish instructions was more a reflection of his own reluctance to act directly on Britain's behalf than of Russian recalcitrance. Far from continuing to demonstrate enmity towards Britain at this time, Osterman had in fact given the British ministers considerable encouragement. In March Rondeau reported that '. . . The obliging behaviour of baron Osterman . . . convinces me that we may be perfectly good friends with this court whenever His Majesty pleases',[59]

53 Liria to De la Paz, 29/11/1728, 'Pis'ma o Rossii', Bartenev, 2 p.115.
54 Rondeau to Harrington, 12/8/1730, PRO SP 91/11, f.158.
55 Rondeau to Townshend, 2/2/1730, PRO SP 91/11, f.21.
56 Rondeau to Harrington, 27/7/1730, PRO SP 91/11, f.152.
57 He wrote, 'When I worked here against the English before the arrival of their consul, Osterman spoke with me on a number of occasions, and repeatedly assured me that, while he was in power, he would never permit reconciliation with Britain, whose King had so cruelly insulted his late master Peter the First' (my translation), Liria to De la Paz, 5/7/1730, 'Pis'ma o Rossii', Bartenev, 3, p.87.
58 *Ibid.*, p.88.
59 Rondeau to Townshend, 30/3/1730, PRO SP 91/11, f.60.

and a month later Osterman repeated his desire for a settlement with Britain.[60] Liria was prepared to serve Spain, but was wary of involving himself in affairs which did not directly relate to Spanish interests. In this way he may have been able to some extent to reconcile his allegiance to Spain with his Jacobite hostility towards the Hanoverian monarchy.

Personal Loyalty: Conflict or Compromise?

Despite Liria's close professional relationship with Rondeau and the Allies of Seville, his Jacobite correspondence continued to demonstrate a strong allegiance to James III. His expressions of support for the Treaty of Seville in his capacity as Spanish ambassador were far from manifest in his private letters to fellow Jacobites. In a letter to Thomas Gordon in August 1729 he wrote pessimistically that the proposed general peace would mean that '. . . all our hopes will be gone for this time', and wished for a more favourable opportunity for the Jacobites in the future.[61] In a further letter to Gordon, written when peace between Britain and Spain was imminent, Liria confirmed that he was as hostile as ever towards George II. He, on the side of the Jacobites, welcomed the possibility that the King of Prussia would open hostilities on Hanover, and declared, '. . . God send he may drubb my friend George and make him change his bullying way of acting'.[62] The private nature of this correspondence would suggest that these sentiments were sincere.

Liria's embassy, however, involved him in a public role which was, on the surface, diametrically opposed to his personal inclinations and to Jacobite interests. In January 1730, James III sought to split the Anglo-French alliance, and instructed his parliamentary supporters to '. . . promote a misunderstanding between the English government and any foreign power, most especially France'.[63] While Liria was attempting to bring Russia into the Treaty of Seville against Austria, and Imperial troops had marched against Spain into Italy, the Jacobites were hoping for Imperial support.[64] It appeared impossible that he could continue to conduct both commissions without compromise, or even damage, to either.

After the conclusion of the Treaty of Seville, the less public manifestations of Liria's Jacobitism continued as before. James III and Liria remained in fairly regular correspondence and letters were forwarded to other Jacobites in Russia under Liria's cover. James continued to regard him as his Jacobite agent at the Russian court despite the fact that he could be of little service.[65] Liria, for his part kept abreast of Jacobite affairs. In December 1729, Thomas Gordon sent him a Jacobite memorial written by the Duke of Wharton, and he welcomed news of the uproar it had caused in Britain. He also employed his influence at

60 Rondeau to Townshend, 20/4 or 1/5/1730, *Ibid.*, f.83.
61 Liria to T.Gordon, 25/8/1729, *HMC Eglinton* etc., p.167.
62 Liria to T. Gordon, 8/9/1729, *HMC Eglinton* etc., p.167.
63 J.Black, *British Foreign Policy*, p.148.
64 James III to Ormonde, 24/3/1730, RA Stuart 135/28.
65 James III to Liria, 1/4/1730, RA Stuart 135/97.

court to the benefit of fellow Jacobites, and in April 1730 he and Thomas Gordon jointly proposed Sir Henry Stirling to the newly vacated post of Vice-President of the College of Foreign Affairs.[66] He had social intercourse with other members of the Jacobite community in Moscow and kept in contact with those attached to the fleet at Cronstadt and St Petersburg.[67]

On an official level Liria's only overtly Jacobite commission after the Treaty of Seville was to present a letter of congratulation from James III to the new Empress Anna Ivanovna, Peter I's niece, after Peter II's sudden death of smallpox in February 1730.[68] It appears that Liria's ambassadorial duties, being of a public nature, were indeed given precedence over his role as an envoy of James III. The international climate had altered greatly since his initial project to launch a Russian-backed Jacobite attack on Britain three years previously. At the same time, the poor state of Jacobite fortunes in Russia meant that opportunities for action in favour of James were greatly reduced. The Russian court showed no inclination to support James III[69] and Thomas Gordon's semi-exile to the fleet at Cronstadt diminished his effectiveness as a Jacobite agent.[70] Liria's Spanish and Jacobite interests did not, therefore, conflict as seriously as they might have done, had a Jacobite conspiracy been under way. To his good fortune, he was able to serve the King of Spain without directly thwarting the Jacobites' plans in Europe. Indeed, although his negotiations diminished their hope of assistance from Russia, his attempts to polarise Austria against the allies of Seville might possibly have served to procure them Imperial support against Britain. Thus he succeeded in maintaining allegiance to Spain and to the Jacobites without injury to himself or to either side.

Liria's Recall and the Second Treaty of Vienna

Almost as soon as it had been concluded the Treaty of Seville encountered insurmountable difficulties. The allies had promised Spain to secure Imperial consent to the introduction of Spanish garrisons into Italy. France, however, refused to guarantee the Pragmatic Sanction, the price of consent, nor did it wish to fight the Emperor. Eventually, in December 1730, Spain grew impatient and the Treaty was annulled.[71]

Meanwhile, Liria had received his recall on 25 July 1730[72] but managed to continue his negotiations in Russia until he was summoned to leave urgently in October.[73] He left Moscow for Warsaw on 19 November.[74] His final months in Russia were made particularly unpleasant by the hostility of Osterman and the

66 T.Gordon to Liria, 26/3/1730, NAS Abercairney GD 24/1/859, f.332; Liria to T.Gordon, 6/4/1730, *HMC Eglinton* etc., p.168.
67 Liria to T.Gordon, 5/10/1730, *HMC Eglinton* etc., p.168.
68 James III to Anna Ivanovna, 1/4/1730, RA Stuart 135/96.
69 James III to Liria, 11/6/1729, RA Stuart 129/27.
70 James III to T.Gordon, 5/3/1729, RA Stuart 125/110; Liria to T.Gordon, 25/8/1729, *HMC Eglinton* etc., p.167; James III to T.Gordon, 18/11/1729, RA Stuart 132/42.
71 B. Williams, 'The Foreign Policy of Britain Under Walpole', *EHR* 16 (1901), p.443.
72 Rondeau to Harrington, 27/7/1730, PRO SP 91/11, f.152.
73 Rondeau to Harrington, 15/10/1730, *SIRIO* 66, pp.243–244.
74 Rondeau to Harrington, 23/11/1730, PRO SP 91/11, f.232.

pro-Austrian faction at the Russian court.[75] In addition, he incurred the wrath of the new Empress by expressing his support for a group of nobles who sought to restrict her autocratic powers.[76] In consequence of this, Osterman had his diplomatic correspondence intercepted and accused him of seeking to establish a republic in order to undermine the Russian minister's own position at the Russian court.[77] Thus, eventually, Liria's efforts to bring Russia into the Alliance of Seville were undermined by factors beyond his control.

Liria's career demonstrated the extent to which the diplomat was subject to the vicissitudes and unexpected realignments of international politics. Even while the Alliance of Seville was in place, Britain's fear of French intrigue with Spain and Austria had led it to engage in secret unilateral negotiations with the Emperor. Soon after Liria left Russia he was posted to Vienna, and in March 1731 became one of the signatories of the Second Treaty of Vienna between Britain, Austria and Spain. Once again he found himself in the camp opposing the Jacobites, who were now seeking the support of France. In the fickle arena of international politics, professional obligation and personal allegiance were, as far as possible, kept distinct, and inconsistency was not necessarily indicative of disloyalty.

Liria's embassy to Russia is illustrative of some of the problems encountered by the Jacobite whose career in exile involved him in a conflict of loyalties. In Liria's case the necessity to perform public diplomatic duties on behalf of Spain inevitably limited his ability to serve the Jacobite cause, yet he nevertheless retained close Jacobite ties. He was fortunate to be able to restrict the extent of this conflict. Firstly, although his allegiance to Spain involved him in confidential relations with British ministers, he managed to avoid directly promoting Britain's ambitions for an Anglo-Russian treaty. Secondly, during the period of his embassy, the absence of Jacobite intrigue involving Russia and the lull in Jacobite fortunes in general meant that his Spanish and Jacobite loyalties were never ultimately tested against each other in action. Had the opportunity for Jacobite intrigue presented itself, his role might well have been different.

---

75 Liria to De la Paz, 15/5/1730, 'Pis'ma o Rossii', Bartenev, 3, p.70.
76 Liria to De la Paz, 9/3/1730, *Ibid.*, 3, p.53
77 Liria to De la Paz, 5/6/1730, *Ibid.*, 3, pp.74–75.

PART FOUR

The Reign of Anna Ivanovna, 1730–1740

CHAPTER FOUR

Jacobites and Politics, 1730–1740

As the Duke of Liria acknowledged in 1730, the political prospects for Jacobites in Russia during the ten-year reign of Anna Ivanovna differed fundamentally from those prior to Catherine I's death. Amicable relations between Britain and Russia now meant that Jacobite loyalty was no longer a motive for embarking on a Russian career, and Russia's involvement in a succession of wars throughout the decade inevitably brought Jacobites into active conflict with powers which were being approached to support the Jacobite cause. The result was a situation rich with irony and duality.

In this political climate individual Jacobites maintained their political allegiances but could only express them within the limitations imposed by their professional obligations to Russia. Indeed, so prominent were their military positions that their role in the Russian armed forces inevitably had negative implications for Jacobite hopes elsewhere in Europe.

The ten year reign of Anna Ivanovna has suffered more than many periods of Russian history from neglect and misinterpretation. This is due, in part, to its unenviable position between the more visionary and tumultuous reigns of Peter I and Catherine II, which were characterised not only by their length, but by their receptivity to Western military and cultural advances. The short decade of Anna's rule, often dismissed as a period of stagnation under Germanic domination, was in fact a time of great military and diplomatic activity, during which Russia demonstrated its military prowess and reinforced its diplomatic status within Europe. The military successes of a number of Jacobite officers in the Russian armed forces made a significant contribution to this process. Indeed, in many respects, Anna's reign can be regarded as encompassing, in a military sense, the high point of the era of the Jacobite diaspora in Russia.

The Collapse of the Anglo-French Alliance

Although the accession to the Russian imperial throne of Empress Anna in February 1730 was greeted with optimism by the Jacobite leadership, it soon became clear that Jacobite hopes from that quarter were at an end. James III sent her a letter of congratulation on her accession in April in which he presented the Jacobite case in detail and requested Russian support. In September, James Keith's unexpected promotion to colonel in the newly-created Ismailovsky guards regiment[1] prompted Thomas Gordon to express the hope that '. . . by this post you will have frequent access to her Imperial person which may be of use to yourself and to your friends'.[2] Nevertheless,

---

1 Rondeau to Harrington, 3/9/1730, PRO SP 91/11, f.176.
2 T.Gordon to J.Keith, 11/10/1730, NAS Abercairney GD 24/1/859, f.338.

attempts to promote the Jacobite cause soon confirmed that prospects of support from the new monarch were poor. In February 1732, Gordon reported that he had '. . . talked seriously with Baron Osterman concerning Jacobite affairs', but was told that 'times are changed'. Russia no longer had any interest in opposing the Hanoverian monarchy. As a result of this rejection, Jacobite hopes were finally moved off the Russian stage and permanently transferred further west. It was now concluded that France and Spain held the only key to a Jacobite restoration.[3]

The collapse of Jacobite hopes in Russia was a reflection of converging British, Hanoverian and Russian interests. After the Anglo-Austrian Second Treaty of Vienna of 16 March 1731 had destroyed the Anglo-French alliance,[4] Anglo-Russian relations underwent a fundamental change as Britain and Russia became alert to a mutual need to prevent France uniting with either Sweden or Prussia and threatening both the Baltic and northern Germany. The French hand was strengthened in 1733 by the conclusion with Spain of the First Family Compact, which set the Bourbon powers in opposition to Britain and Austria.

Empress Anna's accession had renewed Britain's hopes of an Anglo-Russian alliance which would confirm both Britain's commercial and political dominance, and Rondeau in St Petersburg was confident that the sudden death of the young Tsar Peter II would '. . . not turn to our disadvantage . . . for the present Czarina has always loved our nation'.[5] In October 1730, when Count Iaguzhinsky, who favoured closer links with Britain, was promoted to the powerful post of procurator-general and Osterman's influence ebbed, the resumption of Anglo-Russian diplomatic relations appeared imminent, and Rondeau was promised that if George II should now give him the post of minister plenipotentiary, '. . . England and Russia would soon be as good friends as ever'.[6] The following year, after a break of eleven years, Anglo-Russian diplomatic relations were finally resumed; Prince Antiokh Kantemir was appointed Russian Resident in London, and Claudius Rondeau became his official counterpart in St Petersburg. Anglo-Russian relations were further strengthened in December 1734 by the conclusion of a treaty of commerce and friendship encouraging British trade with Russia.[7]

The shift of the Jacobite threat from Russia and Austria to France in 1731, and later to Spain, was a source of great anxiety to Britain, contributing to what has even been described as a 'mid-century crisis'.[8] In spring 1731, rumours that

---

3 T.Gordon to James III, 4/3/1732, RA Stuart 151/187.
4 For details of the Anglo-French rupture, J.Black, *The Collapse of the Anglo-French Alliance 1727–1731* (Gloucester, 1987).
5 Rondeau to Townshend, 19/1/1730, PRO SP 91/10, f.5. Throughout 1730, Osterman continued to assure Rondeau of Russia's goodwill towards Britain. Rondeau to Townshend, 20/4 or 1/5/1730, PRO SP 91/11, f.83.
6 Rondeau to Harrington, 8/10/1730, PRO SP 91/11, f.94.
7 2/12/1734, *PSZ* 6652; for the background to this treaty, D.K.Reading, *The Anglo-Russian Commercial Treaty of 1734* (New Haven, Conn., 1938).
8 For a discussion of this British crisis and Bourbon support for the Jacobites, see J.Black, 'Jacobitism and British Foreign Policy, 1731–5', in Cruickshanks and Black, eds., *The Jacobite Challenge* (Edinburgh, 1988), pp.142–160.

1. Peter I, 'The Great', who ruled Russia from 1682 until his death in 1725. Painting of 1717 by Jean-Marc Nattier (1685–1766). Hermitage, St. Petersburg/ Bridgeman Art Library.

2. View of Moscow, with the Kremlin. From Richter, *Ansichten von St Petersburg und Moskau*, Leipzig, 1804.

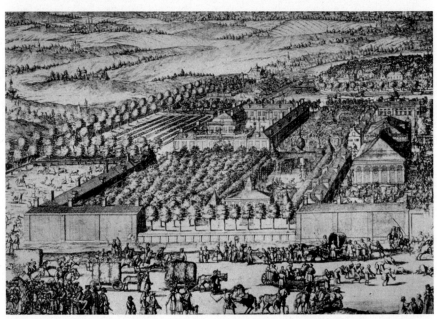

3. The German Quarter, Moscow, c.1705, seen here on the river behind the palace of Count F A Golovin, is from an engraving by Alexei Schoenebeck. This foreign settlement grew up on the banks of the River Yauza in Moscow, and its inhabitants brought with them to Russia a wealth of western culture and talent.

4. The old Tsar's Palace in the Moscow Kremlin. Engraving by Geissler, c.1804.

5. A Russian Town. Although this engraving by Geissler dates from c. 1804, the diversity of building materials and lifestyles depicted would have changed little since Peter I's reign.

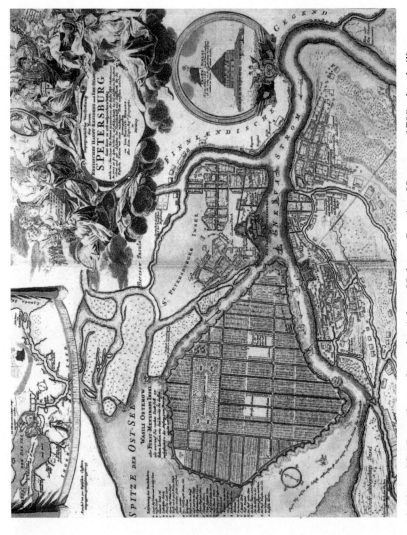

6. Plan of St. Petersburg, from the Atlas of Johann Baptiste Homann, 1725, clearly illustrates the geometric layout of Peter I's 'Window on the West'.

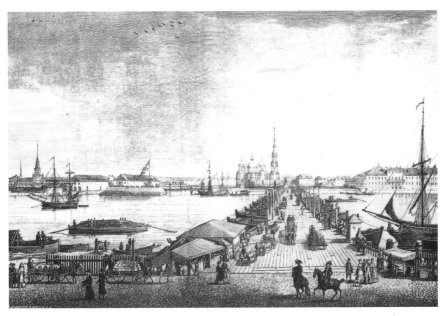

7. View of St. Petersburg. Engraved after a painting by Benjamin Paterssons, 1794.

8. The Winter Palace in St. Petersburg at the time of Peter I. Engraving by Aleksei Fedorovich Zubov, 1717.

9. The Empress Anna Ivanovna, step-niece of Peter I, who ruled Russia 1730–1740. Painting by Louis Caravaque (1684–1754). Tretyakov Gallery, Moscow/Bridgeman Art Library.

10. The Empress Elizabeth Petrovna, daughter of Peter I, who ruled Russia 1741–1761. Painting by Georg Christoph Grooth (1716–1749). Tsarskoye Selo, St. Petersburg/Bridgeman Art Library.

11. James 'III', the 'Old Pretender', by Antonio David (1723). Reproduced by permission of The Blairs Museum Trust.

12. Admiral Thomas Gordon was recruited in Paris in 1717 and was an Admiral by the time of his death in 1741. From a private Scottish collection.

13. Part of the Order of St Alexander Nevsky, awarded to Admiral Thomas Gordon by the Empress Catherine I. Engraved on it are the words, in Russian, 'For feats and homeland'. From a private Scottish collection.

14. Sir Henry Stirling of Ardoch, a relative of the Earl of Mar and nephew of Peter I's physician Dr Erskine, went to Russia in 1716 and was involved in Jacobite affairs there until the death of his father-in-law, Admiral Thomas Gordon, when he and his family returned to Scotland. Painting by Denune, from a private Scottish collection.

15. Miniatures of James 'III' and his sons Charles Edward and Henry Benedict, which were among the possessions brought back from Russia by Sir Henry Stirling in 1741. It is possible that they were sent to Stirling or Thomas Gordon by James III in recognition of their continued loyalty to the Jacobite cause. From a private Scottish collection.

16. Field-Marshall Count Peter Lacy, born in Co. Limerick in 1678, had an outstanding military career in Russia spanning over 50 years. This portrait was in the possession of a descendant of his living in Argentina. From a private collection, artist unknown.

17. James Keith fled Scotland with his brother, the Earl Marischal, after the battle of Glenshiel in 1719. He entered the Russian army in 1728, became a famous general and governor of the Ukraine, but was forced to leave Russian service for Prussia in 1747. He is shown here as Lieutenant-Colonel of the Izmailovsky Foot Guards and General-in-Chief of the Russian Army. Engraved by van Haecken after Ramsay. Reproduced by permission of the Scottish National Portrait Gallery.

18. Kenneth Sutherland, 3rd Lord Duffus. Served in the Royal Navy, then was attainted for taking part in the 1715 Rising. He entered the Russian Navy in 1722 and served for almost ten years as a Rear-Admiral until his death in 1732. He was described by the Duke of Liria as an 'admirable, brave and loyal' Jacobite. Painting by Richard Waitt. Reproduced by permission of the Scottish National Portrait Gallery.

James III had secretly visited France to arrange French military assistance coupled with the movement of French troops to the Channel coast and French naval preparations, gave rise to a ministerial panic that France and the Jacobites were about to invade.[9] The situation was successfully defused by July, but the following year news of Spanish naval armaments ignited a similar scare.[10] Domestic instability in the shape of the Excise Crisis in early 1733, after the failure of a government attempt to introduce a new system of commercial taxation, threatened to topple Walpole.[11] In the wake of this, Chavigny, the French Minister Plenipotentiary in London, and an enemy of Walpole's, attempted to undermine the British government by becoming closely involved with members of the Opposition, particularly Bolingbroke.[12] After the death of Augustus II of Poland on 1 February, which plunged Europe into the War of the Polish Succession, the Jacobites proposed that the French fleet destined for the Baltic be diverted to support a restoration attempt.[13]

Although Britain remained neutral throughout this war, the alliance of France with Spain in late 1733,[14] and fears that James III could gain a foothold in the Polish succession through his father-in-law, Prince James Sobieski,[15] kept the Jacobite threat in the forefront. Thus the outcome of the war, which brought Russia into open conflict with the French in the Baltic, was closely linked both with Jacobite prospects of French support, and with British security. In particular, the military action undertaken by Jacobites in Russia was diametrically opposed to the Jacobite interest.

The War of the Polish Succession, 1733–1735

The prospect of a war in which Britain might intervene against France encouraged James III to rally the support of the military leaders of previous Risings then in exile, both in Russia and throughout Europe. In June 1733, for

---

9 J.Black, *The Collapse of the Anglo-French Alliance,* pp.202–205.

10 Newcastle, the Secretary of State for the Southern Department, repeatedly instructed Waldegrave in Paris to investigate rumours of a Franco-Spanish rapprochement, and to uncover Jacobite intrigue. Newcastle to Waldegrave, 16,17/9/1732, PRO SP 78/202, f.147; 29/10 or 9/11/1732; *Ibid.,* ff.165, 167.

11 For details of this crisis, P.Langford, *The Excise Crisis* (Oxford, 1975).

12 For details of this, see Cruickshanks, 'Lord Cornbury, Bolingbroke and a Plan to Restore the Stuarts', *Royal Stuart Papers* 27 (1986).

13 There was confidence that as few as 3–4000 troops would be sufficient assistance and that, in view of the atmosphere of discontent in Britain, the monarchy could be overthrown 'without a shot'. 'Jacobite plan for an Invasion of Britain', 17/4/1733, RA Stuart 161/37.

14 Newcastle expressed his conviction that both powers were in league with 'the Pretender', without whose restoration to the British throne France would be unable to fulfil its ambitions for 'sovereignty over all Europe'. Newcastle to Waldegrave, 5/16 February 1734, PRO SP 78/206, ff.145–151.

15 In early 1733 Prince James Sobieski actually offered to promote James's candidacy in Poland, but James rejected the offer, declaring that 'La Providence m'a destiné pour une autre'. James III to Prince James Sobieski, 28/3/1733, *HMC Eglinton* etc., p.164. Such was British concern that the ministry issued its minister at Warsaw, Woodward, with confidential instructions to assist secretly in the election of Augustus of Saxony to the Polish throne and to ensure the exclusion of 'the Pretender and his children'. Reading, *The Anglo-Russian Commercial Treaty,* p.143.

example, he instructed James Keith's elder brother, the Earl Marischal, George Keith, to leave Spain for France as soon as French support for an invasion was forthcoming.[16] George was issued with a commission as lieutenant general of the Jacobite forces, with documents to carry to Scotland, and with orders to co-operate with the French commander-in-chief as soon as he should be appointed. Other leading Jacobites, John Cameron of Lochiel and Sir Hector Maclean, were expected to accompany him to Scotland.[17] Although the French attack on Austria in October 1733, which followed the Russian invasion of Poland in August, actually distracted France from a Jacobite invasion of Britain, James III continued to believe, that 'sooner or later' its support would be forthcoming. He therefore attempted to alert exiles of developments and to plan their military participation on the French side.[18] In 1733, George Keith was told that he was now on the list of Jacobite generals chosen to serve in Germany against the Russians.[19] At the same time, James expressed the hope that James Keith would leave Russia, and would make '. . . use ere long of [his] Commission in my service'.[20] His secretary, Edgar, wrote to congratulate Keith on '. . . the honor and glory you are acquiring in the world', but took care to add, '. . . may you soon have occasion to encrease them both by your appearance in your King and Country's cause'.[21]

The success and popularity of exiled Jacobites even as far away as Russia was regarded principally in terms of the benefit this could bring the Jacobite cause. In March 1733 the fantastic rumour was current that '. . . the Empress of Muscovy is with child and has published her marriage with Mr. James Keith, brother to my Lord Marischall'.[22] Before it became clear that this was unfounded, there were hopes that Keith's influential position at the Russian court would augur well for the Jacobites, and Stafford wrote optimistically that '. . . This and other things make me believe indeed the time we want is coming'.[23]

Contact between Russian exiles and the exiled court was maintained by a fairly regular correspondence between James III or his secretary and Thomas Gordon, and James Keith received news of the Jacobites from his brother in Spain. In 1731, Ezekiel Hamilton founded '. . . the most ancient, the most illustrious and most noble order of Toboso', a light-hearted fraternity of exiles whose new members, or 'knights', were chosen for their loyalty.[24] Although its primary purpose was apparently to entertain the two young princes, Charles

16 James III to George Keith, 12/6/1733, RA Stuart 162/76.
17 James III to George Keith, 13/6/1733, RA Stuart 162/83.
18 James III to George Keith, 30/10/1733, RA Stuart 165/219.
19 Daniel O'Brien to George Keith, 1/9/1733, RA Stuart 165/3. This position might have brought George Keith into battle against his own brother!
20 James III to George Keith, 26/9/1735, RA Stuart 183/1.
21 Edgar to James Keith, 17/3/1736, RA Stuart 186/62.
22 J.P.Stafford to Edgar, 16/3/1733, printed in H.Tayler, *Jacobite Epilogue* (Edinburgh, 1941), p.80.
23 *Ibid.*
24 Membership was discretionary on the service record of the applicant; in 1734 the unpopular James Murray, the Jacobite Earl of Dunbar, was debarred from the order for disloyalty. Jacobites in Rome to T.Gordon, 28/1/1733, *HMC Eglinton* etc., p.184.

Edward and Henry Benedict, it also helped to preserve a link with a scattered diaspora. In 1732 William Hay sent Thomas Gordon and Henry Stirling two rings with the insignia of the fraternity.[25] Of the exiles in Russia, James Keith, Thomas Gordon, Thomas Saunders, Kenneth Sutherland, Lord Duffus and Robert Little were members.[26] These efforts to maintain links with Russian exiles were particularly important, not only because of the distance of Russia from the Jacobite nerve centre, but because those who were active on campaign, and represented the best of Jacobite military talent, were frequently separated both from centres of communication and from each other.

Although many Jacobite exiles in France and Spain were ready to rally to James III, not one is known to have left Russian service, either to avoid fighting France, or to lend support for the planned invasion of Britain. Although the claim has been made that '. . . most people, including most committed Jacobites, had pretty well written off any chance of further rebellion by the 1730s',[27] the exiles in Russia cannot simply be accused of political apathy. Despite the fact that prominent military leaders in Russia like Major General James Keith, General Peter Lacy and Vice Admiral Thomas Gordon were now on active campaign against France, they continued to be of service to the Cause from within Russia, regardless of the element of risk to their careers which this involved.

James Keith, who was commanding a regiment in Poland, was prepared to safeguard Jacobite interests as long as they did not openly conflict with his professional responsibilities. During the course of the campaign, and also as he was withdrawing from Poland in June 1736, he ensured that lands and villages belonging to James III's father-in-law, Prince James Sobieski, did not fall victim to damage or pillage at the hands of Russian troops.[28] The difficulty which he experienced in persuading his senior officer, Prince Shakhovskoi, to restrict traditional large-scale devastation of the Polish countryside by Russian plunderers at this time suggests that the favour granted to Sobieski may not have been easily won.[29] General Lacy was also involved in soliciting the favour of the Empress on behalf of Sobieski and his family, and James III sent a letter expressing his gratitude to the Jacobites for their services to his family.[30]

In addition to this, both James Keith and Thomas Gordon carried out a specifically Jacobite commission in early 1735, while Keith was stationed at Javarov, near Sobieski's estate, and Gordon was in chief command of the Russian fleet, still basking in the glory of its victory over the French fleet at Danzig the previous June. James III assigned Keith the unpleasant task of breaking the news to Prince James Sobieski of the death of his daughter Clementina, James's wife. This very personal request fulfilled, Keith was

---

25 William Hay to T.Gordon, 2/2/1732, *HMC Eglinton* etc., p.178.
26 Ezekiel Hamilton, Grand Master, to Members, 22/4/1722, *HMC Eglinton* etc., pp.184,185.
27 B.Lenman, *The Jacobite Cause* (Glasgow, 1986), p.86.
28 James Sobieski to James Keith, 15/6/1736, *HMC Elphinstone*, p.217.
29 J.Keith, *A Fragment*, pp.106–107.
30 James III to T.Gordon, 15/5/1734, RA Stuart 170/79.

approached by Sobieski on a matter of an overtly political nature. Sobieski, knowing him to be a prominent Jacobite, asked him to employ his influence as a military leader at the Russian court to secure the Sobieski succession for James III's younger son, Henry Benedict, the Duke of York. Although Sobieski was primarily concerned with the fate of his estates, the possible significance of this for the Jacobite cause could not be ignored. The intercession of Empress Anna on the Duke of York's behalf would almost certainly have been viewed by Britain as a hostile diplomatic gesture on the part of Russia. Sobieski proposed that Keith pass the responsibility for approaching the Empress and her ministers to Thomas Gordon, he, '. . . having been always employed by the King [James III] in his affairs with Russia'. It was hoped that she would in turn reach agreement with the King of Poland on Sobieski's behalf.[31] Although the outcome of this commission is unknown, it was almost certainly doomed to failure, both by the favourable aspect of Anglo-Russian relations and by the fact that the Duke of York was destined for a cardinalcy in the Church, and never became involved with matters of politics or inheritance. Nevertheless, the readiness of Keith and Gordon to support Sobieski was indicative of a continuing Jacobite commitment in adverse circumstances.

Insignificant as these demonstrations of Jacobite loyalty might appear, they cannot be underestimated. In the context of war against France and Russian hopes of British naval assistance in the Baltic, Jacobite activity in Russia could be seen as tantamount to obstruction of the war effort, and even this low level of Jacobite support could involve considerable risks. The Russian punishment for dereliction of duty was severe, and could mean banishment or even death. Colonel Manstein, who served with Keith in Poland, recorded the strict conditions under which the Russian campaign was conducted. He wrote that

> . . . The general [Keith] received reiterated orders from court not to remain a moment in inaction, but to undertake every thing that might strengthen the party of Augustus and weaken that of Stanislaus.[32]

Keith's assistance of Prince James Sobieski, who supported the French candidate, Stanislaus Lescszynski, would undoubtedly have contravened these orders. Keith himself was recognised as having Jacobite inclinations by foreign ministers in Russia. He was on amicable terms with Villardeau, the French plenipotentiary minister at St Petersburg, and took leave of him before the Polish campaign. Villardeau subsequently commented to the Foreign Minister Chauvelin that Keith was a Jacobite who,

> . . . quoique employé au service de Russie, est in petto [sic] plus ami qu'ennemi de la France et par consequent ses discours me doivent etre moins suspects que ceux de quantité de personnes qui auraient leurs raisons pour me'en imposer.[33]

31 J.Keith to T.Gordon, 20/2/1735, *HMC Eglinton* etc., pp.178–179.
32 Manstein, *Memoirs,* 1770 edn., p.70.
33 Villardeau to Chauvelin, 7/7/1733, *SIRIO* 81, pp.672–673.

Nevertheless, despite Keith's political inclinations, it was the high profile of his military position and the risk to his career which, as much as the lack of favourable circumstances, prevented him from becoming involved in any political capacity with the French minister in Russia. Career considerations inevitably held increasing sway over the exiles' mobility and freedom of decision, and those who held promoted posts in the armed forces enjoyed a status and lifestyle which would not be jeopardised without good reason. In addition to this, even had they wished to leave, the stringently bureaucratic entry and exit procedure, the oath of allegiance binding them to serve the Empress, and Russian reluctance to release its men to serve the enemy, would have posed considerable obstacles.

James III, conversely, trusted in the continued loyalty of his 'subjects', as the aftermath of the episode involving Keith and Sobieski illustrated. As a result of the concern shown for his interests, Sobieski wrote to his son-in-law to recommend Keith for the commission of lieutenant general. James III, who declared to Keith that he was '. . . fully persuaded that your behaviour on that occasion was chiefly influenced by your zeal and attachment to us', complied by granting him promotion, despite the fact that he was in the service of those opposing the Jacobite cause.[34] Although James III did express the hope that '. . . the day may yet come in which you may act as such in my own service', there was a strange irony in the fact that he was effectively furthering the career of an enemy. Indeed, had George Keith, the Earl Marischal, actually fought for France on the Rhine, as the Jacobites had planned, he might well have found himself face-to-face with his younger brother. James III's frequently expressed pleasure at James Keith's success in the Russian army was characteristic of his attitude towards his exiled supporters; their professional allegiances were not seen to compromise their Jacobite identity. Implicit in this was the hope that they could, at some future opportunity, employ their military skill and experience to his advantage.

Jacobite 'Ill Management'

While it is impossible to apportion responsibility for military success to individuals, it appears, with hindsight, that the role of Jacobite commanders in the Polish war had a more detrimental effect on Jacobite hopes of French assistance than either they or the Jacobite leadership were aware.

The Russian naval force which inflicted a decisive defeat on the French fleet off Danzig in June 1734 was commanded by Admiral Thomas Gordon in the flag ship 'Petr I i II', with Robert Little as his first captain.[35] James Kennedy was first rank captain on the 'Narva', and William Thomas Lewis was first captain on the second flag ship.[36] Gordon's journal of the campaign from 14 May to 30 June indicates

34 James III to J.Keith, 6/5/1735, 7/5/1735, *HMC Elphinstone*, pp.215,216.
35 'Spisok flotu', List of the Fleet, 1734, Berkh, *Zhizneopisaniya pervykh rossiiskikh admiralov*, 2, pp.171–172.
36 Vice-Admiral Thomas Saunders, who would have been second in command, had unfortunately died the previous year; Lewis was a Welshman, politics unknown, who was recruited by Saltykov in London in 1714 as a sub-lieutenant, by 1733 was a first captain, and in 1742 commanded a squadron. He had a long and successful career, became Admiral of the fleet in 1762 and died in 1769. Berkh, *Zhizneopisaniya*, 2, pp.51–65.

that he was responsible for co-ordinating the battle movements of the fleet and for initiating the attack, which brought the end of the siege of Danzig on 28 June.[37] James Keith, in a letter of congratulation to Gordon on the victory, wrote,

> . . . All the Poles that I have seen assures me that the so sudden surrender of the town was entirely owing to the appearance of the fleet which cut of all hopes of succours and that therefore they look on you as the main instrument of the loss of their liberty for that is their ordinary term for us who have been emploied on this side of Poland.[38]

The capitulation of Danzig, and the consequent flight of the French candidate to the Polish throne, Stanislas Lescszynski, marked the defeat of the French candidacy and was decisive to the outcome of the war.

The Russian land forces, which had swept into Poland to challenge the election of Lescszynski in August 1733, were commanded by General Peter Lacy, with an additional body of 6,000 men marching from the Ukraine under Major General James Keith. Another Lacy, George, possibly Peter's kinsman,[39] and Keith's kinsman, Robert Keith of Ludquhairn,[40] were among the Jacobites serving in the officer ranks.[41] Peter Lacy besieged the town of Danzig by land in 1734 and prevented French forces from coming to the assistance of Lescszynski.

---

37 Gordon's account in,'Journal of all the Remarkable Accidents and Proceedings of our voyage to Pillow and Dantzig. May 1734', NAS Abercairney GD 24/1/855, ff.110–117, Gordon's instructions and related documents, Ibid., ff.92–107, Extracts of journal printed *HMC Eglinton* etc., pp.191–196.

38 J.Keith to T.Gordon, 20/2/1735, *HMC Eglinton* etc. p.178.

39 According to Edith Kotasek, Peter Lacy had five daughers and three sons by the Livonian Countess Martha Philippina von Loeser, the youngest born in 1725. The eldest son, Michael, served under Eugene of Savoy and died of wounds in 1735, the second, Peter Andreas, was in Saxon service and a colonel during the Seven Years War, and the youngest, Franz Moritz, who was only nine in 1734, became an Austrian field marshal. Edith Kotasek, *Field Marschall Graf Lacy*, pp.2–4; Patrick O'Meara's draft *NDNB* entry for Lacy names his three sons as Peter Anthony, Francis Maurice and Patrick Boris, who became an infantry general. P O'Meara, entry for *New Dictionary of National Biography*, unpublished draft, 2001. In 1741, the French envoy referred to a major general in Russian service as 'Peter Lacy, younger', Peter Lacy's son, *SIRIO* 96, pp.422, 699. George Lacy, a lieutenant colonel in 1734, was probably a relative of the general's. RGVIA F489 o1 d7387.

40 The Keiths of Ludquhairn, in Buchan, were descended from John Keith, the second son of the 14th century Earl Marischal Edward Keith, and received the estates of Ludquhairn in the 15th century. Sir Robert Keith, eldest son of Sir William Keith, and fifth baronet of Ludquhairn, served under James Keith for 15 years in Russia as a captain, left with him for Prussian service, where he was a lieutenant colonel and Frederick II's A.D.C., and finally became a major general in Danish service, marrying Margaret Albertina Conradina von Suhm, daughter of a privy counsellor to Frederick II. *The Scots Magazine* (1750), p.597; R.Douglas, *Baronage*, pp.73–75. Sir William Keith, third baronet, had escaped to the continent after participating in the 1715 rising. A. and H.Tayler, 'The Jacobites of Buchan', in *The Book of Buchan*, ed.J.F.Tocher (Aberdeen, 1943), p.278.

41 Others of Scots origin, possibly with Jacobite connections, included Major Samuel Lindsay, Major 'Semion' Lesley, Lieutenant Colonel 'Vasili' Lesley, Major Andrew Inglis, Major Walmer Douglas, Lieutenant Colonel Charles Ramsay, Lieutenant Colonel Alexander Bruce (son of Robert Bruce, commandant of St Petersburg, and nephew of Field Marshal James Daniel Bruce), Colonel Andrew Johnstone. RGVIA F489 o1 d7387. Also William MacKenzie, D. Fedosov, *The Caledonian Connection*, p76.

In 1735, Lacy and James Keith, now a lieutenant general, jointly commanded a Russian force of eight regiments, 'above thirteen thousand men'[42] which marched to Silesia to join the Imperial army on the Rhine against the French, and encouraged them to seek peace terms. The significance of this campaign in terms of Russian military achievement will be discussed at a later stage. For the Jacobites, the movement of Russian troops against the French army was crucial in that it destroyed their hope of military assistance from France.

Jacobite plans for an invasion had demanded at least four to six thousand French land troops,[43] and their only hope of French assistance lay in the possibility that Britain would be forced to intervene on the Austrian side as a result of French military success. The entry of Britain into the war was the only goad which would prompt France to support an invasion.[44] France, on the other hand, as soon as Russia attacked Poland in 1733, had as first priority to support its candidate, Lescszynski, and to prevent Austria from expanding its control into Poland. To antagonise Britain by openly assisting the Jacobites might break British neutrality, bringing the whole might of the British navy against France and minimising its chances of victory. One of Britain's principal grounds for remaining neutral in the Polish war was a reluctance to antagonise France, which might prompt a Jacobite invasion.[45] This possibility was taken seriously by British ministers, who could not afford to ignore the potential threat of improved Franco-Spanish relations after 1733. As a result, neither Walpole nor Cardinal Fleury was prepared to antagonise the other to the point of open hostility. However, had it reached that point, a Jacobite invasion might have been considered.

In this context, Russia's role was directly detrimental to Jacobite hopes on two counts. Firstly, the physical presence of Russia's land forces on the Rhine and of its fleet in the Baltic ensured that the French army was fully occupied, and could not have spared the troops demanded by the Jacobites for an invasion. Secondly, Russian chances of victory were actually improved by France's reluctance to antagonise Britain. Cardinal Fleury declared that he had refused to send reinforcements to Danzig because he feared that Britain would break its neutral stance and the British navy would attack that of France in the Baltic.[46] James III complained bitterly at the French for their failure to relieve Danzig, and wrote that, '. . . King Stanislaus deserves a better fate than I fear he is like to have'.[47] James Keith concluded in his memoirs that Lescszynski's fatal move to Danzig, which '. . . lost him the crown', was due to his desire to unite with French reinforcements there which did not arrive.[48] The

---

42 Rondeau to Harrington, 31/5/1735, *SIRIO* 76, p.401.
43 Jacobite project of invasion, 17/4/1733, RA Stuart 161/37. Lord Cornbury had told Chauvelin that 14,000 were required. Cruickshanks, 'Lord Cornbury, Bolingbroke and a Plan to Restore the Stuarts, 1731–1735', RSP, 27 (1986), p.8.
44 James III to D.O'Brien, 14/7/1734 n.s., RA Stuart 171/134.
45 Newcastle to Waldegrave, 5/2/1734, in Black, *British Foreign Policy in the Age of Walpole*, p.150.
46 J.Black, *British Foreign Policy in the Age of Walpole*, p.151.
47 James III, 2/7/1734, RA Stuart 171/81.
48 Keith, *A Fragment*, pp.103,104.

presence of French reinforcements might well have altered the course of the war. Thus France's fear of British involvement actually enabled Russia to inflict the defeats on France which meant that British intervention was no longer an issue.

There was, therefore, a strong element of irony in the fact that the cream of Jacobite military talent was commanding the Russian forces and was undoubtedly instrumental in Russian victories. What is more, the Jacobite leadership remained quite unaware of it, and James III commented to George Keith during the Polish campaign that he was '. . . very glad your brother has had so honourable a command in the Czarina's service'.[49] It was George Keith who, a year later, made the comment that '. . . nothing but ill management on this side of the water [on the Continent] has kept or can keep the Elector on the Throne of Britain.'[50] Although he was indeed bemoaning the failure of the Jacobites themselves to coordinate foreign support, he perhaps did not consider that the military contribution of exiles such as his brother to enemy victories might also be seen to constitute a degree of 'ill management' on the part of the Jacobites.

The War with Turkey, 1736–1739

George II's optimism at the opening of Parliament in January 1736 that '. . . the pleasing prospect of peace abroad will greatly contribute to peace and good harmony at home'[51] followed news that France and Austria had initiated peace preliminaries the previous October. Pressure on the government to intervene in the war against France and to maintain an expensive defence force was suddenly lifted. While negotiations for the end of one war were being conducted, however, Russia had been plunged back into another. Controversy with the Tartars and the Ottoman Porte over southern frontier regions had intensified, and in early 1736 preparations were already under way for the first full campaign against Turkey and its allies.

The implications of this war for the Jacobite servicemen in Russia were considerable, in that the remoteness of the campaign from Europe and the Jacobite leadership threatened to cut them off completely from European Jacobite affairs. In early 1736 Field Marshal Lacy and Lieutenant General Keith were ordered to march directly from their units in Bohemia to join Münnich's army in the Ukraine,[52] and contact with Russia was maintained through naval Jacobites like Thomas Gordon who were able to remain with the Baltic fleet. During the 1737 campaign, however, not even Thomas Gordon could contact Keith; several letters were lost on route, and those which arrived had been on the

49 James III to George Keith, 22/10/1734, RA Stuart 174/102.
50 George Keith to Francis, Lord Sempill, 29/8/1736, quoted in Cruickshanks, *The Jacobite Challenge*, pp.43–44.
51 Cobbett, *Parliamentary History* 9, p.969.
52 Keith to Cabinet regarding imperial ukase 2/3/1736, RGADA F117 o1 d27, ll.5,5v; Rondeau to Harrington, 3/4/1736, *SIRIO* 76, p.499.
53 T.Gordon to George Keith, 20/5/1737, *HMC Eglinton* etc, p.188; Edgar to James Keith, n.d. 1737, RA Stuart 203/21.

road for two months.[53] In the latter half of the 1730's, therefore, circumstance as much as choice was distancing exiles in Russia from the Jacobite movement.

This increasingly poor situation for Jacobites in Russia was in sharp contrast to better opportunities elsewhere, the result of Britain's increasing isolation. Rather than providing Britain with the security it expected, the end of the Polish war had given the Jacobites the Austro-French alliance they hoped would permanently sever links between France and Britain, had strengthened both branches of the house of Bourbon, and had left Austria distrustful of its British ally for failing to come to its assistance. Spain, with French support, now began to use force against what it considered illegal British commercial shipping in the West Indies, while in November 1738, France concluded a subsidy treaty with Sweden, arousing fears of French hegemony in the north.

Surrounded by potential enemies, and more vulnerable than in 1733, the British government suspected France, Spain and Austria of Jacobite involvement. In August 1736 there were rumours, later proved false, of Spanish armaments at Barcelona which were '. . . certainly intended against England'.[54] At the same time, a letter from James III to the French minister Chauvelin was delivered, apparently accidentally, to the Earl of Waldegrave.[55] In it James III expressed hopes of enlisting the joint assistance of France and Austria for an invasion of Britain, and referred to a promise of support apparently made to him at an earlier date by Fleury himself. Although Waldegrave did not discount the possibility that this was merely, '. . . a Fetch of the Pretender's to put People in mind of him', the fact that French ministers might be implicated increased British mistrust of French intentions.

Britain's concern over possible Franco-Jacobite co-operation was well-founded; at the end of 1737, Cardinal Fleury actually sanctioned the secret mission of a Jacobite agent to the court of Anna Ivanovna. This envoy, Thomas Arthur Lally Tollendal, an Irish refugee and grenadier captain in French service,[56] was not given official instructions in case of discovery, and travelled on the pretext of conveying a lieutenant's commission to General Peter Lacy's brother,[57] but his unofficial remit was to repair the damage dealt to Franco-Russian relations by the Polish war, which had deprived France of diplomatic representation at St Petersburg. Although he detailed to Fleury the commercial and military benefits which would accrue to France should an alliance with Russia isolate Austria and Britain,

54 Extract of letter Robinson to H.Walpole, 22/8/1736 n.s., encl. in H.Walpole to Keene, 31/8/1736 n.s., BL Add.Ms.32792, ff.108,109,111.

55 James III to [ ], 28/8/1736, BL Add.Ms.32792, ff.353–355, encl. in Waldegrave to Newcastle, 11/10/1736, BL Add.Ms.32792, ff.347–351.

56 Tollendal, whose father commanded the Irish regiment in France, and who has been described as one of those exiles '. . . prepared to exert themselves to the maximum in the hope of Stuart Restoration', was among those closest to Prince Charles Edward, and commander of Lally's regiment with the French auxiliary force poised to invade Britain in 1745. He was unjustly executed in France in 1766 after military disasters in India during the Seven Years War. McLynn, *The Jacobites*, pp.84–85, 134–135.

57 The name of the recipient of this commission, which Fleury had given to Lally, is unknown, (it was not George Lacy, who was an infantry colonel in 1736), Lally to Fleury, 1737, Rambaud, *Recueil*, 8 Russie, p.328.

his political ambition was to dissociate Russia from Britain in the hope of obtaining assistance for the Stuart cause, and Admiral Thomas Gordon had received orders from James III to recommend him to the Russian court.[58]

The poor state of Franco-Russian relations was demonstrated when Lally was forcibly detained on his arrival in Riga in early 1738, and kept on Peter Lacy's estates in Livonia for two months to await the general's return. However, Lacy released him and, with Thomas Gordon's support, gave him both a passport for St Petersburg and a letter of recommendation for Count Osterman.[59] As well as being received by Osterman, Lally also managed, with the assistance of Anna Ivanovna's French chamberlain, M.de la Serre, to obtain audiences on at least two occasions with the imperial favourite, Count Biron, the Duke of Courland. Although Cardinal Fleury's fear of antagonising Britain made him reluctant openly to encourage Lally's mission, or even to correspond with him while in Russia, thus depriving him of the diplomatic credibility and support he required for a significant breakthrough, Lally's efforts did enjoy a degree of success. During the four and a half months of his visit, he received repeated assurances from Biron of '. . . le désir qu'il avoit de les [France and Russia] voir réunies'.[60] Although there was no immediate prospect of Jacobite assistance, his most important achievement both for the Jacobites and for France, was the renewal of Franco-Russian diplomatic relations; in 1738 Prince Antiokh Kantemir was sent to Paris, and Joachim-Jacques Trotti, Marquis de La Chétardie, was accredited to St Petersburg the following year.

Lally's diplomatic success contributed to the crisis which hit the British ministry in 1738, when war with Spain over colonial trading rights became inevitable, despite ministerial fears that it would bring about the alliance between France and Spain which the Jacobites desired.[61] In May 1738, Waldegrave reported that the Queen of Spain had warned that '. . . if we force her to a war, she can raise such troubles in England, as will make us sick of it'.[62] French reluctance to ally with Britain was interpreted as support for Spain, and reports of Jacobite negotiations with French ministers undermined any trust in Cardinal Fleury. In 1739, Waldegrave expressed his suspicion of Fleury, believing that '. . . nobody would go to greater lengths to help the Pretender than ye Cardinal, were he satisfied of a probability of success'.[63] By the time war with Spain was eventually declared in October 1739, the Jacobites had been involved in negotiations with Cardinal Fleury for some time, and had drawn up several invasion projects. James Keith's brother, the Earl Marischal, was sent to

58 Lally to Fleury, 2/10/1738, Lally to Amelot, August 1738, Ibid., pp.333, 336–337.
59 Lally to Fleury, 16/3/1738, Lally to Amelot, August 1738, Ibid., pp.329, 333.
60 Lally to Amelot, August 1738, Ibid., p.334; Lally reasoned that it was in Biron's personal interest to gain the support of France in case the death of the Empress should deprive him of his power, Lally to Fleury, 26/9/1738, *Ibid.*, p.335.
61 In November 1737, Newcastle had declared that Britain would '. . . do everything it could' to avoid war with Spain. Newcastle to Keene, 4/11/1737, BL Add. Ms. 32796, f.111.
62 Waldegrave to Newcastle, 16/5/1738 n.s., BL Add. Ms. 32798, ff.6,7.
63 Waldegrave to Newcastle, early 1739, BL Add. Ms. 32801, f.10; see also Waldegrave to Newcastle, 11/5/1738, PRO SP 78/218, ff.168–172.

Madrid to enlist Spanish support for a rising, and Jacobite optimism was fuelled by news of growing opposition to the Walpole ministry.[64] In a complete reversal of the role of arch-rival, which Russia had played in British foreign policy during the reign of George I, an Anglo-Russian agreement now became Britain's only means of countering the Jacobite threat by regaining the security lost at the rupture with France. By 1739, in a calculated effort to diminish the French influence which Lally had tried to build at St Petersburg, negotiations were under way for the first Anglo-Russian defensive alliance.

James Keith: Jacobite Exile or Russian General?

Only one Russian Jacobite, James Keith, was directly affected by the political situation in Western Europe and had the opportunity to become involved in Jacobite affairs. In March 1738, while Keith was overseeing the Ukrainian defence lines, having to be carried by stretcher between fortifications as a result of a leg wound he had received at the battle of Ochakov, a petition was presented to Parliament on his behalf by his cousin, John Keith, the Earl of Kintore.[65] Its purpose was to procure government consent for James to inherit his cousin's estates, thus circumventing their possible forfeiture, which would result if his attainted elder brother George Keith inherited them on Kintore's death.[66] An Act of Parliament was required to ensure that George's claim could be waived in James's favour. In January James had elicited the assistance of the Russian ambassador Antiokh Kantemir, and, on the advice of the President of the Court of Session in Scotland, had the Empress herself intercede with George II on his behalf the following month.[67] Her letter was a sign of her acknowledgement of the great military service he had rendered to Russia during her reign, and she described, '. . . the particular services and merits, by which Our Lieutenant General Keith perfectly has deserved our Imperial Favour'. Her request was '. . . to confirm in due form of law his Rights to the Possession of the Estates and Titles belonging to the Earl of Kintore and devolving to him after the said Earl's and his Brother's decease'.[68]

---

64 James III wrote to Thomas Gordon that '. . . the general situation of affaires both at home and abroad looks I think favorable enough for my Cause', James III to T.Gordon, 21/1/1739, RA Stuart 213/24. George Keith, hearing news of the war and of domestic unrest, congratulated James on '. . . so fair a prospect at present of your affairs'. G.Keith to James III, 3/8/1739, RA Stuart 216/115.

65 *Journals of the House of Commons*, 23, 1737–1741, pp.70–71.

66 Sir John Keith, 3rd son of William 6th Earl Marischal, had been created Earl of Kintore in 1677. His grandson was the Earl in question, John Keith, 3rd Earl of Kintore (1699–1758), who, being childless, passed the title and estates to his unmarried brother William in 1758. At William's death three years later the closest male descendant was George Keith, 10th Earl Marischal, who had, by Act of Parliament, been enabled, 'notwithstanding his attainder . . . to take or inherit any estate . . .' on 22 May 1760. (*Journals of the House of Lords*, 33 George 2, p.703a.) Balfour Paul mistakenly maintains that his attainder prevented him from inheriting Kintore's estates, and that they lay dormant until he died in 1778. Balfour Paul, *The Scots Peerage* 5, pp.240–241.

67 J.Keith to A.Kantemir, 10/1/1738, Biblioteka Saltykova Shchedrina, Avt.136 ll.2,3; James Erskine to Kantemir, 15/4/1738, NAS Elphinstone GD 156/60, folder 7, f.2.

68 Anna Ivanovna to George II, 18/2/1738, PRO SP 102/50, ff.71–72.

The Bill was presented to the House of Commons on 8th March 1738, '. . . for continuing and securing the succession . . . as if the said George late Earl Marischal had never existed, or had died without ever having been attainted'. The motion to read the Bill before Parliament was passed by a majority of only three votes, and Lord Glenorchy submitted it for its first reading on 4th April.[69] However, as a result of what Keith described as '. . . the peevishness of a minister', probably Robert Walpole himself, it was eventually rejected.[70] The ministry had taken exception to Keith's Jacobitism, and had complained that Keith had not presented his case himself, despite the fact that he had received news of proceedings while in the Ukraine, too late even to respond by letter. In London he was '. . . freely spoke of as an Enemy to our King', although it was observed that '. . . Our Government had granted much greater Favours to profess'd Papists and Jacobites & who were then and afterwards continu'd such'.[71] Kantemir later informed Keith that letters written to both Keith and Kintore regarding the case had gone missing. It is possible, given the political nature of the subject, that the letters had been deliberately intercepted, and that this had a bearing on the outcome of the case, but this remains unconfirmed.

George II managed cleverly to avoid damage to Anglo-Russian relations while using the political implications of Keith's request to state his continued strong opposition to the Jacobites. In his reply to Empress Anna he emphasised that the matter was 'out of our hands', because the Kintore estate had been placed under government control by George I. The principal ground for his refusal was unequivocally political. He wrote,

> . . . the Difficulty that occurs in it is that the said Sieur Keith being justly obnoxious, by the whole Tenour of his past Behaviour to our Government, has not however yet submitted to give any the least assurance either thro' your Czarish Majesty, or otherwise, of his altering his past Conduct, & behaving aggressively towards us for the future.

However, he made the condition that the case would be considered if

> . . . the said Sieur Keith be sincerely disposed to abstain from all farther Misconduct towards us & will give us proper Assurances thereof & of his future Allegiance, before the Opening of the ensuing Session.[72]

Keith's case gives some insight into both British and Russian attitudes towards Jacobite exiles at this time. Russia treated him like the Russian general he was. Not only did he have the support of the Empress and the Russian ambassador, but the state of Anglo-Russian relations was in his favour. They presented his case as though it were not an exile, but a Russian subject whose part they were taking. There was a certain irony in the fact that the Empress

69 *Journals of the House of Commons*, 23 (1737–1741), pp.70–71.
70 J.Keith to [James Erskine, Lord Grange], 11/3/1739, *HMC Mar and Kellie*, p.551.
71 James Erskine (Lord Grange) to Kantemir, 15/4/1738, NAS Elphinstone, GD 156/60 folder 7, f.2.
72 George II to Anna Ivanovna, 2/5/1738, AVPR F36 o1 d131, ll.1–2; PRO SP 102/50, ff.78–79.

emphasised in her letter to George II that the fulfilment of his request would be regarded in political terms, as 'a testimony of friendship' between the two monarchs.[73] This represented a significant diplomatic gesture at a time when an Anglo-Russian treaty was still under negotiation.

In view of increased British sensitivity to the Jacobites in 1738, however, Keith's request was poorly timed. Although Keith had not been actively involved with the Jacobites for twenty years, and had even marched to the Rhine to support Britain's ally, Austria, in the last war, he was still regarded by Britain as a potential threat to British security, a view exacerbated by his brother's Jacobite involvements in Spain. George II took the opportunity of using the case to the benefit of Anglo-Russian relations. The length and distinction of Keith's career in Russia was not sufficient to allow the government to welcome a dissident, Russian general or not, back to Britain.

At the same time, the promise that Keith's case would be reconsidered, should he renounce the Jacobite cause, provided him with a clear incentive to do so and to swear his allegiance to the Hanoverian monarchy. Not only would such a transfer of loyalty bring himself and his descendants material gain, thus removing the necessity of a foreign military career, but it would also cement Anglo-Russian relations and possibly improve Keith's career prospects in Russia. In this way, Keith's Jacobite allegiance was placed in direct conflict with his material and career interests.

It was the leg wound which Keith had received at Ochakov in July 1737 which, ironically, presented him with an ideal opportunity to visit Britain and, should he wish, to renounce the cause which had initially brought him into the service of Russia. In October of that year Keith was flattered to be placed in sole charge of the Ukrainian defence lines, but he was unable to walk more than a few steps unaided.[74] His condition worsened, and in autumn 1738 he was carried to St Petersburg from Poltava, where George Keith had travelled from Spain to visit him. By September, to the consternation of James's friends in Russia, his physician, Dr Horn, believed that the leg would have to be amputated.[75] In November George Keith insisted on seeking the advice of the best Paris physicians before the decision to amputate was taken, and both brothers arrived in Paris in February.[76] In late autumn 1739, after being fully cured of his wound at Barèges in the Pyrenees,[77] James Keith made his first visit

---

73 Anna Ivanovna to George II, 18/2/1738, PRO SP 102/50, ff.71–72.

74 J.Keith to G.Biron, 27/10/1737, RGADA F11 o1 d550, l.3.

75 T.Gordon to James III, 15/9/1738, *HMC Eglinton* etc., pp.188,189.

76 Rondeau to Harrington, 2/12/1738, *SIRIO* 80, p.398; G.Keith to [ ], 16/2/1739, RA Stuart 213/151.

77 There are accounts of Keith's treatment in Paris which describe a long consultation among eighteen doctors and a successful operation to remove a bullet and scraps of cloth and bone from the wound. However, George Keith's own account was more accurate. The surgeons were reluctant to operate due to the proximity of the wound to the main artery, and sent Keith instead to the hot baths at Barèges. Thomas Gordon described how '. . . by the jolting of the coach several small bones are come out of the wound which the Chirurgeons could not come at'. T.Gordon to J.Gordon, 1/9/1738, NAS Abercairney, GD 24/1/855, f.73.

to Britain in twenty years. The decision to go there appears to have made at the last minute because George Keith reported to James III as late as August 1739 that his brother was on the point of setting off for Russia, and he himself for Spain.[78] However, by January 1740, James Keith was not only in London, but actually present at the Hanoverian court.

James Keith's Visit to Britain

Both the *Scots Magazine* and the *London Magazine* recorded in similar terms the audience of James Keith with George II on 25 January 1740, emphasising his military prominence and glossing over his political past. He was described as a 'Russian general in chief', who '. . . went from Scotland in 1716'. Attired in the uniform of the Ismailovsky guards regiment, he was introduced to George II as a Russian dignitary by the Russian ambassador Prince Shcherbatov, and '. . . was graciously received'. The *Scots Magazine* also drew attention to his status and general acceptance in society, writing that, '. . . he is likewise much caressed by the principal nobility'.[79] The political significance of Keith's audience was sufficient to be remarked upon by his contemporaries. The French ambassador in Russia, the Marquis de la Chétardie, heard an account of it from the Saxon envoy while Keith was still in Britain and reported to Amelot that

> . . . à la faveur de son habit des gardes Ismailowsky, on ne l'avait point
> regardé à Londres comme un expatrié; au contraire, le roi de la Grande-
> Bretagne l'avait traité avec beaucoup de bonté.[80]

This official welcome marked a distinct contrast with the unequivocal language of George II's letter, particularly in view of the fact that the Jacobite threat in 1740 had not retreated but had rather intensified.

Not surprisingly, the visit of a notorious Jacobite to the Hanoverian court aroused a great deal of speculation amongst contemporaries. The ministry was disturbed throughout the early part of 1740 by reports of military preparations in Spain and rumours of an invasion attempt from Ireland, and its agents brought reports that George Keith had left James to undertake a Jacobite mission to Spain just prior to the latter's visit to England.[81] What reason could George II possibly have for welcoming an enemy into London at such a crucial time, and why should a Jacobite consent to visit England if not for some secret political end? According to one source, while in England, Keith actually '. . . acknowledged George II for his lawful king'.[82] La Chétardie was led to

78 G.Keith to James III, 28/8/1739, RA Stuart 217/24.
79 *The Scots Magazine* (1740), p.43; *The London Magazine and Monthly Chronologer* (1740), p.48.
80 La Chétardie to Amelot, 23/2 or 5/3/1740, *SIRIO* 86, p.249.
81 Waldegrave to Newcastle, 13/1, 27/1, 31/1, 2/2, 20/2/1740, PRO SP 78/222, ff.1, 54, 59, 73, 98.
82 Sir A.Mitchell, *Memoirs and Papers of Sir Andrew Mitchell*, edited by Andrew Bisset, 2 vols. (London, 1850), 2, p.447; Sir Andrew Mitchell was a close friend of Keith's during his later service in Prussia.

believe, mistakenly, that George II had returned to Keith the estates his brother had forfeited after the 1715 rising. This prompted the conclusion that Keith had come to some agreement with the Hanoverian monarchy:

> . . . il me frappa en ce que la complaisance de SMB (Sa Majesté Britannique) pour être opposée aux constitutions devient si marquée, qu'il est simple de soupçonner, qu'elle est déterminée par de puissants motifs.[83]

There are several possible reasons why Keith should have travelled to London so unexpectedly in early 1740. In a letter of recommendation for Keith to Robert Walpole from Prince Kantemir in Paris in January 1740, Kantemir wrote, '. . . Il s'y rend pour faire sa cour à sa majesté Britannique et pour y solliciter cette affaire qui a été recommandée à sa majesté par l'impératrice, ma souveraine'.[84] In view of the fact that Kantemir had previously supported his inheritance claim, it is probable that the letter referred to the correspondence which had passed between George II and Anna Ivanovna regarding the Kintore estate. This was confirmed in an account of Keith's visit, written by his brother to James III, in which Walpole was reported to have said in private, '. . . Is Mr Keith come to plague us with his damned bill while his brother is going into Galicia against us?'[85] Keith was apparently sufficiently confident of his rights, and prepared to exploit his status as a Russian general by approaching Walpole in person in an attempt to reverse the royal and parliamentary decision. With relation to the Kintore affair, his sojourn in London also happened to coincide with the election of John, Earl of Kintore, to the position of Grand Master Mason of England in March 1740.[86]

Keith's visit might also have been prompted by the state of Anglo-Russian diplomacy. Villeneuve, the French mediator in the peace negotiations which ended the Turkish war in 1739, had succeeded in alienating Russia from Austria, its former ally. La Chétardie, the new French ambassador in St Petersburg, had been instructed to consolidate these efforts to build up French influence in Russia, thus foiling the projected Anglo-Russian treaty. It was also feared that France might use its influence in Sweden against the unpopular Russian-backed monarchy. In early 1740 la Chétardie's intrigues were of particular concern to the ministry because Edward Finch, the successor of the late Claudius Rondeau, had not yet arrived in Russia to continue British negotiations. It is possible, therefore, that Keith was under instructions from the Empress to assess the state of Anglo-Russian relations with regard to the possible implications of French intrigue. Britain's immediate interest in discovering French activities in Russia would explain why Keith, regardless of his

83 La Chétardie to Amelot, 23/2 or 5/3/1740, *SIRIO* 86, p.249.
84 Kantemir to R.Walpole, 14/1/1740, L.N.Maikov, *Materialy dlya biografii kn. A.D.Kantemira* (St Petersburg, 1903), p.157.
85 G.Keith to James III, 29/4/1740, RA Stuart 222/16.
86 On his return to St Petersburg, with Kintore's sanction, Keith became Provincial Grand Master of Russia, B.Telepneff, 'Freemasonry in Russia', in W.J.Songhurst, ed., *Ars Quatuor Coronatorum*, 35, (1922), pp.261–291; A.G.Cross, 'British Freemasons in Russia During the Reign of Catherine the Great', *OSP* ns, 4 (1971), pp.43–44.

own politics, should be granted a court audience. This would certainly explain la Chétardie's concern with the affair. According to Keith's biographer, Varnhagen von Ense, Keith had received secret orders from St Petersburg while in Paris to carry out espionage activity as a result of the expected rupture between Sweden and Russia. Apparently, he discovered that France was secretly fitting out ships at Brest which were bound for the Baltic, and sent detailed reports of this back to Russia.[87] Varnhagen's account is inaccurate; in 1740 a French squadron was preparing to sail to the West Indies. Nor is there any confirmation that Keith was on a secret official mission. Nevertheless, his official reception as a Russian representative at the British court and the personal welcome and reward which awaited him on his return to Russia, strongly suggest this as a possibility. If this were true, Keith's official capacity would once again have been in conflict with Jacobite interests.

Whatever Keith's Russian instructions were, there is evidence that he was also involved in Jacobite negotiations while in Britain, and there is no indication that the alleged promise by George II to secure the Kintore inheritance tempted him while in Britain to renounce his Jacobite allegiance. This was consistent not only with Walpole's reaction to his visit and his failure to win his inheritance, but with the close contact maintained between the Jacobite leaders and the Keith brothers throughout this period. George Keith had intended to fight in the 1738 campaign in the Crimea alongside his brother, and wrote to James III that this '. . . may help me to be good for something, if an occasion offers for our Majesty's Service'.[88] During the course of James Keith's treatment, James III took a great personal interest in his condition, and Thomas Gordon kept him abreast of developments. While in Paris, George Keith was in close correspondence with Edgar, James III's secretary, and in March 1739, he observed with pleasure the unpopularity of the Walpole ministry, with the wish that '. . . we [the Jacobites] may be gainers by the change'.[89] The most conclusive evidence of James Keith's attempts to promote the Jacobite cause during his visit to Britain is contained in a letter written by George Keith to James III from Madrid, just prior to James Keith's audience with George II:[90]

> . . . Mr Keith did what he could for your Service, he had more civility from The Duke of Argyle than from any one, but Argyle never would give him any encouragement to converse of Your Majesty's affairs; they were together when Argyle got a message which vexed him, he said on reading it, Mr Keith, fall flat, fall edge, we must get rid of these people, which might imply both man and master, or only the man. However, Mr Keith resolved on this to speak freely to him . . .'[91]

87 K.A.Varnhagen von Ense, 'Feldmarshall Jakob Keith', *Biographische Denkmäle*, 3rd.edn. part 7 (Leipzig, 1888), pp.41,42.
88 G.Keith to James III, 20/11/1737, RA Stuart 202/59.
89 George Keith to Edgar, 14/3/1739, RA Stuart 214/116.
90 George Keith's letter was dated 15/1/1740 n.s., that is 4/1/1740 o.s. James's audience was on 25/1/1740 n.s, ten days later.
91 G.Keith to James III, 15/1/1740, RA Stuart 222/142.

It is likely that the Duke of Argyll, who was instrumental in Walpole's fall in 1742, was referring to Walpole, the 'man', rather than the 'master', George II. Nevertheless, Keith was actively involved in assessing the level of domestic support for James III in early 1740, while his brother assumed command of the restoration attempt to be launched from Spain.

Unfortunately for the Jacobites, the Spanish invasion plan collapsed under Jacobite suspicions of Spanish insincerity. In February 1740, George Keith had received a commission from James III to be commander-in-chief of all the Jacobite forces in Scotland during the Rising.[92] However, he and Ormonde, waiting in vain for developments, became increasingly doubtful that the Spanish forces gathered at Galicia were intended for any end but to frighten Britain, and the enterprise was eventually called off.[93]

In any case, James Keith had decided to return to Russia even before this fiasco took place. James III had responded to this news with a veiled plea for support, writing that, '. . . I would fain flatter myself that something may yet happen which might incline you to steer your course another way before you arrive there'.[94] It may have been this letter which prompted Keith's decision to make a brief stop in London on the way back to Russia. What is clear, however, is that, despite his personal inclinations, his professional attachments to Russia were by now too strong to justify participation in another Rising.

Whether or not Anna Ivanovna was aware of the fact that Keith might have been tempted to remain in Europe, his reception when he arrived in St Petersburg vindicated his decision to return. It had already been publicised in March that Keith had been appointed to succeed General Rumiantsev to the prestigious position of commander-in-chief of the Ukraine, and the morning after his arrival in June, she invited him to court and presented him with a diamond-studded sword and a gold medallion.[95] To the envy of Field Marshal Münnich, who had coveted the powerful post for himself, Keith had been given both civil and military commands in the Ukraine. Finch observed that

> . . . as both these together are unusual, the command the most lucrative and the same time the most important in the gift of this court, it shews both the favour and the consideration in which he is here.[96]

Nothing was more illustrative than this appointment, which made Keith one of the most powerful and best-respected foreigners in Russia, of the gulf between the real career prospects offered in foreign service and the illusory hopes extended by Jacobitism.

92 Commission dated 2/2/1740, Marquis of Ruvigny and Raineval, *The Jacobite Peerage, Baronetage, Knightage and Grants of Honour* (Edinburgh, 1904), p.245.
93 George Keith to James III, 1/4/1740, 8/4/1740, 15/4/1740, RA Stuart 221/127,148,165.
94 James III to J.Keith, 1/8/1739, RA Stuart 219/114.
95 La Chétardie to Amelot, 8/19 March 1740, *SIRIO* 86, p.260; Finch to Harrington, 10/21 June 1740, also 14/25 June 1740, *SIRIO* 85, pp.52,55.
96 Finch to Harrington, 12/23 June 1740, *SIRIO* 85, p.93; La Chétardie to Amelot, 12/23 July 1740, *SIRIO* 86, pp.488–489.

Conclusion

The circumstances surrounding Keith's unexpected and curiously-timed visit
to the Hanoverian court could not have been better arranged for a case study
of the changing identity of a successful Jacobite exile. How long, for example,
did Jacobite exiles retain their Jacobite identity, not only in their own eyes, and
in those of their host monarch, but with regard to their treatment by Britain?
To what extent was this identity a matter of personal choice, of a conscious
change of allegiance, to what extent a product of international political
tensions? Here was a loyal Jacobite who, by coincidence, after twenty years,
had been transported from the country of his exile to the centre of the conflict
which had exiled him and presented with a free choice to reconsider his past
and redirect his future. Although he arrived at a time when the Jacobite
movement needed him most, and his own brother was about to command an
invasion, he also had a strong material incentive to deny his Jacobitism. His
third option, and the one which he followed, was to return to the secure,
lucrative and prestigious career he had found in exile. His adopted identity,
that of Russian general, served as a unique *passe partout* which allowed him
access to two of the greatest enemies of Jacobitism, Walpole and George II. Yet
the duality of his position remained; although treated as a foreign dignitary, his
Jacobitism was never forgotten. On a personal level his role allowed him
freedom both to view his situation objectively and to speak his mind, which he
did at the Court of St James:

> . . . as to the country here, I never was in one I like less . . . everything is in
> confusion, the one side crying out against arbitrary power; the other
> crying out that it is their mutinous proceedings which oblige them to act
> so.[97]

Russia had become less a place of exile than an escape from hopeless
political compromise. This was clearly demonstrated by Keith's reaction to the
demand, just prior to the royal audience, that he swear the customary oaths of
allegiance to George II, thereby effectively renouncing his Jacobitism. Rather
than committing himself to either, he declared that '. . . having taken them to
the Empresse of Russia, he would take them to no Prince in Europe while he
had the honour to be in her service'.[98] Time and distance, but most importantly, the favourable career conditions in Russia up to and during Anna's
reign, allowed one way of life to be superseded by another. Where possible a
compromise was reached between a lasting personal loyalty to Jacobitism and
more temporary professional obligation, but the latter inevitably prevailed as a
survival practicality, sometimes even at the expense of the former. Keith's
example was mirrored to a greater or lesser extent by all those Jacobites who
were able to establish themselves successfully in Russia.

97 James Keith's account of his court visit, in G.Keith to James III, 29/4/1740, RA Stuart
   222/16.
98 *Ibid.*

SEVEN

The Jacobite as Foreign Mercenary

The Myth of Foreign Favouritism

Despite the shift of Jacobite aspirations further West, to France and Spain, the Polish and Turkish wars encouraged Jacobite mercenaries to remain in Russian service and concentrate on a military career. It is tempting to ascribe their success, as foreigners, to Anna Ivanovna's alleged preference for non-natives, a popular perception of her propagated by her contemporaries and perpetuated by later historians.[1] Although she was Peter I's niece, her marriage to the Duke of Courland, and the retinue of Baltic Germans which followed her to Russia, identified her in the eyes of the native nobility as an incomer. Rondeau, the British minister in St Petersburg, observed in 1731 that

> ... The old russ nobility are very uneasy to see how the affairs of this country are managed and they find themselves entirely excluded from Her Majesty's confidence, who is wholly and absolutely governed by her favourite, count Biron, the two counts Levenwolde, Paul Iwanitsch Jaguginsky and baron Osterman ... As all these gentlemen are foreigners and continually about Her Majesty, she grants no favours but through them, at which the russ are enraged, and even the Czarinna's nearest relations have hardly anything to say.[2]

The most extreme retrospective accounts of foreign infiltration described how

> ... Germans poured down on Russia just like litter from a bag full of holes, clustering around the court, around the throne, sneaking into every profitable place of the administration.[3]

---

1 S.F.Platonov, for example, wrote, 'german overlordship lasted for ten years; for ten years the Russians were humiliated in their best senses and feelings' (my translation), *Leksii po russkoi istorii* (St Petersburg, 1901), p.476; V.O. Klyuchevsky, *Kurs russkoi istorii* (Moscow, 1908); L.G.Beskrovny, 'Armiya i flot, in N.M.Druzhinin et al., *Ocherki Istorii SSSR Rossiia vo vtoroi chetverti XVIIIv:*, (Moscow, 1957), pp.296–309. The 'sickly condition of Russia during Anna's reign' has been blamed on the internal rivalry of influential Russians who failed to 'preserve the Russian national dignity' built up by Peter I and allowed foreigners to occupy all the most prominent positions. Solov'ev, *Istoriya Rossii*, 19, p.1218.

2 Rondeau to Harrington, 4/1/1731 o.s., *SIRIO*, 66, pp.271–273. In early 1732, Lefort, the Saxon foreign minister, observed, '. . . On est sous un regne, où la souveraine veut être obéi sans murmure et l'on a si bien écarté les critiques, qu'il ne paraît pas rester vestige de Russes, dont l'on peut craindre des suites facheuses . . . certainement le parti étranger a le dessus et tient les rênes.' Lefort to Augustus II, 19/2/1732, *SIRIO* 5, p.448. See also Magnan to Chauvelin, 29/11/1731, *SIRIO* 81, p.261; 'Unzufriedenheit der Nation mit dem Regiment der Ausländer', Lefort to Augustus II, 23/9/1732, *SIRIO* 5, pp.464–465.

3 Klyuchevsky, p.390: It is important to note in this context that the Russian word 'nemets', 'german' (lit.'dumb') was a generic term for western non-Orthodox foreigners. Amburger has differentiated between 'inozemets' (a newly arrived or visiting foreigner) *(cont'd)/*

Although the myth of an all-pervasive foreign influence, particularly in civil administration, has been discredited,[4] the power of foreigners in the topmost echelons should not be underestimated. The Cabinet of Ministers, created informally in 1730, then formally by Imperial decree in October 1731, which became the most powerful organ of Russian affairs and exercised ultimate control over domestic administration, legislation and finance, as well as foreign policy, was largely foreign.[5] Moreover, although Münnich, Osterman and Iaguzhinsky had been prominent as individuals during the previous reign,[6] their power had been considerably tempered by the dominance of the Dolgoruky family over Peter II,[7] and Anna's accession and the banishment of the Dolgorukys allowed Osterman and other foreigners to wield their influence more freely. Osterman, initially the only foreign member of the Cabinet, was able to assume control of it.[8] By October 1730, Iaguzhinsky, at the peak of his career as procurator-general, completely dominated the Senate, despite being its only foreign member.[9]

cont'd   and 'nemets' (foreign settler), but in this case the latter was a general term, E.Amburger, 'Die weiteren Schicksäle der alten Einwohnerschaft der Moskauer Ausländer-sloboda seit der Zeit Peters I', *JGO* NF 20 (1972), p.167.

4 Basing her study on statistics of members of the top four service ranks or 'generalitet' of 1730, Brenda Meehan-Waters has concluded that, of 53 who became senators, 4 were foreign; of the 22 members of the 1730 Senate, only the Pole, Iaguzhinsky, was foreign; only one person of foreign descent, Count Jakob (James) Bruce, who was in any case scarcely considered foreign (Solov'ev, 20, p.1171), became a president of a non-military college. During the period of conflict between court factions which marked Anna's accession, none of the many projects either for reform or for maintaining autocracy was signed by any of the 54 top-ranking foreigners: '. . . The overwhelming majority of foreigners in the generalitet were unable to translate their position in the service elite into a place in the political elite . . . in the social elite . . . or in the economic elite,' Meehan-Waters, *Autocracy and Aristocracy, The Russian Service Elite of 1730* (New Brunswick, 1982), pp.58, 61, 142.

5 Copy of Imperial Decree, *SIRIO* 104, intro. by Yur'ev, pp.xxxiv,1,2. Its core membership never exceeded three, and throughout Anna's reign the Westphalian Count Osterman and the Russian Prince A.M.Cherkassky held unbroken office. Of the native nobility, Count G.I.Golovkin, A.I.Ushakov, A.P.Volynsky and Prince N.Yu.Trubetskoi participated at some time in cabinet meetings. The foreigners involved in cabinet decisions were two Germans, Count Osterman and Baron Münnich, who was President of the College of War, one Pole, Count Iaguzhinsky, and the Livonian brothers Counts Friedrich Casimir and Reinhold Gustav Löwenwolde. B.G.Slitsan, 'Organy gosudarstvennogo upravleniya', in Druzhinin et al., *Ocherki istorii SSSR XVIIIv*, pp.269–296.

6 This argument has been put forward, quite rightly, to place the extent of foreign influence in perspective. See P.Dukes, *The Rise of Russian Absolutism*, p.107.

7 Liria reported in 1728 that, since the fall of Menshikov, Osterman had become Vice-Chancellor and was considered the principal minister, but, '. . . being a foreigner, he does not dare to undertake anything on his own initiative', Liria to De la Paz, 10/1/1728 n.s., *RA* 1909, p.345. The Dolgorukys almost destroyed his career (*Ibid.*, p.356) but he made himself indispensable to the favourite, Ivan Dolgoruky; Lefort wrote of Osterman, 'il parait même que la famille brillante sente avoir besoin des conseils d'Ostermann; le favori ne jure que par lui', Lefort to Augustus II, 5/12/1729, *SIRIO* 5, p.334.

8 Lefort observed, 'Des trois membres nommés on ne saurait proprement tabler que sur Ostermann avec Biron, lesquels vont d'accord. Golovkine et Cercaski n'y sont que proforma, pour complaire à la nation et il y a toute apparence que le comte Ostermann et Biron dirigeront tout'. Lefort to Augustus II, 5/11/1731, *SIRIO* 5, p.436.

9 In 1730, Lefort commented that 'Il est facile d'entrevoir que la nomination des membres du sénat n'est qu'un proforma, pour donner le tems d'expulser les pièces de rebut', Lefort to Augustus II, 9/20 March 1730, *SIRIO* 5, p.374; Iaguzhinsky was the one '. . . qui tient le sénat sous ses ordres', Lefort to Augustus II, 16/10/1730, *Ibid., p.385.*

Similarly, Field Marshal Golitsyn's presence at Anna's court in 1730 was by no means an example of Russian influence in court circles, for he owed his position entirely to Osterman, Biron and Löwenwolde, who had bribed him, as a Russian, in order to improve their public image.[10] The wishes of this foreign minority did dictate court decisions, as in early 1731, when Rondeau reported from Moscow that the court was planning to remove to St Petersburg to escape the animosity of xenophobic natives,

> . . . because the favourites think they shall be there out of the daily hearing complaints and in more security than they can be here, for they will be able to hinder the malcontents from coming to that place.[11]

Although the point has been argued that there was division amongst these men, and that the policies they followed were not anti-Russian,[12] there was, in fact, discrimination in favour of other foreigners. Iaguzhinsky's domination of the Senate was attributed to nepotism,[13] and Russians were edged out of the most influential positions. In 1732, it was observed that '. . . nous n'avons pas de Russe, qui ait la confidence ni l'entier secret'. Even Cherkassky's membership of the Cabinet was merely, '. . . proforma pour l'interieur et le clergé'.[14]

Nevertheless, although a handful of exceptional foreigners, occupying high-profile positions at the expense of their Russian counterparts, justifiably became a focus for the resentment which has subsequently coloured the whole decade, this did not constitute 'foreign favouritism' beyond the sphere of power politics. In order to assess the effect of Anna Ivanovna's régime on Jacobite mercenaries it is necessary to distinguish myth from reality by examining the conditions under which they served.

A Haven for Foreign Mercenaries?

A number of misconceptions have grown up around Russian mercenary service during Anna's reign as an extension of the myth of a foreign-dominated Russia. Among these are the assumptions that foreigners were favoured above Russians, were recruited in great numbers and given access to the top military ranks and control over military affairs in general,[15] all to the detriment of

---

10 Liria, 17/3/1730, *RA* 1909, pp.386–387.
11 Rondeau to Harrington, 4/3/1731, *SIRIO* 66, p.272.
12 Alexander Lipski, 'The "Dark Era" of Anna Ioannovna', *ASEER*, 15 (1956), pp.483–488.
13 Lefort wrote, 'la liaison étroite qu'il y a entre lui, Biron et les Loewenwolde n'a pas peu contribué à tout ce changement', J.Hassell, 'Implementation of the Russian Table of Ranks during the Eighteenth Century', *SR* 29 (1970), pp.283–295. In fact, Iaguzhinsky had elicited Löwenwolde's support for his promotion to attorney-general of the Senate by implying that he would remove limits on Livonian privileges imposed by Peter I, Manstein, *Memoirs*, 1770 edn., pp.47–48, 1856 edn., pp.46–47.
14 Lefort to Augustus II, 19/2/1732, *SIRIO* 5, p.449.
15 John Keep, *Soldiers of the Tsar*, p.241; Waliszewski, *L'Heritage de Pierre le Grand, 1725–1741* (Paris, 1911), pp.182ff.

Russia.[16] Prospective foreign mercenaries were also guilty of forming a distorted perception of Russian service.

For their part, the Jacobites, particularly those tired of the constrictive atmosphere of the exiled court, viewed the prospect of military service in Anna's Russia in the 1730s with a romantic fascination. George Keith wrote to his brother from Rome when Jacobite hopes were at a low ebb, '. . . I had much rather live amongst the Calmucks, encamping with them than lead this life',[17] and complained that

> . . . to see some of our old gentlemen, once clever men, turn'd to old women in Rome, is so melancholy a sight that in my oppinion it were better take a pair of colours amongst the Saparosch [Zaparozhe Cossacks] with hopes of rising, than moulder away here.[18]

The Jacobites shared the same primary motive for choosing a career in Russia as many military recruits, the guarantee of active service either in Poland or the Crimea. During the Turkish war, in particular, there was a wave of foreign recruitment to Russia, composed to a large extent of ex-members of the British armed forces. This may have been prompted in part by poor employment prospects in Britain, for John Stuart of Stuartfield, who had served as a British officer for twenty years when he applied to the Russian army in 1739, complained that '. . . the badness of the times' had hindered his promotion. He had therefore decided '. . . to leave his Country and push his fortune as a Soldier under the Russian banner where Honor, vertue and knowledge are in esteem'.[19] There were also those who, like John Lindesay, Earl of Crawfurd, were driven by a lust for military adventure, with a '. . . heart so much enflamed with the love of martial exploits that his noble spirit could no longer bear a confinement in the bounds of classic inactivity'.[20] The Turkish war, in true crusading spirit, was regarded as an honourable conflict against '. . . the common enemy of christianity, liberty, and Europe'.[21]

By contrast, the Russian view of the foreign mercenary was firmly based in a financial and political reality. Service conditions for foreigners were determined pragmatically according to Russian military requirements.

The Russian Military in Crisis

The Russian armed forces traditionally benefited from a greater input of foreign expertise than civil bodies, and Anna's reign was no

---

16 Beskrovny described a foreign 'tyranny', which, in combination with the forcible introduction of alien standards of discipline, apparently destroyed the morale and performance of the Russian army and navy. Beskrovny, 'Armiya i Flot', pp.296–309. Foreign officers have been accused of merciless cruelty against Russian troops, '. . . constantly resorting to sticks, birch rods and whips', which allegedly led to mass desertion and inhuman military conditions, B.Korsakov in *Brockhaus- Efron*, 1, p.340.
17 G.Keith to J.Keith, circa October 1731, *HMC Elphinstone*, p.222.
18 G.Keith to J.Keith, 12/6/1732, NAS Elphinstone GD 156/62, folder 2, f.7.
19 Lord Elphinstone to Thomas Gordon, 4/6/1739, NAS Abercairney, GD 24/1/856, f.243.
20 R.Rolt, *Memoirs of the life of. . . John Lindesay, earl of Crawfurd and Lindesay* (London, 1753), p.48.
21 *Ibid.*, p.116.

exception.[22] However, Russia's need for military strategists and experienced officers was particularly acute in 1730. Firstly, the armed forces, and particularly the navy, had deteriorated through neglect since the death of Peter I. The poll tax, which financed the army, had been so seriously in arrears by 1727 that the War College had been forced to release a half and in succeeding years a third, of its officers on extended leave.[23] As a result, the officer corps suffered a shortage of personnel, and the financial crisis became a military one. The navy had so diminished by 1732, that there was concern about its future. The fleet had fallen from 34 ships-of-the-line, 15 frigates and 77 galleys in 1721 to only 27 ships-of-the-line and 6 frigates in 1732.[24] Moreover, eyewitnesses described many of these as unserviceable.[25] In addition, there was an acute shortage of seamen, and Thomas Gordon had complained as early as 1729 that '. . . our seamen are wearing out and no recruits has been given those three years past'.[26] This was in part due to the unpopularity of this branch of the armed forces with native officers.[27] By 1730 the situation had worsened, and the prospect of war in 1733, and Russia's subsequent military commitments in the course of the decade, naturally increased the demand for foreign expertise.

Foreigners and Military Legislation

The measures taken to combat this crisis gave precedence to military over civil affairs, proposing to maximise the financial and military efficiency of both army and navy for reasons of national security, and, in part, to underpin the authority of the monarch. In two decrees of 1731, Anna Ivanovna ensured that military servitors be better regarded and rewarded than their civil service counterparts and that military ranks prevail over those of civil servants.[28] She also proposed to increase the standing army from 250,000 to 300,000 men.[29] Although the national deficit stood at 15,500,000 roubles in 1732, twice the yearly state income, over two thirds of the yearly budget of 8,000,000 roubles was spent on the armed forces when the Polish war began.[30]

The programme and implementation of military reform was dominated, although not monopolised, by foreigners. Berghard Kristof Münnich, the son

---

22 78% of foreigners in the 1730 generalitet held military rank, as compared with only 58% of natives. Meehan-Waters, *Autocracy and Aristocracy*, p.24.

23 24/2/1727, 'Ob otpuske ofitserov iz polkov v derevni', *PSZ* 5016; 20/12/1729, *PSZ* 5492.

24 Beskrovny, 'Armiya i Flot', p.307.

25 Dashwood, a young tourist and amateur spy for Great Britain (McLynn, *The Jacobites*, pp.174–175), was told in 1733 that only 12 ships were fit to put to sea. Dashwood, 'Sir Francis Dashwood's Diary of his Visit to St Petersburg in 1733' *SEER* 58 (1959–60), p.200; Rondeau put this number at five or six, Rondeau to Harrington, *SIRIO* 66 p.459; see also Solov'ev *Istoriya Rossii* 19, p.1183.

26 T.Gordon to William Hay, 31/7/1729, NAS Abercairney, GD 24/1/859, f.326.

27 From 1737 the punishment inflicted on young nobles who failed the inspection of their academic attainment at the age of sixteen was to be sent to serve in the navy, *PSZ* 7170.

28 13/11/1731, *PSZ* 5877, 5878. See also Hassell, 'The Implementation of the Russian Table of Ranks', p.285.

29 Rondeau to Harrington, 25/4/1732, *SIRIO* 66, p.448.

30 'Anna Ivanovna' by B.Korsakov, in Brockhaus-Efron, *Entsiklopedicheskii slovar'*, 43 vols. (St Petersburg, 1890–1907), 1, pp.340–341.

of an artisan from Oldenburg, whose career had begun under Peter I, was able during Anna's reign to assume supreme control of Russian military affairs. In 1730 he became Master General of the Ordnance and president of the War College,[31] and in March 1732 was promoted to the rank of General Field Marshal.[32] Lefort observed soon afterwards that he had become so powerful that only Löwenwolde dared contradict him.[33] In 1736 he reorganised the War College, placing all military bodies under its jurisdiction, and, at the expense of the Senate, giving it exclusive power in the recommendation and promotion of officers, and thus increasing his own control over the military apparatus.[34] His participation in the reform process was decisive, following his appointment in March 1731 as head of a military commission established by Imperial decree in June 1730 to review and improve all aspects of the Russian army.[35] Involved in the implementation of his reforms were three prominent exiles in the general ranks of the army, Peter Lacy, James Keith and George Brown.

In the navy, an Imperial ukase of 25 January 1732 ordered the creation of a naval commission to co-ordinate improvements in naval administration and the rebuilding of the fleet.[36] Several Jacobites were among the largely foreign contingent which played a major role in the administration of naval reorganisation, including Vice-Admiral Thomas Saunders, who, with Rear-Admiral Bredal, was summoned to St Petersburg as an advisory member of the commission.[37] The position of chief commander of the main port of Cronstadt was dominated almost exclusively by Jacobites; between 1727 and 1742 it was occupied on four occasions by three Jacobites, Thomas Gordon, Thomas Saunders and Christopher O'Brien, with only two short intervals in 1729 and 1732. Although Count Nikolai Golovkin was appointed Inspector General of the Admiralty and Fleet in April 1732, and from 1733 was also President of the Admiralty College, Thomas Gordon, who was chief commander at Cronstadt from 1733 until his death in 1741, assumed responsibility for the introduction of government legislation. Rondeau commented in 1732 that Gordon '. . . passes for a very good officer, nevertheless I believe he will find it very difficult to put the russ fleet on a good footing'.[38] Although Jacobite exiles played a major role in the reform and reorganisation of both branches of the armed forces during Anna's reign, the reform measures themselves did not reflect a particular foreign bias. Münnich's primary objective was to increase the cost-effectiveness of the army without overburdening the tax-paying po-

31 He had been made Master General of the Ordnance in 1729. For an account of his career, C.Duffy, *Russia's Military Way to the West . . . 1700–1800* (London, 1981) p.44, D.N.Bantysh-Kamensky, *Biografii Rossiiskikh generalissimov i general feldmarshalov*, 4 vols. (St Petersburg, 1840–41), 1, p.177.
32 Lefort to Augustus II, 11/3/1732, *SIRIO* 5, p.451.
33 Lefort to Augustus II, 26/4/1732, *SIRIO* 5, pp.451–452.
34 J.P.le Donne, 'Ruling Families in the Russian Political Order, 1689–1725', *CMRS* 28 (1987), p.299.
35 'Ob uchrezhdenii kommisii dlya razsmotreniya sostoyaniya armii . . .' 1/6/1730, *PSZ* 5571.
36 25/1/1732, *PSZ* 5937, Elagin, *Materialy*, 3, p.273.
37 Zhurnal Admiralteistvennoi Kollegii, 26/1/1732, Elagin, *Materialy*, 7, p.348.
38 Rondeau to Harrington, 26/2/1732, *SIRIO*, 66, p.420.

pulation, and much of his legislation reduced the incentives offered to mercenaries and was therefore actually disadvantageous to foreign officers.

Firstly, he annulled Peter I's distinction between the rates of pay of native and non-native officers, declaring, according to Manstein, who served under him, '. . . that they [the Russians] could not subsist upon it, and that it was unjust that foreigners should have a higher pay than the natives'[39] In July 1731, he founded the Noble Land Cadet Corps, designed to provide military education for the children of Russian and Baltic nobles.[40] Although a quarter of the 360 places were to be reserved for non-natives, they were effectively restricted to Baltic Germans; Ukrainian and other nationalities were not admitted.[41] This allowed young nobles to enter active service as commissioned officers rather than enlisted men, and was successful in producing a large number of high-ranking members of the Russian civil administration.[42] The admission of Baltic Germans was primarily to facilitate Baltic integration, rather than a concession to the 'foreign' element. Indeed, in 1739 the Cabinet ordered that foreign children could only enter the Cadet Corps if their parents were in Russian service.[43] Münnich also encouraged the recruitment of Russians and decreased desertion rates by improving conditions for recruits and attempting to ensure that troops were paid regularly.[44]

In early 1737 a decree was issued as a concession to Russian noble families allowing them to retain one son of recruitment age at home to manage their estates. The term of military service for males, previously unspecified, was limited to twenty-five years, upon which the nobleman could retire with promotion of one rank. In the event this clause proved so popular that it had to be suspended until the end of the war with Turkey, but it represented an attempt to make military service a more attractive option for the native nobility, and thereby to improve the morale of native officers.[45] Measures were also taken to ensure by means of periodic inspections that the children of noble families were adequately educated before they entered the armed services, thus increasing the quality of the Russian officer corps. Official restrictions were placed on the recruitment of foreigners; those below the rank of major could only be accepted by Imperial decree, those ranked major

39 'Peter, in forming his army, had instituted three degrees of pay, The foreigners newly entered into the service recieved a very high pay, Those who were born in the country . . . had a somewhat smaller. The Russians had still a less'. Manstein, *Memoirs*, 1770 edn, pp.56–57 (1856 edn., p.56). For details of differentiated pay, 19/2/1711, *PSZ* 2319 (appendix). By 1731 pay scales were equal for natives, 28/10/1731, *PSZ* 5864 (appendix).
40 29/7/1731, *PSZ* 5811; 18/11/1731, *PSZ* 5881.
41 18/11/1731, *PSZ* 5881; 12/5/1732, *PSZ* 6050.
42 Pintner and Rowney, eds., *Russian Officialdom from the Seventeenth to the Twentieth Century* (Chapel Hill, N.Carolina, 1980), p.86.
43 31/3/1739, *PSZ* 7787.
44 Lefort to Augustus II, 3/12/1731, *SIRIO* 5, p.440. Prior to this, in 1728, Lefort had complained that neither the land forces nor the colleges had been paid for eighteen months. Lefort to Saxon King, 22/7/1728, *Ibid.*, pp.309–310.
45 *PSZ* 7142; A.V.Romanovich-Slavatinsky, *Dvorianstvo v Rossii ot nachala XVIII veka do otmeny krepostnogo prava* (St Petersburg, 1870), pp.125, 127.

and above were admitted only if there were vacancies according to the established quota.[46]

In the Russian navy reform was likewise designed to encourage the growth of native talent rather than to encourage foreign recruits. Anna turned her attention to naval affairs immediately after her accession, and Thomas Gordon noted with optimism in 1730 that '. . . I am inform'ed she is resolv'd to follow the schemes of her unkle Petter the great concerning the Imperial Navy we begin already to fynd the effects'.[47] In 1731 and 1732, she demanded details of the state and numerical strength of the fleet, which were duly provided by the four top-ranking officers, including Gordon and Duffus.[48] As a result, new 'shtats' or military quotas were drawn up, upon which subsequent recruitment was based. A decree of July 1731 returned control over district cipher schools from the Synod to the Admiralty College, which supplied them with teachers,[49] presumably to improve the link between education and military service. Steps were also taken to ensure that naval rank was strictly commensurate with skill and merit, and in March 1733 the Admiralty College decided that all naval servicemen requesting promotion first be examined on their knowledge of seamanship.[50] The institution of similar examinations for foreign recruits was evidently necessary, for although Russia needed foreigners, those applying to Russian service included, as Manstein observed, '. . . the most abject wretches that Europe could produce'.[51] Thomas Gordon was largely responsible for setting and conducting these examinations.

Military reform during Anna's reign was, therefore, directly to the benefit of native servicemen at the expense of foreigners, rather than the reverse. This impression is reinforced by the fact that Münnich's legislation was welcomed by the native population, contrary to the opinion of subsequent historians.[52] Nashchokin, in his memoirs, maintained that Münnich's changes were beneficial to the armed forces as a whole.[53] Lefort, likewise, commented that '. . . Il s'est attiré beaucoup d'approbation par les nouveaux règlements, qu'il a établis pour l'armeé'.[54] Manstein concluded that Anna, in selecting Münnich as President of the War College,

46 17/5/1733, *PSZ* 6404; 16/1/1736, *PSZ* 6866.
47 T.Gordon to John Gordon at Rotterdam, NAS Abercairney, GD 24/1/859, ff.333–4.
48 Letter to Empress Anna signed by Gordon, Duffus, Sievers, Sinyavin, 29/11/1731, *SIRIO* 104, p.59; response to Imperial decree 24/1/1732 that all flagmen recommend naval improvements by Lord Duffus, RGAVMF F13 o2 d335, ll.1–4.
49 Decree 2/7/1731, Elagin, *Materialy*, 7, p.529.
50 13/3/1733, Elagin, *Materialy*, 7, p.529.
51 'Among the great number of foreigners who came to this empire since the beginning of this century, there were certainly some excellent officers; but there were also some of the most abject wretches that Europe could produce. Some adventurers, at their last shifts, and who did not know how to dispose of themselves otherwise, got to Russia, and even made their way in the service as well as the best', Manstein, *Memoirs*, 1770 edn. p.406.
52 For example, Beskrovny, 'Armiya i Flot', p.300.
53 V.A.Nashchokin, 'Zapiski Vasillia Aleksandrovicha Nashchokina, generala vremen elizavetinskikh', *RA* 2 (1883), p.273.
54 Lefort to Augustus II, 3/12/1731, *SIRIO* 5, p.440.

... could not have made a better choice, for it was by the care and management of this general that the Russian army was put upon the respectable footing it has since maintained, and a discipline, till then unknown among them, introduced into the troops, thus finishing the work begun by Peter I.[55]

Despite the significant foreign element in military administration, these comprehensive reform measures not only belied claims of the existence of a deliberate policy to favour foreigners, but were evidence that foreign expertise did not damage, but directly benefited, military progress during Anna's reign.

The perception that there were more foreign officers in the armed forces under Anna Ivanovna than during other reigns can best be assessed by analysis of the available service lists. While it is beyond the scope of this study to provide a thorough account of the non-native component of Anna's military leadership relative to that of the preceding and subsequent reigns, these military lists give some impression of the proportion of foreigners to natives in the officer ranks of the army and navy over the second quarter of the century.

For the land forces, statistics have been examined for 1726, 1729 and 1738. According to a list of serving general and staff officers in the land forces[56] drawn up by a decree of November 1726, foreigners comprised 1 of 3 field marshals, 3 of 6 generals, 7 of 11 lieutenant generals, 13 of 44 major generals, and 5 of 22 brigadiers. Of the staff officers, foreigners constitued 38 of 132 colonels, 25 of 113 lieutenant colonels and 18 of 127 majors.[57] Just prior to Anna's accession, in 1729, the situation was approximately the same. The general officer ranks had 1 foreigner of 4 field marshals, 6 of 7 generals, 8 of 21 lieutenant generals, 14 of 38 major generals, 6 of 28 brigadiers, 41 of 129 colonels, 32 of 158 lieutenant colonels and 45 of 180 majors.[58] A similar list drawn up in 1738, towards the end of Anna's reign, shows the following: 1 foreigner of 3 field marshals, 3 of 8 generals, 9 of 15 lieutenant generals, 18 of 36 major generals, 3 of 28 brigadiers, 58 of 154 colonels, 50 of 186 lieutenant colonels and 88 of 327 majors.[59] Although these lists suggest that the army in 1738 was somewhat larger than in 1726, and there was some variation between ranks, the proportion of foreigners to natives in these upper ranks was not uniformly or significantly greater during Anna's reign than it had been under her uncle.

55 Manstein, *Memoirs*, 1770 edn., p.55, 1856 edn., p.54.
56 The general and staff ranks were the first eight ranks of the 1722 Table of Ranks, general field marshal to major and general admiral to third rank captain inclusive. Hassel, 'The Implementation of the 1722 Table of Ranks', p.285; Keep, *Soldiers of the Tsar*, p.9.
57 In response to a protocol of the Supreme Council 18/11/1726, 'Prilozhenie k spisku generalitetu i shtap ofitserom, obretaiyushchimsia pri armeiskikh polkakh i v gvarnizonakh', 22/12/1726, *SIRIO* 56, pp.386–403.
58 'Spisok generalitetu i shtap-ofitseram 1729 goda', RGVIA F489 o1 d7395. These figures were calculated from military ranks, including garrison troops but excluding the Ukrainian landmilitia and administrative ranks.
59 'Spisok generalitetu i stab ofitseram, 1738', RGVIA F489 o1 d7387. See also list for 1735, *SIRIO* 76, pp.555–574.

For the navy, lists of flagmen (general ranks) and staff officers are available for the years 1723, 1732 and 1741, prior to, during, and just after the close of Anna's reign. In 1723 there was 1 Russian general admiral, 1 Russian admiral, 3 foreigners of 4 vice-admirals, 2 of 3 shautbenakht (later rear-admiral), 2 of 3 captain commandores and 20 of 30 first, second and third rank captains.[60] In 1732 there was no general admiral, 1 foreign admiral, 2 foreigners of 3 vice-admirals, 3 of 5 shautbenakht (including two Russians above the quota), 3 of 7 captain commandores (including 3 above the quota), and 22 of 33 first, second and third rank captains (including 2 above the quota).[61] In 1741, after Thomas Gordon's retirement, the only admiral was Russian; there was 1 foreigner of 2 vice-admirals, 2 of 3 rear-admirals, 1 foreign captain commandore, and 13 of 30 captains of all ranks (including 1 above the quota).[62] Again, the proportion of foreign officers changed little between the reigns of Peter I and Anna, and indeed, just after her death it had actually decreased.

The proportion of foreigners to natives in both branches of the armed forces in Russia had traditionally been considerable, particularly in the upper ranks, and it remained so during Anna's reign. There was a tendency, under Anna, probably in response to the demands of war, to maintain numbers in excess of the established quotas. Those recruited above the quotas, however, were not necessarily foreigners. This reinforces the conclusion that, while foreigners still played a crucial role in the Russian armed forces during this period, it is not possible to characterise Anna's reign as dominated to a greater extent than previously by a foreign military element.

Legislation versus Practice

Notwithstanding the spirit of military legislation, there were exceptional cases where non-Russians were employed to counter a hostile native nobility, particularly in view of the attempt of certain Russian nobles to restrict the absolute power of the monarchy at Anna's accession.[63] After the death of Field Marshal Golitsyn in 1730, Anna had the second most powerful Russian field marshal, Vasilii Dolgoruky, imprisoned, leaving the two topmost military positions to be occupied by loyal foreigners.[64] The Ismailovsky horse and foot guards regiments, created in 1730 to protect the monarch,[65] were composed of the cream of the Ukrainian land-militia, and Count Karl Gustav Löwenwolde, brother of the Livonian senator and colonel of the foot guards, was responsible for selecting officers '. . . from various companies and from the service of various nations'.[66] The officer corps selected, which included the

60 'Lichnyi sostav flota, 20/5/1723', RGAVMF F212 o1 d13.
61 'Spisok shtatnomu i nalichnomu chislu chinov korabelnago flota' 1732, RGAVMF F146 o1 d62.
62 'Posluzhnyie spiski flagmanam i shtap-ofitseram', RGAVMF F212 o11 d7.
63 For details of this, see D.A.Korsakov, *Votsarenie Anny Ioannovny* (Kazan, 1880).
64 Solov'ev, *Istoriya Rossii*, 19, p.1217.
65 Mediger, *Russlands Weg nach Europa*, p.92.
66 Nashchokin, *Zapiski*, p.269.

brother of the favourite, Karl Biron, was largely foreign, which aroused the hostility of the two older elite guards regiments, the Semenovsky and Preobrazhensky:

> . . . The two regiments of guards grumble very loudly that the Czarinna or some of her favourites are seen to have a greater confidence in the third regiment, called Ismailovsky, than in the others, which are composed of the best families in the country.[67]

According to Manstein, this reaction was justified, for the Ismailovsky guards were '. . . raised as checks upon the old ones, and to overawe the people',[68] Anna having judiciously ensured that the new guards were of diverse and non-Russian origin in order to maximise their dependence on Imperial favour and to minimise the possibility that they could unite against her.

James Keith benefited directly from this; although he had been '. . . little more than a year in the Empire', and was one of the most junior major generals, he was raised to the prestigious rank of lieutenant colonel of the new foot guards.[69] Such swift promotion after so little experience of Russia was regarded as exceptional, and Keith had good reason to feel honoured,

> . . . As the emploiement is looked on as one of the greatest trust in the Empire, and . . . the officers of the Guards are regarded as domesticks of the Souveraign.[70]

His promotion was not, however, due solely to personal merit, but to his acquaintance with Count Löwenwolde. This is evidence that a degree of nepotism in favour of foreigners, contrary to the spirit of legislation, existed not only in civil, but in military administration. Anna continued to favour the Ismailovsky guards above the other two regiments, and declared herself their colonel in 1735.[71]

It has also been noted that Anna Ivanovna used the support of non-Russian noble families from border areas, like the Ukraine and the Baltic, '. . . to forestall latent anarchy'.[72] During her reign Peter Lacy, governor of Livonia, James Keith, governor of the Ukraine, and Gustav Otto Douglas, governor of

---

67 Rondeau to Harrington, 4/1/1731, *SIRIO* 66, p.272.
68 The guards regiments were traditionally 'kingmakers' who played a major role in palace coups and whose support the prudent monarch would be at pains to secure. Manstein, *Memoirs*, p.46. Liria in Bartenev, *Osmnadtsaty vek*, 3, p.113.
69 The rank of captain lieutenant in a lifeguards regiment was equivalent to full general in the army; lieutenant equalled lieutenant general, sub-lieutenant equalled major-general, adjutant equalled brigadier, ensign equalled colonel etc. *RA* (1880) 2, pp.1–143.
70 Keith, *A Fragment*, pp.89–90.
71 Nashchokin, *Zapiski*, pp.243–352.
72 J.P.Le Donne, 'Ruling Families in the Russian Political Order 1689–1725', *CMRS* 28 (1987), p.311.

Reval,[73] were among a number of foreigners who held administrative posts in these areas. Magnan, the French minister in St Petersburg, ascribed the presence of foreigners in positions of power to her mistrust of native Russians:

> ... On peut aisement comprendre ... combien de défiance à la Czarine de ses sujets naturels, puisqu'elle n'ose pas leur confier le gouvernement de ses provinces frontières, ni même aucun commandement en chef dans ses armées, la Livonie et l'Ingrie, et les troupes qui y sont étant sous les ordres de généraux étrangers comme sont m.m. de Lassi, Munick, Lefort et Hochmut, et l'armée d'Ukraine de même que Kief et la frontière de Pologne sous ceux du général Weisbach.[74]

There may have been some basis for this conclusion, for Walpole had commented on a similar policy during Catherine I's reign,

> ... That persons of great fidelity and particularly officers that are strangers shall be the Governours of the cheif [sic] towns in Livonia etc. and have the principal employments and command of the army to be quartered in those parts.[75]

Nevertheless, the practice of sending foreigners to frontier areas was not peculiar to Anna Ivanovna's administration, and was, moreover, directly linked with the fact that, since the beginning of the previous century, the non-Orthodox in Russia had been forbidden to own Orthodox serfs, forcing them to occupy estates outside greater Russia.[76]

Recruitment from the Royal Navy

The case of James Keith and the Ismailovsky guards was not characteristic of a general trend to secure the monarchy through the enlistment of non-natives, and the recruitment of foreigners by Russia during the 1730's was more closely related to its national military requirements than to fear of civil disruption. Early in Anna's reign the supply of foreign applicants to Russian service actually exceeded demand. In 1732 Rondeau remarked that

> ... Of late a vast number of foreign officers are come to this place to seek service, several of which have been employed, but the Czarinna finding

---

73 Gustav Otto Douglas (General 1738) was the grandson of Robert Douglas, a field marshal in Sweden under Gustavus Adolphus, who was the son of Patrick Douglas of Standingstone in Scotland. Gustav Otto was taken prisoner at Poltava, changed sides, and was made govenor of all of conquered Finland and a count by Peter I. He retired as a general in 1740 and was alive in 1763. He was also the uncle of the Jacobite Chevalier James Johnstone. J.Johnstone, *The Memoirs of Chevalier Johnstone*, 3 vols. (London, 1871), pp.113–114; *SIRIO* 86, p.259; Linklater, 'Scots of the Swedish Service', in Bergand and Lagerkrantz, *Scots in Sweden* (Stockholm, 1962), p.47; Fischer, *The Scots in Sweden* (Edinburgh, 1907), p.139.

74 Magnan to Chauvelin, 6/12/1731, *SIRIO* 81, p.265.

75 Walpole to Newcastle, 8/5/1725 n.s., BL Add.Ms. 32743, f.132.

76 There were exceptions to this; the Catholic General Patrick Gordon, for example, was granted an estate of Orthodox serfs by Peter I. H.H.Nolte, 'Verständnis und Bedeutung der religiösen Toleranz in Russland 1600–1725', *JGO* NF 17, 3 (1969), p.526.

their numbers daily increasing, ordered field-marshal Munich to ac-
quaint them that she had no occasion for any more officers having
already a great many more than she needed.[77]

However, as under Peter I, the demands on the Russian military apparatus
could not be resolved sufficiently quickly by legislation alone, and as soon as
war became imminent there began an active campaign to enlist skilled servicemen from abroad, a situation from which Jacobites, like other skilled foreigners, immediately benefited.

It was in the sphere of military, and particularly naval, recruitment, that the
disparity between military legislation and practice was most marked. In 1733,
the new 'shtat' or quota of ships masters in the navy was supplemented by the
promotion of native steersmen only because foreign recruitment campaigns
would not bear fruit quickly enough.[78] Anna Ivanovna, like her uncle, coveted
British naval officers above other seamen, and one of the prerequisites
demanded by Russia of recruits in 1734 was that they '. . . above all . . . know
and be capable of executing all that relates to their employment as it is done on
British ships-of-war'.[79] Thus the re-establishment of Anglo-Russian diplomatic
relations and the arrival in London of the new minister resident, Antiokh
Kantemir, in March 1732, was secretly welcomed as a possible means of
tempting Britons into Russian service.

Initially, despite the superficial improvement of Anglo-Russian relations,
Britain's own requirements for the build-up of a naval defence force made
great demands on the supply of suitable candidates.[80] In February 1734 George
II actually issued a declaration forbidding any of his subjects with naval
experience to enter the service of foreign powers and ordering those already
in foreign service to return home.[81] Nevertheless, Russia was quite unscrupu-
lous in its efforts, and in April, a mere month after his arrival, Kantemir was
commissioned by Counts Osterman and Alexander Gavrilovich Golovkin, the
plenipotentiary minister in Holland, to look for 'skilled British naval commanders' in response to the Empress's demands.[82] In February 1733 there was
an Admiralty College decision to send abroad Captain William Thomas
Lewis,[83] a Welshman who had served in the Russian navy since 1725, to fill
the new naval quota of ship masters and 'timmermen' (carpenters). Initially he
was instructed to recruit in Dutch ports and to accept only those who could
demonstrate detailed knowledge of the ship-building trade and who were
prepared to be contracted for at least two or three years.[84] A secret clause
added to his instructions, however, ordered him to recruit in Britain should his

77 Rondeau to Harrington, 24/6/1732, *SIRIO* 66, pp.475,476.
78 9/4/1733, Elagin, *Materialy*, 7, p.535.
79 Instructions to Captain Lewis, 1/3/1733, 'Londonskaya missiya', AVPR F36 o2 d33, l.3.
80 Kantemir to Admiralty College, 15/10/1734, *Ibid.*, l.8.
81 Kantemir to Count Golovin, 12/2/1734, RGAVMF F212 o1 d17, l.5.
82 Osterman to Kantemir, 25/4/1732, Elagin, *Materialy*, 7, p.6.
83 His sons John and William also served in the Russian Navy.
84 8/2/1733, Elagin, *Materialy*, 7, p.519; Lewis's instructions and details of recruits' minimum
qualifications in AVPR F36 o2 d33, ll.1–8.

efforts in Holland prove unsuccessful, and the Empress was careful to emphasise that

> . . . the College has written to the Resident of Her Majesty's court, Prince
> Antioch Kantemir, requesting his good offices and assistance in recruit-
> ing these servicemen, but this instruction is to be kept secret according to
> an unofficial [ne reglamentno] decree by Her Majesty.[85]

By May 1733, Lewis had failed to find any suitable Dutch seamen willing to enter
Russian service, and was forced to run the risk of continuing his search in London,
with Kantemir's assistance.[86] One might expect that these conditions early in
Anna's reign, which bore close resemblance to those under Peter I, would tend to
favour Jacobites, and those disenchanted with the British government. However,
this early recruitment campaign failed to attract men of either political leaning
because the financial incentives determined by new Russian military legislation
proved too low. The masters were to receive fifteen to twenty roubles a month, the
'timmermen' ten to fifteen, which was what their Russian counterparts could
expect. By June 1733, Lewis had found only three ship masters willing to enter
Russian service, all reluctant to accept Russian currency at all,[87] and only two of
these were eventually contracted for twenty roubles a month.[88]

By the end of 1734, however, Britain's desire to support Russia, despite its own
neutrality in the Polish war, meant that Russian recruitment campaigns in Britain
received official sanction, and disenchantment with the Hanoverian monarchy
was no longer an issue. In 1735, Kantemir received permission from Admiral
Wager to recruit six British seamen to serve as captains in the Russian Navy.[89] This
followed a decree from Anna Ivanovna in February 1734 to fill the new quota of
captains, lieutenants and steersmen from the British Navy.[90] In addition to this,
Russia continued its attempts to recruit British naval craftsmen.

Improved Anglo-Russian relations alone, however, were not sufficient to
attract the expertise Russia so urgently required. Instead, measures had to be
taken to offer foreigners a larger salary than their Russian counterparts, thus
contravening the legislative trend in Russia towards both cost-cutting and the
encouragement of the native population.

In order to recruit British naval craftsmen, the Admiralty was forced to augment
the financial incentives offered to masters to thirty roubles a month and to
redouble its campaign.[91] In 1736 the Jacobite Captain Christopher O'Brien, who
was himself applying to enter Russian service, took over Lewis's commission to

---

85 Instructions to Lewis, 1/3/1733, AVPR F36 o11 d33, 1.6v.
86 Lewis to [Golovin], 28/5/1733, RGAVMF F212 o11 d3/657, ll.9–10.
87 Report from Lewis, 19/6/1733, RGAVMF F212 o11 d3/657.
88 Golovin to Kantemir, 7/2/1737, AVPR F36 o1 d71, 1.3.
89 3/6/1735, RGAVMF F212 o1 d17, 1.58. Also, in a letter of 17/5/1735 to Newcastle,
   Kantemir recorded that he had royal permission to recruit two British naval officers, and
   had chosen Captain Mathews. Maikov, *Kantemir*, p.31.
90 Instructions from Golovin to Admiralty College to recruit six captains and six lieutenants,
   27/2/1734, RGAVMF F212 o11 d3/657, 1.33.
91 Report from Lewis, 19/6/1733, RGAVMF F212 o11 d3/657, f.31.

recruit eighteen further 'timmermen'. It was hoped that his contacts in the British Navy, which he had just left, would ensure him greater success than his predecessor.[92] In early 1737 Captain John Opie, also a recruit from the Royal Navy, was likewise instructed to recruit 'timmermen' and boatswains.[93] The fact that the Russian ship-building industry benefited greatly from an influx of British seamen and technicians during this period suggests that these efforts were well rewarded. There are records of passports for numerous British carpenters and boatswains,[94] and the prolific shipbuilders, Yeames Lambe and Alexander and his brother John Sutherland, were also recruited at this time. It has been calculated that between 1726 and 1750 British shipbuilders produced half of all new Russian ships-of-the-line and nearly two thirds of the frigates in the Baltic fleet.[95] Between Peter I's death in 1725 and 1740 British shipbuilders were responsible for eight-and-a-half of eighteen ships-of-the-line and four of seven frigates built for the Baltic fleet. Native shipbuilders made a total of only nine ships and frigates; the remainder were built by foreigners.[96]

Similarly, legislative measures were overlooked in order to attract British naval officers. According to an Imperial decree of 1734, lieutenants recruited from Britain were to be paid fifteen roubles a month and captains forty roubles, the established rate in 1732, and Russians and foreigners were to be paid equally, as Münnich had intended.[97] This was approximately the same rate as in 1717, when Peter I had offered foreign lieutenants twenty roubles a month and foreign first-rank captains forty roubles, significantly less than they would have received in Britain but more than their native counterparts.[98] However, as had been the case with the tradesmen, this salary was insufficient to attract suitable officers. Two of them, Captain William Kenzie and Lieutenant Richard White demanded more, and Kantemir promised them seventy and twenty-five

92 Golovin to Kantemir, 27/1/1736?, AVPR F36 o2 d71, l.11v.
93 Letters from Admiral Golovin to Kantemir, 18/1/1737, AVPR F36 o2 d81, l.2: Opie arrived in St Peterburg in June 1736 under the alias 'captain Speedwell', with a companion, M.Cagnoni, and they were suspected by Rondeau of intending to damage British trade by using the Empress's authority and shipping for commercial enterprises with China and the East Indies. Osterman disapproved of their project and they joined Russian service instead. Although their political affiliations are unknown, their loyalty to the Hanoverian monarchy was apparently not strong. Rondeau to H.Walpole, 12/6/1736, *SIRIO* 76, p.522; H.Walpole to Rondeau, 25/7/1736, *Ibid.*, p.547; Rondeau to Harrington, 15/10/1737, *SIRIO* 80, p.213.
94 These included: carpenters Thomas Brazier, Henry Styers, Edward Camberden, John Beatie, William Chandler, John Weshmore, John Hawkes, Thomas West, George Nelson, Vesen Ward, John Carswell, John Collet, James Robertson, boatswains John Racy, James Benbrook, William Smith. Passports 1734–37, AVPR F36 o1 d119, l.1; also recruited, boatswain William Adamson, *Obshchi morskoi spisok* 2, p.2.
95 M.S.Anderson, *Mariner's Mirror*, 42, p.134.
96 Calculated from F.F.Veselago, 'Spisok russkikh voennykh sudov s 1668 po 1860 god' (St Petersburg, 1872), pp.20–716.
97 'Spisok shtatnomu i nalichnomu chislu chinov korabelnogo flota, s ukazaniem okladov poluchaemogo imi zhalovaniya, 1732', RGAVMF F212 o1 d17, l.255; AVPR F36 o2 d60, l.16; RGAVMF F146 o1 d62.
98 George Paddon to William Hay, 9/6/1717, RGAVMF F233 o1 d163, l.545. In 1733 the rouble was calculated at between four and five shillings, approximately the same as in 1717, AVPR F36 o2 d60, l.6.

roubles a month respectively.[99] Although Kantemir denied having made any
promise to Captain Kenzie, and his case was dropped, the Admiralty decided to
raise not only White's salary, but those of the other lieutenants recruited, to
twenty roubles a month to avoid embarrassment.[100]

Britain's acquiescence in Russian recruitment, and augmented financial
incentives, markedly increased the number of ex-British naval recruits.[101]
Those for whom material reward was of secondary importance, like the
Jacobite Christopher O'Brien, who did not reach agreement on a minimum
rate of pay before signing his contract and delayed any financial negotiation
until he had reached Russia,[102] nevertheless gained from the favours extended
to loyal Britons in the new climate of Anglo-Russian amity.[103]

Jacobites from the Royal Navy benefited additionally from enhanced promotion prospects which were extended to British officers, despite the existing
legislation to restrict foreign promotion and encourage native talent.[104]

 99 Golovin to Kantemir, 7/10/1735, AVPR F36 o2 d60, l.16.
100 Report of the Admiralty College on the Recruitment of Englishmen, 22/1/1736, RGAVMF
    F212 o1 d17, l.255.
101 RECRUITED 1734–35: Capts.John Thomas, William Kenzie, William Griffiths, Somerset
    Masters, Arthur Trevor, Nathaniel Oris (Oris and Trevor were discharged for
    incompetence, drunkenness, and ignorance of the Russian language in 1738, RGAVMF
    F227 o1 d4), Lts. George Lesley, Robert Gorson (went home, never returned), Richard
    White, John Smallman, Robert Porter (died 12/1/1737), [John] Eckles, Peter Anderson,
    Dennis Avery, surgeon Richard Duffin, Ship Masters Thomas Atkins, Thomas Bell, William
    Wilkins, Thomas Swallow, Instrument Master Benjamin Scott, also Francis Allen, William
    Hall, Alexander Craig, James Mitchell, David Hubert, William Clark, John Latham,
    William Norton.
    RECRUITED 1736: Capt.John Opie, Lts.James Glasford, [David] Ogilvie,* Ship Masters
    Alexander Sutherland, John Atkinson, Thomas MacKenzie,* Duncan Willison.
    RECRUITED 1737: Rear Admiral Christopher O'Brien,* Capt.William Talbot, Lts.
    Alexander Gordon,* John Geitch, William Kenzie jr., M'men Samuel Stokes, Machine
    Master John Cleeves, Master Builder Yeames Lambe.
    RECRUITED 1738: Lts. Thomas Cunningham, Alexander Binnings, Midshipman James
    Young.*
    RECRUITED 1739: Lt.Christopher O'Brien jr., M'man Lucius O'Brien*
    (AVPR F36 o1 d119; RGAVMF F212 o11 d3/657, d17/712, d17/733; F227 o1 d4).
    * = known Jacobites or their relatives.
102 Christopher O'Brien to Osterman, 27/6/1737, regarding contract of April 1737, AVPR
    F35 o1 d607, l.11.
103 O'Brien was prepared to travel to Russia at his own expense and to accept the relatively
    low Russian salary, and had left Britain before Kantemir could advance him the money for
    his passage, Kantemir to [Golovin], 21/7/1737, RGAVMF F212 o11, d17/733, l.144.
    According to one source, O'Brien had served as a rear-admiral under Peter I between
    1714 and 1718 and returned to the Royal Navy as a captain until about 1736. His initial
    departure from Russia has been ascribed to 'the frequent indications of a rupture
    between the courts of Moscow and London', Charnock, *Biographia Navalis*, 4, pp.48–49.
    (The first part of his Russian career is absent from Russian sources, incl. *Obshchi morskoi
    spisok*, 2, p.296.) In 1718 he was on a list of British naval officers well-affected to the
    Jacobites, July/August 1718, *HMC Stuart*, 7, p.116.
104 24/2/1730, *PSZ* 5503, Supreme Council decree to accept foreign engineers at their
    former rank, on condition that they had a commission and permission from their own
    government; 18/8/1735, *PSZ* 6789, Imperial decree that foreign recruits should be
    'accepted at the same rank at which they previously served', rather than being promoted
    by one rank. This echoed Peter I's decree of 28/2/1722 that foreign volunteers should
    serve at lower ranks than native Russians, *PSZ* 3913.

Although many of the craftsmen and ship builders recruited from Britain filled the same position in Russia, and there was an attempt on the part of the Admiralty to restrict, where possible, the promotion of foreigners on entry,[105] in most cases a compromise was reached. In 1738, for example, both Thomas Cunningham and Alexander Binnings were initially offered their former British naval ranks of midshipman and lieutenant, but after they had protested at this, their demands for promotion were met, on the condition that they could demonstrate the requisite naval skills.[106] Russia's need for foreign naval officers meant that there was frequently such a disparity between policy and practice, and in the case of British naval officers such as these, promotion on entry was not only common but was virtually taken for granted. This was due, in part, to the fact that both Russia and Britain were aware that favour shown to British subjects would benefit Anglo-Russian relations. In 1735, Wager had granted Kantemir permission to recruit lieutenants from Britain only on the condition that they be promoted to the rank of captain in the Russian navy. Russia's readiness to oblige was a positive response to Britain's move to promote military co-operation in place of the rivalry which had for decades been most acute in the area of naval affairs.[107]

There was, therefore, a certain irony in the fact that the policy of promoting experienced British naval officers to cement Anglo-Russian relations also benefited Jacobites from the Royal Navy. Christopher O'Brien had been commanding a war ship in Jamaica when Captain Mathews of the Royal Navy returned from Russia, having failed to receive the promotion to the rank of admiral he had demanded. Subsequently, Admiral Wager recommended to George II that O'Brien apply to the Russian Navy, which he did, via Kantemir, in May 1736.[108] In November, apparently with Thomas Gordon's intercession, Kantemir was ordered by Imperial decree to send O'Brien immediately, and his contract was signed in April 1737.[109] To ensure that he be immediately promoted to the rank of rear-admiral[110] and be guaranteed good career prospects,[111] he included in the contract the special proviso that '. . . his Christoffer O'Briens being a foreigner shall be no impediment or hindrance to his advancement, whenever a vacancy shall happen, according to his services and merits'.[112] Both his promotion to rear admiral and his subsequent career

---

105 Some unreasonable demands were rejected. Commodore Mathews of the Royal Navy arrived in Russia in August 1735 requesting immediate promotion to the rank of admiral on the strength of Anglo-Russian amity. Anna was prepared to grant him the rank of first vice-admiral, but refused to yield to his excessive demands and he was forced to return home, Rondeau to Harrington, 16/8/1735, 6/9/1735, *SIRIO* 76, pp.435,442.

106 RGAVMF F227 o1 d4 ll.145, 182, 183, 213, 245.

107 3/6/1735, RGAVMF F212 o1 d17, l.58.

108 O'Brien to Osterman, 1/1/1738, AVPR F35 o1 d607, ll.20–20v.

109 C.O'Brien to T.Gordon, 3/5/1736, NAS Abercairney, GD 24/1/856 f.215; Imperial decree of 6/11/1736, in report 12/5/1737, RGAVMF F212 o11 d17/733, l.44.

110 He had apparently held this rank before. Charnock, *Biographia Navalis*, 4, pp.48–49.

111 Golovin to Kantemir, Sept.1737, AVPR F36 o2 d81,l.10; also Berkh, *Zhizneopisaniya*, 2, p.193.

112 Contract between O'Brien and Kantemir, 1/4/1737, RGAVMF F212 o11 d17/733, ll.46,47.

were therefore a direct result of improved relations between Russia and the Hanoverian Government. His Jacobite inclinations, of which Britain was apparently unaware, and his participation in the 1745 Jacobite Rising, in a promoted position thanks to his Russian career, must be seen as a curious twist in Anglo-Russian diplomatic efforts.

O'Brien's sons also gained from Russia's readiness to concede to the demands of ex-British naval officers. Soon after his arrival in Russia, he asked the Admiralty College to accept Lucius and Christopher O'Brien, a midshipman and a first lieutenant respectively in the Royal Navy, with promotion of one rank. When the College would only agree to promote them after three years, O'Brien protested that British seamen had always been promoted on arrival and sent his sons back to Britain to prevent their case serving as a precedent for others.[113] Russia eventually conceded, and both are recorded as having entered the Russian navy with the requested promotion in 1739.[114]

As well as being accorded the favour extended to British naval officers, Jacobites also benefited from a Russian readiness to overlook official legislation in the cases of those with friends already in Russian service. Officers who were recruited above the established quotas for their rank commonly owed their positions to relatives already in Russian service.[115] In the case of the Jacobites, such requests were made not only for relatives, but also for fellow-Jacobites. Christopher O'Brien had sought Admiral Gordon's intercession and, judging by the speed with which he was accepted, probably received it.[116] In 1737 O'Brien, in turn, recommended two engineers, Henry Brown and his friend Jean de la Roche, who might well have had Jacobite connections, and who planned to manufacture their own more efficient design of bronze cannon.[117] In 1738 Thomas Gordon petitioned the Admiralty to accept his grandson, James Young, who had been working aboard trading ships in the Mediterranean and was now a volunteer in the Baltic, at the rank of midshipman.[118] The shipmaster Thomas MacKenzie, who became engaged to Admiral Gordon's granddaughter, Ann Young, in 1738, two years after coming to Russia, kept in correspondence with Sir Henry Stirling's neighbour in Scotland, John Drummond of Blairdrummond, and possibly owed his recruitment to Jacobite contacts. His future grandfather-in-law must have played a role in his swift

---

113 Berkh, *Zhizneopisaniya*, 2, p.194.

114 R.C.Anderson, 'British and American Officers', *Mariner's Mirror*, 33, p.25.

115 This naturally applied to some non-Jacobites where their immediate family was involved, like Midshipman William Griffith, son of Captain William Griffith, who entered the navy as a lieutenant above the quota, 'for his father's sake', Golovin to Kantemir, AVPR F36 o2 d71, f.4; Captain William Kenzie's son was likewise admitted with promotion to the rank of lieutenant as a favour to his father although the quota had already been exceeded. Golovin to Anna Ivanovna, 7/3/1737, RGAVMF F212 o11 d17/733, l.47; Captain William Thomas Lewis's two sons, William and John, enjoyed similar favour.

116 C.O'Brien to T.Gordon, 3/5/1736, NAS Abercairney, GD 24/1/856 f.215.

117 Letter by Christopher O'Brien accompanying list of Conditions by Henry Brown and Jean de la Roche for entry into Russian service, 25/10/1737, AVPR F35 o1 d607, ll.10–13v.

118 Petition by T.Gordon, November 1738, RGAVMF F227 o1 d4, ll.277–278.

promotion to lieutenant by 1738 and his subsequently very successful career.[119] Cosmo George, third Duke of Gordon, approached Admiral Gordon on behalf of 'Mr Ogilvie'[120] in 1736, and the Admiral immediately '. . . obtain'd for him the Post of Lieutenant in the Imperial Navy of Russia', with a promise to assist his further career.[121] The veteran Jacobite John Gordon of Glenbucket, wrote to Admiral Gordon in April 1737 explaining, on his son Alexander's behalf, the desperate predicament of Jacobites in the British navy, complaining that '. . . considering the Times [neither] he nor his children are Entitled to our Governments Favours' and,

> . . . as matters now go, the young man may continue in his present station of a midshipman, till he looses his Feet before he is advanced in the Navy, which Consideration Encourages & obliges him to push his fortune abroad under your Protection and Countenance.[122]

By August, through Gordon's intercession, Alexander Gordon was recruited and promoted from midshipman to lieutenant, despite the fact that the quota excess of lieutenants in the Russian Navy had risen to sixteen.[123] Contrary to what one might expect, therefore, Jacobite naval officers actually profited from the improvement of Anglo-Russian relations.

Jacobites and the Land Forces

The recruitment of foreign officers in the land forces was less structured than that in the navy, and although experienced commanders were in demand in the army, Russia could apparently rely on a natural influx of mercenaries to fill its requirements. No particular favour was shown towards Britons, therefore the state of Anglo-Russian relations did not play the same role as it did in naval recruitment.

In the 1730's, the Russian army attracted mercenaries and adventurers of all nationalities, including Jacobites, with the promise of active service. The great losses incurred during the Turkish war, in particular, meant a greater depen-

---

119 T.Gordon to John Young, 24/4/1738, T.Gordon to J.Gordon, 24/11/1738, 11//3/1740, NAS Abercairney, GD 24/1/855, ff.69,74,81; Thomas MacKenzie to John Drummond, 2/8/1736, SRO GD 24/3/368; He became a captain in 1754, and finally a rear-admiral in 1765, before his death the following year. *Mariner's Mirror* 33, p.24; *Obshchi morskoi spisok* 2, pp.245–247.

120 Although Cosmo did not risk his estates by active Jacobite participation, his father Alexander, 2nd Duke of Gordon, had fought under Mar at Sheriffmuir in 1715 while still Marquess of Huntly, and his younger brother Lewis was exiled after the 1745 rising. Ogilvie was possibly David, eldest son of John 4th Earl of Airlie, later 'out' in the 1745 rising, or else a relative of that family, whose earldom had been forfeited in 1715, and with whom the Gordons were closely connected. Sir J.B.Paul, ed., *The Scots Peerage*, 9 vols., 4, (Edinburgh, 1907), pp.551–554; Douglas, *The Peerage of Scotland*, 1, pp.126–127.

121 T.Gordon to Cosmo, Duke of Gordon, 12/1/1737, NAS Gordon Castle Muniments, GD 44/43/13, f.33; 18/8/1736, Report by T.Gordon to Golovin on recruiting Ogilvie from British navy, RGAVMF F212 o1 d17/712, l.59.

122 John Gordon of Glenbucket to T.Gordon, 20/4/1737, NAS Abercairney, GD 24/1/856, f.220.

123 31/8/1737, 7/9/1737, RGAVMF F212 o11, d17/733, ff.178,179.

dence on foreign recruitment as the most direct way of replenishing the officer complement.[124] Many of the non-Jacobites to arrive were volunteers, more interested in adventure than career security or financial reward. Manstein recorded that in June 1737 the Russian army was '. . . joined by several foreign officers, who came to make the campaign in the quality of volunteers'.[125] John Lindesay, Earl of Crawfurd, arrived in Russia in 1738 with Alexander Cumming, son of Sir Alexander Cumming of Culter, Mr Barrow or Burrard, and his groom James Graham, and was followed by 'captain Clifton and m-rs. Harris Pour and Gaven', all of whom set off to serve as volunteers in the Ukraine.[126] Lindesay was an adventurer of independent means who also joined the Imperial army, and who, unlike the exiles, could afford to fight as a volunteer without committing himself to one monarch. His attraction to the Russian army dated from 1735, when he had been greatly impressed by the discipline of the Russian auxiliary force as it passed through Pilsen on its way towards the Rhine campaign.[127] Another military adventurer, Major Ramsay, whom Manstein has described as 'a jacobite refugee in France', came to Russia by a curious route. As an officer in French service, he was at the Porte training Turks in Western military tactics when Anna Ivanovna intervened and offered him a post in the Russian army.[128]

The war also created good career opportunities for foreign physicians in the armed forces, including several Scots, whose political affiliations are unknown. Dr James Grieve, Dr James Mounsey and Dr John Cook came to Russia at this time. Grieve arrived in 1734 and later became physician to Empress Elisabeth. Mounsey signed a contract with Kantemir to work as a physician in the Naval Hospital in St Petersburg in 1736, but was sent within a year to the Ukrainian front to treat the outbreak of plague in Munnich's army. He became a close friend of James Keith, treated his wounded knee, and travelled with the Keith brothers to Paris.[129] Cook, a native of Hamilton, went to Russia in 1736, worked

---

124 Münnich himself complained to Osterman in July 1736, during the campaign in the Crimea, of an insufficiency of skilled officers, and suggested that more be recruited. Münnich to Osterman, 17/7/1736, RGVIA F846 o16 VUA no.1557 ch.2, ll.35v,36.

125 Manstein, *Memoirs*, 1770 edn., p.146, 1856 edn. p.150.

126 Rondeau to Harrington, 10/6/1738, *SIRIO* 80, p.315. Although Crawfurd was not a Jacobite, his status as one of the sixteen Scottish peers elected to sit in the House of Lords earned him a warm welcome from Thomas Gordon and Peter Lacy. Rolt, pp.117–118. Alexander Cumming and James Graham took advantage of the career prospects in Russia and became professionals; the former rose to the rank of colonel and served under James Keith in the Swedish war, the latter became Princess Elisabeth's chief groom, and later captain of a cuirassier regiment. Rolt, pp.117,122; RGVIA F846 o16 VUA 1622, ll.132,134.

127 Rolt, p.50.

128 Manstein, *Memoirs*, 1770 edn., pp.86–87, 1856 edn., pp.87–88. According to Dimitri Fedosov, who is currently researching the influence of Scotsmen in Russia, this was Bogdan Adrianovich Ramsay, of Scots descent, who was created a count in 1737, assumed the name 'Balmaine', after a Scottish line, and was killed at Wilmanstrand in 1741. Neither his own politics nor his political origins have been confirmed.

129 In 1757 he became First Physician to Elisabeth, then Chief Imperial Physician or 'archiator' to Peter III on a salary of 7000 roubles a year, retired to Dumfriesshire in 1761 and died in Edinburgh in 1773. Innes Smith, 'James Mounsey of Rammerscales', *Edinburgh Medical Journal*, 33 (1926), p.276; RGADA F16 o1 d322 pt.1 l.89v; J.Wilson, 'Three Scots in the Service of the Czars', *The Practitioner*, 210 (April, May, 1973), pp. 569–574, 704–708.

with Mounsey in the St Petersburg General Naval Hospital, and in 1738 also went to the Don region to treat plague and scurvy among the troops.[130]

The recruitment of Jacobites continued to flourish, as it had under Peter I, through the offices of those already established in Russia. During Peter's reign, when Jacobite attention had been focused on Russia, and exiles had sought service there for political reasons, the efforts of this network of Jacobite contacts in the sphere of recruitment had been a natural progression from political activism. Under Anna Ivanovna, despite the absence of such a political motive, the network flourished naturally, and, in the army as in the navy, served to counter any disadvantage to Jacobite recruitment which might have resulted from the Anglo-Russian rapprochement of the 1730's.

Thomas Gordon, Peter Lacy and James Keith, whose military success must have attracted other exiles, were the main intermediaries for Jacobites hoping to enter the Russian army. George Keith, for example, spurred on by his brother's great career, intended on several occasions to join him in Russia, but in 1730 was too poor to make the journey to St Petersburg, and calculated that it would take him two years to save sufficient funds.[131] After the death in spring 1732 of Francis Atterbury, the Bishop of Rochester, he looked to Russia as an escape from the consequences of having his own incriminating letters found among Atterbury's seized correspondence.[132] It was not until James Keith was injured at the battle of Ochakov in 1737 that he eventually received permission to travel to Russia, but on this occasion his hope of participating in the Turkish war himself was disappointed by his brother's poor health.[133]

Nevertheless, George Keith, writing mainly from Spain, used his brother's position to find employment for Jacobite exiles in Russia. In 1732 he recommended a friend, 'Don Marcos' (probably Mark Carse, Jacobite exile and member of the Order of Toboso), who wished to make a career in the Russian army, observing to his brother that

> . . . A subaltern officer in your service I believe has not a very pleasant or easy life, but then I hope there is good prospect of rising, when one has as much merit as Don Marcos.[134]

In the same year he recommended 'young St Clair . . . the best natured, honorable lad, I have met with',[135] and 'Stewart a son of Bog who was killed at

130 For a colourful account of his visit to Russia between 1736 and 1751, including details of medical procedures, see his memoirs, *Voyages and Travels through the Russian Empire, Tartary and part of the Kingdom of Persia*, 2 vols. (Edinburgh, 1770).

131 G.Keith to J.Keith, 12/7/1730, NAS Elphinstone, GD 156/62, folder 2, f.9.

132 He planned '. . . to get away with the least noise', G.Keith to J.Keith, 6/5/1732, *HMC Elphinstone*, p.222.

133 G.Keith to James III, 20/11/1737, RA Stuart 202/59; G. Keith to Edgar, RA Stuart 202/58.

134 G.Keith to J.Keith, 12/6/1732, NAS Elphinstone, GD 156/62, folder 2, f.7. This may well be the same Carse who had applied to enter Russian service in 1728.

135 This was a relative of John Master of St Clair of Roslin (Rosslyn), hereditary guardian of the Scottish relics, who had escaped to Orkney after his part in the 1715 rising. Young St Clair was then a supernumerary officer in the Swiss army. NAS Elphinstone, G.Keith to J.Keith, 30/10/1732, 15/4/1732, GD 156/62 folder 2, ff.8,28.

Sheriffmoor'. Stewart was serving in the Spanish dragoons in Tuscany, and later entered Russian service.[136] There were other Jacobites who had come to Russia from Spain, like Le Clerc, who left Spanish service for Russia after being involved in a duel.[137] George Keith apparently also sent a chaplain to Russia, for he asked his brother in 1731 '. . . what progress my chaplain makes in the propogation [sic] of the Gospel, by which I hope to gain Glory among our Ancestors the Scytes'.[138]

James III, likewise, approached his supporters in Russia to recommend other Jacobites to Russian service, including, in 1736, Colonel Bret, who had previously been involved in reporting British political affairs to the exiled court.[139] Bret was apparently attracted to Russia by the prospect of promotion, and James had granted him the commission of major general, although he was not in fact recruited.[140] James was also among those who recommended Robert Fullarton, the exiled younger son of the Jacobite Laird of Dudwick, who was recruited to Russia in 1738 and eventually became one of Catherine II's foremost officers, having risen to the rank of lieutenant general and been accorded the coveted title of Knight of St Catherine.[141] Besides James, he had several influential Jacobite referees who must have contributed to the success of his application, including the Earl of Aberdeen, the Laird of Pittodrie, John Gordon of Glenbucket and James Moir of Stoneywood.[142] Fullarton's father had lost an estate worth £400 a year and been exiled for his Jacobite activities, but his elder brother John continued to fight for the cause and was later charged with treason after Culloden. Both Thomas Gordon and Peter Lacy interceded on Robert's behalf in 1738 to secure him a military post in the Russian army which would not have been accessible to him in Britain. He was described as '. . . a pretty young Gentleman, and has had a very good Education, and is related to many familys of very good account in this country'.[143] Gordon commissioned the Prince of Hessen Homburg in the Crimea to promote Robert Fullarton's career, and he was consequently recommended to the commander Field Marshal Münnich himself.

Admiral Thomas Gordon was approached not only by seamen, but by

136 He was a cadet of about 20, of 'a very good character . . . has studied well, speaks high dutch perfectly . . .' George Keith to James Keith, 30/10/1732, NAS Elphinstone, GD 156/62 folder 2, f.8; John Stewart of Bogs, near Cairnfield, was younger brother of Andrew Stewart, 4th laird of Tanachie, and was killed fighting on the Jacobite side at Sheriffmuir, Tayler, *Jacobites of Aberdeenshire and Banffshire in the Rising of 1715*, p.192.
137 G.Keith to J.Keith, 17/1/1731, NAS Elphinstone, GD 156/62 folder 2, f.15.
138 G.Keith to J.Keith, 6/3/1731, NAS Elphinstone, GD 156/62, folder 2, f.2. This may have been the Rev. Thompson, of whom Thomas Gordon wrote to a friend in London, asking him '. . . to engage Mr Thompson [a chaplain] to come over hither with the first shipping', T.Gordon to W.Browne, 24/1/1727, NAS Abercairney, GD 24/1/859, f.309.
139 Colonel Bret to Daniel O'Brien, 9/9/1734 o.s., RA Stuart 173/45.
140 James III to James Keith, 4/3/1738, RA Stuart 205/64.
141 T.Gordon to Williams [James III], 20/7/1738, *HMC Eglinton* etc., p.188; Grant, 1889, p.49; A.Francis Steuart confuses Robert with his elder brother John, Earl of Dudwick, *Scottish Influences*, p.113.
142 Thomas Gordon to referees, 21/7/1738, NAS Abercairney, GD 24/1/855 f.72.
143 Kelly, Earl of Aberdeen, to T.Gordon, 29/3/1738, NAS Abercairney, GD 24/1/856 f.228.

prospective army recruits. In 1738 William Geddes, a Jacobite friend of Gordon's, requested his intercession on behalf of his son.[144] In the same year, Gordon recommended Hugh Eccles, who was recorded as having arrived in Russia by 1740.[145] Francis Hay, the son of the Jacobite Laird of Pitfour,[146] was recommended to Gordon by his maternal grandmother, the Countess of Errol, who wrote,

> . . . he has been bred Chirurgeon and Phisician and as our country is overstock'ed with them of that Profession, he goes to try his fortune abroad and would wilingly put himself under your protection.[147]

Although Hay could have taken advantage of the opportunities for military doctors in the Crimea he chose instead to serve as a major in the Russian army.[148]

James Keith recruited a number of Jacobites, as well as furthering the military career of his young relative Robert Keith, the orphaned son of Keith of Ludquhairn, who came to Russia in 1732 with his cousin's assistance and left with him for Prussia in 1747.[149] James III wrote to him in 1738 to thank him for having assisted in the recruitment of a young Jacobite, the son Alexander of '. . . a friend of mine at home of your own name'.[150] In 1738, then aged eighteen, James Johnstone, the Jacobite 'Chevalier de Johnstone', whose later memoirs recorded his part in the 1745 Rising, travelled to Russia to seek a career with the assistance of his two uncles there. One, James Hewitt, also a Jacobite and Johnstone's mother's brother, had been President of the College of Commerce under Peter I, but had retired, a wealthy man, at the Tsar's death.[151] The other was General Gustav Otto Douglas, governor of Reval. Hewitt's influence was such that he was able to introduce Johnstone to his

---

144 T.Gordon to William Geddes, 21/7/1738, NAS Abercairney, GD 24/1/855, f.72.
145 T.Gordon to Hugh Eccles, 4/2/1738, NAS Abercairney, GD 24/1/855, f.66; T.Gordon to John Gordon, 29/6/1740, *Ibid.*, f.86.
146 Francis was the Laird of Pitfour's second son. The politics of the father were characteristically reflected in the names of his children: James, Francis, Edward, Charles and Louise. Burke, *Commoners of Great Britain*, 1 p.508; Douglas, *Baronage*, 1, p.483.
147 Countess of Errol to T.Gordon, 23/6/1737, NAS Abercairney, GD 24/1/856 f.224.
148 Burke, *Commoners*, 1 p.508.
149 His name was recorded as 'Roman' or 'Robert' Keith in the Azov regiment in the military list of 1741, and in 1744 he was a lieutenant-colonel of infantry in the Novgorodski regiment. 'Spisok generalitetu i shtap ofitseram', 1741, 1744. RGVIA F489 o1 d7367, d7339.
150 James III to James Keith, 29/1/1738, RA Stuart 204/89. This may have been Alexander Keith, elder son of Keith of Uras, who died young. His younger brother Robert, however, was later educated in Prussia under the direction of James and George Keith, and became a lieutenant-colonel in the British army. Douglas, *Baronage*, 1, p.589.
151 Johnstone described Hewitt as '. . . a man of distinguished merit. He had a great deal of good sense, spirit, attainments, and experience . . . in his youth he had been as much a libertine as myself'. He had been colonel of a regiment, but after being injured at the battle of Narva, was a counsellor of the College of Commerce, 1719–1727, then took charge of the sugar factory in St Petersburg in 1732. He was a native of Edinburgh, and his son William Henry was the town physician of Moscow. J.Johnstone, *Memoirs*, 2, pp.113–115; *SIRIO* 60, p.181; E.Amburger, 'Die Zuckerindustrie in St Petersburg', *Jahrbücher für Osteuropäische Geschichte*, 38 (Berlin, 1986), pp.352–391.

friends, the Secretaries of State Count Golovin and Prince Kurakin, while they were dining at his house, and to procure the assistance of his other close friend, General Keith. Within days, with Keith's intercession, Johnstone was given the commission of a lieutenant, and promised a company at the end of the 1739 campaign against the Turks. Unfortunately, he was forced to decline the offer under threat of disinheritance by his father, and returned to London in 1739.[152] His account, however, gives a strong impression both of the romantic attraction Russia held for a young adventurer, and of the influence exerted in Russian court circles by a number of powerful Jacobites, many of whose careers had begun under Peter I, which kept the Jacobite community alive.

Selectivity and Success

Russian concessions to British naval officers and to those, like the Jacobites, with acquaintances in the Russian armed forces, tend to create the impression that recommendation through the correct channels was sufficient to guarantee recruitment. This was far from the case; even the best-connected applicants were only accepted if they could pass the relevant military examinations and if their specific skills were in demand, allowing them to be recruited above the established quota for their rank. Alexander Gordon's experience as a midshipman in the Royal Navy, including five years service in the Mediterranean and the West Indies, and his success in the lieutenants' examination, was a prerequisite for acceptance, even with Thomas Gordon's intercession. The recruitment of Gordon's grandson, James Young, was conditional on evidence that Young could pass the midshipman's examination, and even then, he had to be content with the meagre salary received by a Russian of the same rank. Indeed, in 1738 Thomas Gordon actually rejected the son of Commissar Paterson of Kirktoun, a distant relative, who wanted to enter the Russian army as '. . . not altogether fit for this countrey [sic] service'.[153]

Anglo-Russian amity notwithstanding, Anna was more discriminating than Peter I had been. A Captain Hasher, claiming to have served in the Royal Navy, had his request for promotion into the Russian service as a rear-admiral rejected because documentation of his previous career was lacking.[154] In 1737, despite the need for officers, ten applicants were rejected as unsuitable. In 1739 an Imperial decree was issued to the Senate forbidding the recruitment of any naval officers but those best qualified and experienced.[155] A decree was issued in the same year that recruitment should not exceed the established quotas.[156]

The restriction on recruitment was largely the result of a shortage of money. The Admiralty was operating on a reduced budget, and offers of pay incentives to a few skilled foreigners, though necessary, led to Kantemir being disciplined in 1736 for his liberal use of Treasury funds, and he had to account in full for

---

152 J.Johnstone, *Memoirs*, 2, pp.114–117.
153 NAS Abercairney, GD 24/1/855, f.78.
154 Golovin to Kantemir, 27/1/1736, AVPR F36 o1 d71, l.1.
155 Imperial decree, April 1739, RGAVMF F230 o1 d42.
156 31/3/1739, *PSZ* 7787.

his expenditure. Between 1733 and 1737 the naval recruitment campaign in Britain cost Russia 5141 roubles 36 kopecks, or approximately £1142. Meanwhile, the Admiralty College complained that it had insufficient resources to complete its ship-building projects.[157] Military lists indicate that promoted officers in Russia remained for some time at their former salary rate despite holding higher rank. There could, therefore, be no question of mass foreign recruitment; mercenaries were not simply an option preferred by a minority of powerful foreigners in Russia but an expensive necessity to supplement a lack of native expertise.

Moreover, native opposition to any preferential treatment of foreigners forced the military authorities to maintain parity, where possible, between foreign and native employment conditions. When Kantemir first offered financial incentives to British recruits, for example, he was reprimanded by the Admiralty College because some native officers were already protesting that they were treated unfairly, and two Russian lieutenants receiving only ten roubles a month demanded fifteen.[158]

This selectivity, and the patronage Jacobites enjoyed from those already established in Russia, may to some extent explain both the generally high quality of Jacobite recruits, and the disproportionate success of exiles and their relatives in the Russian army and navy. By the end of the decade of Anna's reign Peter Lacy had become a field marshal, James Keith was a general, Alexander Bruce, George Lacy, Theodore Gordon[159] and George Brown were colonels, Ramsay of Balmaine[160] was a lieutenant colonel. In the navy, Thomas Gordon had attained the pinnacle of his career as admiral of the fleet. Thomas Saunders had reached the rank of vice-admiral, Kenneth Lord Duffus, had been a shautbenakht (rear-admiral) at the time of his death in 1732, Christopher O'Brien became a vice-admiral, his sons a lieutenant and a captain respectively, Alexander Gordon was a lieutenant, Robert Fullarton a major and Robert Little a first rank captain. Unlike rich young adventurers like Lindesay of Crawfurd, some faced the alternative of poverty at home or in the narrow confines of the exiled court, where those '. . . that have spirit are suffer'd (and suffer) because, not having bread elsewhere, they are forced to silence'.[161] One might speculate that their reliance on a successful military career, either for reasons of enforced exile from Britain or of continuing professional discrimination, acted as an additional spur to their ambition.

157 RGAVMF F212 o11 d3/657, ll.64,65; Report of Admiralty College, 5/1/1737, *Ibid.*, d3/733, l.18.
158 Report to Admiralty College, RGAVMF F212 o1 d17, l.147.
159 This was the son of Peter I's Jacobite General Patrick Gordon.
160 He was described by Manstein as a Jacobite exile from France.
161 G.Keith to J.Keith, c.1731, *HMC Elphinstone*, p.222.

EIGHT

Jacobites in Battle, 1730–1740

Anna's reign marked a high point in terms of the military contribution made by Jacobites in Russia. This was, of course, ultimately due to the Polish and Turkish wars, which both attracted Jacobites and enabled them to practise the military skills for which they had been recruited. The extent of their influence was reflected in the acclaim they received as military leaders even among their contemporaries. In 1739 the *Scots Magazine* boasted of the number of Scots in the Russian army:

> . . . The empire of Russia has . . . gained great honour by the valour and conduct of its troops which indisputably is in good measure owing to the great resort of Gentlemen from other countries . . . We may surely be indulged to take a little rational pride, in finding no action of consequence performed in which Gentlemen of this nation are not in particular manner distinguished for their bravery and resolution: At the head of the Russian fleet we find a GORDON; in the highest rank of the army a KEITH, and DOUGLAS, LESLEY,[1] and many more, send their names from the extremities of that vast empire, and even from the inmost plains of Tartary.[2]

Of those mentioned, Gordon and Keith, of course, were Jacobites, and Douglas had Jacobite relatives. It was ironic that the *Scots Magazine* should draw attention to the success enjoyed by these Jacobites abroad, as though to national heroes, when they had effectively been driven from their native land on grounds of political allegiance, and were thus unable to employ their talents at home. However, it was significant that men formerly regarded as mere political dissidents should so quickly have been able to achieve such international acclaim. The military role of individual Jacobites during Anna's reign not only enabled them to overcome the discrimination and oblivion to which their political disaffection had consigned them at home, but helped to reinforce the dominance Russia had acquired in European military and diplomatic affairs over the course of the previous three decades.

1 Colonel [George/Yuri] Lesley was of Scots descent, but his political inclinations are unknown. Lesleys had been mercenaries in Russia for at least a century, and if he was already russified, his political sympathies would be at best cool, unless stirred by home contacts. General Sir Alexander Leslie of Auchintoul was one of the 445 foreign officers in the Russian army in 1624, and the surname was first recorded in the Foreign Quarter in Moscow in 1630. This Lesley distinguished himself in both the Polish and the Turkish wars, and, as a major-general, was killed by Tartars while drunk in 1737. Barnhill and Dukes, 'North-East Scots in Muscovy', pp.52–53; Amburger, 'Die Einwohnerschaft', p.417; *RA* 4 (1898), p.485; Manstein, *Memoirs*, 1770 edn., p.139, 1856 edn., p.143; Cook, *Travels*, 1, pp.119–200.

2 *The Scots Magazine*, 1 (1739), p.4.

Poland

The most decisive battles of the War of the Polish Succession, fought over control of Poland after the death of King Augustus II in early 1733, owed much to Jacobite leadership. The war was fought on two fronts, in Poland and Germany. Hostilites began in 1733 when Russia launched a military intervention in Poland in support of the Austrian Imperial candidate, Augustus Elector of Saxony, and against his rival, the French-backed candidate, Stanislas Leszczynski. Soon afterwards France declared war on Austria and initiated the offensive on the Rhine. The former conflict was effectively decided by the surrender of Danzig to Russian troops in 1734, and hostilities on the Rhine ended with peace preliminaries between France and Austria in October 1735, although the Treaty of Vienna was not concluded until 1738.

Unfortunately, by 1733 two of the generation of Jacobites to have joined Peter I's navy, Vice-Admiral Thomas Saunders, and Rear-Admiral Kenneth Sutherland, 3rd Lord Duffus, had died. Until shortly before his death on 25 December 1733, Saunders had been of great service in directing the 500 men involved in the harbour, dock and canal construction at Cronstadt, and the British residents, Forbes and Rondeau, described his death as '. . . a considerable loss to this court, he being the only good naval officer they had'.[3] Duffus, who had died on 2 April 1732, was also greatly missed, by the navy as well as the Jacobite community.[4]

Nevertheless, the accretion of new members to those remaining of the older generation helped to offset this loss. One of the old guard whose Russian career, launched in 1699, was only just reaching its peak under Anna Ivanovna, was General Peter Lacy, perhaps the most experienced, competent and popular commander of the Russian campaign. Although the military ambitions of Field Marshal Münnich deprived him of chief command, Lacy's long service under Peter I and his understanding of the Russian troops were acknowledged. The Duke of Liria, who had met Lacy during his posting as Spanish ambassador to Russia, wrote that he, '. . . was beloved and an honest man . . . incapable of doing any evil', and that he '. . . knew his job to perfection'.[5] Rondeau commented that Lacy, although a foreigner, did not encounter hostility from the Russians under his command, but on the contrary was '. . . very much beloved by the troops'.[6]

Having learned on 23 February 1733 that he was to enter Poland, Lacy took great care in selecting good recruits and adequate provisions, prior to gathering 30,000 men near Riga. He insisted on postponing his departure in order to

---

3 Memoirs of Francis Dashwood, *SEER* p.200, n.34. This deprecation of Russian naval officers was rather exaggerated. Forbes and Rondeau to Harrington, 29/12/1733 o.s., *SIRIO* 76, p.158.

4 He left his widow Charlotte and two daughters in Russia, and his son and heir Eric, in Britain, Rondeau to Harrington, 11/4/1732 o.s., *SIRIO* 66, p.446. In 1734, Eric married his cousin, the third daughter of Sir James Dunbar of Hempriggs, and they had two sons. J.Gordon to T.Gordon, 19/12/1734, NAS Abercairney, GD 24/1/856, ff.205–206.

5 Liria, 'Zapiski Diuka Liriiskago', p.403.

6 Rondeau to Harrington, 3/4/1736, *SIRIO* 76, p.499.

ensure that his troops were fully supplied with ammunition, horses and food, and did not set off for Warsaw until August. The Russian authorities greatly complicated his supply problems during the march by insisting that he use Russian currency in Poland, and he experienced terrible difficulties as wet weather turned his route into a sea of deep mud, which delayed his arrival until the end of September. Although he was too late to bring Russian force to bear on the outcome of the Polish elections, his mission was nevertheless instrumental in turning the war in Russia's favour.

While on the march he impressed the local population with the discipline of the Russian troops under his command by restraining them from pillaging, an achievement almost unheard of in the eighteenth century. More importantly, his arrival in Warsaw forced the elected opposition candidate, Leszczynski, to abandon the city, and to flee to Danzig with a part of the Polish nobility, a move which, as discussed in an earlier chapter, left Leszczynski vulnerable to encirclement by Russian troops.[7] Lacy's presence also enabled a 'seim' (parliament) to be held, which elected Augustus King of Poland. Unfortunately, when he was sent to besiege Danzig with 12,000 men in November 1733, his reluctance to storm the town and risk the lives of his men brought him into conflict with the more precipitate Münnich, who then assumed command of the siege. The attempted storming was unsuccessful, as Lacy had anticipated, yet his men, decimated by enemy fire, refused to obey Münnich's orders to retire until Lacy himself issued them.[8] Lacy led his troops to victory in 1734 at the batle of Wisiczin. At the decisive battle of Busawitza, although outnumberd ten to one, he heavily defeated Leszszynski's forces. His success earned him the Order of the White Eagle of Poland

As discussed earlier, the decisive leadership of Admiral Thomas Gordon played a key role in the fate of Danzig. With a squadron of 14 ships-of-the-line, five frigates and two bomb-ships he successfully prevented the French fleet from relieving Danzig, took possession of the island of Wechselmunde, and forced the surrender of Danzig on 28 June 1734.[9] This capitulation, perhaps the most important single victory in the Polish campaign, was, with justification, attributed to Gordon's leadership.[10] He was by nature a man of independent opinion, and throughout his career preferred a position of sole command to one of subordination.[11] On receiving his instructions from the Cabinet for a possible naval encounter at Danzig, he declared them 'all well digested', but insisted that an article be added granting him discretionary power.[12] After the French fortifications had capitulated, he overruled Field Marshal Münnich's

7 Keith, *A Fragment*, p.103.
8 *Russkii Biograficheski Slovar'*, 25 vols. (St Petersburg, 1896–1918), 10, pp.80–86.
9 Elagin, *Materialy*, 7, pp.624–635; 'Boevaya letopis' russkogo flota', ed.N.V.Novikov (Moscow, 1948), pp.72–74; Solov'ev, *Istoriya Rossii*, 20, p.1294.
10 J.Keith to T.Gordon, 20/2/1735 o.s., *HMC Eglinton* etc., pp.178,179.
11 In 1732, for example, during the reorganisation of the navy, Gordon had protested hotly the decision to give his junior, Admiral Golovin, superiority over him on the grounds that Golovin was President of the Admiralty College. Elagin, *Materialy*, 7, p.591.
12 T.Gordon to Cabinet, May 1734, NAS Abercairney, GD 24/1/855, f.107.

order to send men and ammunition for the continuing siege, having received news of the imminent arrival of additional French ships, and instead gave priority to evacuating the French prisoners and securing his victory.[13]

The war with Poland established James Keith as one of the most respected Russian commanders, and earned him promotion to the rank of lieutenant general. After his career had been launched by his selection to the Ismailovsky guards, he had, in 1732, been appointed one of three military inspectors assigned to maintain standards in the armed forces in accordance with military reform. The large area for which he was responsible stretched from the Polish border near Smolensk to the Asian frontier demarcated by the Volga and Don rivers, and between June and December he travelled over 4500 miles and inspected more than thirty regiments.[14] This task was one involving considerable responsibility and hardship, and a preparation for his role in the Polish war. Soon after his return to St Petersburg, he was placed in command of 6,000 men, one of three bodies of troops preparing to defend Russian interests in Poland, and ordered to march back to the Ukraine to enter Poland through Volynia. He crossed the frozen Dnieper to Poland in December. Overcoming the incompetence of Lieutenant General Prince Shakhovskoi, a superior officer sent after him by the War College, whom Keith had on one occasion to dissuade from pillaging enemy property and thus putting the Russian army 'in hazard of dying of hunger',[15] he demonstrated excellent military judgement and independent leadership. In spring 1734 he disregarded General Weisbach's orders, which were irrelevant by the time they reached him, and marched his men towards the main enemy force in the town of Brodi. Despite a numerical disadvantage, he managed to drive off an enemy attack, and in June, after the arrival of Hessen Homburg, who replaced Shakhovskoi, Brodi was besieged and taken with very few losses. Keith was subsequently put in command of the siege of the fort of Zbarage, which was surrendered without Russian loss. The competence of field commanders like Keith and Lacy was well demonstrated by the battle situation, in which communication difficulties with military headquarters often forced them to act on their own initiative.

The Rhine Campaign

In early summer 1735 Russia made its first direct intervention in European military affairs by sending eight regiments of Russian troops from the borders of Silesia to aid the Emperor's army on the Rhine against the French.[16] The first 12,000 men were to be joined by an additional 8,000 as soon as recruits enlisted in Russia could reach Poland.[17] Once more, it was the Jacobites,

13 Gordon, 'Journal of all the Remarkable Accidents and Proceedings of our voyage to Pillow and Dantzig', NAS Abercairney, GD 24/1/855, ff.110–117. Ironically, as previously discussed, Gordon's great service to Russia was simultaneously in direct opposition to Jacobite interests. James III to [], 2/7/1734, 24/7/1734, RA Stuart 171/81, 171/174.
14 Keith, *A Fragment*, p.97.
15 Keith, *A Fragment*, p.107.
16 RGVIA, F846 o16 VUA 1557 ch.1, l.33.
17 Rondeau to Harrington, 16/3/1735, *SIRIO* 76, p.380.

General Peter Lacy, in chief command of the force, and the newly promoted Lieutenant General James Keith who, as two of the foremost officers in Russia, took charge of the campaign, along with Major General Biron. Rondeau observed to Harrington that

> . . . Those gentlemen are reckoned as good officers as any in the country, and I humbly believe . . . the russ troops will not be the worst soldiers in the imperial army.[18]

The Rhine campaign was highly significant in terms of Russia's military reputation in Europe. Firstly, Russian troops were marched further west than ever before, and it said much for Russian military confidence that they were prepared to make such a prominent show of force so far from home. The march marked the full entry of Russia into the European military and political arena as a powerful ally and a daunting enemy. Secondly, Russia's impressive performance in Poland had confirmed that it was quite capable of defending its interests in Europe, and the professionalism of the force sent to the Rhine created a great impression on eyewitnesses. Manstein reported that

> . . . Everyone admired [them], and was astonished at the good discipline [and order] they observed on their march and in their quarters.[19]

Indeed, it was the appearance of this organised body of Russians which prompted the French to concede to peace negotiations, and hastened the end of the Polish war. Thirdly, the march marked the acknowledgement by the Emperor at Vienna of Anna's imperial title. In one notable incident, the Austrian officer who received Keith persisted in referring to the Empress as 'Tsarina'. In response, Keith called the Emperor Charles VI simply 'Archduke' and, as a consequence, the Austrian was ordered to recognise Anna's title as Empress of Russia. Although this appeared to be an insignificant matter of diplomatic form, it was, in fact symbolic of the recognition and respect Russia was gaining in Europe, largely as a result of the military dominance which Jacobite commanders were instrumental in building.

The Crimea

The Turkish war erupted in 1735 following Tartar incursions beyond Kabarda, which threatened to cut Russia off from Georgia and Persia. The Turks had long coveted the strategically important Kabarda, and Russia sought to protect its southern borders.[20] This, coupled with Field Marshal Münnich's personal ambition to reclaim Constantinople for Russia and to secure Russian access to the Black Sea, initiated a savage four-year war in which Russia gained little but military experience, and lost thousands of men, largely to disease.

After a short preparatory campaign in 1735, Münnich led the full offensive in 1736. That season the Russians broke down the defenses of Perekop, occupied

---

18 Rondeau to Harrington, 31/5/1735, *SIRIO* 76, p.401.
19 Manstein, *Memoirs,* 1770 edn., p.88, 1856 edn., p.85; [ ] only in 1856 edn.
20 Beskrovny, *Russkaya armiya i flot v XVIII veke,* p.245.

the Crimean capital, Bachshiserai and took the town of Azov. The following, and bloodiest year, an army under Münnich had a great victory at the capture of Ochakov, while Lacy fought in the Crimea. Austria joined the war on the Russian side. However, in 1738, Russia lost Ochakov and Kinburn again, retaining only Azov. Münnich was enjoying greater success in 1739, and had won Khotim and Moldavia, when the Austrians brought the war to an unexpected end with the Treaty of Belgrade in September. In military terms the war was unsatisfactory for Russia; there was little net territorial gain for great human loss. Nevertheless, the Crimea proved to be a testing ground for Russian discipline and tactics, and gave individual Jacobites the opportunity of more active service.

The capture by Field Marshal Lacy of the strategic fortress of Azov in July 1736 was one of the major achievements of the campaign both for Russia and for Lacy himself. According to Field Marshal Münnich's plans, Azov was the primary military objective of the Russian army, and he commenced the siege himself in March 1736 as the first part of the campaign.

Lacy had been promoted to the rank of field marshal in February 1736 in recognition of his role in the Polish war and particularly the Rhine expedition. He met Münnich in Tsaritsyn in the Ukraine in April on his return from that campaign, was appointed commander of half of the Russian army in place of the deceased General Weisbach, and was immediately sent to oversee the siege of Azov.[21] Münnich, meanwhile, set off with the first army towards the Crimea. It was intended that Azov should serve to divert part of the Turkish force away from Münnich and the Crimea, and Lacy arrived before the city on 15 May 1736, new style, and assumed command from General Levashev. Although Münnich had originally predicted that the inhabitants would surrender by May, the siege drew out until late June, despite continuous Russian artillery bombardment of the fortress. Lacy himself led frequent sallies towards the city walls, and received a gunshot wound in the leg on 14 June. The tide eventually turned in Russia's favour when a powder magazine within the walls was exploded by a Russian bombshell, causing great destruction. On 28 June, Lacy followed this with a night attack using 1600 of his best troops, accompanied by bombardment and gunfire from the Russian batteries and the fleet under Vice Admiral Bredal, and the following day capitulation terms were agreed, and the inhabitants of the fortress sent back to Turkey. The Russian victory was won at little expense. Of a total force of 25,000 men, fewer than 200 were killed, and only 1,500 injured.[22]

This campaign spread Lacy's military reputation abroad, and the *Scots Magazine* praised him as second only to Münnich, who was now regarded as '. . . the greatest General Europe can now boast'.[23] Indeed, for a short time after the end of the siege of Azov, it appeared that he might even replace Münnich as chief commander of the Russian forces. Münnich's march into the

21 Manstein, *Memoirs*, 1856 edn., p.125.
22 Manstein, 1770 edn. pp.123–127, 1856 edn., pp.124–128; Solov'ev, *Istoriya Rossii*, 20, p.1345.
23 *The Scots Magazine*, 1 (1739), p.5.

Crimea in 1736 had been hindered primarily by poor organisation and supply of provisions,[24] and although Lacy had warned him from Azov that he could send no assistance, Münnich subsequently blamed Lacy for failing to send either food or reinforcements. At the end of the season, Lacy was instructed by the War College to send details of the condition of Münnich's army, and the latter, in order to escape Imperial disapproval, claimed to be prepared to resign his command to Lacy on grounds of ill health. As expected, the Empress refused his request, naturally regarding the resignation of the chief comman-der in the midst of war as a gross dereliction of duty. Münnich thus succeeded both in salvaging his reputation and re-asserting his superiority over the less ambitious Lacy. Nevertheless, this episode was evidence of Lacy's military status, a fact which Anna Ivanovna acknowledged early the following year by granting him a Livonian estate worth thirty-seven thousand roubles.[25]

Colonel George (Yuri Yurevich) Brown, who had been promoted from captain since entering Russian service in 1730, was severely wounded at the siege of Azov, but this did not curtail his career. He recovered to fight at Ochakov in 1737, and in 1739, while on a special mission in the Austrian army, was taken prisoner by the Turks at Krotzka. John Lindesay, Earl of Crawfurd, who had served with Brown under Münnich and had been wounded at Krotzka, recorded that he and Brown were permitted to meet frequently in September 1739.[26] Brown was of particular service to Russia during his captivity; after being resold on three occasions and acquiring Turkish military secrets, he was eventually assisted by the French envoy at the Porte, who helped him to escape. On his return to St Petersburg, the intelligence he was able to communicate earned him promotion to major general.[27]

Also under Lacy at Azov was his kinsman, Colonel George Lacy of the Kazanski regiment,[28] probably the messenger described as the field marshal's son, who travelled to St Petersburg with news of the victory.[29] According to Dr John Cook, the Scottish physician who came to Russia in 1736, Lieutenant Innes of Aberdeen served as a volunteer in the Horse Guards and was under Münnich's command in the Turkish war. He would, therefore, have seen active service in the siege of Azov, and his absence from the 1738 military list can be attributed to his volunteer status. Cook described him as '. . . the brave Innes, the soldiers' friend, and beloved of all good men'.[30]

24 'Turetskaya voina pri imperatritse Anne', contemporary manuscript, *RA* 1878, 1, 3, pp.255–274.
25 Rondeau to Harrington, 9/4/1737, *SIRIO* 80, p.128.
26 Rolt, *John Lindesay*, p.282.
27 Brockhaus-Efron, 8, pp.739–740; *DNB*, 3, p.45.
28 'Spisok generalitetu i shtap ofitseram', 1738, RGVIA F489 o1 d7387.
29 Rondeau to H.Walpole, 3/6/1736, *SIRIO* 76 p.532.
30 John Cook, *Voyages and Travels through the Russian Empire*, 2 vols. (Edinburgh, 1770); 'Captain' Innes, had been a volunteer in the Russian army in 1734 and it was hoped would soon be promoted to lieutenant colonel, John Ouchterlony (Jacobite merchant at Riga) to T.Gordon, 5/12/1734, NAS Abercairney, GD 24/1/856, f.202; Grant, in his work on prominent Scotsmen, recorded him as 'lieutenant Innes' in the Russian army, Grant, *The Scottish Soldiers of Fortune*, p.19.

Lieutenant General James Keith's bravery in the siege of Ochakov in 1737 not only contributed to the greatest Russian victory of the year but earned him promotion to the rank of full general at the end of the campaign.[31] On 22 April 1736, Keith, at Neuhausen, had received orders to march with all haste to the Ukraine to join the Russian army under Lacy and Münnich.[32] Once more, the exemplary discipline of his troops, maintained on pain of immediate and severe punishment, impressed eyewitnesses, and, after wintering in the Ukraine, they joined the main Russian army under Münnich for the 1737 campaign.[33]

Münnich arrived at the citadel of Ochakov in late June 1737, and on 12 July, without preparation, launched a bombardment, unaware that he was attacking the best-fortified position.[34] Fortunately, just before dawn of 13 July, a fire broke out inside the battlements, and Münnich sent orders to Keith and Löwendahl on the left wing to approach to within musket shot of the glacis to prevent the garrison from extinguishing it. According to Manstein, who was a major general participating in the siege, Keith answered Münnich that he was already less than that distance from the enemy, and was sustaining considerable losses. Nevertheless, Münnich sent him further orders to advance with his men without cover to the foot of the glacis, although they lacked equipment to cross the moat of the first rampart. Keith obediently remained there under heavy fire until a sally by the Turks drove him and his men back with heavy losses. At this point, Keith himself was shot in the thigh and severely wounded. Münnich, rather hypocritically, blamed Keith for advancing too close to the enemy and bringing on the counter-attack too early, to which Keith responded by threatening to take the matter to court martial. As it transpired, it was Keith's bravery in diverting Turkish attention which had allowed time for the fire in the fortress to reach the munitions store, which subsequently exploded, killing 6,000 of the enemy occupants. It was this event which forced the Seraskier to surrender and won Ochakov for Russia. Manstein wrote,

> . . . it was owing to the over-great ardour of Keith that the assault had been made and had successed . . .[35]

As well as promoting Keith to the rank of full general, Empress Anna was so concerned by the severity of his wound that she permitted his brother George to visit him in Russia, and provided 5000 roubles in addition to the sum granted him on his promotion, 'to defray his charges' and to enable him to return with

---

31 Münnich informed Keith of his promotion in March 1738. Anna also granted him 5,000 roubles as a reward for his services. Münnich's report, *Vse. Donosheniya Minikha*, pp.292–293; also Rondeau to Harrington, 18/3/1738, *SIRIO* 80, pp.284–285.
32 Keith to Cabinet, 25/4/1736, RGADA F177 o1 d27, 1.10.
33 Keith to Cabinet, 7/5/1736, *Ibid.*, ff.12,13.
34 For accounts of the siege, Manstein, *Memoirs*, 1770 edn., pp.151–157, 1856 edn., pp.155–162; Nashchokin, RA (1883), 2, pp.277–278; Rondeau to Harrington, 19/7/1737 o.s., 6/8/1737 o.s., *SIRIO* 80, pp.173,179; Varnhagen von Ense, *Feldmarschall Jakob Keith*, p.37.
35 Manstein, *Memoirs*, 1856 edn., p.162.

George to Paris for treatment.[36] Her intercession on his behalf with George II to secure him the Earl of Kintore's estates, was, likewise, in recognition of his service to Russia. Even Münnich, who had known him since the beginning of his Russian career, described him in 1737 as

> . . . A general whose deeds and bearing are inspired with loyalty to the throne, courage and good-nature. One cannot fault his character in any particular.[37]

His military talents gave him, in the judgement of John Hill Burton, '. . . a place in history and . . . a fortune far above the home respectability, affluence, and rank from which calamity had driven [him]',[38] and he is regarded as one of the greatest commanders in Russia, not only of the 1730's and 1740's, but of his century. According to A.G.Cross, even, '. . . The Russian army during Catherine's reign could boast of no Scottish officers of the stature of Field Marshall James Keith'.[39]

Lieutenant Innes also distinguished himself at Ochakov, and in the plundering which followed the victory, intervened to save a Turkish child from being slaughtered by a Russian grenadier. He beheaded both the guardsman and his companion, for which, according to Dr John Cook, he was 'greatly commended', and his action '. . . encouraged some other officers, who soon thereafter got the soldiers brought to a sense of their duty'. Münnich was so impressed by his bravery that he made honourable mention of him in his dispatches to Empress Elisabeth, and procured for him the commission of Colonel of dragoons.[40]

Robert Fullarton, son of the Laird of Dudwick, who arrived in Russia towards the end of the war in 1738, and was recommended to Field Marshal Münnich,[41] joined the campaign at the same time as John Lindesay, Earl of Crawfurd, and, like Crawfurd, probably first served as a volunteer, for his name does not appear on the military lists for 1738.[42] Fullarton saw active service during the last full campaign in the Crimea, and by 1741 was a successful professional soldier with the rank of lieutenant colonel.[43] Colonel Innes continued to serve under Münnich, and in 1738, Rondeau reported that '. . . Captain Innis, a scotsman in Russian service' had been sent by Field Marshal Münnich from the Russian army to report on a Russian victory over 25,000 Turkish janissaries by the river Bilotch.[44] In 1739, when pirates were harrying passengers on the Volga, including Russian officers, Innes and his spies, dressed as peasants,

36 Rondeau to Harrington, 2/12/1738, *SIRIO* 80, p.398.
37 Report by Münnich, 1737, RGVIA F846 o16 VUA 1556 ch.2, 1.26.
38 J.Hill Burton, *The Scot Abroad* (Edinburgh, 1881), p.331.
39 A.G.Cross, 'Scoto-Russian Contacts in the Reign of Catherine the Great (1762–1796)', in *The Caledonian Phalanx*, Publications of the National Library of Scotland, p.24.
40 J.Cook, *Travels*, 1, pp.204–206.
41 Prince of Hessen-Homburg to T.Gordon, 6/6/1738, *HMC Eglinton* etc., pp.164–165.
42 T.Gordon to James Moir of Stoneywood, 21/7/1738, NAS Abercairney, GD 24/1/855, f.72.
43 Finch to Harrington, 29/8/1741, *SIRIO* 91, p.263.
44 Rondeau to Harrington, 26/8/1738, *SIRIO* 80, p.351.

surrounded and killed many of them, for which, according to Dr John Cook, '. . . everyone applauded the conduct and bravery of Mr Innes'.[45] Unfortunately, he was later arrested for distributing the pirates' spoil amongst his men, and apparently died while in custody.[46] This was, however, almost certainly the same Innes who figured in the military list of 1744 as a colonel in the Reval regiment, having been promoted to that rank in November 1740. Although his name does not subsequently figure in the military list of 1748, he may not have died as early as Cook claimed.[47]

Although Christopher O'Brien's contract with Kantemir dated from April 1737, he was not on active service during the war with Turkey. Instead, on arrival in St Petersburg, he was ordered to advise the Admiralty College on improving ship-building and docking facilities at Cronstadt. Although not himself an engineer, he inspected every part of the fortifications, and was sufficiently informed of the construction of English docks to assist Major General Lubras, the chief engineer at Cronstadt. O'Brien consulted closely with Admiral Gordon, and reported that, to acquire as much knowledge of Cronstadt as possible, '. . . I convers with all I can, from the highest to the lowest'.[48] The fruits of his efforts were sketches of the Cronstadt canal which he submitted with suggestions for structural improvements. He also made detailed reports to the Admiralty of the latest British artillery developments, and invited cannon manufacturers to design, '. . . a Canon a considerable deale shorter, lighter and to require less powder which can carry a shott double or twice the distance that Canon usually doe at present'. He also proposed to produce a newly invented water pump capable of drawing 'ten tuns in a minute'.[49] In 1738, after commanding a squadron in the Baltic, he made a number of suggestions for improving ship design which were subsequently adopted.[50] Despite his lack of formal engineering training, his inventive talent benefited the Russian navy during the last years of the war with Turkey.

Many of the British naval officers recruited in the late 1730's were sent in early 1737 to Bryansk on the Dnieper and Tavarov on the Don to command ships which had recently been built there for the Turkish campaign. Of the nine captains and other officers sent, '. . . there [were] five english captains and a great many english lieutenants,'[51] including Jacobites Lieutenant Ogilvie, who commanded the Ovod in the area of Azov and Midshipman Alexander Gordon, who was drowned in 1739. Others remained in the Baltic; Thomas MacKenzie, made a lieutenant in 1738, was on campaign in the ships Riga and

45 J.Cook, *Travels,* 1, pp.351–355.
46 *Ibid.,* p.356.
47 'Spisok generalitetu i shtap ofitseram', 1738, 1744, 1748, RGVIA F489 ol d7387, d7367, d7386.
48 O'Brien to Osterman, 24/7/1737, AVPR F35 ol d607, ll.3–4.
49 O'Brien's report on Artillery Improvements, AVPR F35 ol d607, ll.10,12,13.
50 Berkh, *Zhizneopisaniya,* 2, pp.194–5.
51 The word 'english' was often used to mean British. Rondeau to Harrington, 22/1/1737, *SIRIO* 80, p.99; Talbot and Somerset Masters were sent to the Dnieper the following year, Rondeau to Harrington, 25/2/1738, *SIRIO* 80, p.279.

Rossiya sailing between Cronstadt and Krasnaya Gorka,[52] and Thomas Gordon's grandson, James Young, was a volunteer on the Riga in 1738, before being recruited as a midshipman.

Albeit brief and selective, this account of the military careers of better known Jacobites in the wars of the 1730's gives some indication of the extent to which their professional success in Russia raised them above their dissident past. In terms of providing exiles with the opportunity for active service, Anna's reign was second only to that of Peter I. There was a belief among contemporaries that foreign officers were essential to the effective discipline and leadership of Russian troops, that

> . . . Russians are capable of undertaking and executing everything when they are well led; but it is requisite they should have a number of foreign officers, as the soldiers have more confidence in them than in those of their own nation.[53]

The Jacobites formed only a small percentage of the foreign officer contingent, yet their presence in the foremost ranks of the Russian army and navy in every campaign of Anna Ivanovna's reign gives grounds for speculation that Russian troops would not have fared as well as they did in international conflicts, had it not been for the leadership and experience of such men as Thomas Gordon, Peter Lacy and James Keith.

52 *Obshchi morskoi spisok*, 2, pp.245–247.
53 Manstein, *Memoirs*, 1770 edn., p.187, 1856 edn.,p.193.

PART FIVE

The Regencies and the
Reign of Elisabeth, 1740–1750

NINE

The End of An Era

The year 1740 was like a touch paper, setting ablaze conflicts which would rage throughout Europe for the rest of a momentous decade. The deaths within a short time of three great monarchs, Empress Anna Ivanovna of Russia, the Holy Roman Emperor Charles VI and King Frederick Wilhelm I of Prussia, impelled the division of Europe into rival camps, which began squabbling amongst themselves over former Imperial possessions to defend their territorial interests. Every corner of Europe was affected, from Sweden and Russia to Turkey and Spain. In Russia domestic jockeying for power was reflected in two successive coups, the latter of which was supported by Russia's European rivals and involved it in war with Sweden. Most importantly, in 1745 the Jacobites, aligning themselves as always with Britain's enemies, were able at last, with the promise of French assistance, to launch a Rising. Preoccupied as Russia was with internal upheavals and with strife on its own borders against Britain's enemies, it had no interest in Jacobite involvement. Nevertheless, Jacobites in Russia did not, and indeed could not, escape the repercussions of events in the West. The diplomatic and military importance of Russia as an ally heightened the political sensitivities of French and British rival camps at the Russian court, and had a decisive effect on the fate of Jacobites there. In addition, the early 1740's marked a sharp decline in the number of Jacobites in Russia that was not motivated by politics alone; worsening conditions in Russia for foreigners in general told on the foreign military population. Nevertheless, the decade which saw the successful beginning and ultimate failure of the last Jacobite Rising in Britain also brought to an end the era in which Jacobites in Russia, albeit not always voluntarily, had played a political as well as a military role.

Spark and Fire: Jacobite Attempts and the 1745 Rising

James Keith arrived back in St Petersburg late on 20 June 1740, fresh from his sojourn in France and England, having reported to Jacobites in Paris as much intelligence as he could glean from his conversations with British politicians. What he had learned of the unpopularity of Walpole was very encouraging, and he reported to his brother through the safe channel of an agent in Paris, that '. . . animositys are now run to such a pitch, that nothing but the ruin of the Minister will satisfy'. Not only were bribery and favouritism rife in political circles, Keith observed, but Walpole had incurred the hatred of naval officers, and had neglected the fleet, Britain's primary defence. British ships, he wrote, were '. . . in a very bad condition, most of them built of green wood, and many which were never at sea nor in condition to be employed'.[1]

1 George Keith to James III, 29/4/1740, RA Stuart 222/16.

Although now far from the centres of Jacobite intrigue himself, having been sent immediately on his return to his prestigious new post as governor of the Ukraine, Keith intended his information to be of assistance in a planned invasion of Britain with Spanish assistance in summer 1740.[2] It was to command this enterprise that George Keith, together with the Duke of Ormonde, had travelled to Spain while his brother was in England.[3] Unfortunately, it became apparent to both the Earl Marischal and Ormonde, who waited in Madrid and Barcelona for several months, that the Spanish co-ordinator, the Count of Montemar, had no serious intention of aiding the Jacobites. Despite his promises of ships and men to set off from Galicia, the main purpose was, '. . . to alarm the English Government', against sending a fleet to fight the Spanish in the West Indies.[4] These suspicions prevented the twenty-year-old Prince Charles Edward Stuart, James III's elder son and the 'Young Pretender', from travelling to Spain, and by May the attempt was abandoned. Britain, in any case, remained undeceived by Montemar's intrigue; as early as February the Dutch minister, Van der Meer, had warned Trevor at the Hague of Spain's real motives.[5]

From this point until the Rising of 1745, therefore, France became the principal object of Jacobite attention, particularly after the invasion of Silesia by Frederick II of Prussia in December 1740 had brought Europe into open war. Although France did not actually declare war on Britain until 1744, it supported Britain's enemies from the outset. Jacobite hopes were fanned not only by Anglo-French enmity, but by the success of Walpole's political adversaries at home. Supported by the Duke of Argyll, with whom James Keith had held lengthy interviews in 1740, they greatly diminished Walpole's majority in the 1741 general election, forcing his resignation in February 1742. In addition to this, the death of the cautious and conciliatory Cardinal Fleury in January 1743 opened new prospects for a more actively antagonistic French stance against Britain.

It was French losses in the war in Germany, combined with a Jacobite request for armed French intervention, which finally drove Louis XV to action.[6] In autumn 1743, convinced of British domestic support, France collaborated in the hatching of an invasion project, and French ships were positioned on the Channel coast. While part of this fleet distracted the British navy, some 10,000 French troops under Marshal de Saxe were to be ferried to Essex under armed escort. Charles Edward undertook a harrowing journey from Rome in early 1744 to be ready on the French coast at Gravelines,[7] while the Earl Marischal and Lord Elcho prepared to cross with the main invasion force from Dunkirk.

---

2 Finch to Harrington, 10/21 June 1740, *SIRIO* 85, p.52; La Chétardie to Amelot, 14/25 June, *SIRIO* 86, p.406.
3 James III to G.Keith and Ormonde, 2/2/1740, RA Stuart 220/72.
4 G.Keith to James III, 15/4/1740, RA Stuart 221/165; see also RA Stuart 221/41, 127, 148, 165; 222/16, 75, 146. See also G.Keith, 'Two fragments of Autobiography', pp.362–365.
5 Trevor to Harrington, 18/3/1740 n.s., PRO SP 84/384, f.78.
6 Cruickshanks, *Political Untouchables*, p.38.
7 RA Stuart 255/163.

Unfortunately, by the end of February, the British ministry had been alerted to these plans and took immediate defensive action. Characteristic Jacobite ill-fortune played a role when two storms in March destroyed many of Saxe's transports and some of Roquefeuil's fleet. By this time even Charles's assurances that some British naval officers had defected to the Jacobite side were insufficient to rekindle French enthusiasm.[8] Moreover, the Earl Marischal, who was in any case on poor terms with the Prince, further damaged their relationship by discouraging him from further action, and the attempt was abandoned.[9] The only positive outcome of the affair for the Jacobites was the declaration of war by France on Britain on 20 March.

Despite this setback, Charles continued to lay plans for an invasion, and was encouraged by the embassy of John Murray of Broughton to Paris in the autumn of 1744. He sent Murray home with instructions to coordinate Highland support and then detailed his own proposals to Louis XV. Receiving little positive commitment from the French, however, he resolved to undertake the journey to Scotland unsupported.[10] His landing on Eriskay on 23 July 1745[11] marked the beginning of the most remarkable year in Jacobite history. By December his leadership brought the Jacobite army as far south as Derby and alarmingly close to London. For a short time, until the army's controversial retreat back to Scotland, and ultimate defeat at Culloden in April 1746, both monarchy and ministry lived in fear. Unfortunately, the failure of either the French or of English Jacobites to lend military assistance, despite another planned French invasion in early 1746, sealed the fate of the enterprise, and, after months of concealment, Charles escaped to France in September 1746. In the months that followed, government forces employed the most ruthless and brutal means to ensure that the 1745 rising would be the last.[12]

The ripples which this created were felt throughout the decade as far away as Russia, even after the Rising had been put down. Although, with hindsight, any Jacobite venture lacking timely foreign assistance might appear doomed from the outset, this was by no means the view of contemporaries. Moreover, the possibility that the French would bring the war in Europe onto British soil posed an increasing threat, particularly after 1743, when the presence of George II's Pragmatic army on the continent made the option of attacking Hanover less attractive. The ministry's attempts to root out Jacobite conspiracy

---

8 One of these, Captain Christopher O'Brien, commander of the 'Royal Sovereign', had left Russian service two years previously.

9 G.Keith to Charles, 5/3/1744, RA Stuart 256/92; 13/3/1744, 256/126; 16/3/1744, 256/134.

10 Charles to Louis XV, Autumn 1744, RA Stuart Box 1/201.

11 W.B.Blaikie, ed., *Itinerary of Prince Charles Edward Stuart*, Scottish History Society (Edinburgh, 1897), p.2.

12 Ironically, John Lindesay, Earl of Crawfurd, who had fought alongside James Keith and Peter Lacy in 1738, and had accompanied Keith to take the waters in 1743, was, from February 1746, one of the principal Hanoverian commanders involved in the brutal suppression of the Jacobite Rising. Blaikie, *John Murray*, p.26; Rolt, *John Lindesay*.

redoubled during the course of the decade,[13] and it came as a serious shock to the government, therefore, to learn of the 1744 plot only days before it was to be executed. The speed with which Carteret requisitioned 6,000 Dutch troops and reinforcements from Ireland, and the wave of Jacobite arrests which followed the news, reflected the extent of ministerial anxiety. The terror which the Jacobite march to Derby in 1745 and the rumoured French invasion struck into the London population has been well documented; George II was on the point of flight, and the Duke of Cumberland wrote in panic to Newcastle that he could not receive reinforcements before the Jacobites seized the throne.[14]

It was, however, in the context of the war in Europe, in particular of Anglo-French relations, that Jacobite activity and ministerial concern registered on the wider scale of international diplomacy. The Jacobites served as a wedge, driving Britain and France further apart, and heightening British political sensitivity to possible French support at all foreign courts in any way involved with the war. In Russia, Jacobitism became closely identified with pro-French or anti-British sentiment, and the conflicts facing military Jacobites were exacerbated by the fact that they constituted Russia's most competent and experienced commanders, and as such wielded considerable influence in Russian military affairs.

Russian Domestic Turmoil, 1740–1741

While Anglo-French hostility was reaching boiling point over the issue of French support for a Jacobite invasion, Jacobites in Russia were preoccupied, from 1740, with weathering a period of political change. James Keith's return to St Petersburg was closely followed, on 17/28 October 1740 by the death of Anna Ivanovna and the rise to supreme power of Count Ernst Biron, acting as regent for her grand-nephew and heir, the infant Ivan VI. Biron lacked support, and within a month, on the night of the 6/17 November, was overthrown in favour of the child's parents, Prince Anton Ulrich of Braunsch-weig-Lünebourg and his wife Anna Leopoldovna.

The response of western Jacobites was to attempt to persuade their friends in Russia to return home. During the months following the coup, members of the exiled Jacobite court, concerned for the safety of James Keith, Thomas Gordon and others experiencing '. . . the present confusion and unsettled government in Muscovy', expressed their fears by letter.[15] Those in Russia wisely ignored this concern, for, despite outward appearances, the Braunschweig regency, which lasted only twelve months, was a short but surprisingly fruitful period in the careers of certain Jacobites. This owed more to coincidence than to any change of policy, but it did distract them from the intrigues preoccupying the exiled court.

13 As early as January 1740, Newcastle, having received intelligence that an invasion was to be launched from Spain, ordered Waldegrave to probe his invaluable agent, the French diplomat François de Bussy, 'to get the most exact and fullest information . . . relating thereto', Newcastle to Waldegrave, 22/1/1740, BL Add.Ms. 32802, f.25.

14 Cruickshanks, *Political Untouchables*, pp.92,93.

15 Edgar to G.Keith, 4/1/1741, RA Stuart 229/167; James III to T.Gordon, 6/2/1741, RA Stuart 230/163.

James Keith, now military and civil governor of the Ukraine, found himself in the highest esteem at court and earned the nickname 'the English Prophet', when he refused to take the oath of allegiance to Biron. Instead, he directed his letter to Prince Anton Ulrich who, by the date of its arrival, had indeed replaced Biron as regent. According to the French ambassador, La Chétardie's account, Keith had kept to his room on the pretext of illness, and had then ordered his men to swear allegiance to Ivan VI.[16] Dr John Cook maintained that Keith had sent a secret messenger to St Petersburg.[17] There were other rumours that his soldiers had refused to honour the unpopular Biron. In fact, although this speculation served Keith well, it is probable that he had been genuinely ill with an eye infection, and, moreover, had had to conceal the news of Anna's death until he had ensured that the Turkish ambassador, who was at that time journeying to St Petersburg for an Imperial audience, would not turn back. His letter, which was unaddressed, was directed automatically to the parents of the young Tsar.[18]

This incident had a dramatic effect on Keith's career. In May 1741, despite being of subordinate rank to the Prince of Hessen Homburg, he was recalled from the Ukraine and given command of an army of 30,000 men preparing to fight Sweden in Finland. Peter Lacy, likewise enjoying the Regents' favour, became the most senior field marshal in Russia, replacing Münnich, whom the Braunschweigs mistrusted.[19] In July the two Jacobites, Keith and Field Marshal Lacy, set off independently for the Swedish border of Finland, and at the end of August Lacy joined Keith to assume supreme command. General Keith's detailed military journal of the Swedish campaigns is evidence of the professionalism with which he and Lacy pursued and harried the Swedish army, after news of the Swedish declaration of war had been leaked to the Russian leadership on 22 August n.s. 1741.[20] Within two weeks, on 3 September, the Russian army had inflicted a decisive defeat on General Wrangel's Swedes and had taken the fortress of Wilmanstrand.[21] In recognition of this victory, Anna Leopoldovna rewarded her commanders generously; Lacy received land in Livonia to a value of £10,000, Keith an annual pension of 4,000 roubles.[22] Finch, the British ambassador, reported in November '. . . the great reputation

---

16 La Chétardie to Amelot, 2/13 Dec. 1740, *SIRIO* 92, p.134.
17 According to Cook's version, Keith, knowing that the parents of the heir disliked Biron, '. . . dispatched a major . . . dressed as a peasant . . . to apply to the Grand Duchess or her royal husband personally'. Biron was arrested the night the major arrived. Cook, *Voyages and Travels*, 1, pp.451–452.
18 Finch to Harrington, 29/11/1740, *SIRIO* 85, pp.410,411; *Ibid.*, 5/12/1740, p.421; George Napier to Henry Stirling, 5/12/1740, NAS Abercairney, GD 24/1/454, f.10.
19 La Chétardie to Amelot, 13/5/1741, *SIRIO* 96, pp.12,13; Finch to Harrington, 2/10/1741, *SIRIO* 91, p.99.
20 'Journal de la Campagne de Finlande des Années 1741, 42 et 43 écrit par le Lieut. Colonel de Keith aux services de l'Imperatice de Russie', RGVIA F846 o16 VUA 1627. Keith's contemporary, Manstein, and his biographer, Varnhagen von Ense, recorded the declaration of war as the Emperor's birthday, 13/24 August. Manstein, p.299; Varnhagen von Ense, *Feldmarschall Jakob Keith*, p.47.
21 For an account of this battle, see *Ibid.* ll.10–15; also Manstein, p.302.
22 Finch to Harrington, 15/9/1741, *SIRIO*, 91, pp.274,275; La Chétardie to Amelot, 30/9/1741, *Ibid.*, 96, pp.442,443.

Keith very deservedly has in this service and that he is the officer in these troops
the most capable of supplying the loss of the field-marshal Lacy whenever that
may happen'.[23]

Although the Braunschweig regency was generally more favourable for
Jacobite servicemen than the reign which followed it, the Swedish campaign
of 1741 and the Russian victory at Wilmanstrand were costly in terms of Jacobite
casualties. Major General Ramsay, the self-styled 'Comte de Balmaine', who was
in the vanguard leading the foot grenadiers, was among a number of officers
killed on the palisade of the town.[24] His death, according to Keith, angered the
army into storming and capturing Wilmanstrand.[25] George Lacy, recorded in
the 1741 service list as a full general, died of his wounds in Viborg a week after
the battle.[26] Robert Fullarton was more fortunate; although wounded in three
places, he recovered and was promised promotion.[27] Major Douglas, a 'scotch
gentleman' of uncertain origin, whose name appeared in the 1738 military list
as second major 'Count Walmer' Douglas of the Nizhegorodskii regiment,
received a leg wound, but was supposed '. . . not in danger of life or leg'.[28]

By the end of 1741, the Jacobite ranks had been further diminished by other
losses. On 18/29 March the great Jacobite naval commander, Admiral Thomas
Gordon had died before a ship could take him back to Scotland. In failing
health, and with the support and intercession of James Keith and Sir Henry
Stirling, he had been petitioning for permission to return home since the
previous July. His Jacobite activities and illegal departure from the Royal Navy
in 1716, however, made complete discharge from Russian service and consequent subjection to British law on his return too great a risk. Unfortunately,
he fell foul of Russian political upheavals; Biron granted his congé but was
overthrown before the order could be executed.[29] Tragically, Gordon died

23 Finch to Harrington, 17/24 November 1741, *SIRIO* 91, p.335; Lacy, although in 1741 in
    his sixty-third year, did not, in fact, die until 1751.
24 Although Manstein, who was himself wounded at Wilmanstrand, described Ramsay as a
    colonel, he was recorded in the 1741 service list as a major-general. Manstein, p.88;
    RGVIA F489 o1 d7006.
25 Keith, 'Journal de la Campagne . . .', RGVIA F846 o16, VUA 1627, l.14.
26 Finch to Harrington, 15/9/1741, *SIRIO* 91, p.275; RGVIA F489 o1 d7006.
27 George Napier to Henry Stirling, 28/10/1741, NAS Abercairney, GD 24/1/855, f.11;
    Finch to Harrington, 29/8/1741 o.s., *SIRIO* 91, p.263.
28 This was, however, almost certainly first Major 'Charles' Douglas, who was promoted in
    1739 and recorded in the 1741 list as having died, probably of this wound. Two or more
    Douglases have been confused; one source maintains that the Douglas who died was a
    lieutenant-colonel described as 'Charles Douglas, a younger son of Mr Douglas of
    Dorwick, and a branch of the Duke of Queensberry's family'. This same Douglas had
    apparently been recommended by the Episcopalian Bishop Robert Keith to his nephew
    General Keith, who mourned him particularly. The only Lieutenant-Colonel Douglas in
    the service list of 1741 was indeed a count, but he was not killed at Wilmanstrand, for his
    name reappears in 1744, and as Count Robert William Douglas in 1758. The acquaintance
    of the Major Charles Douglas with Keith was not corroborated, and his identity, Jacobite
    or otherwise, remains unconfirmed. Finch to Harrington, 29/8/1741 o.s., *SIRIO* 91, p.263;
    RGVIA F489 01 dd.7367, 7387, 7340.
29 T.Gordon to Duke of Courland, 12/7/1740, NAS Abercairney, GD 24/1/855, f.87;
    T.Gordon to Lord Golovin, 5/12/1740, Ibid., f.88; T.Gordon to John Gordon, 14/2/1741,
    Ibid., f.91.

before Prince Anton Ulrich could respond to his request, or the spring thaw could free Cronstadt harbour for shipping. Another Jacobite Gordon in the Russian fleet, Alexander Gordon, son of Glenbucket, had died in the Black Sea late in 1739, at the end of the campaign against the Turks. He was still a young man in his twenties, and his untimely death was much regretted by his father's Jacobite friends in Russia.[30] Thomas Gordon, however, was the greatest loss, not only to the Russian navy, but to the Jacobite community. Following his death, the number of Jacobites in Russia was further reduced by the departure for Scotland of his daughter Ann, her husband Sir Henry Stirling, and all their children.[31]

Jacobite Pawns and Politicians

Even while enjoying professional success under the Braunschweigs, prominent Jacobites in Russia were unable to evade the changing tides of politics in a war-torn Europe. By the end of the decade, the diminution of the Jacobite population through 'natural' causes such as death and departure, had been exacerbated by political pressures, which were related to the Jacobite restoration attempts discussed above, and began to make themselves felt much earlier.

The War of the Austrian Succession, set in motion by Frederick II's sudden invasion of Silesia in December 1740, left Russia particularly vulnerable to French intrigues in the north. While Britain's chief concern was for the security of Hanover and its possessions, Russia opposed Prussian aggrandisement at the expense of Austria, and feared the burgeoning French influence directed against it in Sweden. Although the convergence of Russian and British interests bore fruit in the form of a defensive treaty against France and Prussia, signed on 4 April 1741, the French party at St Petersburg and Stockholm continued, undeterred, to vie for dominance.[32] As well as seeking to divert Russian military attention from central Europe by inciting Russo-Swedish hostilities over the Baltic provinces, their efforts to reinforce French power in St Petersburg involved a plot to overthrow the pro-British Braunschweig regency and place Peter I's daughter Elisabeth on the imperial throne. The principal instrument of this intrigue in Russia was la Chétardie, who had been resident as French ambassador since 1739.

Meanwhile, members of the exiled Jacobite court chose this moment of increased Russo-French and hence Anglo-French tension to recall James Keith from Russia to lead a French-backed restoration attempt. Keith was favoured above other possible commanders on several grounds. Not only was he of the family of the Earl Marischal of Scotland, with a traditional right to military leadership, but he was by now one of Europe's best-known and most successful generals, whose exploits were frequently recorded in the gazettes. Moreover,

---

30 T.Gordon to John Gordon of Edinburgh, 13/12/1739, NAS Abercairney, GD 24/1/855, f.80; John Gordon of Glenbucket to T.Gordon. 8/5/1740, *HMC Eglinton* etc. p.198.
31 George Napier to Sir Henry Stirling, 12/8/1741, NAS Abercairney, GD 24/1/454, f.14.
32 For details of the negotiations leading to this, see R. Lodge, 'The First Anglo-Russian Treaty, 1739–42', *EHR* 43 (1928), pp.354–375.

his recent visit to Britain and France in 1740 had persuaded other Jacobites of his continued loyalty.

In June and July 1741 James III wrote to Keith, who was just setting off for Viborg, to inform him that many Jacobites wanted him as their commander.[33] A letter from William Drummond of Balhaldie on the same subject, written in circuitous terms, '. . . lest some accident should disclose the mater [sic]', implied that Keith had actually offered while in Paris '. . . to quitt some presente advantages' and lead an insurrection. Reminding Keith of this 'offer', he proposed that the Keith brothers assume joint command in the projected rising.[34] It is doubtful, given Keith's prompt return to Russia in 1740, and his loyal service to the Russian monarch, that he ever expressed his willingness to support the Jacobite cause in more than general terms. Balhaldie was also well aware that Keith's participation would ruin his Russian career, due to

> . . . the engagements your Court is under to the Duke of Hannover, and that upon your coming to us you are to act in a direct opposition to what they take to be their interest.[35]

Nevertheless, the Jacobites deliberately imposed on Keith's professional obligations to Russia, not only to regain Keith's military expertise, but to deprive France's enemy, Russia, of one of its foremost commanders.

Once again, however, the Jacobites' demands were poorly timed. By the time the letters arrived, Keith was already completely committed to pursuing the Swedes through the bogs of Finland. Moreover, the favour bestowed on him by the Braunschweigs had aroused the suspicions of the pro-French party to such an extent that they regarded him as an enemy. La Chétardie had interpreted Keith's coincidental oath of allegiance to Prince Anton Ulrich rather than to Biron on Anna Ivanovna's death as calculated political expediency in favour of the Braunschweigs, and in January 1741 Amelot warned the French ambassador that Keith's support for the Regency would be one of the major obstacles to the proposed coup in favour of Elisabeth.[36] Keith and Lacy's decisive victory for Russia at Wilmanstrand reinforced this mistrust by effectively destroying French hopes of co-ordinating the planned Swedish attack on Russia with a revolt against the Regency in St Petersburg.[37] Indeed, after Wilmanstrand, la Chétardie attempted to blacken Lacy's reputation by reporting the rumour that the German version of the battle had had to be destroyed, because Lacy, in his 'extreme devotion' to the regent, had referred throughout to Anton Ulrich rather than to the Tsar.[38]

Paradoxically, it was the Jacobite commanders' professional obligation to oppose French interests which prompted a curious attempt in 1741 to oust

---

33 James III to James Keith, 14/6/1741, RA Stuart 233/89, also 18/7/1741 RA Stuart 234/172.
34 W.Drummond to J.Keith, July 1741, RA Stuart 234/81.
35 Ibid.
36 Amelot to la Chétardie, 23/1/1741, *SIRIO* 92, p.238.
37 This fact also tends to exclude the possibility that either Jacobite was in the plotters' confidence.
38 La Chétardie to Amelot, 30/9/1741, *SIRIO* 96, p.442.

them from Russia, with unwitting Jacobite assistance. While in Valencia in early autumn, George Keith received a letter purporting to be from Don Sebastian de la Quadra, the King of Spain's minister, ordering him to write to his brother James in the King's name, accepting his alleged request for entry into Spanish service at the rank of lieutenant general. According to his own account of the affair, George was immediately put on his guard, having heard nothing of such an intention from his brother. He therefore replied to de la Quadra that the King should send the letter of acceptance by his own channels, as James Keith was obviously too concerned with maintaining strict confidentiality to risk use of the public post. In confirmation of George's suspicions, de la Quadra claimed complete ignorance of the matter, and laid it at the door of the French ambassador at Madrid, the Bishop of Rennes. George, now in Avignon, therefore sent his brother a warning through the secure channel of Kantemir in Paris, of what he described as the '. . . très vilain trouve, qu'on a voulu lui jouer'.[39] Soon after receiving his brother's information, James Keith informed the British ambassador in St Petersburg, probably in order to clear his own reputation. Finch reported to Harrington in November that Keith claimed complete innocence of the intrigue and blamed it on la Chétardie and other members of the French party, whose intention it was '. . . to give some jealousies and suspicions of his fidelity to the crown of Russia'.[40] Keith cleverly added force to his disclaimers by accosting la Chétardie, in the presence of Finch and Field Marshal Lacy, to demand an explanation. It appeared, on further investigation, that la Chétardie himself was not involved, for in March 1742, the French minister Amelot admitted to him, in response to Keith's demands, that the plot had been instigated by Cardinal Fleury with the purpose of recruiting Keith's renowned military expertise for Bourbon service.[41] What Amelot did not mention, as James Keith later discovered from the Swedish minister Nolcken, was that the plot devised by Cardinal Fleury was in collaboration with Sweden. One of its aims was to take advantage of Lacy's absence on leave to have Keith removed on a charge of treason from his position of sole command of the Russian forces, thus enabling the Swedes to launch an unopposed attack on Russia and facilitating Elisabeth's coup. According to George Keith's account, the Swedes also intended to exploit existing Russian distrust of foreigners to discredit other foreign officers, particularly Major General George Brown and Patrick Stuart, Peter Lacy's son-in-law, who had been promoted to major general the previous year for bringing news of the Russian victory over Sweden to St Petersburg.[42]

39 G.Keith to Kantemir, 21/10/1741, NBSS (St Petersburg) AVT.136 no.35. The secret letter to James Keith has apparently not survived; it was directed to be burned after reading.

40 Finch to Harrington, 17/28 Nov. 1741, *SIRIO* 91, pp.332–334.

41 '. . . m. le cardinal ne désavouera pas d'en avoir été l'auteur, et connaissant le mérite et la capacité de ce général, d'avoir conseillé à S.M.Chr. de se l'attacher . . .' Amelot to la Chétardie, 12/3/1742, *SIRIO* 100, p.102.

42 Wich to Carteret, 6/9/1740, *SIRIO* 99, pp.57,59; 'Two Fragments of Autobiography', *SHS Misc.* 3rd series, 5, p.365; 'Spisok generalitetu', 1741, RGVIA F489 o1 d7006; Stuart's Christian name confirmed, RGVIA F9 o3 d808, 1.5.

The targeting of these commanders, motivated by a tacit acknowledgement of their indispensability to Russia's military machine, illustrated that military prowess could have political implications, even for those, like Keith, Lacy, Brown and Stuart, not personally involved in politics. In the context of its role in the war in Europe, France's intrigues in Sweden and Russia and its relationship with the Jacobites were closely linked. The timing of the plot to displace Russian officers, designed to take effect with the planned Russian coup in autumn 1741, coincided with an increase in Jacobite activity in the West. In August and September rumours were circulating of an imminent Jacobite invasion after Charles was reported to have left Rome.[43] British anxieties were compounded by the advance of a French army under Marshal Maillebois across the Rhine and into Hanover, prompting George II to sign a neutrality agreement and accept the French candidate as Holy Roman Emperor. In December, the Jacobites took advantage of this opportunity to issue a confident, if unfounded, declaration that France would only leave Hanover when the British monarchy had been overthrown.[44]

Britain, meanwhile, secretly informed Russia of French subsidies to Sweden, French and Spanish collaboration against Austria,[45] and French-supported Swedish negotiations with Prussia to obtain financial support for a Russian invasion.[46] There was also evidence that, quite apart from weakening Russia's military leadership, Cardinal Fleury was genuinely eager to recruit Keith to fight against Britain, if not for Spain, then for France.[47] The transfer of a well-known Jacobite from the enemy to command the French army at such a crucial point in Anglo-French relations, would not only have served French military ends, but would have been a significant challenge to both Russia and Britain. Although Fleury had no intention of aiding an armed Jacobite rising at this point, he successfully exploited British fears of French and of Jacobite plans.

James Keith and his brother suspected a close link between the intrigue of Fleury and the Bishop of Rennes, and their own Jacobite affiliations. In early 1742, just after being informed of the plot, Keith admitted to la Chétardie that his great anxiety to discover its source was largely due to recent news from England of the possibility of '. . . une révolution prochaine en faveur du roi Jacques.[48] George Keith viewed what amounted to French exploitation of the

43 Spy report to Mr Thompson, 18/8/1741, BL Add.Ms 32802, f.258; H.Mann to Harrington, 22/8/1741, PRO SP 98/44, ff.463–4; H.Mann to Newcastle, 22/8/1741, *Ibid.*, ff.465–466; J.Conraud to H.Mann, 3/9/1741, PRO SP 43/108, unfol; Account of Meeting at Whitehall, 15/9/1741: Newcastle informed Whitehall of Shcherbatov's warning of a planned French-backed Jacobite invasion of Scotland and Ireland, claiming that the French were 'sorry to hear of the return of Sir John Norris with his squadron to the English coasts'. PRO SP 48/108, unfol.
44 H.Walpole, December 1741, PRO SP 98/44, f.526. This Jacobite declaration of French intentions, although unfounded, served France by reinforcing its show of strength.
45 Harrington to Finch, 17/3/1741, Finch to Harrington, 28/3/1741, *SIRIO* 91, pp.25,31.
46 Finch to Harrington, 13/24 June 1741, *SIRIO* 91, p.147.
47 Fleury alluded to this wish the following spring. La Chétardie to Amelot, 9/4/1742, *SIRIO* 100, p.141; 1/6/1741, *Ibid.*, p.193.
48 La Chétardie to Amelot, 10/2/1742, *SIRIO* 100, p.75.

Jacobites in a more critical light. Fleury's plot, a demonstration of French self-interest, which, as he appreciated, could easily have resulted not in his brother's recruitment to the opposition, but in his punishment for treason in Russia, so disgusted him that he was on the point of completely severing all links both with the Jacobites and with France and of retiring to Russia '. . . pour la reste de mes jours'.[49] The whole affair, likewise, made James Keith and others in Russian service alert to the fact that their success in Russia did not protect them from becoming the unwitting tools of politicians.

Elisabeth in Power

The revolution which raised Elisabeth to the Russian throne on the night of 25 November 1741 o.s. was as distrusted by Britain as it was naively welcomed by western Jacobites. Finch saw his recent treaty rendered void and his credibility with the new monarch diminished by his efforts to forestall the coup. Aware that it was France's intention to weaken Russia, he believed that the Russians had been '. . . more infamously duped than ever anybody was'.[50]

James III, the memory still fresh of the encouragement given to his cause by Elisabeth's parents, Peter I and Catherine I, placed his hope in her much publicised intention to reinstate 'Russian' Petrine policies in place of the allegedly detrimental period of 'foreign' rule which had prevailed since 1730.[51] He was further encouraged by the poor state of Britain's affairs; Walpole's resignation was by now only a matter of time, Russia and Sweden had declared a ceasefire, Spain was at war with Britain, and France on the point of it. Britain had demonstrated its unreliability as an ally of the new Empress by signing a treaty with the Braunschweigs. In January, therefore, James III took the opportunity to write to Keith, outlining a project for joint Russo-Swedish assistance, which he believed would be, '. . . more acceptable to our Country-men than either French or Spaniards'. With the same post he sent Peter Lacy instructions to co-operate with Keith, enclosing letters of congratulation to the Empress on her accession from himself and his son to provide the two commanders with a pretext to seek an Imperial audience.[52]

By the time the letters arrived, however, the precarious nature of Elisabeth's hold on power made support for the distant Jacobite cause unthinkable. La Chétardie's attempts to reconcile Russia with Sweden were failing, and Russia was already preparing to resume the Swedish war. The French party at court had been severely discredited following the interception of a letter revealing that France was indeed intent on weakening Russia and had actually asked

49 George Keith to Kantemir, 21/10/1741, NBSS (St Petersburg), Avt. 136, no.35.
50 Finch to Harrington, 5/12, 19/12/1741, 5/1, 6/2/1742, *SIRIO* 91, pp.354,382,408,444, 446.
51 For a discussion of the idealisation of Peter I as an embodiment of 'Russian' values and the simultaneous denigration of the previous decade, see E.V.Anisimov, *Rossiya v seredine XVIII veka*, in *V borbe za vlast*, pp.24–282.
52 James III to James Keith, 26/1/1742, RA Stuart 239/128; James III to Peter Lacy, 26/1/1741, RA Stuart 239/142; James III to Elisabeth, RGADA F4 ol d50; Charles Edward to Elisabeth, Ibid. d.86.

Turkey to launch an invasion on its southern borders.[53] Alexei Petrovich Bestuzhev-Riumin, who strongly favoured close ties with Austria and Britain, was gaining in influence, having been appointed as an aide to the elderly Chancellor Cherkassky. Moreover, the change of administration threatened the careers of those, like Lacy and Keith, who had enjoyed favour under the Braunschweigs and had not been involved in the coup. Lacy narrowly escaped the arrest and exile suffered by Field Marshal Münnich by assuring Elisabeth's guards on the night of the revolution that he was loyal to 'whichever party was in power'. Keith and Vice Admiral O'Brien astutely took the first opportunity in January to pay their court to the new Empress.[54]

Difficulties for individual Jacobites were echoed in the suspicion with which James III's letters were regarded. Not only were they intercepted and read, presumably by the Empress and her ministers, before Keith and Lacy received them, but when Keith, in Vyborg, entrusted copies of them to the Jacobite Colonel Innes, to send to Elisabeth's private physician, Lestocq, they received no acknowledgement. James Keith observed in his reply to James III that the Stuarts had been omitted from the 1742 Russian almanac, a point which clearly implied a rejection by Russia of their right to the British crown. Keith had received, '. . . some indications on Elisabeth's part', in the Jacobites' favour, but this was countered by the disinterest or opposition of all those in positions of influence, particularly Bestuzhev. In a political climate in which support for Austria and Britain was gaining the ascendant, Keith's correspondence with the Jacobites was unfortunately interpreted as evidence of French sympathies. Indeed, the Jacobite letters not only met with complete failure at the Russian court, but almost certainly fostered the distrust between Keith and the future Grand Chancellor Bestuzhev which would eventually lead to Keith's departure from Russian service.

Career Difficulties

James III's hope for a strengthening of Jacobite support in Russia after Elisabeth's accession was further disappointed by a marked deterioration in service conditions for foreign mercenaries, which prompted the departure of most of Russia's remaining Jacobites. Elisabeth had been raised to power on a wave of reactionary ardour directed against what many in Russia viewed as a decade of domination by a clique of foreigners. The guards who supported her coup, and who, as recent research has indicated, were mainly of peasant and non-noble origin, tended to idealise her as embodying the patriotic qualities they attributed to her father, Peter I.[55] In the aftermath of the coup, therefore, particularly in 1742, she paid lip-service to their patriotic, and inevitably

---

53 Amelot to de Castellan, 12/1/1742. A copy of this reached the Austrian ambassador in
     May. Anisimov, *Rossiya v seredine XVIII veka,* p.118.
54 Finch to Harrington, 26/1/1742, *SIRIO* 91, p.484.
55 Fifty-four of the 308 guards were from the nobility, 137 were of peasant origin, see
     Anisimov, *Rossiya v seredine XVIII veka,* p.50. Popular opinion tended to overlook the fact
     that the coup had been planned by foreigners, La Chétardie, Lestocq and Schwarz, with
     the support of Sweden and France.

xenophobic desire to rid Russia of alien influences. This, in turn, was taken as a sanction for the persecution of foreigners, and violent incidents erupted in several places against foreign officers accused of collaboration with the Swedes.

Manstein recorded how, on Easter Day 1742, some Russian officers picked a quarrel with a foreign officer, and, chasing him into a house full of foreigners, began a fight which left Peter Lacy's aide and Captain Brown severely injured. Lacy was forced to post full-time guards in every street to prevent the escalation of xenophobic violence.[56] In June, James Keith had to put down a mutiny of two regiments of foot guards who had seized and beaten a Swedish messenger and drummer boy. According to Manstein, who had first-hand experience of such insubordination, Keith

> . . . threw himself without the least hesitation into the thickest of the rebellious troops; seized with his own hand one of the mutineers, and ordered a priest to be called to confess him, saying he would have him shot on the spot.

Although Elisabeth took steps to punish the offenders, and seventeen men were exiled the following April, Manstein gave Keith the credit for suppressing a potentially volatile situation:

> . . . it is certain that, if it had not been for the spirited resolution of general Keith, the revolt would have spread far and wide, as no Russian officer would have undertaken to oppose himself to the rage of the soldiery.[57]

La Chétardie, likewise, recorded that Keith, as lieutenant colonel of the Ismailovsky guards, was the only foreigner to command the respect and obedience of the rebellious element, and Elisabeth was forced to take the precaution of sending to Finland a native officer, General Rumiantsev, recently promoted lieutenant colonel of the Preobrazhenski guards, to maintain discipline.[58] Foreign diplomats continued to report high levels of antagonism towards foreigners, particularly throughout the first years of Elisabeth's reign.[59]

Such incidences of anti-foreign violence undermined the morale of foreign servicemen, a trend which was exacerbated by a corresponding fall in their material situation. The British ambassador in Russia, Cyril Wich, warned a potential recruit to Russian service in 1742

> . . . that a captain in this service does not get above four pound a month; so that if he has no fortune of his own, it will be very difficult for him to live upon his pay, and foreign officers are not advanced at present in the russian service so fast, as they were formerly; nor are they upon such an

56 Manstein, *Memoirs*, 1856 edn., pp.350,351.
57 Manstein, *Memoirs*, 1856 edn., p.357; Solov'ev, v.11, pp.178,179.
58 La Chétardie to Amelot, 5/10/1742, *SIRIO* 100, p.386.
59 Pezold to Brühl, 29/3/1742, *SIRIO* 6, p.419; Wich to Carteret, 24/4/1742, *SIRIO* 91, p.464; La Chétardie to Amelot, 12/7/1742, *SIRIO* 100, p.280.

agreeable foot, as they were under former reigns, and if some things are not redressed, I know a great many of foreign officers which will demand their dismission from service at the end of the campaign.[60]

Military finances suffered neglect when the newly re-established Senate took over the administration of many areas of military affairs from the War College, and foreign servicemen were among those to complain of pay arrears. In October 1742, Pezold, the Saxon envoy, noted that mismanagement by Chancellor Cherkassky had brought the army to an unprecedented state of bankruptcy.[61] In November the Prussian envoy, Mardefeld, reported that officers in Russia had not been paid for ten months, and that the penniless Admiralty was urgently in need of 50,000 roubles to prevent the fleet from deteriorating entirely.[62] Plans to economise by putting the army on half pay threatened to drive the foreign contingent from Russian service,[63] and the military found itself in worsening financial straits throughout Elisabeth's reign.[64] Foreign officers were further disenchanted by Elisabeth's annulment of all promotions and rewards granted during the regency, including the estates and the pension which Lacy and Keith respectively had received for the victory at Wilmanstrand. Officers were paid for one post only rather than a full salary for each position held.[65] Individual financial difficulties were compounded by the relatively high cost of living in Russia, which caused Wich to complain that he '. . . should prefer three pounds a day in any other part of Europe to whatever sum may be given [him] in this country'.[66] By June 1742, Keith was so deeply in debt that he could not have left Russia even had he wished to.[67]

By late 1742, this combination of financial uncertainty and the hostile atmosphere engendered by anti-foreign violence, compounded by the end of the war with Sweden, encouraged many foreigners to leave Russian service altogether. It also acted as a deterrent to prospective recruits. A list of land officers compiled for 1758, which included the year of entry into Russian service, indicated that a large proportion of the foreign officers of 1758 came to Russia in the early and late 1730s, and that numbers of foreign recruits declined after 1741.[68] Among the outstanding foreign officers who applied for discharge were several Jacobites. As early as June, at the time of the anti-

60 Wich to Carteret, 6/8/1742, *SIRIO* 99, p.34.
61 Pezold to Brühl, 29/10/1742, *SIRIO* 6, p.450.
62 Mardefeld to Frederick II, 8/11/1742, Waliszewski, *La Dernière des Romanov*, p.191.
63 Pezold wrote, '. . . Dieses sei gerade das Mittel, die ausländischen Offiziers, welche die eigentliche force der Kaiserin ausmachten, vollends zu vertreiben'. Pezold to Brühl, 17/11/1742, *SIRIO* 6, p.456.
64 In 1749 the War College owed the Treasury over 240,000 roubles, and in 1761 the Treasury needed 301,000 roubles to pay the army for the previous year. See Waliszewski, *La Dernière des Romanov*, pp.191, 192.
65 Manstein, *Memoirs*, 1856 edn., pp.373–374.
66 Wich to Carteret, 24/5/1742, *SIRIO* 91 p.480.
67 La Chétardie to Amelot, 1/6/1742, *SIRIO* 100, p.193.
68 According to this list, 45 foreign army officers from the rank of 2nd major up to field marshal entered Russian service in 1732, 26 in 1736, and 29 in 1738, as opposed to only 17 between 1741 and 1747. RGVIA F489 o1 d7340.

foreign riots and while the campaign was still in progress, there were rumours that James Keith intended to resign at the first opportunity. The large estate in Rannenburg, near Riga, which he had recently been granted in lieu of the confiscated pension, was apparently not sufficient to keep him in Russia.[69] Lacy, likewise, hoped to retire from service to his Livonian estates as soon as the fighting season was over.[70]

In September Colonel Stuart carried the news to court that Lacy and Keith had finally forced a Swedish surrender at Helsingfors, and with the end of the campaign, Keith was one of many who immediately sought to leave Russia. The extent of his military reputation was reflected in the fact that Frederick II had offered him a command in the Prussian army even before his request for discharge had been approved.[71] Lacy applied for retirement. Christopher O'Brien left the Russian fleet the same year, a few months after his son Lucius, and, like him, rejoined the British Navy.[72] Both suffered a drop in rank; Lucius from captain to lieutenant, his father from vice-admiral to captain, but the latter was still able to offer the ship under his command, *The Royal Sovereign*, to the Jacobites for the planned rising of 1744.[73]

The death of Admiral Gordon in 1741, followed by the threatened resignation of Keith and Lacy, meant that, in the space of a few months, Russia would be left without its foremost commanders in both branches of the forces. These losses alone would have had serious consequences for Russia's military role in Europe. In December 1742, Wich, noting that the majority of foreign officers had applied to leave Russian service, alerted Britain to the devastating blow this would deal Russia's military prowess:

> . . . if all the foreign officers persist in their resolution of leaving this country, the russian army will not make that figure in the world it has done for some years past, and as for the fleet, it is in a very bad condition and without one single officer to command it.[74]

Such was the gravity of the situation that Russia's debt to its foreign commanders and administrators began to be openly acknowledged, and the anti-foreign insubordination which had characterised the first year of Elisabeth's reign to be discouraged.[75] Recognising the importance of her two Jacobite

---

69 Imperial decree signed 25/4/1742 by Senate. Keith was granted land of 23 'gaky' in Rannenberg in the Vendenski district, RGVIA F11 d774, ll.6–7v.

70 La Chétardie to Amelot, 1/6/1742, *SIRIO* 100, p.193.

71 Mardefeld to Frederick II, 11/10/1742, Frederick II's reply (recorded by cabinet secretary) 1/11/1742, *Politische Correspondenz*, 2, p.288.

72 R.C.Anderson, *Mariner's Mirror* 33, p.25.

73 Defectors had arranged through Lt.Richard Barry of the Royal Navy to signal their intentions by means of a white flag. Of these, two, Christopher O'Brien and the Hon. Fitzroy Lee, were friends of Barry's and commanders of two of the larger ships. O'Brien had left Russia in 1742, but unfortunately his death at sea in 1744 precluded any further Jacobite activity. *The Gentleman's Magazine*, 1744, pp.53, 108; E.Cruickshanks, *Political Untouchables*, p.55.

74 Hyndford to Harrington, 9/12/1742, *SIRIO* 99, p.172.

75 Pezold to Brühl, 20/12/1742, *SIRIO* 6, p.470.

commanders, the Empress attempted to dissuade them from resigning. Keith was rewarded for his service, and made a knight of the prestigious Order of St Andrew, as well as being given chief command of the army in Finland.[76] Fortunately, Sweden's refusal to cede Finland and the consequent continuation of the Swedish war in 1743, provided both Lacy and Keith with an incentive to remain in active service. Nevertheless, there remained an element of hostility towards foreigners which could not be masked by the demands of military expediency, and as many as eight hundred foreign officers are known to have left Russia in the first four years of Elisabeth's reign.[77] This inevitably told on the Russian armed forces, and as late as 1745 Hyndford commented that '. . . the army here is in the same weak condition as the ministry, for there is hardly one russian officer fit to command a regiment'.[78]

James Keith in Sweden

The decline in Jacobite numbers in Russia during the 1740's was largely due to death or to voluntary departure in the worsening climate for foreign mercenaries. However, in one important case, that of James Keith, the close link between his Jacobite identity and his virtual expulsion from Russian service in 1747, was evidence of the continuing influence of Jacobitism as far away as Russia, long after the 1745 Rising had been extinguished and Keith himself had ceased to be politically involved. His experiences shed light on the development of Jacobitism as a powerful instrument of diplomacy, surviving on international political conflicts and increasingly independent of the movement in Britain.

The age and infirmity of Field Marshal Peter Lacy enabled Keith to achieve recognition as Russia's foremost military commander after the end of the Swedish war, raising him to new international military and political prominence. Not only was he entrusted with the chief command of the Russian army in Finland in 1743, but in September, a month after the Treaty of Abo ended the Swedish war, he was posted to Stockholm with the dual role of commander of the Russian force sent to protect Sweden from Denmark, and of Russian diplomatic representative in what was a politically sensitive area.[79] Its particular political significance stemmed from the fact that Sweden continued to focus the conflicting interests of the warring factions in Europe, France and Britain. Britain still sought to safeguard its Hanoverian possessions by destroying the French party at the Swedish court, France to strengthen its position in both

---

76 J.Keith to Empress Elisabeth, 21/11/1742, RGVIA, F84 o16 VUA 1622 pt.2, ll.130–131; 21/12/1742, *Ibid.*, l.127.
77 Pezold to Brühl, 2/3/1743, *SIRIO* 6, p.479; Hyndford to Harrington, 3/9/1745, *SIRIO* 102, pp.330–331.
78 Hyndford to Harrington, 3/9/1745, *SIRIO* 102, pp.330–331.
79 The death of Queen Ulrika Eleonora in December 1742, which left her elderly husband, Friedrich of Hesse-Cassel, to rule Sweden, had initiated an international wrangle over the succession. Danish fears for the security of Sleswig had been aroused by the election of Adolf Friedrich of Holstein as the Swedish heir, necessitating a Russian presence in Sweden.

Sweden and Russia with the aim of obstructing Russian military support for Austria. During his stay in Stockholm, from November 1743 until June 1744, Keith found himself at the crux of this conflict, and after his return, became the victim of rivalry at the Russian court between the pro-British Bestuzhev, who became Grand Chancellor in July 1744, and Vice Chancellor Mikhail Illarionovich Vorontsov, who by 1744 had become closely identified with French interests and Russian non-intervention.

Once again, Jacobite activity in the West directly affected Keith's reputation in Russia. Preparations for the French-supported Jacobite Rising of 1745–46 were under way, and the death of Cardinal Fleury in January 1743, combined with the movement of British troops to the Austrian Netherlands for an invasion of France, revived Jacobite hopes of participating in a French retaliation. As in 1741 and 1743, George Keith, Earl Marischal had been appointed commander of the projected rising, but there was a strong body of opinion among the Jacobites, including Charles Edward's secretary John Murray of Broughton, the Duke of Perth and Cameron of Lochiel, who disliked his 'high and forbidding manner'. Instead, they favoured his brother James for the position, '. . . who they understood was of a very mild and humane temper and in whose abilitys they had great confidence'.[80] Murray approached James III with this idea, emphasising that in the Highlands James Keith enjoyed the status of folk hero, '. . . the Highlanders having the same notion of him as they formerly had of Lord Dundee'.[81] This strong popular support for Keith in Scotland undoubtedly owed much to the international reputation he had earned during his service to Russia.

As had been the case two years previously, Keith's professional commitments precluded a return to the Jacobites. Although James III attempted to contact Keith through the Earl Marischal, he was informed that letters to Russia frequently went missing, and that George himself had not heard from his brother for months.[82] In view of the fate of the first Jacobite letters to Elisabeth and of Keith's subsequent treatment, it is reasonable to suspect that Jacobite correspondence to Russia was being intercepted. Had James Keith been approached in autumn 1742, when he had wanted to leave Russia, he might perhaps have joined the Rising, but by 1743 he had cancelled his application for discharge. James III was justly sceptical that he would leave Russia, correctly observing that '. . . one of his rank and distinction cannot well quite [sic] the service he is in either abruptly or upon an uncertainty'.[83]

Although James Keith chose to remain in Russian service, Bestuzhev was, without doubt, aware that his political prominence and Jacobite connections made him a political liability. While in Sweden he would have been in a position to

80 Meeting between Murray and Duke of Perth, January 1743, Blaikie, *Origins of the Forty-Five*, p.7.
81 *Ibid.*, p.26.
82 James III to George Keith, 13/3/1743, RA Stuart 248/53; George Keith to James III, 6/4/1743, RA Stuart 248/173.
83 James III to John Murray, 11/3/1743, in Blaikie, *Origins of the Forty-Five*, p.31.

promote the French parties in Stockholm and St Petersburg, thus hindering Russian military support for Austria and Britain and freeing French troops for an invasion of Britain. Rumours, in fact, implicated Keith in the intrigues of opposing sides. The British government, Guy Dickens, ambassador in Sweden, and his counterpart in Russia, were convinced that Keith was involved in subverting British interests. On the other hand there were rumours, hotly denied by Carteret, that he was acting together with Britain in a plot for '. . . changing the constitution of the government and giving his Swedish majesty absolute sovereignty over it'.[84]

The suspicions of the two parties were fuelled by Keith's unenviably central position as Russia's diplomatic representative. In December 1743, Carteret was encouraged by news that he had approached Guy Dickens, and that the latter had the intention of

> . . . entering into all proper and possible measures with him [Keith], and our Swedish friends towards the removal of the partizans of France from the ministry and destroying the influence of that Crown there.

Carteret added that

> . . . The French party seem hitherto to have no manner of suspicion of Keith, but I believe rather look upon him as their friend, so that he must have acted his part with great dexterity.[85]

Inevitably, given Keith's powerful, and largely independent position in Sweden, the question arises whether he really was secretly promoting Jacobite interests while going through the motions of supporting Guy Dickens and Bestuzhev.

On his arrival in Sweden, Keith was under Bestuzhev's orders to report the activities of the French ambassador, la Chétardie, who was passing through Stockholm on his way to arrange a treaty with Russia. La Chétardie also intended to engineer the fall of Bestuzhev, who was in the pay of Britain, Austria and Saxony, and posed the single greatest obstacle to French and Prussian plans.[86] Keith's official reports back to the Russian court, and his correspondence with Korf, the Russian minister at Copenhagen, preserved in the Archive of Foreign Affairs in Moscow, were a record of the extent to which he appears to have served Russian and British interests. Not only did he report as instructed on la Chétardie, but he provided Bestuzhev with the first warning of the French ambassador's designs against him.[87] He also complained repeatedly of France's attempts in Stockholm to reinstate its superiority in the north and to undermine the British party at the Russian court.[88] In early 1744, he insisted on Elisabeth's behalf that she hold the right to approve the peace terms being negotiated between Denmark and Sweden at Copenhagen,

84 Carteret to Tyrawly, 18/5/1744, *SIRIO* 102, pp.41,42.
85 Carteret to Dickens, 13/12/1743, Chance, ed., *Diplomatic Instructions*, 5 Sweden 1727–1789, p.112.
86 Wich to Carteret, 8/11/1743, *SIRIO* 99, p.441; A.P.Bestuzhev to J.Keith, 24/11/1743, AVPR F96 o1 d11, f.1.
87 Bestuzhev to J.Keith, 16/1/1744, NAS Elphinstone, GD 156/60 folder 6, f.21.
88 J.Keith to Korf, 4/12/1743 o.s., AVPR F96 o1 d11, ll.12–13.

in case they compromise the interests of the Holstein heir.[89] He also earned the praise of Bestuzhev for exposing a plot by the Swedish minister Nolcken to negotiate a defensive treaty with Prussia without Russia's knowledge.[90]

Nevertheless, suspicion began to fall on Keith when it became clear, during the course of 1744, that Russia's position in Sweden was worsening, and that Bestuzhev's instructions were not being fulfilled. Swedish ministers negotiating in Denmark ignored Russian wishes, to the detriment of Holstein, and popular Swedish hostility towards the Russian 'occupation' increased after Frederick II's sister was promised to the Swedish Crown Prince Adolf Friedrich. Although Elisabeth was not opposed to this marriage, which followed the treaty between Russia and Prussia signed in March 1743, Frederick II was actively involved with la Chétardie in attempting to overthrow Bestuzhev. His plans for an invasion of Bohemia, which he executed in 1744, gave him a particular interest in preventing Russian intervention at any cost. Not only had he paid the non-interventionist Vorontsov 50,000 roubles, but he had even sought to discredit Britain by spreading the false rumour that the British ambassador in Russia, Lord Tyrawly, intended to launch another revolution in Russia.[91] By May 1744 Keith's failure to safeguard British interests in Sweden prompted suspicions on the part of Guy Dickens and the British party that Russia was on the point of concluding an alliance with Sweden, France and Prussia against Denmark.[92] In June, Hyndford, then ambassador to Prussia, warned of a plot between France and Prussia against Britain and Russia.[93] France's declaration of war on Britain in March, in conjunction with the projected Jacobite invasion from the French coast, increased British sensitivity to the strong link between French activity in Sweden and the Jacobite threat.[94]

As the principal Russian diplomatic representative in Sweden, and a man whose background did not predispose him to serve the British government, particularly at this juncture, it was James Keith whose loyalties were scrutinised. Correspondence intercepted by Bestuzhev between la Chétardie and Elisabeth's physician Lestocq, who was in receipt of a French pension, revealed that the latter was in contact with General Keith through la Chétardie.[95] La Chétardie did write to Keith in 1744, with the intention of winning him over to the French and Prussian camp against Bestuzhev.[96] In May Mardefeld

89 J.Keith to Empress Elisabeth, 13/1/1744, AVPR F96 o1 d9 ll.24–25v.
90 J.Keith to Bestuzhev, 14/1/1744, AVPR F96 o1 d9, ll.20v-21, 46–48v.
91 Lodge, 'Russia, Prussia and Great Britain', p.605; Carteret to Hyndford, 6/7/1744, BL Add.Ms. 11376, ff.149–150; Carteret to Tyrawly, 6/7/1744, *SIRIO* 102, p.73.
92 J.Keith to Empress Elisabeth, 4/5/1744, AVPR F96 o1 d9, ll.280–281.
93 Hyndford to Weston, 6/6/1744, BL Add.Ms. 11376, ff.69–70.
94 Hyndford to Harrington, 9/3/1745, *SIRIO* 102, pp.241–242.
95 Lestocq to J.Keith, February 1744, *SIRIO* 105, 213–214; *Arkhiv Vorontsova*, 1, pp.516–518, 582.
96 La Chétardie wrote that his letter to Keith was meant to convince him that Elisabeth's interests were met by French policy and thereby to win him to his opinion; '. . . en le mettant à l'aise sur les dispositions véritables de sa Maîtresse, le ramenera nécessairement de plus en plus à vous'. La Chétardie to Lanmary, 23/2 or 5/3/1744, *SIRIO* 105, p.207; Amelot wrote to la Chétardie, 'Quant à la lettre secrète que vous avez fait écrire sur ce sujet au général Keith . . . il faut espérer, qu'elles ne pourront aussi produire que de bons effets', *SIRIO* 105, p.259; Solov'ev, p.271.

reported to Frederick II the contents of a letter from Keith to Lestocq concerning the need to win the confidence of Count Tessin, Swedish state counsellor, who had conducted Swedish peace negotiations with Denmark and had arranged the engagement of the Swedish Crown Prince Adolf Friedrich to Frederick II's sister. Lestocq and la Chétardie's other associate, the chief marshal at the Russian court, Petr Fedorovich Brummer, wanted Frederick II to influence his future brother-in-law to this end.[97] In early June, Frederick, encouraged by la Chétardie's opposition to Bestuzhev and by what he saw to be Keith's complicity, responded by ordering Mardefeld to warn Elisabeth through Lestocq to expel Bestuzhev from the chancellorship. He maintained that she was exploited by her ministers, a fact which '. . . la dernière lettre du digne général Keith . . . servait de nouvelle preuve'.[98]

Quite apart from this, Keith is also known to have had personal links with the Swedish minister Nolcken, who was suspected of trying to conceal Swedish-Prussian negotiations from Bestuzhev in January 1744.[99] Keith, who had been Provincial Grand Master of the Brotherhood of Freemasons in Russia since 1740, had founded lodges both in St Petersburg and during his stay in Sweden, in Stockholm.[100] Nolcken was also a Freemason, possibly even a member of Keith's lodge, and later corresponded with him concerning the Swedish King's induction into the order. Although masonic contacts did not necessarily have any bearing on political allegiance, Keith's secret acquaintance with a man whom Bestuzhev condemned for his 'deceitful cunning', gives some food for speculation that Keith's true sympathies might not have been what they appeared.

Before concluding that Keith was in fact paying only lip-service to the interests of Bestuzhev, Britain and Austria while secretly encouraging their enemies, however, Frederick II's motives should be considered. He had an interest in using Keith to lend credibility to his campaign against Bestuzhev, and, as the case of Tyrawly illustrates, was not above manufacturing rumours to achieve his ends. Keith was on amicable terms with the Swedish king, who was known to prefer Britain to France, and expressed his deep disapproval of the

---

97 Mardefeld to Frederick II, 7/5/1744, *Politische Correspondenz*, 3, p.166 n.2.
98 Frederick II to Mardefeld, 2/6/1744, *Politische Correspondenz*, 3, p.166.
99 J.Keith to Bestuzhev, 14/1/1744, AVPR F96 o1 d9 ll.20v.,21,46.
100 Keith was Worshipful Master of a Lodge in St Petersburg in 1732, during the office of the first known Provincial Grand Master, Captain John Philips. In 1740 he was appointed Provincial Grand Master in Russia by Kintore, who was then Grand Master in England, and he founded the second Swedish lodge in Stockholm in 1743, where at least four members of the Swedish government were masons. Both Keith brothers were members of lodges in Prussia (Frederick II had been initiated in 1738). However, there is no evidence that Keith's lodges were of an overtly Jacobite or political nature. G.Behre, 'Gothenburg', pp.113; R.F.Gould, *Military Lodges. The Apron and the Sword or Freemasonry under Arms* (London, 1899), pp.203,208; B.Telepneff, 'Freemasonry in Russia', *Ars Quatuor Coronatorum*, 35 (1922), pp.261–291; A.N.Pypin, *Russkoe masonstvo XVIII i pervaya chetvert' XIX v.*, ed. G.V.Vernadsky (Petrograd, 1916); A.G.Cross, 'British Freemasons in Russia during the Reign of Catherine the Great', *OSP* ns 4, (1971), pp.43–45; Brockhaus-Efron, 72, pp.502–509. For links between Freemasonry and Jacobitism, see N.Paton, *The Jacobites: Their Roots, Rebellions and Links with Freemasonry* (Hampshire, 1994).

conduct of la Chétardie in Russia and satisfaction at his expulsion by Bestuzhev in June 1744.[101] In July, acting on imperial orders, Keith warned the Swedish Crown Prince against la Chétardie's attempts to win him to the French side, noting with apparent satisfaction that '. . . Le Prince me paroit être fort sur ses gardes contre les insinuations de la faction françoise'.[102] It was Bestuzhev's own assessment of Keith's loyalties while in Sweden which most conclusively undermined British suspicions. In March 1745 Hyndford, who had arrived to replace Tyrawly as Russian ambassador in December 1744, asked Bestuzhev's opinion of Keith's conduct in Sweden, and was told that

> . . . he was not in the french interest. On the contrary, while he commanded in Sweden, he had withstood great temptations, and had more than once remonstrated against private orders sent to him in the Empress's name, by M.Chétardie, Lestock, and of that party. In short, the chancellor commends his whole conduct extremely, and I think it is my duty to disabuse your lordship with regard to that part of general Keith's character . . .[103]

This judgement, made despite the mutual antipathy which existed between the future Chancellor and his general, suggests that if Keith supported the French party while in Sweden, he did so with great discretion and on a limited scale.

Lord Hyndford's Offensive

Within a year of Keith's return from Sweden, and only months after Bestuzhev had exonerated him in the eyes of the British ambassador of any involvement in French intrigue, Hyndford began a ruthless campaign against him, which was later backed by Bestuzhev. Given the increasing pressure for close Anglo-Russian relations, their sudden hostility was less a reaction to any change in Keith's own conduct, than to political expediency.

The conclusion of the dispute between Denmark and Sweden in spring 1744 was soon followed by a formal demand by the Swedish King and Senate for the return to Russia of Keith's auxiliary troops. When Keith eventually arrived in St Petersburg in August, the unpopular intrigues and expulsion of la Chétardie, combined with Frederick II's recent invasion of Bohemia and the Jacobite threat to Britain from France, had united Russian and British defence interests against France and Prussia, strengthening the hand of Bestuzhev and the British faction. In July Bestuzhev had been promoted to Grand Chancellor, and Vorontsov remained subordinate to him as Vice-Chancellor. Carteret approached Russia to join against Frederick II in a defensive alliance with the United Provinces and Saxony, and decided to transfer the more experienced diplomat, Lord Hyndford, from Berlin to St Petersburg to replace Tyrawly, for the purpose of negotiating this with Bestuzhev.[104] This state of

---

101 Bestuzhev to J.Keith, 6/6/1744, AVPR F96 o1 d8 ll.128–131; J.Keith to Empress Elisabeth, 26/6/1744, AVPR F96 o1 d9, ll.346–347v.
102 J.Keith to Empress Elisabeth, 3/7/1744, AVPR F96 o1 d9 l.358v.
103 Hyndford to Harrington, 9/3/1745, *SIRIO* 102, pp.241,242.
104 Carteret to Tyrawly, 10/8/1744, *SIRIO* 102, p.88.

affairs, combined with British demands for a subsidy agreement with Russia, served to polarise the divergent interests of the Grand and Vice-Chancellors, and redoubled British hostility against supporters of Vorontsov.

Keith and the twelve thousand Russians under his command were immediately sent to Reval and then to Riga to fulfil British demands for a force to safeguard Hanoverian possessions against Prussia, according to the Anglo-Russian treaty. The strategic and political importance of Keith's troops was increased by Frederick II's declaration of war on Saxony in May 1745, and by the victory of Marshal de Saxe with a Jacobite Irish brigade over the Duke of Cumberland at Fontenoy in the Austrian Netherlands, followed by the capitulation of Ghent, Bruges and Ostend to French forces. Meanwhile, in Russia, Hyndford's proposals for a subsidy agreement had met with an unacceptable Russian counter-project, drawn up with Vorontsov's collaboration to forestall Russian intervention in the war. Thus Anglo-Russian relations and Russian internal politics were brought to a state of extreme tension, and once more, fate placed James Keith, as Russia's most able commander, in a position which exposed him to the full force of Russian domestic divisions.

Had Keith, like Field Marshal Lacy, remained aloof from the rift between Vorontsov and Bestuzhev, his career might have survived. As it was, he tended to be identified with Vorontsov and his policy of non-intervention, rather than with Bestuzhev and British interests. Hyndford reported that his alleged, '. . . conection [sic] and intimacy with Lestock and Brummer and the princess of Zerbst, has lost much of his credit with Her Majesty'.[105] The fact that neither Keith nor Lestocq were admitted to the Empress's grand council in September 1744 to discuss giving aid to Saxony, was evidence that this observation had some basis.[106] Keith's reputation stood in sharp contradiction both to his command in Livonia and to Anglo-Russian negotiations, and Hyndford, naturally, felt obliged to protest vehemently against his suitability as commander of the force, which, raised to thirty thousand men, was now to be sent from Livonia to oppose Frederick II's invasion of Saxony. He argued that, despite Keith's '. . . great personal merit . . . his discourses tend entirely towards defeating our project of obtaining any assistance from this country [Russia]'. He also suspected that, '. . . his [Keith's] aim in all this is to save the king of Prussia as a good ally of France', and was anxious lest Keith carry out an intention which had '. . . escaped him . . . in the heat of discourse', of using the Russians under his command, now augmented to thirty thousand, to, '. . . make peace in what manner [the Empress] pleased'. There was also concern that Keith could assist the French Marshal de Saxe in his aspiration to become Duke of Courland.[107]

Keith's reputation with Bestuzhev and Hyndford was further undermined by Frederick II's continued interest in acquiring his services for Prussia. Frederick had kept Keith under Mardefeld's close watch ever since his declared intention

105 Hyndford to Harrington, 1/10/1745, *SIRIO* 102, p.346.
106 21/9/1745, *Ibid.*, pp.337,338.
107 Hyndford to Harrington, 3/9/1745, *SIRIO* 102, pp.331,332; 19/7/1746; 103, p.85.

to leave Russia in 1742, and in April 1745 ordered his ambassador to offer him the rank of field marshal in his army with an annual salary of eight to ten thousand ecus.[108] Mardefeld's response, that Keith was '. . . des généraux russes le seul capable de commander une armée', redoubled Frederick's determination to reach an agreement with him.[109] Mardefeld took advantage of the Prussian victory over Austria at Hohenfriedberg in June to approach Keith secretly with the king's attractive offer.[110] Although there is no evidence that Keith was prepared to accept Prussian proposals at this point, Bestuzhev, Hyndford and the Russian court were well aware of Frederick's approaches, and their mistrust of Keith grew correspondingly. This did, however, bring Keith some short-term benefits. One reason for giving him command of the troops opposing Frederick II was to keep him in Russian service; Russia could not risk losing its most competent and experienced general to the enemy.[111] Even without the added element of Jacobitism, Hyndford's attack on Keith had a strong military and political basis in the context of the war in Europe.

Hyndford's objections to Keith on the grounds of his alleged Jacobitism were not expressed until some time after the beginning of the 1745 Jacobite Rising in August. The complex political manoeuvring which motivated his attack make it difficult to determine whether he used allegations of Jacobitism to dispose of Keith before the latter jeopardised British plans, or whether he genuinely believed Keith's enmity towards Bestuzhev and friendship with Vorontsov to be based on Jacobite sentiments.

There was no evidence that Keith was in any way involved with the Jacobite Rising, apart from his acknowledged opposition to the British subsidy agreement, which would bring Russia to the aid of Austria and Britain, and by implication, divert French energies away from support of the Jacobites. Neither the Earl Marischal nor even James III, Keith's former correspondents on Jacobite affairs, was privy to Charles Edward's plans, and George Keith was in any case convinced that a restoration attempt was doomed to failure.

Anglo-Russian relations experienced a setback when George II, having temporarily abandoned hope of securing Russian assistance, and in great need of an ally, signed the Treaty of Hanover in August 1745 with Prussia, its former enemy. The fact that neither the Empress nor even Hyndford was informed of the move illustrated that Russia was not perceived as a threat. Yet even at the height of Russian anger in the aftermath of the treaty, Elisabeth had no time for the Jacobites. Charles Edward chose this critical period to write to her from Edinburgh on behalf of the people of Scotland, reminding her that she had placed Adolf Friedrich on the Swedish throne, and requesting her assistance in the Rising he was now leading.[112] Although some rumours

---

108 Frederick II to Mardefeld, 7/4/1745, *Politische Correspondenz*, 4, p.113.
109 Mardefeld to Frederick II, 24/4/1745, Frederick II to Mardefeld, 13/5/1745, *Politische Correspondenz*, 4, p.117.
110 Mardefeld to J.Keith, 18/6/1745, NAS Elphinstone, GD 156/60 folder 6, f.26.
111 Hyndford to Harrington, 12/10/1745, *SIRIO* 102, pp.352,353.
112 Charles Edward to Empress Elisabeth, 9/10/45 n.s., RA (1865) 2, pp.347–352.

circulated in Britain that Russian troops would actually be sent to overthrow the Hanoverian monarchy, the fact that the British ministry's preoccupation with the domestic insurrection had caused it to neglect Hyndford and Russian affairs completely suggests that these were not taken seriously.[113] In the event, Elisabeth did not respond to Jacobite requests.

Whatever Hyndford believed to be Keith's motives for opposing British interests in Russia, his attack on Jacobitism was no less genuine for being less to do with the Rising in Britain than with the poor state of Anglo-Russian relations. He himself had been deeply shocked to learn at second hand as late as October of the Treaty of Hanover, which was not only a betrayal of all his efforts, but had dealt his credibility in Russia a considerable blow and damaged the reputation of Bestuzhev in Russian eyes. Hyndford described it as a crisis in Anglo-Russian relations, and protested to Harrington that

> . . . the maritime powers must either secure the friendship of the empress or lose it for ever, and the standing or falling of Count Bestucheff, the only friend we have in this country, entirely depends upon the measures which we shall now take.[114]

In the aftermath of the Treaty Hyndford was excluded from exerting any influence in Russia; he was even kept ignorant of Austro-Russian negotiations leading to the 'treaty of the two Empresses' in June 1746.

When it became known in July 1746, therefore, that George Keith intended to travel to Russia, only three months after the battle of Culloden had ended the Jacobite Rising, his visit was perceived as a serious threat in the light of Britain's already insecure diplomatic position. The level of concern registered in Hyndford's reports to Harrington was evidence not only that the Jacobite threat remained an issue, but that it continued to have political consequences as far afield as Russia. He summarised the possible damage George Keith might inflict on Britain and its allies:

> . . . either to work for the interest of count Saxe in Courland, or to stir up a rebellion in this country, or . . . to have produced a commission as ambassador from France at this court, which he very possibly may have in his pocket, or some other pernicious scheme, for it can never be imagined, that a person who has lived so long in France, Spain and Italy, could think of spending the remainder of his days at Archangel or Astracan.[115]

While James Keith was meeting George at Mittau, having requested Bestuzhev's permission for him to settle in Russia, Hyndford approached Elisabeth through Bestuzhev to have him turned back at the frontier without even the luggage which had been sent ahead to Riga. He also procured the promise from

---

113 McLynn, *The Jacobites,* p.43.
114 Hyndford to Harrington, 29/10/1745, *SIRIO* 102, p.362.
115 Hyndford to Harrington, 29/7/1746, *SIRIO* 103, pp.86,87; see also 19/7/1746, *SIRIO* 103, p.85.

Bestuzhev, '. . . in the Empress's name, that Her Imperial Majesty will never grant her protection to any Rebel against the King my Master'.[116] Bestuzhev then wrote personally to both James and George Keith to prevent the latter's entry into Russia unless he renounced his Jacobitism.[117]

Hyndford's suspicions of the Keith brothers, although evidently not to be taken lightly, were in fact quite unfounded. George had intended for several years to retire to Russia, and even in his correspondence with James III attached no political significance to the visit.[118] Nevertheless, this incident illustrated the extent to which the war in Europe extended the sphere of the Jacobite threat to include every area of British foreign policy in which French and British interests conflicted.

Hyndford was not content merely to safeguard British interests in Russia through the extradition of a Jacobite, but used the incident to manipulate both Russian domestic and foreign policy to Britain's advantage. Firstly, by securing the Empress's promise, '. . . not to give refuge to any rebels against the king', he began the process of cementing the Anglo-Russian bond damaged by the Treaty of Hanover. Harrington responded on behalf of the king that George II considered it '. . . a particular mark of her friendship and regard towards him'.[119] She, in turn, described the measure as '. . . due from one good ally to another'.[120] Secondly, Hyndford attempted to undermine Vorontsov's reputation in both British and Russian eyes, while promoting that of Bestuzhev, by reporting that the former had transmitted letters of recommendation from George Keith to members of the Russian court. He hoped that '. . . this will contribute to the discredit of the Vice-Chancellor with the Empress, and will show to some other courts, who depend upon him, that his interest is not so great as they imagine'.[121] At the same time he emphasised Bestuzhev's role in procuring the prohibition, earning the Chancellor the gratitude of George II and the ministry.[122]

His efforts were an unqualified success. The Empress requested a full-length portrait of, 'our young hero', the Duke of Cumberland, victor at Culloden.[123] Vorontsov, who had recently returned from a year's congé in Europe, was forced to admit, in the Empress's presence, that he had met with George Keith both at Mittau and at Aix-la-Chapelle, a confession which confirmed the suspicions of the anti-French faction, Elisabeth and Bestuzhev, that he had

---

116 Hyndford to Harrington, 2/8/1746, BL Add.Ms. 11382, f.7.
117 Bestuzhev to George Keith, draft approved by Empress, 15/8/1746, letter sent 20/8/1746, AVPR F35 o1 d706 ll.2–2v; James Keith to George Keith, 28/10/1747, *HMC Elphinstone*, p.223.
118 James III wished George Keith in Russia '. . . all the quiet and satisfaction you can propose to yourself', 18/7/1746, RA Stuart 275/152. George later protested at being debarred from 'living quietly' with his brother, James Edgar to Charles Edward, 6/1/1747, Tayler, *Jacobite Epilogue*, p.87.
119 Harrington to Hyndford, 26/8/1746, *SIRIO* 103, p.96.
120 Hyndford to Harrington, 2/9/1746, *Ibid.*, pp.97,98.
121 Hyndford to Harrington, 29/7/1746, *Ibid.*, p.87.
122 Harrington to Hyndford, 5/9/1746, *Ibid.*, pp.98,99.
123 Hyndford to Harrington, 9/8/1746, *Ibid.*, pp.89–90.

been conspiring against them during his absence, and significantly damaged his credibility and influence at the Russian court. In November, when Lord Chesterfield, who had replaced Harrington, instructed Hyndford to reach agreement with Russia for the provision of 30,000 men, the British ambassador, Bestuzhev and Elisabeth largely succeeded in excluding Vorontsov from the negotiation process.[124] It was the exclusion of George Keith which, to a large extent, had paved the way for this new rapprochement.

James Keith's Departure from Russia

The fate of the Earl Marischal provided incontestable proof of the superiority of the British faction in Russia, and prompted James Keith and some other sympathisers to request their discharge from Russian service. In Keith's case, however, the final decision to leave was reinforced by the persistence of Hyndford and Bestuzhev's anti-Jacobite campaign, closely linked to their efforts to engineer the fall of Vorontsov, which was now directed against him.[125]

The activities of Charles Edward, and particularly the hero's welcome he received in France in the aftermath of the Rising, continued to strengthen the anti-Jacobite bond between George II and the Empress. In November, Bestuzhev passed Hyndford a copy of an intercepted letter from D'Argenson in France to D'Allion, la Chétardie's successor as ambassador in St Petersburg, reporting that Charles Edward intended to launch another invasion of Britain with French assistance. According to this, Charles had declared publicly that '. . . If the English force us to lay aside all sort of management with them, we do not want the means to raise new disturbances in their Islands . . .'[126] George II was grateful for Bestuzhev's information, which redoubled his determination to weaken the pro-French influence of Vorontsov at the Russian court.[127] Hyndford's main objective, the Anglo-Russian subsidy agreement, became inextricably linked with his efforts to have James Keith excluded from commanding the subsidy troops.

Hyndford began his plot to oust Keith by extracting a promise from Field Marshal Lacy that he would not decline the command if offered it.[128] Although Lacy was a personal friend of Keith's and a Jacobite exile, his indifference to politics, and obedience to whomsoever happened to hold authority were well recognised. In this case there is evidence that Hyndford claimed that Keith had slandered Lacy in order to win his support.[129] Hyndford then had Bestuzhev request Elisabeth's assistance against Keith. His intrigue was uncovered when Bestuzhev inadvertently confirmed in Vorontsov's hearing that the Empress

---

124 Chesterfield to Hyndford, 4/11/1746, BL Add.Ms. 11382, f.201.
125 Hyndford to Harrington, 8/11/1746, BL Add.Ms.11382, f.228v.
126 Extract of D'Argenson to D'Allion, 31/10/1746, enclosed in Hyndford to Harrington, 22/ 11/1746, BL Add.Ms. 11382, f.255v.
127 Chesterfield to Hyndford, 23/12/1746, BL Add.Ms 11382, f.355v.
128 Hyndford to Chesterfield, 23/12/1746, BL Add.Ms.11382, f.347v.
129 Hyndford to Chesterfield, 23/12/1746, *SIRIO* 103, pp.162–163; J.Keith to G.Keith, 28/10/ 1747, *HMC Elphinstone*, p.223.

had sanctioned his proposal to deprive Keith of the command. Hyndford succeeded in turning the tables on Vorontsov, however, by countering the latter's warm recommendation of Keith's military skill and experience, with his own protest against Keith's Jacobitism. According to his own account, he told the Vice-Chancellor '. . . that my only reason for objecting against him was because he had been twice in a rebellion against the King my Master', which '. . . put an end to the encomium upon Mr Keith'.[130]

Hyndford not only won his confrontation with Vorontsov by raising the issue of Keith's Jacobitism, his victory served to inflict further damage on Vorontsov's standing at court. After this incident, Vorontsov, although Vice-Chancellor, was actually excluded from a meeting between Bestuzhev, Lacy and the Empress concerning the subsidy troops. The Empress's wish to retain Lacy in Russia left the 30,000 Russians Britain required without a single competent commander, but Bestuzhev chose Prince Repnin instead of his superior, Keith, on purely political grounds.[131] As in the case of George Keith, the label of Jacobite had become a blanket justification for action against an individual whose pro-French sympathies posed a much wider political threat. It was, moreover, a label against which Vorontsov could not protest.

Keith applied to leave Russian service on 30 January 1747, as soon as he realised the extent to which his political affiliations were affecting his military career. Problems arose, however, when Bestuzhev, having achieved his aim of removing one of Vorontsov's supporters from a position of responsibility, but unwilling to lose Keith's skills, was reluctant to release him. After winning time by refusing to submit Keith's application, trying to tempt him with an inferior command, then maintaining the application had been made too late, he eventually resorted to threats, claiming, falsely, that Keith had once requested Russian lands and was therefore debarred from leaving the country.[132] Eventually, in May, he bound Keith's departure to the condition that he sign a document promising '. . . never to serve directly or indirectly against Russia'. Refusal to do so would be punished by immediate arrest. Field Marshal Lacy, who administered the signing in July, was, according to Keith's account, clearly opposed to Bestuzhev, but dared not disobey his orders. Keith was forced to sign, but was unwise enough to comment that '. . . if ever they should take me alive serveing against Russia I was willing they should make a new article to condemn me'.[133] Fearing severe punishment for disrespect, he boarded the first ship bound for Britain. By August 1747 one of the last great Jacobites to serve in Russia had managed to flee it with his life.

By a curious twist of fate, Keith suffered in Russia the very penalties for Jacobitism which he had gone there to escape twenty years before, and was,

---

130 Hyndford to Chesterfield, 27/12/1746, BL Add.Ms.11382, f.363.
131 Hyndford to Steinberg, 10/1/1747, BL Add.Ms.11383, f.19v.
132 James Keith to Peter Lacy, two letters January and February 1747, *HMC Elphinstone*, p.227; Bestuzhev to J.Keith, 12/2/1747, *Ibid.*, pp.227–228; Keith to Bestuzhev, late February, *Ibid.*, p.228.
133 J.Keith to G.Keith, 28/10/1747, *HMC Elphinstone*, p.223.

moreover, innocent of the charges against him. Hyndford's objection to his Jacobitism was not simply a pretext for dismissal; later, sending Chesterfield a copy from Bestuzhev of Keith's request for discharge, in which Keith had declared his intention of repurchasing the family estate in Scotland, Hyndford warned the ministry to '. . . keep a watchful eye over that gentleman's conduct in Scotland, for he is as much a jacobite as ever he was'.[134] Nevertheless, Hyndford also gave both Keith brothers an auxiliary role in his diplomatic mission by exploiting their Jacobitism in the service of improved Anglo-Russian co-operation.

There was an additional irony in that the Jacobite cause had by this time already sustained its greatest defeat, and its adherents in Britain were being systematically and brutally suppressed. The unlikelihood of a further rising was borne out by the fact that Charles Edward, in his ignorance of international politics, even resorted to fantastic projects to win Russian assistance. In April 1747, just as Keith was attempting to leave a Russia which had demonstrated its utter hostility towards Jacobitism, Charles Edward wrote to his father with the proposal

> . . . to find a proper person to go to ye Zarina from me along with a letter from you proposing to Marry her and your portion to be twenty thousand men to be sent over immediately in England . . . the only difficulty I finde is who to pitch upon to carry the messages.[135]

James III, who was more aware of the state of Anglo-Russian politics and knew the fate of the Earl Marischal, firmly quashed the plan as so ridiculous as to be potentially damaging to the reputation of the cause.[136]

A Transfer of Allegiance

After his mistreatment at the hands of Bestuzhev and Hyndford, James Keith found an effective revenge. Throughout the difficult process of obtaining his discharge, he had always maintained that he intended to return to Britain, and even went as far as to board a British ship sailing from Russia.[137] This may have been his original intention, for he had corresponded with the Earl of Kintore the previous year on the possibility of returning to Scotland to stand for election to parliament in the Banffshire area.[138] However, by 1747, this only served to conceal his real desire to go into Prussian service. He left the British ship at the Danish coast, deliberately letting it be known that he was on his way to Holland. In fact, immediately on his arrival in Denmark on 1 September, having rejected a position in Danish service, he had written offering his services to Prussia, and had then travelled to Hamburg, where he received news of his

---

134 Hyndford to Chesterfield, 30/3/1747, *SIRIO* 103, p.253.
135 Charles Stuart to James III, 3/4/1747, RA Stuart 282/128.
136 James III to Charles Stuart, 25/4/1747, Browne, *History of the Highlands*, 3, p.498.
137 J.Keith to P.Lacy, two letters, January, n.d. *HMC Elphinstone*, p.227; J.Keith to Bestuzhev, February, *Ibid*, p.228.
138 Kintore to J.Keith, 27/10/1746, *HMC Elphinstone*, pp.228–229.

acceptance. He arrived in Berlin on 11 October and two days later was officially declared field marshal of the Prussian army.[139]

Frederick II, likewise, was reluctant to attract international attention to the transfer of such a prominent commander. Having heard rumours of Keith's imminent departure from Russia, he was so anxious to gain his services for Prussia that he wrote repeatedly to his envoys in St Petersburg for information.[140] He sent him a letter of welcome in Hamburg as soon as he received his offer of service in mid-September. However, in late September, when Mardefeld reported news from Holland that Marshal de Saxe was trying to acquire Keith for the French, Frederick gave orders that he should encourage him to travel via Berlin, 'pour aller en Hollande', well knowing that Keith would remain in Prussia.[141] Frederick then attempted to conciliate Russia by ordering his minister at St Petersburg, Count Finckenstein, to claim that Keith had come to Berlin on his own initiative, and he had been unable to refuse his request for military service.[142] His concern to conceal the details of Keith's recruitment was a reflection both of the deteriorating state of Russo-Prussian relations, and of the great military asset which Keith was seen to represent. According to the gazettes of the time, Keith's expertise was so greatly in demand when he left Russia that, according to his brother, he could have entered military service not only in Denmark and Prussia, but also in Britain, France, Holland or Venice.[143]

Keith's defection to Prussia dealt Russia a double blow. Firstly, the Russian army was deprived of its most capable commander not long before the build-up to the Seven Years War. Lacy could not supplant this loss, for he died in 1751, aged 73.[144] The absence of Keith was compounded by the departure of other leading officers, who accompanied him into Prussian service. These included Major John Grant, nephew of Patrick Grant of Dunlugus, who had been aide-de-camp to Field Marshal Lacy,[145] and his own kinsman, Robert Keith of Ludquhairn.[146] According to Hyndford, a number of other Britons, who possibly shared Keith's political views, followed Keith, '. . . leur Général Keith',

139 J.Keith to G.Keith, 28/10/1747; G.Keith to J.Keith, 7/11/1747, *HMC Elphinstone*, p.223.

140 Frederick II to Wasendorf, 6/5/1747, Frederick II to Finckenstein, 29/7/1747, *Politische Correspondenz*, 5, p.446.

141 Mardefeld to Frederick II, 26/9/1747, Frederick II to Mardefeld, 29/9/1747, *Politische Correspondenz*, 5, p.487.

142 Frederick II to Finckenstein, 28/10/1747, *Politische Correspondenz*, 5, p.511.

143 G.Keith to J.Keith, 7/11/1747, *HMC Elphinstone*, p.223.

144 E.Kotasek, *Feld Marschall Graf Lacy*, p.2.

145 Grant belonged to the branch of the Grants of Dalvey, but he succeeded to the estate of Dunlugus, near Banff. Born in 1700, he had gone to Russia as a cadet, and Keith had procured him a commission under Empress Elisabeth. He later became Frederick II's favourite ADC during the Seven Years War, was on two missions to England, and died as governor of Neisse in 1764. His early political affiliations are uncertain, but by 1758 the exiled Jacobite Andrew Hay of Rannes considered seeking his mediation and Frederick II's influence to secure a pardon in Britain. Tayler, *A Jacobite Exile*, pp.90,91; Fischer, *The Scots in Germany*, pp.128,287; Grant, *The Scottish Soldiers*, pp.63,64; Bisset, *The Memoirs of Andrew Mitchell*, pp.286–288.

146 See previous note, also Grant, *The Scottish Soldiers*, pp.62,63; *Scots Magazine*, (1750), p.597.

having also been recruited by Mardefeld before the latter's recall in 1746.[147] Secondly, Prussia gained an invaluable source of intelligence on the military affairs of its great enemy, Russia, and Frederick made frequent use of Keith's knowledge to complement Finckenstein's dispatches from St Petersburg.[148] His advice would also prove useful during the Seven Years War. Moreover, Keith himself was financially so much more secure than he had been in Russia that he was at last able to invite his brother George to join him at the Prussian court.[149] He could also support his mistress, Eva Merthens, the daughter of the Mayor of Gothenburg, whom he had met while in Sweden.

Neither Hyndford nor Bestuzhev forgave Keith for his defection to Prussia. When Hyndford passed through Berlin on his return to England, having been recalled from Russia in September 1749, he reported to Bestuzhev that Keith had declined to visit him on grounds of ill health. For his part, he refused to admit to his house any of those who had left Russia, regarding them '. . . comme une éspèce de deserteurs'.[150] He also maintained that they appeared to have gained nothing for their infidelity, apparently disregarding the fact that, by 1749, James Keith had been appointed Governor General of Berlin and awarded the highest Prussian decoration, the Order of the Black Eagle, while John Grant and Keith of Ludquhairn had been promoted. Hyndford's criticism of mercenaries for transferring into what Britain regarded as 'enemy' service is interesting, however, in that it predated the time when the concept of fighting for money, rather than national loyalty, would no longer be considered morally acceptable.

Hyndford's disapproval, of course, derived more from his immediate concern that the defectors would be detrimental to British interests than from any judgement on mercenary service *per se*. His fears were indeed justified, for the Keith brothers continued to be associated with Jacobite intrigue while in Prussia. In January 1748 Frederick II wrote in a letter to Charles Edward that

> . . . You are frequently the subject of my conversation with General Keith, whom I have had the good fortune to engage in my service, and besides his consummate knowledge in military affairs, he is possessed of a thousand aimable [sic] qualities. Yet nothing endears him to me so entirely as his entertaining the same sentiments with regard to your Royal Highness that I do.[151]

147 Hyndford to Bestuzhev, 6/1/1750, BL Add.Ms.32819, ff.287–288.
148 Frederick II to Finckenstein, 26/3/1748, *Politische Correspondenz*, 6, p.68. Also, in April 1749 when Sweden feared a Russian attack on Finland, Keith advised the Queen of Sweden, Frederick II's sister, to retreat and allow the Finnish winter to defeat the Russians. In March 1753, Keith advised Frederick on the state of Russian finances. *Ibid.*
149 He wrote, '. . . I was to have eight thousand crowns a year, with which I can live easilier here than with twelve in Russia where our immense equipages eats up all our income', J.Keith to G.Keith, 28/10/1747, *HMC Elphinstone*, p.223.
150 Hyndford to Bestuzhev, 6/1/1750, BL Add.Ms. 32819, ff.287–288.
151 Frederick II to Charles Edward, 12/1/1748 (letter dated 1747 o.s.), *The Lyon in Mourning*, 3, p.254.

In 1752, while George Keith was Prussian ambassador at the court of Louis XV[152], the Keith brothers were implicated in the 'Elibank Plot', as called after its organiser, Alexander Murray, younger brother of the fifth Lord Elibank. The Earl Marischal encouraged Frederick II to promise support for a rising in Scotland in conjunction with the assassination of George II and his family. James Keith was to land in Scotland at the head of Swedish troops. The plot failed, however, in 1753. Frederick, like so many monarchs, was only interested in exploiting the Jacobite threat for political ends, and a Jacobite double agent, believed to have been Alasdair MacDonnell of Glengarry, betrayed the affair to the ministry.[153] Nevertheless, this not only confirmed Hyndford's suspicions of James Keith, but showed that he was potentially as great a political liability to Russia's allies outside Russia as within.

Conclusion

Despite these late sparks of Jacobite intrigue in Europe, the Jacobite movement was in its dying stages when James Keith left Russia in 1747. Charles Edward's relations with Louis XV deteriorated the following year, when the Treaty of Aix-la-Chapelle, ending the War of the Austrian Succession, required his expulsion from France. As late as 1759, during the Seven Years War, the French foreign minister, Choiseul, had plans for a united naval offensive with Jacobite co-operation by France, Russia and Sweden to force Britain and Prussia to make peace terms. These were, however, conclusively put to rest in November by the destruction of the French Brest fleet by Britain's Admiral Hawke at Quiberon Bay, which ended forever French attempts to restore the Stuarts.

In Russia Keith's departure coincided with the decline and disappearance of the Jacobite element which had been a constant presence in Anglo-Russian politics since the reign of Peter I. The handful of Jacobite exiles who remained in Russian service acquired military prominence but no longer exerted the same political influence. The greatest of these, Field Marshal Peter Lacy, had died soon after Keith left Russia, in 1751. Of the rest, Robert Fullarton attained the rank of lieutenant general for his services in the Seven Years War.[154] In 1768 he returned to Scotland to inherit the lairdship of Dudwick from his brother John, where he died in 1786.[155] One Drummond, who might also have

---

152 George Keith's appointment to this post in 1751 prompted a formal protest by the ministry on the grounds that it contravened the terms of the 1717 Triple Alliance, '. . . that no Subject of His Majesty, under Attainder for Rebellion, shall be haboured or received in the Dominions of his most Christian Majesty'. Holdernesse to Yorke, 26/8/1751, PRO SP 78/242, ff.41,42; Yorke to Holdernesse, 15/9/1751 n.s., *Ibid.* 78/241, ff.104–108.

153 For a detailed account of this plot, see Andrew Lang, *Pickle the Spy*, (London, 1897). For evidence of both Keith brothers' part in it, see *Politische Correspondenz*, v.9, pp.356–358, 366, 436–438, 456–457.

154 During the reign of Catherine II, Fullarton, together with Lieutenant Colonel Drummond of the Nisovsk regiment and Captain O'Hara of the Narva regiment, took part in the recruitment of skilled British veterans of that war, under the supervision of General Brown. General Brown to Catherine II, 19/3/1763, RGADA F21 o1 d57, ll.4–8.

155 Tayler, *Jacobites of Aberdeenshire and Banffshire*, pp.198–199; Grant, *The Scottish Soldiers*, p.46.

had Jacobite connections, had entered Russian service in 1740, and was a major during Elisabeth's reign.[156] George Brown was promoted to the rank of full general in 1756, and remained at that rank during the reign of Catherine II.[157] James Hewitt and Gustav Otto Douglas, uncles of the Jacobite exile of the 1745 rising, Chevalier James Johnstone, were still in Russia in 1746, when their nephew intended to visit them.[158] Daniel Cumming was promoted to the rank of major general in 1755, and was serving in Russia in 1758.[159]

During the 1740's, Russia's reputation for attracting military foreigners suffered, and this, in conjunction with the general improvement in Anglo-Russian relations over the course of the previous ten years, meant that there was no equivalent influx of Jacobites to Russia immediately after the 1745 rising as there had been after the rising of 1715. Although the reign of Catherine II, from 1762, initiated a whole new era of foreign influence in Russia, which included large-scale recruitment of foreign military commanders, Jacobite exiles were not prominent among their number. In Russia, by the 1750s, Jacobitism as a political force had ceased to exist.

Between the early years of the century and 1750, however, Jacobites played a key role in shaping Russia's rise as a military power and in placing it firmly on the stage of European diplomacy. There remains the legacy of these coura-geous and talented people, particularly of the military leaders and diplomats who carved successful careers, raised families and built communities in one of the most exotic but also most challenging of countries. The extent of their impact was out of all proportion to their numbers; they trained Russian troops, led them to innumerable military victories, governed Russian-owned lands and helped to steer the course of international diplomacy at a critical period in Russian history. The British government was justifiably wary of the breadth of their influence, and it became clear over the course of the century that the Jacobite talent lost to the British Isles was, decidedly, to Russia's lasting gain.

156 Lieutenant-Colonel Drummond was probably John Drummond, who entered Russian service in 1740 and was a first major in 1758, RGVIA F489 o1 d7340, military list 1758. His politics are unconfirmed, although the Jacobite banker, George Napier, sent Sir Henry Stirling 'Drummond's bill' in 1742. NAS GD 24/1/454, f.19. A Simon Drummond was made an army brigadier in 1728, but was no longer present in 1738. RGVIA F489 o1 d7395 military list 1729.

157 RGVIA F489 o1 d7340, military list 1758.

158 Chevalier de Johnstone, *A Memoir of the '45*, 1820. There were several other Johnstones in Russian service. One, the brother of the Marquis of Annandale, applied to serve in Russia as early as 1709, 23/12/1709, PRO SP 91/107. A William Johnston arrived at Riga in 1719, RGVIA F495 o1 d114, l.5v; John Johnson was in the Russian navy until his death in 1727, *Obshchi morskoi spisok;* Andrew Johnstone was made a lieutenant colonel in 1725 (RGVIA F489 o1 d7395, military list 1729), a colonel in 1730 (*Ibid.*, d7387, military list 1738), but did not appear in the 1758 military list (*Ibid.*, d.7340).

159 This was almost certainly the son of Alexander Cumming of Culter on Deeside, recommended to Thomas Gordon in 1738 (Sir Alexander Cumming to T.Gordon, 10/4/1738, NAS Abercairney GD 24/1/856) His date of entry into Russian service was recorded, probably wrongly, as 1736 and he was a colonel in 1742 (RGVIA F846 o16 VUA 1622, ll.132ff.).

Bibliography

Manuscript Sources

ALOII Kollektsii 39, 150 (letters of James Keith, 1740).

AUL

    Ms.2707 1/1/1 and 1/1/2, Mss of A.W.Keith Falconer, The Life of Marshal Keith, and related papers 1928–39.

    Ms.2708.

    Ms.2709, 'Correspondence of James Keith Soldier' (photostat copies).

    Ms.2710.

    Ms.2711/1–12. Correspondence, Family and Estate Papers of Keith Family, 1550–1787.

    Ms.3163 Mss of H.Godfrey, 'Field Marshal James Keith; Mercenary and Jacobite'.

    Ms.3295 'Documents from Marischal Keith's Despatch Box'.

AVPR

    F9 o1 dd.2, 3.

    F10 (Religious Affairs: Foreign Religions) o1 dd.1,6.

    F13 o2 d.335.

    F15 o158/3 dd.14, 24, 35, 86, 107, 160, 185.

    F24 o2 dd.22, 47, d53.

    F35 o1 dd.495, 505, 506, 507, 508, 518, 520, 607, 706, 809, 829.

    F36 o1 dd.115, 116, 119, 131, 144, 199.

    F36 o2 dd.18, 21, 33, 36, 46, 55, 60, 68, 71, 72, 81, 94, 110.

    F96 (Russo-Swedish Relations) o1, dd.3a/968, 5, 7, 9, 10 (Keith's letters from Sweden 1743) dd.9a, 11.

BODLEIAN LIBRARY

    French e.20 (Letters of Cardinal G.Alberoni).

BRITISH LIBRARY

    Stowe 231, 231

    Additional Manuscripts 11376, 11382, 11383, 28129, 32686, 32743, 32744, 32745, 32746, 32747, 32792, 32798, 32801, 32802, 32819, 33005, 33199.

CAMBRIDGE UNIVERSITY LIBRARY Cholomondeley (Houghton) Mss. 1250, 1251

GUILDHALL LIBRARY

    Court Minute Books of the Russia Company Mss. 11741/4, 11741/5, 11741/6.

    Diocese of London, Register of the British Factory in Russia 1706–1815, Ms.11192b.

NAS

    Abercairney Mss., GD 24/1/450, 451, 454, 464/F-M, 846, 854–862.

    Airth Writs, GD 37/328, 329.

    D and J.H. Campbell W.S., GD 253/144/4, 5, 9.

    Elphinstone Muniments, GD 156/62 folders 2, 4.

    Farquharson of Invercauld Muniments, GD 0061.

    Gordon Castle Muniments, GD 44/43/13.

    Hume of Marchmont Mss., GD 158/1643.

    Seaforth Muniments, GD 46/6/97A.

NBSS

    Avt.136 (Letters of James Keith).

NLS

    Murray of Ochtertyre papers, Ms.21175, 21184.

PUBLIC RECORD OFFICE
  State Papers 35/15, 35/27, 35/28, 35/50, 35/64, 35/71, 42/77, 43/7, 43/8, 44/65,
  44/280, 48/108, 74/92, 75/49, 75/185, 78/202, 78/206, 78/218, 78/222, 78/242, 80/
  55, 80/56, 80/58, 82/42, 84/290, 84/295, 84/384, 90/19, 90/20, 91/9, 91/10, 91/11,
  91/107, 94/93, 94/94, 94/95, 94/214, 95/30, 95/36, 95/37, 95/38, 95/39, 95/41, 95/
  42, 95/43, 95/46, 95/47, 98/44, 100/52, 102/50
RA Stuart vols.
  66, 67, 68, 69, 71, 72, 73, 78, 79, 80, 81, 82, 83, 101, 103, 104, 105, 106, 107, 108, 109,
  112, 113, 114, 115, 116, 117, 118, 119, 121, 122, 124, 127, 128, 129, 132, 133, 135, 138,
  139, 142, 144, 151, 155, 169, 170, 183, 185, 186, 192, 193, 199, 203, 204, 205, 213, 219,
  220, 230, 233, 234, 239, 241, 252, 352, 360.
RGADA
  F4 o1 d86 (Royal letters).
  F9 'Kabinet Petra Pervogo', o5 d1 pt.1 (letters Kurakin to Peter I), d1 pt.2, d1 pt.7,
  d29.
  F11 Razdel II dd.419, 531, 577, 590, 607, 774, 816, 817.
  F16 o1 dd.98, 322, 369, 450, 558, 856.
  F20 (Military Affairs) o1 dd.78, 126, 127, 158.
  F21 (Naval Affairs), o1 dd.25, 41, 57.
  F22 o1 ed.kh.110.
  F35 o1 pt.1 dd.338, 481.
  F149 o1 ed.kh.187. (letters of James Keith).
  F177 'Kabinet Ministrov', o1 d27.
  F179 o1 d217.
  F181 o13 ed.kh.1224.
RGAVMF
  F146 (Affairs of the Military Naval Commission) o1, dd.56, 61, 62 (list of those in fleet,
  incl. pay 1732), 63 (list of naval servicemen c.1732), 64 (list of fleet 1732), 65, 66.
  F212 (Affairs of the Admiralty College) o1, dd.13 (list of flagmen, ober ofitsery 1723),
  17, 54, 55, 56.
  F212 (State Admiralty College), o11, dd.2/516 (list of officers 1727), 3/157, 3/657, 3/
  719, 7 (establishment of fleet 1741), 7/558, 7/791, 17/531, 17/733, 18, 31, 1102, 32/
  546, 33/271, 34/189, 41a/447, 45, 55/212, 142, 173, 189, 712.
  F227 o1 d4/681.
  F233 o1 dd.93, 118, 142 (special collection A, o2 no.558), 142, 162, 163, 165, 176, 177,
  178, 179 (special collection A, o2 no.560), 189, 190, 192, 196, 198, 199, 201, 203, 251,
  252, 255, 256, 257, 258, 259.
RGVIA
  F8 o1 d45
  F16 o1 'Inostrannaya ekspeditsiya Kantselariya voennoi kollegii'.
  F160 o1/212 d9 folder 107.
  F489 o1 'Formulyarnye spiski' (lists of officers in land forces), dd.7006 (1741), 7122
  'Spisok kavalergardov' (list of cavalry guards 1724–31), 7339 (1744), 7367 (1744),
  7340 (1758), 7386 (1748), 7387 (1738), 7389 (1744), 7390 (1745), 7395 (1729).
  F490 o2 d50 'Ofitserskie skazki' (career accounts for 1720–21).
  F495 o1 dd.104 (Petition of capt. T.Saunders to enter Russian service), 114 (list of
  foreigners entering Petersburg 1719–21).
  F846 o16 VUA no.1556 parts 1 and 2 (campaign against Turkey), VUA no.1557 pts.1–
  4 (campaigns against the Turks 1733–37), VUA no.1565 (Turkish War), VUA no.1622
  pt.2 (letters of commanders in Swedish War, 1742–43.), VUA no.1624 (Bibikov's
  Account of the Swedish War 1743), VUA no.1627, 'Journal de la Campagne de
  Finlande des Années 1741,42 et 43 écrit par le Lieut. Colonel de Keith aux services de
  l'Imperatrice de Russie'.

Primary Printed Sources

D'Alembert, Jean le Rond, *Oeuvres Philosophiques, Historiques et Littéraires de D'Alembert*, edited by J.F.Bastien, 18 vols. (Paris, 1805), including 'Lettres à D'Alembert sur Milord Maréchal', 5, pp.415–460.

———., *Éloge de milord Maréchal par m. D . . .* (Berlin, 1779).

Algarotti, Count F., *Lettres du Comte Algarotti sur la Russie . . . avec L'histoire de la guerre de 1735 contre les Turcs* (London, 1769).

Anon., '*Turetskaya voina pri imperatritse Anne: sovremennaya rukopis*', RA, 3 (1878), pp.255–274.

Anon., '*Prevratnosti sud'by . . .*', '*Vospominaniya polyaka na russkoi sluzhbe v tsarstvovaniyakh Anny Ioannovny: Yelizavety Petrovny: perevod iz neizdannoi rukopisi*', RA, 4 (1898), pp.479–508.

Anon., 'La cour de la Russia en 1761', taken from the library of Gr.Prince Konstantin Nikolaevich in Pavlovsk, author unknown, but notes in hand of La Fermière, secretary to Grand Prince Paul Petrovich, transl. from French), RA, 23 (1878), pp.187–206.

Arkhiv Knyazya F.A. Kurakina, 10 vols. (St.Petersburg, 1890–1901).

Arkhiv Knyazya Vorontsova, 40 vols. (Moscow, 1870–95).

Bell, J. *Travels from St Petersburg in Russia to Diverse Parts of Asia* (London, 1764).

Bruce, P.H., *Memoirs of Peter Henry Bruce, Esq. A Military Officer in the services of Prussia, Russia and Great Britain* (London, 1782).

Chance, J.F., ed., *British Diplomatic Instructions, 1689–1787*, Publications of the Royal Historical Society, Camden third series, 1 Sweden 1689–1727 (London, 1922), 3 Denmark (London, 1725), 5 Sweden 1727–1789 (London, 1728).

Cook, J., *Voyages and Travels through the Russian Empire, Tartary and part of the Kingdom of Persia*, 2 vols. (Edinburgh, 1770).

Cracraft, J., ed., *For God and Peter the Great: The Works of Thomas Consett, 1723–1729* (New York, 1982).

Dashwood, F., '*Sir Francis Dashwood's Diary of his Visit to St.Petersburg in 1733*', intr. and notes by B.Kemp, SEER, 38 (1959–60), pp.194–222.

Deane, J., *History of the Russian Fleet during the Reign of Peter the Great by a Contemporary Englishman* (1724), ed. by Vice-Admiral Cyprian A.G.Bridge, Navy Records Society 15 (London, 1899).

Elagin, S.I. & F.F.Veselago, *Materialy dlya istorii russkogo flota*, 17 vols. (St.Petersburg, 1865–1904).

Erskine, R., 'Letters and Documents relating to Robert Erskine, Physician to Peter the Great, Czar of Russia', ed. Rev. Robert Paul, Publications of the Scottish History Society, *Miscellany 2* (Edinburgh, 1904), pp.371–430.

Frederick II, *Politische Correspondenz Friedrichs des Grossen*, 39 vols. (Berlin, 1879–1925).

Geffroy, A., ed., *Recueil des Instructions Données aux Ambassadeurs et Ministres de France, depuis les Traités de Westphalie jusqu'à la Révolution française*, 4 Suède (Paris, 1885).

The Gentleman's Magazine (London, 1731–1758).

Gordon, A., *The History of Peter the Great, Emperor of Russia, to which is prefixed a short General Account of the Country, from the rise of that Monarchy, and an account of the Author's life, with a map of Russia, the heads of Czar Peter, Prince Menzikoff, and the Author, engraved from original paintings*, 2 vols. (Aberdeen, 1755).

Greig, J.Y.T., ed., 'Two Fragments of Autobiography', by George Keith, Earl Marischal, *Fifth Miscellany of the Scottish History Society*, 21, third series (Edinburgh, 1933), pp.359–374.

Historical Manuscripts Commission:

Report on the Muniments and other Family Papers belonging to the Right-Honourable William Buller Fullerton Elphinstone, Lord Elphinstone, Appendix to Ninth Report (London, 1883), pp.182–229.

——, *Reports on the Manuscripts of the Earl of Eglinton, Sir John Stirling-Maxwell, Bart., C.S.H. Drummond Moray, Esq. C.F.Weston Underwood Esq. & Sir Wingfield Digby Esq.* (London, 1885).

——, *Report on the Manuscripts of the Earl of Mar and Kellie* (London, 1904).

——, *The Manuscripts of the Earl of Mar and Kellie, suppl. report.* (London, 1930).

——, *Report on the Manuscripts of Lord Polwarth*, ed. by Rev. Henry Paton, 5 vols. (London, 1911–1961).

——, *Calendar of the Stuart Papers Belonging to His Majesty the King, Preserved at Windsor Castle*, 7 vols. (London, 1902–1923).

Hughan, W.J., ed., *The Jacobite Lodge at Rome, 1735–1737* (Torquay, 1910).

Johnstone, J., *Memoirs of the Chevalier de Johnstone*, ed. by C.Winchester, 3 vols. (Aberdeen, 1870–1871).

——, *A Memoir of the Forty Five*, ed. by B.Rawson (London, 1958).

Journals of the House of Commons

Journals of the House of Lords

Keith, J., *A Fragment of a memoir of Field-marshal James Keith. written by himself, 1714–1734*, (Berlin, 1789), reprint from original manuscript, Spalding Club (Edinburgh, 1843).

Ker, John of Kerseland, *The Memoirs of John Ker of Kersland, containing His Secret Transactions and Negotiations in Scotland, England, the Courts of Vienna, Hanover and other Foreign Parts* (London, 1726).

Korb, J.G., *Diary of a Secretary of Legation at the Court of Czar Peter the Great*, translated from original Latin and edited by Count MacDonnell, 2 vols. (London, 1863).

Lefort F., 'Unzufriedenheit mit dem Regiment der Ausländer', *SIRIO* 5, pp.464–465.

Legg, L.G.Wickham, *British Diplomatic Instructions*, Camden Society third series, 4 France 1721–1727 (London, 1727), 6 France 1727–1744 (London, 1730).

Liria, J.F., 'Zapiski diuka Liriiskago', *RA* I (1909), pp.337–429.

Liria, J.F., 'Pis'ma o Rossii v Ispaniyu Duka de Liria, in Bartenev, *Osmnadtsatyi vek istoricheskii sbornik* (Moscow, 1869), 2, pp.5–198, 3, pp.27–132.

The London Magazine: or Gentleman's monthly intelligencer, known as *Monthly Chronologer*, 1736–1746, vols. 1–52 (London, 1732–1783).

Manstein, C.H.von, *Memoirs of Russia, Historical, Political, and Military, from the Year MDCCXXVII to MDCCXLIV . . .*, translated from the original manuscript of General Manstein and edited by David Hume (London, 1770).

——, *Contemporary Memoirs of Russia from the Year 1727 to 1744 by General Christopher Hermann v. Manstein*, re-edited and compared with the original French by a Hertfordshire encumbent (London, 1856).

Milton, J., *A Brief History of Muscovia: and of other less known Countries lying eastward of Russia as far as Cathay* (London, 1682).

Mitchell, Sir A., *Memoirs and Papers of Sir Andrew Mitchell*, edited by Andrew Bisset, 2 vols. (London, 1850).

Münnich, B.K., *Vsepoddanneishiya Donoseniya Gr.Minnikha po spisku poruchika zapasa arm. kav. M.N.Prokopovicha*, pt.1 doneseniya 1736 i 1737 godov, ed. by Myshlaevskii, Moskovskoe otdelenie arkh. glav. Shtaba (St.Petersburg, 1897).

Murray of Broughton, John, *Memorials of John Murray of Broughton, 1740–1747*, edited with an introduction, notes and an appendix by R.F.Bell, Publications of the Scottish History Society (Edinburgh, 1898).

Nashchokin, V.A., 'Zapiski Vasiliia Aleksandrovicha Nashchokina, generala vremen elizavetinskhikh', *RA*, 2 (1883), pp.243–352.

Paton, Henry, ed., *The Lyon in Mourning or A Collection of Speeches, Letters, Journals etc. Relative to the Affairs of Prince Charles Edward Stuart by the Rev. Robert Forbes, A.M., Bishop of Ross and Caithness, 1746–1775*, Publications of the Scottish History Society, 20–22, 3 vols. (Edinburgh, 1895–6).

Perry, J., *The state of Russia under the Present Czar* (London, 1716).

Polnoe Sobranie Zakonov Rossiiskoi Imperii s 1649 goda, 1st series,46 vols. (St.Petersburg, 1825–1839).

Poze, J., 'Zapiski Pridvornago Brilyantchika Poze o Prebyvanii ego v Rossii s 1729 po 1764 g'., *RS* (1870) 1, 16–27, 77–103, 197–244.

Preis, J., 'Izvlechenie iz donesenii shvedskago kommisions-sekretara Preisa o prebyvanii Petra Velikago v Gollandii v 1716 i 1717 gg.', *ChIOMU*, 2 (1877), Book 4, 1–12.

Rae, P., *The History of the Rebellion, Rais'ed against His Majesty King George I. By the Friends of the Pretender . . .*, 2nd edn. (London, 1746).

Rambaud, A., ed., *Recueil des Instructions Données aux Ambassadeurs et Ministres de France, depuis les Traités de Westphalie jusqu'à la Révolution française,* 8 Russie (Paris 1890).

Rosebery, Earl of, ed., *A List of Person concerned in the Rebellion, transmitted to the Commissioners of Excise by the several supervisors in Scotland in obedience to a general letter of the 7th May, 1746 . . .*, Publications of the Scottish History Society, 8 (Edinburgh, 1890).

Sbornik Imperatorskogo Russkogo Istoricheskogo Obshchestva, 148 vols. (St.Petersburg, 1867–1916).

Seton, Sir Bruce Gordon, and Jean Gordon Arnot, eds., *The Prisoners of the '45, edited from the State Papers,* Publications of the Scottish History Society, third series, 13–15, 3 vols (Edinburgh, 1928–1929).

Shuvalov, I.I., 'Letters to Ivan Ivanovich Shuvalov', *SIRIO* 9, pp.444–522.

Sinclair, John, Master of, *Memoirs of the Insurrection in Scotland in 1715,* with notes by Sir W.Scott (Edinburgh, 1858).

Songhurst, W.J., ed., *The Minutes of the Grand Lodge of Freemasons of England, 1723–1739,* Masonic Reprints of the Quatuor Coronatorum Lodge 2076 (London, 1913).

Spilman, J., *A Journey through Russia into Persia by two English Gentlemen who went in the Year 1739 From Petersburg, in order to make a Discovery how the Trade from Great Britain might be carried on from Astracan over the Caspian,* Paper dedicated to Sir John Thompson, governor of The Russia Company (London, 1742).

The Scots Magazine, Containing a general view of the religion, politicks, entertainment etc. in Great Britain, 65 vols. (Edinburgh, 1739–1804).

Tayler, A. and H., ed., 'Letters of George, Tenth Earl Marischal', *Third Spalding Club Miscellany,* 1, pp.67–95.

Tayler, H., ed., *Jacobite Epilogue, A Further Selection of Letters from Jacobites among the Stuart Papers at Windsor* (Britain, 1941).

Vaucher, P., ed., *Recueil des Instructions Données aux Ambassadeurs et Ministres de France, depuis les Traités de Westphalie jusqu'à la Révolution française,* 25 Angleterre (Paris, 1965).

Weber, F.C., *The Present State of Russia* [by Friedrich Christian Weber], *with several other pieces relating to Russia* [by L.Lange and others], translated from High Dutch, 2 vols. (London, 1723).

Whitworth, Sir C., *An Account of Russia as it was in the Year 1710,* (Strawberry Hill, 1758).

Guides to Archival Sources

Grimsted, P.K., *A Handbook for Archival Research in the USSR,* (Princeton, 1989).

———, *Archives and Manuscript Repositories in the USSR: Moscow and Leningrad,* (Princeton, 1972).

Hartley, J.M., *The Study of Russian History from British Archival Sources,* (London, 1986).

———, *Guide to Documents and Manuscripts in the United Kingdom relating to Russia and the Soviet Union* (London, 1986).

McGowan, I.D., *Russian Material in the National Library of Scotland: a guide for readers* (Edinburgh, 1981).

Secondary Printed Sources

Aberg, A., 'Scottish Soldiers in the Swedish Armies in the Sixteenth and Seventeenth Centuries', in G.Simpson, ed., *Scotland and Scandinavia,* (Edinburgh, 1990), pp.90–99.

Alabin, P.B., 'Ivan Ivanovich Buturlin General-anshef, biograficheskii ocherk', *RA*, 23 (1878), pp.161–186.

Aldridge, D., 'Jacobitism and Scottish Seas', in T.C.Smout, ed., *Scotland and the Sea* (Edinburgh, 1992), pp.76–93.

Aleksandrenko, V.N., *Russkie Diplomaticheskie Agenty v Londone v XVIIIv.*, 2 vols. (Warsaw, 1897).

Allworth, E. *et al, Soviet Nationality Problems* (London, 1971).

Amburger, E., *Geschichte des Protestantismus in Russland* (Stuttgart, 1961).

———, *Geschichte der Behördenorganisation Russlands von Peter dem Grossen bis 1917* (Leyden, 1966).

———, 'Die weiteren Schicksäle der alten Einwohnerschaft der Moskauer Ausländer-Sloboda seit der Zeit Peters I', *JGO* NF 20 (1972), pp.412–426.

———, *Fremde und Einheimische in Wirtschafts und Kulturleben des Neuzeitlichen Russland* (Wiesbaden, 1982).

———, 'Die Zuckerindustrie in St Petersburg', *JGO* 38 (1986), pp.352–391.

Anderson, James, *The New Book of Constitutions of the Most Ancient and Honourable Fraternity of Free and Accepted Masons* (Dublin, 1951).

Anderson, M.S., 'Great Britain and the Growth of the Russian Navy in the Eighteenth Century', *Mariner's Mirror*, 42 (1956), pp.132–146.

Anderson, R.C., 'British and American Officers in the Russian Navy', *Mariner's Mirror*, 33 (1947), pp.17–27.

Anisimov, E.V., *Rossiya v seredine XVIII veka*, in *V borbe za vlast* (Moscow, 1988), pp.24–282.

———, *Vremya Petrovskikh reform* (Leningrad, 1989).

Appleby, J.H., 'British Doctors in Russia, 1657–1807', Ph.D.thesis, Univ. of East Anglia (1979).

———, 'Through the Looking Glass: Scottish Doctors in Russia 1704–1854', in National Library of Scotland Publications, *Caledonian Phalanx* (Edinburgh, 1987), pp.47–64.

———, 'James Spilman F.R.S. (1680–1763) and Anglo-Russian Commerce', *Notes and Records of the Royal Society of London*, 48, 1 (1994), pp.17–29.

Atlas Geographus: or, A compleat system of geography, ancient and modern, 5 vols. (London, 1711–1717).

Bantysh-Kamensky, D.N., *Biografii Rossiiskikh generalissimusov i general feldmarshalov*, 4 vols. (St.Petersburg, 1840–41).

———, *Reliatsii chrezvychainnago vo Frantsii posla knyazya Kantemira, 1738 i 1739 godov.* (St. Petersburg, 1873).

Bantysh-Kamensky, N.N., *Obzor vneshnykh snoshenii Rossii po 1800 god*, 4 vols. (Moscow, 1894–1902).

Barrow, J., *Memoir of the Life of Peter the Great*, 3rd edn. (London, 1839).

Barskov, Y.L., ed., *Perepiska moskovskikh masonov XVIIIgo veka* (Moscow, 1915).

Barsukov, A.P., *Spiski gorodovykh voevod i drugikh lits voevodskogo upravleniya Moskovskogo gosudarstva XVII stoletiya* (St.Petersburg, 1902).

Bartenev, P.I., ed., *Osmnadtsatyi vek: istoricheskii sbornik*, 4 vols. (Moscow, 1868–1869).

Bartlett, R.P., *Human Capital: The Settlement of Foreigners in Russia, 1762–1804* (Cambridge, 1979).

Baugh, D., *British Naval Administration in the Age of Walpole* (Princeton, 1965).

Behre, G., 'Gothenburg in Stuart War Strategy, 1649–1760', in G. Simpson, ed., *Scotland and Scandinavia* (Edinburgh, 1990), pp.107–118.

Bergand, J. & Bo Lagerkrantz, *Scots in Sweden* (Stockholm, 1962).

Berkh, V.N., *Zhizneopisaniya pervykh Rossiiskikh admiralov ili opyt istorii rossiiskogo flota*, 4 vols. (St.Petersburg, 1831–1836).

Beskrovny, L.G., 'Reforma armii i sozdanie voennomorskogo flota', in N.M.Druzhinin *et al,* eds., *Ocherki istorii SSSR, Period feodalizma, Rossiya v pervoi chetverti XVIIIv.* (Moscow, 1954).

———., 'Armiya i flot', in N.M.Druzhinin *et al,* eds., *Ocherki istorii SSSR, Period feodalizma, Rossiya vo vtoroi chetverti XVIIIv.* (Moscow, 1957), pp.296–309.

————, *Russkaya armiya i flot v XVIIIv.* (Moscow, 1958).

Black, J., 'Anglo-Russian Diplomatic Relations in the Eighteenth Century', *SGER*, 12 (1984).

————, 'Parliament and the Political and Diplomatic Crisis of 1717–18', *PH*, 3 (1984), pp.77–101.

————, 'The British Navy and British Foreign Policy in the First Half of the Eighteenth Century', in J.M.Black and K.W. Schweizer, eds., *Essays in European History in Honour of Ragnhild Hatton* (Lennoxville, Quebec, 1985), pp.137–155.

————, *British Foreign Policy in the Age of Walpole* (Edinburgh, 1985).

————, 'Russia's Rise as a European Power 1650–1750', *HT*, 36, 8, August (1986), pp.21–28.

————, *Natural and Necessary Enemies* (London, 1986).

————, *The Collapse of the Anglo-French Alliance, 1727–1731* (Gloucester, 1987).

————, and P.Woodfine, eds., *The British Navy and the Rise of Naval Power in the Eighteenth Century* (Leicester, 1988).

————, *Jacobitism and British Foreign Policy Under the First Two Georges*, Publications of the Royal Stuart Society, Royal Stuart Papers 32 (Huntingdon, 1988).

————, *Knights Errant and True Englishmen. British Foreign Policy, 1660–1800* (Edinburgh, 1989).

————, *Robert Walpole and the Nature of Politics in Early Eighteenth Century England* (London, 1990).

————, *Culloden and the '45* (New York, 1990).

Blaikie, W.B.,ed., *Itinerary of Prince Charles Edward Stuart*, Publications of the Scottish History Society (Edinburgh, 1897).

————, *Origins of the Forty-Five and other papers relating to that Rising*, Publications of the Scottish History Society, second series, 2 (Edinburgh, 1916).

Bogoyavlensky, S.K., 'Moskovskaya Nemetskaya sloboda', *IAN* SSSR Seriya istorii i filosofii, 4, 3 (1947), pp.220–232.

Bonner-Smith, D., 'The Authorship of "The Russian Fleet under Peter the Great"', *Mariner's Mirror*, 20 (1934), pp.373–376.

Bourgeois, E., *La Diplomatie Secrète au 18e. siècle*, 3 vols. (Paris, 1909).

Brockhaus-Efron, *Entsiklopedicheskii slovar*, ed. by I.E. Andreevskii, K.K. Arsenev, F.F.Petrushevsky, 43 vols. (St.Petersburg, 1890–1907).

Brown, K.M., 'From Scottish Lords to British Officers: State Building, Elite Integration and the Army in the Seventeenth Century', in N. MacDougall, ed., *Scotland and War* (Edinburgh, 1991), pp.133–169.

Browne, J., *A History of the Highlands and of the Highland Clans*, 4 vols. (Glasgow, 1835–1838).

Bruce, M.W., 'Jacobite Relations with Peter the Great', *SEER* 14 (1936), pp.343–362.

Bulloch, J.M., *The Gay Gordons. Some strange adventures of a famous Scots family*, (London, 1908).

Burke, J., *A Genealogical and Heraldic History of the Commoners of Great Britain and Ireland*, 4 vols. (London, 1833–1838).

Burton, J.H., *The Scot Abroad* (Edinburgh, 1881).

Carmichael, J., *The Cultural History of Russia* (London, 1968).

Carswell, J., *The South Sea Bubble* (London, 1909).

Cassels, L., 'The Czarina and her Advisers', in *The Struggle for the Ottoman Empire 1717–1740* (London, 1966), pp.29–43.

Chance, J.F., 'Northern Affairs in 1724', *EHR*, 27 (1912), pp.483–511.

————, *The Alliance of Hanover* (London, 1909).

————, *George I and the Northern War* (London, 1909).

————, 'George I and Peter the Great after the Peace of Nystad', *EHR*, 26 (1911), pp.278–309.

Charnock, J., *Biographia Navalis, or Impartial Memoirs of the Lives and Characters of Officers of the Navy of Great Britain, From the Year 1660 to the Present Time*, 6 vols (London, 1794–1798).

Childs, J., *Armies and Warfare in Europe, 1648–1789* (Manchester, 1982).

Christie, I., 'Samuel Bentham and the Russian Dnieper Flotilla, 1787–1788', *SEER* 50, 119 (1972), pp.173–197.

Clemow, F., 'Medicine Past and Present in Russia', supplement to *The Lancet* 7/8/1897, pp.343–374.

Clendenning, P., 'Admiral Sir Charles Knowles and the Russian Navy, 1771–1774, *Mariner's Mirror* 65, 1 (1975), pp.39–49.

———, and R.Bartlett, *Eighteenth Century Russia: A Select Bibliography of work published since 1955* (Newtonville, 1981).

Cobbett, W., *The Parliamentary History of England*, 36 vols. (London, 1806–1820).

Colley, L., *In Defiance of Oligarchy: The Tory Party, 1714–60* (Cambridge, 1982).

Collyer, A. D'Arcy, 'Notes on the Diplomatic Correspondence between England and Russia in the First Half of the Eighteenth Century', *Transactions of the Royal Historical Society, new series*, 14 (1900), pp.143–174.

Coxe, W., *Memoirs of the Life and Administration of Sir Robert Walpole, Earl of Orford, With Original Correspondence and Authentic Papers, Never Before Published*, 3 vols. (London, 1798).

———, *Memoirs of Horatio, Lord Walpole, Selected from His Correspondence and Papers and Connected with the History of the Times from 1678–1757* (London, 1802).

———, *Memoirs of the Kings of Spain of the House of Bourbon, 1700–1788* (London, 1813).

Cracraft, J., 'The Succession Crisis of 1730: A View from the Inside', *CASS*, 12, 1 (1978), pp.60–85.

Cromarty, Gillen et al., *Scots in Russia 1661–1934: Eleven Scots who Visited Russia from the Seventeenth to the Twentieth Centuries.*, Scotland's Cultural Heritage (Edinburgh, 1987).

Cross, A.G., 'John Rogerson, Physician to Catherine the Great', *CASS*, 4, 3 (1970), pp.594–601.

———, 'British Freemasons during the Reign of Catherine the Great', *OSP* N.S. 4 (1971), pp.43–62.

———, *Russia under Western Eyes, 1553–1815* (London, 1971).

———, 'Chaplains to the British Factory in St Petersburg, 1723–1813', *ESR*, 2 (1972), pp.125–142.

———, 'The Sutherland Affair and its Aftermath', *SEER*, 50, 119 (1972), pp.257–275.

———, 'The British in Catherine's Russia, a Preliminary Survey', in J.G. Garrard, ed., *The Eighteenth Century in Russia* (Oxford, 1973), pp.233–263.

———, 'Samuel Greig, Catherine II's Scottish Admiral', *MM*, 60, 3 (1974), pp.251–265.

———, ed., *Anglo-Russian Relations in the Eighteenth Century*, catalogue of an exhibition 5–9 July 1977 (University of East Anglia, 1977).

———., *Great Britain and Russia in the Eighteenth Century: Contacts and Comparisons* (Newtonville, 1979).

———, 'The Drummond Hoax' *SGER*, 7 (1979), pp.9–11.

———, 'Scoto-Russian Contacts in the Reign of Catherine the Great', in Publications of the National Library of Scotland, *Caledonian Phalanx* (Edinburgh, 1987), pp.24–46.

———, *Anglo-Russica: Aspects of Cultural Relations between Great Britain and Russia in the Eighteenth and Early Nineteenth Centuries* (Oxford, 1993).

Crowther, P.A., *A Bibliography of Works on Russian History to 1800* (Oxford, 1969).

Cruickshanks, E., *Political Untouchables: the Tories and the '45* (London, 1979).

———, 'Lord Cornbury, Bolingbroke and a Plan to Restore the Stuarts, 1731–1735', *RSP*, 27 (1986).

———, ed., *Ideology and Conspiracy: Aspects of Jacobitism, 1689–1759* (Edinburgh, 1982).

———, and J.Black, eds., *The Jacobite Challenge* (Edinburgh, 1988).

Crummey, R., 'Russian Absolutism and the Nobility', *JMH*, 49, 3 (1977), pp.456–68.

Cuthell, E., *The Scottish Friend of Frederick the Great: The Last Earl Marischall*, 2 vols (London, 1915).

Danielson, J.R., *Die Nördische Frage in den Jahren 1746–1751 Mit einer Darstellung Russisch-Schwedisch-Finnische Beziehungen, 1740–1743* (Helsingfors, 1888).

Danilevsky, H.Ya, *Rossiya i Evropa*, 4th edn. (St.Petersburg, 1889).

Dickson, W.K., *The Jacobite Attempt of 1719*, Publications of the Scottish History Society, 19 (Edinburgh, 1895).

le Donne, J.P., 'Ruling Families in the Russian Political Order, 1689–1725', *CMRS*, 28 (1987), pp.233–322.

Donnert, E., *Russia in the Age of Enlightenment* (Leipzig, 1986).

Douglas, Sir Robert, *The Peerage of Scotland, containing an historical and genealogical account of the nobility of that kingdom* (Edinburgh, 1764).

————, *The Baronage of Scotland, containing an historical and genealogical account of the gentry of that kingdom*, (Edinburgh, 1798).

Druzhinin, N.M. *et al*, eds., *Ocherki istorii SSSR period feodalizma, Rossiia vo vtoroi chetverti XVIIIv.* (Moscow, 1957).

Duffy, C., *Russia's Military Way to the West: Origins and Nature of Russian Military Power, 1700–1800* (London, 1981).

————., *The Wild Goose and the Eagle: A Life of Marshal von Browne ,1705–1757* (London, 1964).

Dukes, P. and J.W.Barnhill, 'North-east Scots in Muscovy in the seventeenth century', *Northern Scotland*, 1 (Dec.,1972), pp.49–63.

————, comp. and ed., 'V.N. Tatishchev: "The Voluntary and Agreed Dissertation of the Assembled Russian Nobility about the State Government, c. 1730"', in *Russia under Catherine the Great*, 1 (Newtonville, Mass., 1978).

————, and B.Meehan-Waters, 'A Neglected Account of the Succession Crisis of 1730: James Keith's Memoir', *CASS*, 12, 1 (1978), pp.170–182.

————., 'Some Aberdonian Influences on the Early Russian Enlightenment', *CASS*, 13, no.4 (Winter 1979), pp.437–439.

————, *The Making of Russian Absolutism, 1613–1801* (New York, 1982).

————, 'How the Eighteenth Century Began for Russia and the West', in A.G.Cross, ed., *Russia and the West in the Eighteenth Century, SGER* 1981 (Mass., 1983), pp.2–19.

————, 'Peter the Great and Freemasonry', *SGER*, 10 (1982), pp.71–72.

————, 'Scottish Soldiers in Muscovy', in Publications of the National Library of Scotland, *Caledonian Phalanx* (Edinburgh, 1987), pp.9–23.

Egan, D.R., and M.A. Egan, *Russian Autocrats from Ivan the Great to the Fall of the Romanov Dynasty: An Annotated Bibliography of English Language Sources to 1985* (London, 1987).

Fedosov, D., *The Caledonian Connection: Scotland – Russia Ties, Middle Ages to early Twentieth Century, A concise biographical list* (University of Aberdeen, 1996).

Fischer, T.A., *The Scots in Germany* (Edinburgh, 1902).

————, *The Scots in East and West Prussia* (Edinburgh, 1903).

————, *The Scots in Sweden* (Edinburgh, 1907).

Florinsky, M.T., *Russia: A History and an Interpretation*, 2 vols. (New York, 1955).

Forfar, J., 'The Czarina Elizabeth', *GM*, 250 (May, 1881), pp.598–614.

Formey, J.H.S., *A Discourse on the Death of Marshal Keith*, transl. from original French (Edinburgh, 1764).

Fraser, Sir William., *The Stirlings of Keir and their Family Papers* (Edinburgh, 1858).

————, *The Douglas Book* (Edinburgh, 1885).

————, *The Sutherland Book* 1 (Edinburgh, 1892).

Fritz, P., 'The Anti-Jacobite Intelligence System of the English Ministers, 1715–1745', *HJ*, 16, 2 (1973), pp.265–289.

————, *The English Ministers and Jacobitism between the Rebellions of 1715 and 1745* (Toronto, 1975).

Garrard, J., *The Eighteenth Century in Russia* (Oxford, 1973).

Goldberg, J., 'Poles and Jews in the 17th and 18th Centuries, Rejection or Acceptance', *JGO*, 22 (1974), pp.248–282.

Golikov, I.I., *Deiyaniya Petra Velikago mudrago preobrazitelya Rossii*, 2nd edn., 15 vols. (Moscow, 1837–1843).

Goltsev, V.A., *Zakonodatelstvo i nravy v Rossii XVIII veka* (St.Petersburg, 1886).

Goltsyn, N.N., *Ukazatel imen lichnykh upominaemykh v dvortsovykh razryadakh* (St.Petersburg,?).

Gould, R.F., *Military Lodges. The Apron and the Sword or Freemasonry under Arms* (London, 1899).

Grant, J., *The Scottish Soldiers of Fortune* (London, 1889 [1888]).

——, ed., *The Old Scots Navy from 1689–1711*, NRS, 44 (London, 1914).

Grasshoff, H., *A.D.Kantemir und Westeuropa* (Berlin, 1966).

Gregg, E., *Jacobitism* (London, 1988).

Gribovsky, V.M., *Pamyatniki Russkogo zakonodatelstva*, 1 Epokha Petrovskaya (1907).

Hans, N., 'Henry Farquharson, Pioneer of Russian Education, 1690–1739', *AUR*, 38 (1959–60), pp.27–29.

Hassel, J., 'Implementation of the Russian Table of Ranks during the Eighteenth Century', *SR*, 29 (1970), pp.283–295.

Hatton, R., *Diplomatic Relations between Great Britain and the Dutch Republic, 1714–1721* (London, 1950).

——., ed., *Captain James Jeffreyes' letters to the Secretary of State, Whitehall, from the Swedish Army, 1707–1709*, Historiska Handlingar Del 35:1 (Stockholm, 1954).

——, *George I: Elector and King* (London, 1978).

Hayes, R., *Biographical Dictionary of Irishmen in France* (Dublin, 1949).

Hayes-McCoy, G.A., ed., 'Ireland and the Russian Navy', in *The Irish Sword*, 2 (Dublin, 1954–6), pp.229–230.

Hellie, R., *Enserfment and Military Change in Muscovy* (Chicago, 1971).

——, 'The Petrine Army: Continuity, Change and Impact', *CASS*, 8 (1974), pp.237–253.

Henderson, A., *Memoirs of the life and actions of James Keith, Field-Marshal in the Prussian armies* (London, [1757]).

Herd, G.P., 'General Patrick Gordon of Auchleuchries – A Scot in Seventeenth Century Russian Service', Unpubl. Ph.D. thesis (Aberdeen University, 1994).

Hervey, Lord John, *Memoirs of the Reign of George the Second*, 2 vols. (London, 1848).

Hill, B.W., *Sir Robert Walpole* (London, 1989).

Horn, D.B., *The British Diplomatic Service, 1689–1789* (Oxford, 1961).

——, ed., *British Diplomatic Representatives, 1689–1789*, Camden Society, third Series, 46 (London, 1932).

Hughes, L., *Russia in the Age of Peter the Great* (New Haven and London, 1998).

Insh, G.P., *The Scottish Jacobite Movement* (Edinburgh, 1952).

Jacob, Ilse, *Beziehungen Englands zu Russland und zur Türkei in den Jahren 1718–1727* (Basel, 1945).

Jones, G.H., *The Mainstream of Jacobitism* (Cambridge, Mass., 1954).

Jordan, J., 'John Delap: An Irish Seaman in Russia', *The Irish Sword*, 2 (Dublin, 1954–6), pp.54–56.

Kappeler, A., *Russlands Erste Nationalitäten: Das Zarenreich und die Völker der Mittleren Wolga vom 16 bis 19 Jahrhundert*, BGO, 14 (Köln, 1982).

Keep, J.L.H., 'The Secret Chancellery, the Guards and the Dynastic Crisis of 1740–1741', *FOG*, 26 (1978), pp.169–93.

——, 'From the Pistol to the Pen: The Military Memoir as a Source on the Social History of Pre-Reform Russia', *CMRS*, 21 (1980), pp.295–320.

——, *Soldiers of the Tsar: Army and Society in Russia, 1462–1874* (Oxford, 1985).

Kemp, P., ed., *History of the Royal Navy* (London, 1969).

Klier, J., 'The Ambiguous Status of Russian Jewry in the Reign of Catherine II', *SR*, 35 (1976), pp.504–517.

Klyuchevsky, V.O., *Sochineniya*, 8 vols. (Moscow, 1956–58).

Kohn, H., *The Idea of Nationalism* (New York, 1956).

Komarov, A.A., 'Razvitie takticheskoi mysli v russkoi armii v 60kh-90kh gg. XVIII v ', *VMU*, series 8, 3 (1982), pp.57–66.

Korsakov, D.A., *Votsarenie Anny Ioannovny* (Kazan, 1880).

Kotasek, E., *Feld Marschall Graf Lacy: Ein Leben für Österreichs Heer* (Horn, N.Österreich, 1956).

Krotov, P.A., 'Sozdanie lineinogo flota na Baltike pri Petre I', *istoricheskie Zapiski* 116 (Moscow, 1988), pp.313–331.

———, 'Stroitelstvo Baltiiskogo flota v pervoi chetverti XVIII veka', avtoreferat dissertatsii na soiskanie uchenoi stepeni kandidata istoricheskikh nauk (Leningrad, 1987).

Lang, A., *Pickle the Spy or the Incognito of Prince Charles* (London, 1897).

———, *The Companions of Pickle* (London, 1898).

Latkin, V.N., *Zakonodatelnaya kommisiya v Rossii v XVIIIv.* (St.Petersburg, 1887).

Lecky, W.E.H., *The History of Ireland in the XVIII Century*, 4 vols. (London, 1896).

Lenman, B., *The Jacobite Risings in Britain, 1689–1746* (London, 1980).

———, *The Jacobite Clans of the Great Glen* (London, 1984).

———, *The Jacobite Cause* (Glasgow, 1986).

———, and John. S. Gibson, *Rebellion and Conspiracy, 1688–1759: England, Ireland, Scotland and France* (Edinburgh, 1990).

Lipski, A., 'The "Dark Era" of Anna Ivanovna: a Re-examination', *ASEER*, 15 (1956), pp.477–488.

———, 'Some Aspects of Russia's Westernisation During the Reign of Anna Ivanovna, 1730–1740', *ASEER*, 18 (1959), pp.1–11.

Lodge, R., 'The Treaty of Abo and the Swedish Succession', *EHR*, 43 (1928), pp.540–571.

———, 'The First Anglo-Russian Treaty, 1739–1742', *EHR* 43, pp.354–372.

———, 'Russia, Prussia and Great Britain, 1742–1744', *EHR*, 45 (1930), pp.579–611.

———, 'Lord Hyndford's Embassy to Russia', *EHR*, 46 (1931), pp.48–76, 389–422.

Longinov, M., 'Russkii generalitet v nachale 1730 goda po spisku P.F.Karabanov', in Bartenev, *Osmnadtsatyi vek, istoricheskii sbornik*, 3 (Moscow, 1869), pp.161–177.

Longworth, P., *The Three Empresses: Catherine I, Anne and Elizabeth of Russia* (London, 1972).

Löwe, H-D., 'Nationalismus und Nationalitätenpolitik als Integrationsstrategie im zarischen Russland', in *Die Russen - Ihr Nationalbewusstsein in Geschichte und Gegenwart* (Köln, 1990), pp.55–79.

MacDougall, N., ed., *Scotland and War AD 79–1918* (Edinburgh, 1991).

MacKintosh, J., *Historic Earls and Earldoms of Scotland* (Aberdeen, 1898).

Maclean, N.N., *Memoir of Marshal Keith, with a sketch of the Keith family* (Peterhead, 1869).

McLynn, F., *France and the Jacobite Rising of 1745* (Edinburgh, 1981).

———, 'Issues and Motives in the Jacobite Rising of 1745', *The Eighteenth Century*, 23 (1982), pp.897–133.

———, *The Jacobites* (Edinburgh, 1985).

———, *Bonnie Prince Charlie, Charles Edward Stuart* (Oxford, 1991).

MacLysaght, F., *A Short Study of a Transplanted Family in the Seventeenth Century* (Dublin, 1935).

MacMillan, D.S., 'The Russia Company of London in the Eighteenth Century: the effective survival of a "Regulated" Chartered Company', *The Guildhall Miscellany*, 4 (1973), pp.222–236.

de Madariaga, I., *Russia in the Age of Catherine the Great* (London, 1981).

Maikov, L.N., *Materialy dlya biotrafii kn. A.D.Kantemira* (St Petersburg, 1903).

Marriott. J.A.R., *Anglo-Russian Relations, 1689–1943* (London, 1944).

Mediger, W., *Moskaus Weg nach Europa* (Brunswick, 1952).

———, *Mecklenburg Russland und Russland-Hanover, 1706–1721* (Hildesheim. 1967),

Meehan-Waters, B., *Autocracy and Aristocracy, The Russian Service Elite of 1730* (New Brunswick, N.J., 1982).

Menning, B.W., 'The Emergence of a Military-Administrative Elite in the Don-Cossack Land, 1708–1836', in Pintner and Rowney, eds., *Russian Officialdom*, pp.130–161.
Merritt, A.K., *The Keith Book* (Minnesota, 1934).
Milyukin, A.S., *Priezd inostrantsev v Moskovskoe gosudarstvo* (Moscow).
Mitchison, R., ed., *The Roots of Nationalism: Studies in Northern Europe* (Edinburgh, 1980).
Mottley, J., *The History of the Life of Peter the First, Emperor of Russia*, 3 vols., 2nd edn. (London, 1740).
——, *The Life and Reign of the Empress Catharine* (London, 1744).
Müller, Michael G., 'Russland und der Siebenjährige Krieg', *JGO* NF 28 (1980), pp.198–219.
Munro, R.W., *Kinsmen and Clansmen* (London, 1971).
Murray, D., *The York Buildings Company* (Edinburgh, 1883, repr. 1973).
Myshlaevsky, A.Z., *Ofitserskii vopros v XVII veke: Ocherki iz istorii voennogo dela v Rossii* (St.Petersburg, 1899).
National Library of Scotland, *The Caledonian Phalanx: Scots in Russia* (Edinburgh, 1987).
National Maritime Museum, *The Commissioned Sea Officers of the Royal Navy, 1660–1815* (London, 1954).
Nerwood, H.W., comp., *To Russia and Return: An Annotated Bibliography of Travelers' English Language Accounts of Russia from the Ninth Century to the Present* (Ohio, 1968).
Nikoforov, L.A., *Russko-angliiskie otnosheniya pri Petre I* (Moscow, 1950).
Nikol'ski, N.M., *Istoriya Russkoi tserkvi* (Moscow, 1988).
Noble, P.S., 'Soldiers of the North-East', in *The Book of Buchan*, ed. by J.F.Tocher (Aberdeen, 1943), pp.167–189.
Nolte, H.H., *Religiöse Toleranz in Russland, 1600–1725*, Göttinger Philosophische Dissertation, 41 (Göttingen, 1969).
——, 'Verständnis und Bedeutung der religiösen Toleranz in Russland, 1600–1725', *JGO* NF 17,3 (1969), pp.494–530.
Nordmann, C., *La Crise du Nord au début du XVIIIe siècle* (Paris, 1956).
——, 'Louis XIV and the Jacobites', in Ragnhild Hatton, ed., *Louis XIV and Europe* (London, 1976), pp.82–114.
Novikov, N.V. ed., *Boevaya letopis' russkogo flota. Khronika vazhneishikh sobytii voennoi istorii russkogo flota s IX v. po 1917 g.* comp. V.O.Egorov, V.A.Divin *et al* (Moscow, 1948).
O'Callaghan, J.C., *History of the Irish Brigades in the Service of France* (Dublin, 1854).
Paton, N. *The Jacobites, their Roots, Rebellions and Links with Freemasonry*, Sea-Green Ribbon Publications (Fareham, Hampshire, 1994).
Paul, Sir J.B., ed., *The Scots Peerage, Founded on Wood's edition of Sir Robert Douglas's Peerage of Scotland*, 9 vols. (Edinburgh, 1904–14).
Petrie, Sir Charles, 'The Elibank Plot, 1752–3', *Transactions of the Royal Historical Society*, fourth series, 14 (1931), pp.175–196.
——, *The Jacobite Movement: The First Phase, 1688–1716* (London, 1948).
——, *The Jacobite Movement: The Last Phase, 1716–1807* (London, 1950).
——, *The Duke of Berwick and his Son, selected from the private papers of The Tenth Duke of Berwick and 17th Duke of Alba* (London, 1951).
Pintner, W.M., 'Russia as a Great Power, 1709–1856: Reflections on the Problem of Relative Backwardness, with Special Reference to the Russian Army and Russian Society', in *Kennan Institute for Advanced Russian Studies Occasional Paper* no.33 (Washington, 1978).
——, and D. Rowney, eds., *Russian Officialdom from the Seventeenth to the Twentieth Century* (Chapel Hill, N.Carolina, 1980).
——, 'The Eighteenth-Century Military: What Kind of Costs', *SGER*, 10 (1982), pp.9–10.
——, 'Russian Military Style, Russian Society, and Russian Power in the Eighteenth Century', in Cross (ed.), *Russia and the West in the Eighteenth Century*, SGER 1981 (Mass., 1983).
Platonov, S.F., *Moskva i Zapad* (Berlin, 1926).

————, *Leksii po russkoi istorii* (st Petersburg, 1901).
Pushkarev, S.G., *Rol' Pravoslavnoi tserkvi v istorii Rossii* (New York, 1985).
Pypin, A.N., *Russkoe masonstvo XVIII i pervaya chetvert XIXv.*, ed. by G.V.Vernadsky (Petrograd, 1916).
Rabinovich, M.D., 'Sotsialnoe proiskhozhdenie i imushchestvennoe polozhenie ofitserov reguliarnoi russkoi armii v kontse Severnoi voiny', in Pavlenko, ed., *Rossiya v period reform Petra I* (Moscow, 1973), pp.133–171.
Raeff, M., 'Patterns of Russian Imperial Policy Toward the Nationalities', in E. Allworth, ed., *Soviet Nationality Problems* (London, 1971), pp.22–42.
————, 'The Well-Ordered Police State and the Development of Modernity in Seventeenth and Eighteenth Century Europe: An Attempt at a Comparative Approach', *AHR*, 80, 5 (1975), pp.1221–1244.
Ransel, D., 'The "Memoirs" of Count Münnich', *SR*, 30, 4 (1941), pp.843–852.
Reading, D.K., *The Anglo-Russian Commercial Treaty of 1734* (New Haven, Conn., 1938).
Rice, T.T., *Elizabeth, Empress of Russia* (London, 1970).
Rogger, H., *National Consciousness in Eighteenth Century Russia* (Cambridge, Mass., 1960).
Rolt, R., *Memoirs of the life of . . . John Lindesay, earl of Crawfurd and Lindesay* (London, 1753).
Romanovich-Slavatinsky, A.V., *Dvorianstvo v Rossii ot nachala XVIII veka do otmeny krepostnogo prava* (St.Petersburg, 1870).
Russkii biograficheskii slovar, edited by A.A.Polovtsov, 25 vols. (St,Petersburg, 1896–1918).
Ruvigny and Raineval, Marquis of, *The Jacobite Peerage, Baronetage, Knightage and Grants of Honour* (Edinburgh, 1904).
Rzhevsky, S.M., 'O Russkoi armii vo vtoroi polovine yekaterinskogo tsarstvovaniya . . .', *RA*, 3 (1879), pp.357–62.
Schuyler, E., *Peter the Great, Emperor of Russia*. 2. vols. (London, 1884).
Scouller, R.E., *The Armies of Queen Anne* (Oxford, 1966).
Sedgewick, Romney, ed., *The History of Parliament: The House of Commons, 1715–54*, 2 vols. (London, 1970).
Simpson, G., ed., *The Scottish Soldier Abroad, 1247–1967*, The Mackie Monographs 2 (Edinburgh, 1992).
Slitsan, B.G., 'Organy gosudarstvennogo upravleniya', in Druzhinin *et al* eds., *Ocherki istorii SSSR period feodalizma, Rossiya vo vtoroi chetverti XVIIIv.* (Moscow, 1954), pp.269–296.
Smith, R.W.Innes, 'Dr. James Mounsey of Rammerscales', *Edinburgh Medical Journal* (May, 1926), pp.274–279.
Solov'ev, S.M., *Istoriya Rossii s drevnieshikh vremen*, 3rd edn., 29 vols. and index in 6 books (St Petersburg, Obshchestvennaya pol'za, 1911).
Steuart, A.F., *Scottish Influences in Russian History from the End of the Sixteenth to the Beginning of the Nineteenth Century* (Glasgow, 1913).
————, 'Sweden and the Jacobites, 1719–1720', *SHR*, 23 (1927), pp.119–127.
Stevens, L., and S.Lee, *The Dictionary of National Biography*, 63 vols. (London, 1885–1900).
Stevenson, D., *The First Freemasons: Scotland's Early Lodges and their Members* (Aberdeen, 1988).
————, *The Origins of Freemasonry, Scotland's Century, 1590–1710* (Cambridge, 1988).
Storch, H., *Tableau Historique et Statistique de l'Empire de Russie*, 1 (St.Petersburg, 1802).
Sumner, B.H., *Survey of Russian History* (London, 1944).
————, *Peter the Great and the Emergence of Russia* (London, 1951).
Tayler, A. and H., *Jacobites of Aberdeenshire and Banffshire in the Forty Five* (Aberdeen, 1928).
————, A., *The Jacobite Cess Roll for the County of Aberdeen* (Aberdeen, 1932).
————, A., *1715: The Story of the Rising* (London, 1936).
————, A. and H., *Jacobites of Aberdeenshire and Banffshire in the Rising of 1715* (Edinburgh, 1934).

———, H.,   *The Jacobite Court at Rome in 1719* (Edinburgh, 1938).

———, H.,   *A Jacobite Miscellany* (Edinburgh, 1938).

———, A. and H.,   *1745 and After* (London, 1938).

———, A. and H.,   *The Stuart Papers at Windsor* (London, 1939).

———, H.,   *Jacobite Epilogue* (Edinburgh, 1941).

———, A. and H.,   'The Jacobites of Buchan' in,   *The Book of Buchan* ed. by J.F.Tocher (Aberdeen, 1943), pp.269–280.

———, H.,   *The History of the Family of Urquhart* (Aberdeen, 1946).

Telepneff, B., 'Freemasonry in Russia', in W.J.Songhurst, ed., *Ars Quatuor Coronatorum,* 35 (1922), pp.261–291.

Terry, C. Sanford, *The Chevalier de St George and the Jacobite Movements in his Favour, 1701–1720* (London, 1901).

Troitskii, S.M., *Russkii absolyutizm i dvorianstvo XVIIIv: formirovanie byurokratii* (Moscow, 1974).

Ustryalov, N., *Russkaya Istoriya,* 5 vols. (1840).

Varnhagen von Ense, K.A., 'Feldmarshall Jakob Keith', *Biographische Denkmäle,* 3rd edn., 7th part (Leipzig, 1888).

Vaucher, P., *Walpole et la Politique de Fleury, 1731–1742* (Paris, 1924).

Veliko, K.I. *et al,* eds., *Voennaya entsiklopediya* (St.Petersburg, 1912).

Vernadsky, G.V., *et al,* eds., *A Source Book of Russian History from Early Times to 1917,* 3 vols. (New Haven and London, 1972)

Veselago, F.F., *Spisok russkikh voennykh sudov s 1668 po 1860 god* (St.Petersburg, 1872).

———, comp., *Opisanie del arkhiva Morskogo Ministerstva za vremya s poloviny XVII do nachala XIX stoletiya,* 11 vols. (St.Petersburg, 1880–1906).

Waliszewskii, K., *La Dernière des Romanov: Elisabeth 1re, Impératrice de Russie* (Paris, 1902).

———, *L'Heritage de Pierre le Grand, 1725–1741* (Paris, 1911).

———, *Pierre le Grand* (Paris, 1914).

Walton, Col. C.,   *The British Standing Army, AD 1660–1700* (London, 1894).

Williams, B., 'The Foreign Policy of Britain under Walpole', *EHR* 16 (1901).

———, *Stanhope* (Oxford, 1932).

Wilson, J.B., 'Three Scots in the Service of the Czar', *The Practitioner,* 210 (1973), April pp.569–574, May pp.704–708.

Wilson, R.T., *Brief Remarks on the Character and Composition of the Russian Army* (London, 1810).

Wood, S., *The Scottish Soldier* (Manchester, 1987).

Yanov, A., 'The Drama of the Time of Troubles', *CASS,* 12, 1 (1978), pp.1–59.

Yazykov, *Prebyvanie Petra Velikago v Sardame i Amsterdame v 1697 i 1717 godakh* (Berlin, 1872).

Zaionchevsky, P.A., ed., *Istoriya dorevoliutsionnoi Rossii v dnevnikakh i vospominaniyakh,* 1, XV-XVIII veka (Moscow, 1976).

Index

Aland Islands, peace congress 56, 57
Alberoni, Cardinal, Spanish minister in
   France 57
Alliance of Hanover 108, 116, 121
Alliance of Seville 140
Anglo-French alliance 90
Anglo-Russian relations 3, 21, 41, 50,
   144
Anna Ivanovna, correspondence on
   Kintore Estate 159
Anna Ivanovna, Empress of Russia,
   1730–40 4, 14, 139, 140, 143, 155,
   156, 170, 175, 176, 186, 194, 195,
   201
Anna Leopoldovna, of Braunschweig-
   Lunebourg 204, 205
Anne, Queen of Great Britain 39
Anti-British sentiment 105
Anton, Ulrich, Prince, of Braunschweig-
   Lunebourg 204
Apraksin, Admiral 36, 51, 53, 100, 102
Atterbury Plot, 1721–22 69, 71
Atterbury, Francis, Bishop of Rochester
   70, 75, 121, 183
Augustus II, King of Poland 145, 189
Augustus, Elector of Saxony 189
Azov, siege of 193, 194

Balmerino, James Elphinstone, 5th Lord
   31
Barrow, Mr. 182
Bassewitz, Holstein minister to Russia
   110
Beretti Landi, Marquis de, Spanish
   ambassador at the Hague 60, 66
Bernstorff, Baron Andreas Gottlieb von
   41
Bestuzhev-Riumin, Alexei Petrovich 212,
   217, 218, 220, 225
Bestuzhev-Riumin, Mikhail, Russian
   ambassador to Great Britain 69
Binnings, Alexander 179

Biron, Count, Duke of Courland 154,
   165, 173, 204
Bolingbroke, Henry St John, Viscount
   145
Bourbon, Louis Henri, Duke of 87, 89
Bredal, Vice Admiral 168, 193
Bret, Colonel 184
Britain, alliance with Prussia and
   Sweden, 1719
British Factory in St. Petersburg 100
British navy 23, 27, 109, 122; pay 27;
   Peter I's admiration for 27, 29;
   poor state of 201
British squadron 121, 129
Brown, George 15, 22, 31, 168, 187, 194,
   209, 232
Brown, Richard 102
Brown, shipbuilder 35
Bruce, Alexander 187
Bruce, James Daniel (Jakob Wilimovich)
   15, 16
Bruce, Peter Henry 9, 10, 11, 13, 33, 54
Bruce, Robert 15
Bruce, Thomas 23
Bruces of Clackmannan 54

Calendar, Gregorian xiii
Calendar, Julian xiii
Cameron, John, of Lochiel 146, 217
Campbell, of Glendarule 21
Campredon, Jacques, French minister to
   Russia 17, 72, 78, 81, 90, 97, 111,
   113
Carse, Mark (also Kerse) 133, 183
Carteret, John, 1st Earl Granville 77, 84,
   89, 91
Catherine I, Empress of Russia, 1725–
   1727 97, 116, 118, 120, 121
Catherine II, Empress of Russia, 1762–
   1796 232
Charles I, King of Great Britain 38
Charles II, King of Great Britain 38

Charles VI, Emperor of Austria 135, 192

Charles VI, Holy Roman Emperor 201

Charles XII, King of Sweden 59, 60, 61, 62

Charles Edward Stuart, Prince (Young Pretender) *see* Stuart

Chavigny, French Minister Plenipotentiary to Great Britain 145

Cherkassky, Prince 137

Clark, Father, confessor to Philip V of Spain 130

Consett, Thomas 15, 78, 103

Cook, David 55

Cook, John, physician 8, 10, 16, 182, 194

Cooper, William 17, 26, 32, 55

Cousins, Richard, shipbuilder 35

Crawfurd, Thomas 50

Cronstadt 7

Culloden, battle of 203

Cumming, Alexander, son of Sir Alexander Cumming of Culter 182

Cumming, Daniel 232

Cunningham, Thomas 179

Danzig, surrender of 190

Dashwood, Francis 7, 13, 14

De la Vie, French envoy in Russia 49, 50, 58, 105

Deane, John 10, 13, 29, 35, 37, 51

Deane, John, mission to St. Petersburg 101, 102, 106, 112

Dillon, Arthur 45

Dillon, General 70, 71, 73, 75, 79, 80, 89

Dolgoruky, Prince Ivan 57, 131, 133

Dolgoruky, Prince Vasilii, Russian ambassador to France 74, 79, 80, 81, 82, 83, 84, 85, 102, 107, 133, 164, 172

Don Carlos, Prince 136

Douglas, Gustav Otto 173, 185, 232

Douglas, Major General 36, 188

Douglas, Count Walmer 206

Drummond, John of Blairdrummond 180

Drummond, Major 231

Drummond, William of Balhaldie 208

Dubois, Guillaume, Cardinal 84, 85, 86

Duffus, Kenneth Sutherland, 3rd Lord 22, 56, 114, 147, 170, 187

Eccles, Hugh 185

Elibank Plot, 1751–52 231

Elisabeth Petrovna, Empress of Russia, 1741–61 14, 207, 211, 212

English merchants 38

Erskine, Charles 48, 50

Erskine, John, of Alva 44, 45, 50

Erskine, Robert, physician 16, 22, 41, 42, 43, 44, 45, 46, 47, 48, 49, 50, 51, 52, 53, 54, 56, 58, 61, 62; recruitment of Jacobites 35

Erskine, William 48

Excise Crisis, 1733 145

Farquharson, Henry 16

Ferguson, James 55

Finch, Edward, British ambassador to Russia 159, 161, 211

First Family Compact (France and Spain), 1733 144

Fleury, André Hercule de, Cardinal 89, 151, 153, 154, 209, 210

Foreigners in Russia 15, 211, 212

Frederick II, King of Prussia 202, 222

Frederick Wilhelm I, King of Prussia 98, 201

Fullarton, Robert, son of Laird of Dudwick 22, 31, 184, 187, 196, 231

Geddes, Alexander 34, 35, 52

Geddes, William 185

George 1, King of Great Britain, Elector of Hanover 3, 22, 39, 41, 42, 46, 47, 49, 51, 90, 93, 97, 119, 121, 122, 137, 156

George II, King of Great Britain, Elector of Hanover 129, 152, 155, 156, 158, 159, 225

German Quarter (nemetskaya sloboda), Moscow 11, 12

Gibraltar, siege of 123, 130

Golitsyn, Field Marshal 165, 172

Golitsyn, Prince 119, 134

Golitsyn, Senator 102

Golovkin, Alexander Gavrilovich,
Russian Minister Plenipotentiary to
Netherlands 175
Golovkin, Count Nikolai, 104, 109, 114,
133, 168, 186
Golovkin, President of the College of
Foreign Affairs 102
Gordon, Alexander, of Auchintoul 9, 22,
38, 43
Gordon, Alexander, son of John Gordon
of Glenbucket 181, 186, 207
Gordon, Ann, daughter of Thomas
Gordon 15
Gordon, Cosmo George, 3rd Duke of
181
Gordon, John, of Glenbucket 181, 184
Gordon, General Patrick of
Auchleuchries 3, 9, 12, 38
Gordon, Theodore 187
Gordon, Thomas, 50, 52, 54, 55, 56, 58,
59, 72, 73, 75, 79, 83, 84, 85, 87, 98,
99, 103, 107, 113, 132, 133, 138,
139, 143, 146, 147, 149, 154, 160,
168, 170, 179, 180, 181, 183, 184,
186, 187, 188, 190, 206
Görtz, Baron von, Swedish ambassador
at the Hague 41, 42, 43, 45, 46, 47,
48, 51, 56, 59, 60
Graeme, John, Jacobite minister in
Vienna 115, 118
Graham, James, physician
Grant, Major John 229
Grieve, James, physician 182
Gyllenborg conspiracy, 1716–17 41, 43,
45, 49
Gyllenborg, Count Karl, Swedish
minister to Britain 42, 45, 46, 47,
48, 50, 51

Hadley, shipbuilder 35
Hall, William 54
Hamilton, Ezekiel 146
Hanover, House of 39
Hay, Francis, son of Laird of Pitfour
185
Hay, John, of Inverness 99
Hay, le Sieur 100
Hay, Captain William 34, 36, 56, 90, 98,
99, 103, 106

Hease, William 107, 108, 111, 113, 147
Hessen Homburg, Prince of 184, 191
Hewitt, James 133, 185, 232
Holstein, Duke of 62, 72, 91, 97, 99,
101, 113, 118, 119, 120
Home, George of Whytfield 23
Huguenots 14
Hyndford, John, 3rd Earl of, British
ambassador to Prussia 219; British
ambassador to Russia, campaign
against James Keith 221, 222, 224

Iaguzhinsky, Paul 69, 102, 104, 137, 144,
164, 165
Innes, James 54
Innes, Lieutenant 196
Ismailovsky regiment, foreigners in 172,
173, 174
Ivan VI, infant Tsar of Russia 205

Jacobite court 3, 24
Jacobite diaspora 2, 3, 4
Jacobite diplomatic activity 4
Jacobite Rising, 1715 3, 21, 22, 39, 40,
42, 51, 63
Jacobite Rising, 1745 1, 180, 201, 223
Jacobites and Russia, plans for support
84, 166
Jacobites, Acts of Attainder against 22
Jacobites, Austria 1
Jacobites, English 1
Jacobites, exiled court 166
Jacobites, France 1, 3, 24
Jacobites, in Russian military 163, 166
Jacobites, Irish 1
Jacobites, Italy 1, 26
Jacobites, Scots 1
Jacobites, Sicily 24
Jacobites, Spain 1, 24
Jacobites, Sweden 1, 24
James II 3
James III 3, 21, 39, 40, 41, 48, 51, 52,
57, 59, 68, 71, 76, 79, 80, 81, 82, 83,
84, 85, 87, 88, 89, 90, 98, 113, 117,
118, 123, 131, 132, 134, 145, 149,
151, 158, 160, 184, 185, 212
James VI and I 38
Jaupain, François 77
Jefferyes, James 37, 61, 63, 66, 68

Jerningham, George 47, 48, 57, 60, 66
Johnstone, James 185, 186, 232

Kantemir, Antiokh 144, 155, 156, 159,
    175, 176, 177, 178, 179, 182, 186, 187
Keene, Benjamin 117, 118, 119
Keith, George, 10th Earl Marischal 17,
    118, 146, 149, 152, 154, 157, 158,
    160, 161, 166, 183, 184, 195, 201,
    203, 210, 217, 224, 225
Keith, James 17, 31, 54, 71, 129, 133,
    143, 152;, brings news of death of
    Clementina Sobieska 147, 149, 151,
    155; Bill to Parliament for
    inheritance 156, 157, 159, 160, 161,
    168, 173, 174, 182, 183, 184, 187,
    188; at the Siege of Danzig 190,
    191, 192, 195, 196, 201, 204,
    'English Prophet' 205; invited to
    lead Jacobites 207, 212, 213; estate
    at Rannenburg, Livonia 215; chief
    command of army in Finland 216,
    217; diplomatic representative in
    Stockholm 218, 219; and Russian
    Freemasonry 220, 222, 224, 225,
    226, 227; entry to Prussian service
    as field marshal 228, 229; Governor
    General of Berlin 230
Keith, John, 3rd Earl of Kintore 155,
    159, 228
Keith, Robert of Ludquhairn 150
Keith, Robert, son of Keith of
    Ludquhairn 185, 229
Kennedy, James 55, 149
Kenzie, Captain William 177
Kurakin, Prince Boris, Russian
    ambassador to the Netherlands 51,
    54, 68, 85, 88, 89, 90, 107, 186

La Chétardie, Joachim-Jacques Trotti,
    Marquis de 154, 158, 159, 160, 207,
    213, 219, 221
Lacy, George 150, 187, 194, 206
Lacy, Peter 31, 36, 38, 56, 106, 147, 150,
    151, 152, 154, 168, 173, 183, 184,
    187, 189, 190, 192, 193, 194, 205,
    212, 215, 226, 229
Lambe, Yeames 177
Lane, Edward 102

Lawless, Patrick 60
Lawrence, James 54
Le Clerc, M 184
Lescszynski, Stanislaus 148, 189
Lesley, George 188
Lewis, William Thomas 149
Lewis, William Thomas, recruitment of
    foreigners 175, 176
Lindesay, John, 20th Earl of Crawfurd
    166, 182, 194
Liria, James Fitzjames, Duke of 22, 113,
    117, 118, 123, 124, 130, 132, 133,
    134, 135, 136, 137, 138, 139, 140
Little, Robert 36, 53, 133, 147
Logan, John 55
Louis XV, King of France 97, 202
Löwenwolde, Count Karl Gustav 165,
    172, 173

MacDonnell, Alasdair, of Glengarry 231
MacKenzie, George, British resident in
    St Petersburg 40
MacKenzie, Thomas 15, 180, 197
Maclean, Sir Hector 146
Manstein, Christopher Hermann von
    148
Mar, John Erskine, 6th Earl of 22, 24,
    41, 43, 44, 45, 46, 47, 50, 52, 53, 56
Mary of Modena, wife of James VII and
    II, 52
Mecklenburg 41, 50
Menshikov, Count 100, 102, 121
Menzies, John 25, 74
Merthens, Eva, mistress of James Keith
    230
Milton, John 16
Moir, John of Stoneywood 184
Montemar, Count of 202
Moscow 6, 7, 33, 38
Mottley, John 43
Mounsey, James, physician 182
Munnich, Baron 164
Munnich, Berghard Kristof 167, 168, 170
Munnich, Field Marshal 184, 192, 193,
    194, 195, 196, 205
Murray, Alexander, brother of 5th Lord
    Elibank 231
Murray, John, of Broughton 203, 217

Naki, William 55
Newcastle, Thomas Pelham-Holles, 1st
    Duke of 97, 108, 119, 122
Ney, Joseph, shipbuilder 35, 102
Norris, Sir John, Admiral of British Navy
    40, 42, 50, 59, 61, 69
Nystad, Peace of 71

O'Brien, Christopher 168, 176, 178, 179,
    180, 187, 197, 215
O'Brien, Christopher, son of
    Christopher O'Brien 180
O'Brien, Daniel 57, 77, 78, 82, 83, 84,
    85, 86, 87, 88, 89, 91, 92, 99
O'Brien, Lucius, son of Christopher
    O'Brien 180
Ochakov, battle of 155, 183, 195
O'Connor, Edmund 106, 107
Ogilvie, Lieutenant 197
Opie, Captain John 177
Orléans, Philip, Duke of 70, 85, 87
Ormonde, James Butler, 2nd Duke of
    56, 58, 74, 75, 79, 110, 113, 202
Osterman, Count 102, 133, 135, 137,
    139, 140, 154, 164, 165, 175
Oxford, Earl of 51

Paddon, George 34, 54
Paterson, James of Prestonhall 26
Paterson, Sir Hugh of Bannockburn 24,
    26, 47, 53
Perth, Duke of 217
Peter I (the Great), Tsar/Emperor,
    1682–1725 2, 3, 4, 6, 61, 68, 71, 72,
    76, 80, 81, 85, 86, 87, 88, 89, 90, 92;
    visit to western Europe, 1697–8, 6,
    13, 16, 21, 25; recruitment of
    Jacobites 25, 31, 38, 39, 40, 41, 42;
    visit to western Europe, 1716–17, 6,
    42, 43, 45, 46, 47, 50, offer of
    daughter in marriage to James III 57
Peter II, Emperor of Russia, 1727–1730
    131, 132, 139, 164
Philip V, King of Spain 57, 118, 123,
    124, 130, 131, 132
Pittodrie, Laird of 184
Polwarth, Lord, British Minister
    Plenipotentiary in Copenhagen 50,
    62

Poyntz, Stephen, Hanoverian envoy to
    Sweden 98, 100, 106, 111
Preobrazhensky regiment 173

Quadruple Alliance, 17, 18, 60, 61, 90

Radzivil, Prince 132
Ramsay, Bogdan Adrianovich 'of
    Balmaine' 187, 206
Ramsay, Major 182
Ramsay, shipbuilder 35
Rank, General 57
Religion, Protestant, churches in Russia
    14; Roman Catholic 14; Russian
    Orthodox 11, 13, 14, 15; Tolerance
    Manifesto, 1702 14
Repnin, Prince, Governor of Riga 83
Reval (Tallin) 55
Rhine campaign 191
Ripperda, Jan Willem, Baron de 97, 100,
    117, 118, 119, 122
Robertson, Alexander of Struan 51
Robertson, Duncan, brother of 17th
    laird of Struan 22, 51
Robethon, Jean de, Hanoverian minister
    62
Robinson, Thomas, British
    representative in France 100
Rondeau, Claudius 129, 133, 134, 136,
    137, 138, 144, 165, 168, 174
Russia, attitude to foreigners 9; crime
    and punishment 10; cultural life in
    17; education in 16; land ownership
    6; population 6
Russia Company 15, 30
Russian army, financial crisis in 167;
    recruitment of foreigners 181
Russian military, conditions for
    foreigners 34; financial crisis in
    214; foreigners in 167, 171;
    Jacobites in 49; ranks of foreigners
    32, 33, 175; rates of pay for
    foreigners 33
Russian navy 26, 54, 109, 168; British
    shipbuilders 64; career
    opportunities for Jacobites 26, 27,
    28; financial crisis in 167; number
    of ships 63, 64; recruitment from
    British navy 28, 174, 178, 187;

recruitment of foreigners 28, 165,
172, 186, 187

St-Germain-en-Laye 3
St Leger, Samuel 111
St Petersburg 6, 32
Saunders, Rear-Admiral Thomas 23, 51,
52, 53, 54, 56, 147, 168, 187, 189
Saxe, Marshall Maurice de, attempt to
recruit James Keith 222, 229
Schaub, Luke 70, 76
Schleinitz, Baron, Russian minister to
France 72
Seissan, General 110
Semenovsky regiment 173
Serocold, John 51, 111, 114
Shakhovskoi, Lieutenant-General Prince
191
Shcherbatov, Prince 158
Siege of Azov 193, 194
Siege of Danzig, 1734 149, 151
Siege of Gibraltar 123, 130
Sievers, Rear-Admiral 29
Sinclair, John, 8th Master of Sinclair 24,
26
Sinzendorf, Chancellor 124
Sobieska, Clementina 131
Sobieski, Prince James 132, 145, 147,
148, 149
South Sea Company, 'South Sea Bubble'
70
Spain 60; joins Quadruple Alliance 17,
20, 68
Sparre, Baron Eric, Swedish minister to
France 42, 45, 47
Stanhope, James, Ist Earl of 30, 44, 49,
57, 61, 68, 117, 118, 119, 122
Stirling, Sir Henry of Ardoch 15, 22, 44,
46, 48, 50, 59, 68, 73, 76, 80, 84,
103, 107, 108, 133, 180, 207
Stobs, Captain 55
Stokes, Thomas 31
Stuart, Prince Charles Edward (Young
Pretender) 3, 147, 202, 223
Stuart, Prince Henry Benedict, later
Cardinal York 3, 147, 148
Stuart, James Francis Edward *see* James III
Stuart, John of Stuartfield 166
Stuart Papers 79, 85

Stuart, Patrick 209
Sunderland, Charles Spencer, 3rd Earl
of 70
Sutherland, Alexander, boatbuilder 177
Sutherland, John, boatbuilder 177
Sutherland, Kenneth, 3rd Lord Duffus
31, 54, 56, 189
Sutherland, William, shipbuilder 30
Sweden 39; alliance with Poland,
Prussia, Denmark, 1720 68

Thirlby, Charles, minister to the British
Factory in Russia 15
Tilson, George 76
Toboso, Order of 146
Tollendal, Thomas Arthur Lally 153, 154
Tolstoi, Petr 102, 121
Treaty of Aix-la-Chapelle, 1748 231
Treaty of Charlottenburg 86
Treaty of Commerce and Friendship,
1734 144
Treaty of Hanover, 1725 110, 112, 114
Treaty of Hanover, 1745 223
Treaty of Seville, 1729 131, 135, 136, 138
Treaty of Stockholm, 1724 115, 117
Treaty of Utrecht, 1713 3
Treaty of Vienna, 1725 98, 100, 108,
114, 117, 120, 122, 130
Treaty of Vienna, 1731 139, 140, 144
Treaty of Vienna, 1738 189
Tyrawly, Lord, British ambassador to
Russia 219, 220

Urquhart, Adam 36, 51, 53
Urquhart, John, of Newhall 53

Veselovsky, Russian ambassador to
Britain 44
Vienna Alliance 134
Villardeau, French Minister
Plenipotentiary at St Petersburg 148
Vorontsov, Mikhail Illarionovich, Vice-
Chancellor 217, 222, 225
Vratislavsky, Count 133, 135

Wade, General George 108, 109
Wager, Sir Charles, Vice-Admiral 116,
117, 119, 120, 121, 176, 179
Waldegrave, James, 1st Earl 153

Walpole, Horatio, 1st Baron Walpole 111

Walpole, Sir Robert, 1st Earl of Orford 76, 91, 92, 93, 108, 109, 110, 112, 129, 145, 151, 201; intelligence network of 76, 79

War of Austrian Succession, 1742–48 207

War of Polish Succession, 1733–35 145, 189

War, Rhine Campaign, 1735 191

War, Russo-Turkish, 1736–39 192

War, Seven Years War, 1756–63 231

War, with Sweden, 1741–43 38, 207

Ward, Thomas 129

Waters, William 107

Weber, Friedrich Christian, envoy of Hanover in Russia 29, 58, 62, 68

Wharton, Philip, Duke of 109, 110, 113, 115, 117, 119, 138

Whigs, in Danzig 82

White, Lieutenant Richard 177

Whitworth, Charles 34

Wich, Cyril 111, 213, 214

Wilmanstrand, siege of 205

Wisheart, Thomas 55

Wogan, Charles 57

Wolfenbüttel, Augustus Wilhelm, Duke of 131

Young, Ann, granddaughter of Thomas Gordon 15

Young, James 111, 186, 198

Young, John 15